Get the eBooks FREE!

(PDF, ePub, Kindle, and liveBook all included)

We believe that once you buy a book from us, you should be able to read it in any format we have available. To get electronic versions of this book at no additional cost to you, purchase and then register this book at the Manning website.

Go to https://www.manning.com/freebook and follow the instructions to complete your pBook registration.

That's it!
Thanks from Manning!

Usability Matters

Usability Matters

MOBILE-FIRST UX FOR DEVELOPERS AND OTHER ACCIDENTAL DESIGNERS

MATT LACEY

MANNING
SHELTER ISLAND

For online information and ordering of this and other Manning books, please visit www.manning.com. The publisher offers discounts on this book when ordered in quantity. For more information, please contact

Special Sales Department
Manning Publications Co.
20 Baldwin Road
PO Box 761
Shelter Island, NY 11964
Email: orders@manning.com

Manning Publications Co.
20 Baldwin Road
PO Box 761
Shelter Island, NY 11964

Development editor: Marina Michaels
Technical development editor: Damien White
Review editor: Ozren Harlovic
Project manager: Tiffany Taylor
Copy editor: Frances Buran
Proofreader: Alyson Brener
Typesetter: Dennis Dalinnik
Cover designer: Leslie Haimes

ISBN: 9781617293931
Printed in the United States of America
1 2 3 4 5 6 7 8 9 10 – DP – 23 22 21 20 19 18

To Chrissie, Izaak, and Phoebe: thank you for giving me the time and space to write this book. You can have Daddy back now.

brief contents

1 ■ Introduction 1

PART 1 CONTEXT **25**

2 ■ Who's using the app? 27
3 ■ Where and when is the app used? 57
4 ■ What device is the app running on? 83

PART 2 INPUT **103**

5 ■ How people interact with the app 105
6 ■ User-entered data 126
7 ■ Data not from a user 155

PART 3 OUTPUT **175**

8 ■ Displaying items in the app 177
9 ■ Non-visible output 207

PART 4 RESPONSIVENESS 227

10 ■ Understanding the perception of time 229
11 ■ Making your app start fast 248
12 ■ Making your app run fast 268

PART 5 CONNECTIVITY...285

13 ■ Coping with varying network conditions 287

PART 6 RESOURCES...307

14 ■ Managing power and resources 309

contents

preface xvii
acknowledgments xviii
about this book xix

1 *Introduction 1*

1.1 What's usability, and why does it matter? 1

Usability matters to everyone 2 ▪ Usability, UX, and design 2 The formula for app success 3 ▪ Great usability experiences are intuitive 5

1.2 Six components of great app experiences 6

Context of use underpins everything in an app 6 ▪ Input includes all ways data and information get into the app 7 ▪ Output includes and goes beyond what is shown onscreen 8 Responsiveness: how output is perceived 8 ▪ Connectivity changes and isn't always guaranteed 9 ▪ Resources are finite and must be managed 10

1.3 How considering all six components can make apps better 10

Example 1: an email client 11 ▪ Example 2: a news app 13 Example 3: a tower defense game 15

1.4 Why you need to consider the six components in your apps 17

Experience is an important differentiator 17 ▪ Meet the expectations of those who'll use your app 20 ▪ Planning for success 21

PART 1 CONTEXT 25

2 ***Who's using the app? 27***

2.1 You aren't your users 28

How you're different from your users 28 ▪ You're not an average user 31 ▪ Be aware of the effects on your thinking 32

2.2 Who's the app for? 33

Who'll get value from your app? 34 ▪ Understanding the potential user base 35 ▪ Are there enough people who want the app? 36 Targeting groups of individuals 39 ▪ Putting on a persona, or several 40 ▪ Enterprise app usage 42

2.3 People aren't all the same 43

Consider people's differing abilities 44 ▪ Consider people's differing expectations 45 ▪ Consider people's differing goals 47

2.4 What are people doing? 49

What are people doing with the app? 49 ▪ What else are people doing? 53

3 ***Where and when is the app used? 57***

3.1 Where is the app used? 57

App usage at a macro-geographic level 58 ▪ App usage at a micro-geographic level 60

3.2 The regional impact on an app 61

Considering support for multiple languages 61 ▪ How culture and locale can impact an app 65

3.3 When is the app used? 70

Consider the time of day 70 ▪ Consider the day of the week 72 Consider the time of year 73 ▪ How long is the app used? 74

3.4 What activities are being undertaken while using the app? 78

Is the person using the app moving or stationary? 78 ▪ Is the user dedicated or distracted? 79 ▪ Is use isolated or in conjunction with something else? 80 ▪ Are they standing, sitting, or lying down? 81

4 *What device is the app running on?* 83

4.1 Write once, run everywhere? 84

4.2 Supporting multiple operating systems 86

OS-imposed restrictions 86 ▪ Looking like you belong on the OS 87 ▪ Belonging on a version of the OS 89 ▪ Belonging in the enterprise 89

4.3 Maintaining brand identity and differentiation 90

Branding vs. visual identity 91 ▪ Separating your brand from the OS 91 ▪ Maintaining OS conventions while still reflecting a brand 93

4.4 Supporting different device capabilities 93

Handling multiple physical device sizes 94 ▪ Variations in internal hardware capability 97 ▪ Accounting for software variations 100

PART 2 INPUT 103

5 *How people interact with the app* 105

5.1 Supporting different pointing devices 106

Providing input with a finger 107 ▪ Providing input with a stylus 112 ▪ Providing input with a mouse and the keyboard 114

5.2 Using a pointing device to provide input 116

Supporting gesture-based input 116 ▪ Supporting multi-touch input 119

5.3 When pointing and touch input become difficult 121

Touch events don't always do what the user wants 121
Raw input events need special attention 123

6 *User-entered data* 126

6.1 The goals of the people using the app 127

Improve tasks by minimizing input 128 ▪ Improve tasks with defaults and suggestions 134 ▪ Improve tasks with alternative inputs 136

6.2 How to ask for data to be entered in forms 138

Optimizing how the form is arranged 138 ▪ Simplify how text is entered 143 ▪ Password entry requires special consideration 146
Simplifying entry from a fixed set of options 149 ▪ Validation and required fields 151

7 *Data not from a user 155*

7.1 Data from web-based resources 156

Dealing with the data you directly request 156 ▪ Dealing with data pushed to the app 158

7.2 Getting data from the device 161

Input from the operating system 162 ▪ Data from the filesystem 163 ▪ Data from other apps 164

7.3 Getting data from sensors 166

Transparency and permission when using sensor data 166
Allow for variations in sensor input 168

7.4 Using heuristics and inferring input 171

Enhancing the app experience based on an individual's usage 171
Enhancing the app experience based on the usage of all people 172

PART 3 OUTPUT 175

8 *Displaying items in the app 177*

8.1 The fundamentals of good visual output 178

Focus on the person using the app and their goals 178 ▪ Meet the expectations of the people using the app 178 ▪ Account for the specific device being used 179 ▪ Respect standards and conventions 180

8.2 Laying out controls on a screen 181

Implying meaning and relationships through alignment and hierarchy 182 ▪ Implying meaning and relationships through consistency 183 ▪ Implying meaning and relationships through proximity 184

8.3 Navigating within the app 186

Common navigation patterns 186 ▪ Special navigation considerations 188

8.4 Avoiding discrimination with what you display 191

Ensure your UI works for everybody 191 ▪ Saying the same thing to everybody who uses the app 192

8.5 Many factors affect the display of images 193

One size doesn't fit all 193 ▪ Physical size isn't everything: consider formats and formatting too 196 ▪ Customizing image placeholders 198

8.6 Use distinct icons with specific meanings 200

8.7 Allow for extremes of connectivity and content 202

Content that loads slowly or doesn't load at all 202
When content isn't available 203 ▪ Avoiding empty states 203

9 ***Non-visible output 207***

9.1 Physical and audio output support changes onscreen 208

Give your app a voice 208 ▪ Haptic feedback starts with vibration 210

9.2 Output to other apps and devices 212

9.3 Communicating from your backend 214

Allowing for multichannel communication 215 ▪ Sending effective push notifications 216 ▪ Using badges with push notifications 219

9.4 Communication via channels beyond the app 221

Using email to communicate with your users 221 ▪ Using SMS to communicate with your users 223 ▪ Using third-party messaging services to communicate with your users 223

PART 4 RESPONSIVENESS 227

10 ***Understanding the perception of time 229***

10.1 How people perceive mobile time 230

Context influences the perception of responsiveness 230
Perception is about feelings, opinions, and comparisons 231
Being responsive with notifications 233 ▪ Meet expectations, don't just be as fast as possible 234

10.2 Influencing the perception of responsiveness 236

Answer questions about what the app is doing 236
Show appropriate progress when something's happening 240
Animation can hide delays 240 ▪ Usable isn't the same as finished 241

10.3 Perceptions associated with the age of your app 243

11 ***Making your app start fast 248***

11.1 Doing the minimum to start the app 249

Deciding what to do on startup 249 ▪ Displaying a splash screen when launching the app 252

11.2 Preloading content to make the app faster 254

Preloading content to distribute with the app 254 ▪ Preloading content for the app's next use 255

11.3 Preformatting content retrieved by the app 257

11.4 Caching content to save time and money 259

Using in-memory and disk-based caches 260 ▪ Checking for new versions of cached items 262 ▪ When to invalidate and delete cached items 264

12 ***Making your app run fast 268***

12.1 Using eager loading so people don't have to wait 269

Eager loading complements preloading content 270 ▪ Beware of being too eager 272 ▪ Knowing what to load eagerly 272

12.2 Parallel operations take less time 273

Synchronous and asynchronous operations 275 ▪ Advice when working in parallel 276

12.3 Combining requests for improved speed and control 279

Controlling the server your app connects to 279 ▪ Getting faster responses by combining requests 280 ▪ Simplifying the client by combining requests 281 ▪ Combining requests and local files 282

PART 5 CONNECTIVITY...285

13 ***Coping with varying network conditions 287***

13.1 Not all connections are the same 288

Securing your connection 288 ▪ Connection speed can vary 289 Connection cost can vary 290

13.2 Occasionally connected is the norm 292

Connections may not be possible 292 ▪ Connections may be lost 294 ▪ Connections may change 294

13.3 Optimizing for subprime conditions 296

Caching improves the experience in subprime conditions 296 Compression improves the experience in subprime conditions 296 Deferring actions increases what's possible in subprime conditions 297 Batch operations in subprime conditions 297 ▪ Automatic retries improve the experience in subprime conditions 298

13.4 Balancing usability and a poor connection 299

Prioritizing important activities in poor conditions 300
Adjusting network usage based on network conditions 301

13.5 Keeping the user in control when conditions are poor 302

PART 6 RESOURCES 307

14 *Managing power and resources 309*

14.1 When it's gone, it's gone 310

14.2 Do you really need it? 313

Lazy loading reduces wasted effort 314 ▪ Using alternatives to save resources 315

14.3 How often are you going to use it? 318

Managing resources that are only used once 318 ▪ Managing resources that are used repeatedly 319

14.4 Do you still need it? 320

Turning off resources when finished 321 ▪ Responding to changing circumstances 322

appendix A Exercise answers 324
appendix B Put it into practice 335
appendix C Recommended reading 348
appendix D Bibliography 350

index 357

preface

I don't like bad software. I don't want to make it, and I don't want others to make it. It's not just that I don't want to use it; I don't think anyone should have to use it. Unfortunately, what constitutes bad software is often difficult to define, which makes it hard to avoid creating it.

More than a decade ago, I set about trying to learn how to make better software so I could avoid contributing to the body of bad software that exists. As a developer, this meant learning about a lot of new topics, especially design. As I learned more, I started to share what I'd discovered with other developers at conferences and in user groups. Developers couldn't understand or relate to the language and terminology of design, and they often weren't interested in learning it, but they *were* interested in making better software.

It was at this time I developed the idea of the six components of an app that form the six parts of this book. These components allow developers to think about software (particularly mobile apps) in a way that goes beyond just the writing of code, but without needing to become a designer. This book aims to bring these ideas to a wider audience to help more developers improve their apps.

This is a book by a developer for developers—developers who want to build great apps, but realize that doing so takes more than just the ability to write code. Although there's more to creating a successful app than any one book can cover, I hope that the contents of this book will help you to think about developing apps in new ways and improve the experiences of the people who will use them.

acknowledgments

Several people have helped shape my career and approach to work. I will always be eternally grateful to Barney, Pete, Ian, Will, Seth, and Hugh. Thank you.

I'd also like to thank those people I've worked with who've taught me to write better software or about the mobile industry. A big thanks to Alan, Alec, Alex, Andy C., Andy W., Anna, Ben, Clint, Craig, Dave, David K., David M., Ewan, Garry, Glenn, Jaime, James, Keith, Louise, Marcus, Martin, Mike T., Nelson, Nicholas, Nick, Pat, Paul B., Paul F., Paul L., Paul M., Rafe, Riaz, Richard, Scott, Simon C., Simon S., Steve, Stuart L., Stuart R., Tom, and anyone I've forgotten.

Finally, I want to thank everyone at Manning who has made this book possible, including publisher Marjan Bace and everyone on the editorial and production teams. My thanks especially to Greg Wild, without whom I wouldn't have started this book, and Marina Michaels, without whom I don't think I would have finished. I also can't thank enough the technical peer reviewers led by Ozren Harlovic: Damien White, Clive Harber, Giuliano Bertoti, Alan Lenton, Matthew Heck, Dmytro Lypai, Clifford Kamppari-Miller, Desmond Horsley, Alberto Chiesa, Amit Lamba, Alvin Raj, Jessica Lovegood, Xan Gregg, Paulo Nuin, and Saara Kamppari.

about this book

This book exists to help people create better mobile apps. When anyone can create an app, it takes more than just an app's existence to make it stand out from the millions of others out there. There's also a massive difference between a simple app and something that people appreciate, value, and repeatedly use to improve their lives. This book gives practical advice and guidance on how to take a mobile app, on any platform, and make it better.

Who should read this book

This book is for people who are creating mobile apps. The primary audience is developers, but there's plenty of information for anyone involved in app creation: designers, testers, project managers, any other stakeholders, or a combination thereof. This book doesn't teach how to write code or use a set of APIs or frameworks. Instead, this book teaches many other things you need to know to create a successful mobile app that the people using it will love and will enjoy using.

Much of what this book covers loosely falls under the broad topic of user experience (UX), but this isn't a UX book. It won't teach you to be a UX expert, and it isn't for UX practitioners. This book is for people creating mobile apps, who have a desire to improve the apps they've already built or to build better ones in the future.

Note that despite this being a book for developers about creating apps, it doesn't include any code. This is because the ideas this book covers are bigger than any single platform, technology, or programming language. The contents of this book aren't limited to the people who use a single language and are meant to encourage you to think beyond the code to the actual use of the software and experiences you produce.

How this book is organized: a roadmap

This book has 14 chapters, divided into 6 parts:

- Chapter 1 provides details of the six conceptual components of an app that are reflected in the six parts encompassing the rest of the book.

Part 1, "Context":

- Chapter 2 covers the importance of understanding the different people who are using or will use your app and how knowledge of them can affect the app and its use.
- Chapter 3 looks at the importance of knowing about the different times and places an app is used, because these can alter what people want from the app and how they will use it.
- Chapter 4 highlights the ways devices can vary, and how to support those differences and keep a unique identity while still looking like the app belongs on the device.

Part 2, "Input":

- Chapter 5 covers capturing input with different pointing devices and supporting advanced and custom input techniques.
- Chapter 6 discusses capturing data in forms and doing so in a way that aligns with the goals of the people using the app.
- Chapter 7 looks at working with data from the web, data that's stored on the device, and data that comes from sensors on the device.

Part 3, "Output":

- Chapter 8 covers the fundamentals of good UI, how to lay out controls on the screen, and navigating within the app.
- Chapter 9 looks at what the app can do beyond displaying things onscreen. This includes audio and physical feedback, as well as sending details to other apps and communicating with the person using it in ways that go beyond the app itself.

Part 4, "Responsiveness":

- Chapter 10 looks at how time plays a part in the experience of using an app and how this can be used to influence the experience of the people using it.
- Chapter 11 focuses on different methods and techniques for helping an app to start as quickly as possible.
- Chapter 12 covers the different ways apps can load, store, and use data to increase the speed with which it becomes accessible to the person using the app.

Part 5, "Connectivity":

- Chapter 13 looks at the different connectivity scenarios in which mobile apps have to work and what can be done to limit any negative impact on the experience of using the app.

Part 6, "Resources":

- Chapter 14 looks at strategies for making the best use of the finite and potentially limited resources available in a mobile environment.

This book is intended to be read from cover to cover, but each chapter is self-contained so that you can read it in isolation if you wish. The first four chapters provide the fundamental underpinning for the ideas in the rest of the book and so should be read before any other chapters if you don't wish to read the book from cover to cover.

After chapter 1, each chapter contains exercises and "Put it into practice" sections. The exercises are to help you confirm that you've understood the preceding section. Answers to the exercises are in appendix A.

The "Put it into practice" sections include tips, comments, and suggestions for how you can apply what you've just read to your apps. Appendix B includes copies of all the "Put it into practice" sections in a single place for easy reference or to use as a checklist.

About the author

Matt Lacey is an independent mobile developer and consultant. He's built, advised on, and contributed to apps for social networks, film and TV broadcasters, travel companies, banks and financial institutions, sports companies, news organizations, music streaming services, device manufacturers, and electronics retailers. These apps have an installed base of more than 500,000,000 users and are used every day around the world.

Matt previously worked at a broad range of companies, doing many types of development. He has worked at startups, small ISVs, national enterprises, and global consultancies, and written software for servers, desktops, devices, and industrial hardware in more languages than he can remember. He lives in the UK with his wife and two children.

1 Introduction

This chapter covers

- What usability is, and why it matters
- How user experience contributes to success
- The six components of great apps
- Why each component is important

As someone involved in the creation of mobile apps or games, you'll want what you create to be as successful as possible. Regardless of how you define success, you can't overlook the factor that the experience you create for the people using your app plays a role in achieving it. Throughout this chapter, I'll introduce six components that contribute to great, successful app experiences, but I'll start by defining what I mean by usability and the experience of using an app.

1.1 What's usability, and why does it matter?

When it comes to creating apps, you'd probably rather spend most of your time focusing on code. Sadly, the successful developers I know say that the code only accounts for between 10% and 40% of their success. Many factors contribute to a successful app, but I believe that expanding your focus to also think about the experience of using an app is the easiest way to make simple, tangible improvements.

In this book, you'll learn how to think about usability and the experience you'll want your app to convey. Plus, you'll gain lots of practical tips and general advice for changes you can make to improve them. Rather than tell you how to address specific scenarios, I'll give you the knowledge to address all scenarios. These aren't the things you'd normally see in a book about design—that's because this book is specifically for developers like you.

Usability beyond mobile apps

You can apply the principles, knowledge, and lessons in this book to more than mobile apps. While this book focuses on mobile app examples, the principles behind the advice can be applied to websites and apps that run on any device.

In some ways, building for all the constraints of mobile can make other software development seem easier. If you can create an app that works on multiple devices, it's much easier to build something that has to work only on one. Similarly, if you're able to optimize for multiple forms of input or output, then non-mobile software that doesn't need to account for as many situations can seem simple by comparison.

1.1.1 *Usability matters to everyone*

If you're making the conscious decision to expand your app development knowledge beyond just code, or you're looking for a way of making your app stand out among the competition and keep people using it, usability should matter; it matters to the people who use the app. Usability is about how easy your app is to use. People don't want to spend their time trying to work out how to use your app or remembering how it's different. An app that's easy and intuitive will keep people using it repeatedly. They'll also be more inclined to tell others about it in a positive way.

1.1.2 *Usability, UX, and design*

Design and *designer* are terms loaded with nuance and interpretation. They mean different things to different people and cover a broad array of concepts and topics. Everything from graphic design to branding, animation to copywriting, iconography to user interfaces, usability to human-computer-interaction, and user experience (UX) to information architecture, all fall under the umbrella of design. You don't have to be an expert in each area of design, but knowledge and awareness of each will help. This book covers many aspects of design, but two that need special mention are usability and UX:

- *Usability*—An aspect of design that looks at how easy something is to use. The only way to measure usability is by testing it with real people who use apps. We'll come back to testing many times throughout this book, because getting feedback from the people who will use and are using your apps is important. To learn how to run your own usability tests, I recommend reading *Rocket Surgery Made Easy* by Steve Krug (New Riders, 2009).

- *UX*—A popular term that many people have appropriated in recent years. It's a formal discipline with recognized practices and techniques. More than just focusing on software design, it encompasses all aspects of interaction with a product, service, or company.

This book isn't trying to teach you to be a UX expert or to give you license to call yourself a designer. This book will enable you to take the apps you're already developing and create better experiences for the people using them so you (and your app) can be successful.

1.1.3 The formula for app success

App success is based on three important factors: value, experience, and luck. You can be successful with one, but striving to address all three is best. The distinction between these factors can sometimes be blurry, but this book focuses on the second. It's about the experience that you design for the people using the app.

Please don't make the common mistake of thinking that usability and UX are only about how your app looks. The experiences created by using your app can be much richer and more nuanced when you consider more than just the visuals. If this weren't the case, this would be a book about user interface design rather than usability and the user's experience. In this section, I define the three success factors:

- *Value*—What a person gets from using an app. This could be a single benefit or many.
- *Experience*—Relates to how the value is provided. It's about the feelings and emotions that a person has when using an app.
- *Luck*—The variable that you don't have complete control over.

Let's look at value first. Some ways that your app can provide value for the people using it are

- By making a task possible
- By making a task simpler
- By making a task faster
- By earning a person money
- By saving a person money
- By entertaining
- By informing
- By educating
- By serving as a distraction or way to pass the time (although this is rarely a good reason for creating something)

Your app's ability to meet the needs and desires of the people using it is part of the value it provides. You need to make sure you're building the right thing for the people looking for the value you provide, not just making something possible. Sometimes a mobile app isn't the best way to meet a person's needs or to provide the value they seek.

NOTE Meeting user needs is the fundamental principle of providing value. If you can't provide value, it doesn't matter how good the experience is. People won't use the app.

The experience you create for the user is dependent on the value you're providing. There may be some overlap between the two when defining the context of use and the target market for the app. Experience is also, in part, about how you deliver value. The experience you create for the people using the app is what impacts success. Traditional UX tasks, such as user research and testing, can contribute to the experience you create, but they aren't the same thing. In most cases, you'll want the experiences you create to be positive, but this isn't always the case.

When you might want to create a negative experience

You will want to consider two occasions when it might make sense to provide a negative experience. The first is to discourage bad or negative behavior. For example, if a player was to turn on their teammates in your game, you might want to do something to discourage them from doing this again. You could reduce the effectiveness of their armor, restrict the strength of their weapons, artificially limit the responsiveness of the game, or include another creative way of letting them know the consequences of doing things they shouldn't. Or, your app can force a negative experience upon the person using it when they do something that's detrimental to the other people who use the app. If someone's repeatedly reported for spam or offensive content in your chat app, you may choose to limit the length or frequency of messages they can send.

The second reason for deliberately creating a negative or challenging experience is if you want to increase positive emotion in the future. (This is a common strategy used in games to keep people playing.) If someone must struggle and fail a few times to achieve something, such as completing a level or defeating an opponent, they'll feel much better when they do achieve their goal. In this scenario, the positive feeling will be higher after they've failed a few times than it would've been if they had achieved their goal on the first attempt.

Creating a great experience in your app is important because you can't rely on luck. For example, large companies that have had success in the past release new games to a muted response. Or, individual developers have seen their games suddenly become viral hits months after release. Luck is as good as any name for this factor, but it isn't totally out of your control. Becoming a viral hit, being repeatedly featured in the app store, or having positive reviews in the press isn't something anyone can guarantee, but there are things you can do to increase your chances of these happening and the luck you and your app experience.

In the first century AD, the Roman philosopher Seneca said, "Luck is what happens when preparation meets opportunity." It still applies today. You can't guarantee the opportunities you'll have, and you may even have to work to create them. But if they do come and you're not prepared, you'll miss out.

You're more likely to create something lots of people use if it's something they want. People will share an app more if it's easy and there's a benefit. The press and websites are more likely to write about your app if it's unique, if it's high quality, and if you tell them about it and ask for a review. Stores are more interested in featuring apps that are new, of high quality, and show the unique features of the platform.

This book is about experience, as that's the easiest factor for you to control in a way that can be beneficial to your app and help it stand out from the competition. Value is often easy to compete with as functionality is easy to copy. Luck is partially out of your control, so it isn't something you can rely on. The experience of an app is embedded deep in its design, and that's the hardest to replicate. But a great, intuitive experience can enhance its value and increase your opportunities for luck.

1.1.4 Great usability experiences are intuitive

Intuitive is a word that's often used to describe apps. I regularly see release notes claim, "Now, more intuitive to use." There's a problem with such a claim. It's that whether something is intuitive is subjective—for something to be intuitive, it must meet the expectations of the person using it.

You'll find some official lists of things software should do to be considered usable at www.usabilitynet.org/tools/r_international.htm, but you can't tick off the items on a checklist and then claim your app is intuitive. You can claim that something is intuitive for you, or you can mention other people who've said they find it intuitive, but you can't claim something is intuitive for me. Only I can say if I find your app intuitive once I've used it.

To find out if people think your app is intuitive, you must ask them. This raises the question, "How can this book show how to increase the usability of an app and make it more intuitive if that can only be determined by the people who use it?" This is a good question and shows you're paying attention. Before releasing them more widely, test the apps you create based on the advice given in this book with a sample of real people the apps are intended for. Only the people the app is intended for can say if it's right for them.

This book provides guidance and instruction on improving your apps based on common conventions, best practices, and many years of investigating what features of hundreds of apps led to people having a positive, intuitive experience. Making something intuitive is like the ideas behind the principle of least surprise: software should behave as the person using it expects it to. Applying these concepts to an app isn't intuitive itself. To help you think about all aspects of an app, I've broken the app experience into six components, which I'll introduce now.

1.2 Six components of great app experiences

You can think about or visualize the structure of an app in many ways. Throughout this book, we'll look at six different components of an app experience:

- Context
- Input
- Output
- Responsiveness
- Connectivity
- Resources

Five of these components relate to logical areas of functionality, or parts of the architecture of an app. The sixth, context, is about how to view the app, so we'll look at that first.

1.2.1 Context of use underpins everything in an app

Context is the situations and circumstances surrounding the use of an app. It's about looking at the big picture and seeing how the app fits into the wider environment. Think of considering context as looking at your app through a pair of glasses with three lenses, like that shown in figure 1.1. Each lens allows you to see a different aspect of the app's context, and it's only when you see all of those that you get the complete picture.

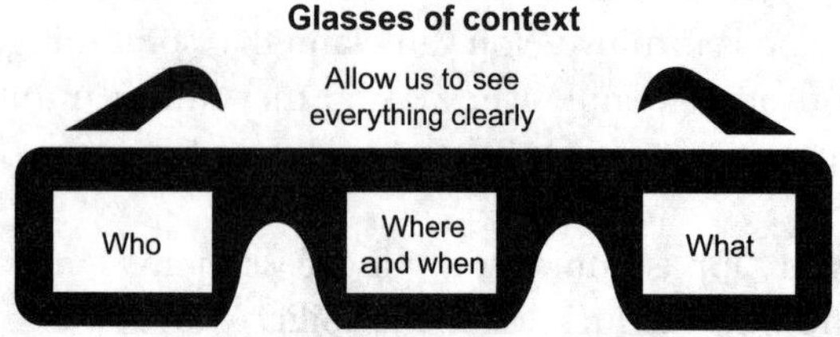

Figure 1.1 Considering context is like looking at an app and seeing three different aspects of its use.

An app that considers context appropriately provides an experience that fits seamlessly into the life of the person using it; it meets their needs and works as expected. An app experience that doesn't fully consider context can end up not working for the audience it was intended for, because it lacks what they want and performs poorly on the devices they're using. Ultimately, people will struggle with the motivation to keep using the app. Different people have different needs, expectations, and requirements. Considering the people who'll use your app allows you to be sure you're providing what's right for them.

Also, the environment where the app is used can influence how a person interacts with it, and the location can provide extra hints to help optimize what a person experiences from an app. Knowledge of the capabilities possessed by the devices your app will run on allows the creation of an app that makes use of the facilities and functionality available to it. This knowledge also enables the creation of an app that can integrate with the wider experience of using the phone and the other apps installed on the device.

Ignoring context is like only testing your app with a mouse in the simulator on your PC while sitting at a desk when real people using the app will do so by hand, in the field, with poor connectivity, and while distracted by another part of their job. In chapters 2 through 4, I'll take you through the elements that make up the circumstances of use to consider as the context.

1.2.2 *Input includes all ways data and information get into the app*

Input encompasses all the ways of supplying data and instructions to the app. It's the first of the components that relate to the high-level structure of the app. Figure 1.2 shows these components (in bold) and their relationships.

Input for a mobile app can be about much more than tapping a screen and filling out a form. An assortment of input sources and mechanisms are available from the

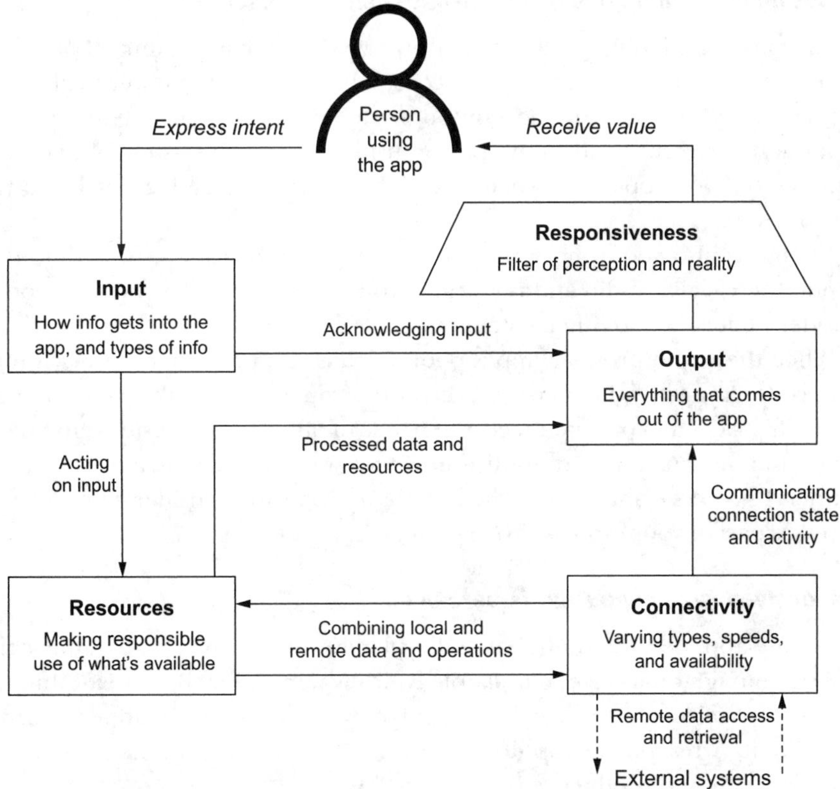

Figure 1.2 How the five structural components of an app relate to each other, the user, and external systems

device, the person using it, and remote sources. For the people using the app, it's rarely their aim to use an app just to gather input. Whether saved for later use or to give an immediate reward, aim to optimize the input-gathering elements of an app to the point where the people using the app can receive the maximum benefit from their input.

> **NOTE** You can avoid much direct input, but when necessary, gather it quickly, simply, and accurately. Whether the input is optional or necessitated by the app, input is a means to an end and not an end in itself.

If you're not considering input fully, you may end up creating a long, slow, tedious, and error-prone process that degrades the experience of the people using it to one that frustrates and annoys. As an example of how input can impact usability, consider the need to get a person's location. Three ways of doing this, each with different user experiences, are using the device's GPS, tapping a point on a map, or typing in a street address. Chapters 5, 6, and 7 dig deeper into considerations of how your app can handle input.

1.2.3 Output includes and goes beyond what is shown onscreen

When considering output, the first thing you'll probably think of is the screen. Devices in use today have screens that cover a broad spectrum of physical dimensions. You can't always use the identical output on a 3 in. screen, on a 10 in. screen, or in a response that's read aloud to the person using the app. It's essential that everything displayed on any supported device is readable, usable, helpful, attractive to view, and easy to navigate.

Output is also about more than what's displayed onscreen. In addition to visual output, there's also audio and physical output to consider. Beyond that, you need to consider what is sent to other systems and services as well.

When the output from an app is poor, it leads to an experience that's unusable in some contexts or by some people. Why would you want to make your app unusable? On the flip side, an app that meets the needs of all use cases ensures that people can receive the information and notifications they want in a simple and easy-to-consume manner. Chapters 8 and 9 cover the options and specific considerations for providing output as part of your mobile app experiences.

1.2.4 Responsiveness: how output is perceived

People use apps because of the value they'll gain from doing so. Sometimes the experience is enough on its own, but people typically want value. Because of this, it's beneficial to optimize for that and to avoid having people wait unnecessarily before providing it. A responsive app doesn't waste people's time, but helps them use their time efficiently and productively.

Responsiveness is the filter through which a person interprets the amount of time a task is perceived to take. To create an app that's responsive involves controlling and influencing the perception of the time a task takes. Often this means making something as fast as possible and then giving the impression that it takes even less time.

Responsiveness is about more than just speed; it also ensures that what's output is appropriate and targeted to the circumstances of the people using the app. It's the difference between someone being unsure about the app (because it shows a blank screen while it's presumed to be doing something), and someone confident that the app is busy working as hard and as fast as possible for the desired outcome. Part 4 of this book is about responsiveness and what you can do to objectively improve the time your app takes, and to improve the subjective perception of how long a task takes.

1.2.5 Connectivity changes and isn't always guaranteed

While some games and utility tools, like a calculator or flashlight, need no form of connectivity, the majority of apps depend on data that will change. So they'll need to be updated or will be dependent upon interaction with another person, machine, system, or service, such as a backend server. Because apps are designed to help the person using them, it's incredibly frustrating when a connectivity issue leads to lost work or unavailable information that's needed.

If an app that needs server connectivity suddenly loses it, the experience of the person using the app is determined by how the app handles the situation. If the app loses data and stops functioning, or crashes, it reflects poorly. For apps built to survive such scenarios, people can continue using the app, confident that if there's a temporary setback, their information is safe, their progress is remembered, and everything will carry on as normal once connectivity returns. There's a lot more to consider about connectivity, but the implications of not handling the loss or lack of connectivity are easy to appreciate.

If you're fortunate enough to live in a part of the world where a 4G signal is readily available and Wi-Fi is ubiquitous, it's easy to think that everyone else also has the same situation. This isn't the case for a large part of the world. Care should be given to what happens in an app when someone doesn't always have a fast, cheap, reliable connection. The way variations in connectivity are handled in an app can be the difference between an app that's unusable and one that always provides some value, even if that's showing older, cached data or saving gathered information to upload later.

Chapter 13 explains what to consider when regarding connectivity. In it, I'll talk about how the type of connection can vary, how the connection can't and won't always be possible, and what you can do to create the best experience for people when they don't have perfect network conditions.

1.2.6 Resources are finite and must be managed

Due to their portable nature, mobile devices have several constraints and restrictions. Device manufacturers must balance the size and number of components they can fit into the dimensions of a specific device. Similarly, they must balance the cost of the components against the cost people are willing to pay for a device.

All this leads to a situation where your app will often end up running on devices without the space, power, or capabilities you'd choose. Yes, there are people with devices containing several hundred gigabytes of storage, more CPU and GPU cores than you can count on your fingers, and more sensors than you might believe can fit inside the space available. But these are the outliers. Even if you're in the position of being able to know that all the people using your app have super-high-specification devices, you can improve the experience of using your app by fully considering how to use the available resources. Doing so will also help anyone who doesn't have such plentiful resources.

The most important resource to consider is power. As a mobile device isn't always connected to a power source, power must be considered as limited. Aside from some line-of-business scenarios, people use their devices for many things, and in all parts of their lives. If using your app drains the battery, you don't just prevent that person from continuing to use your app, you also stop them from living their lives as they want or performing other, possibly more important tasks. Your app or game is important. It just might not be *as important* as an email about a job offer, a phone call from a relative, or messages from a romantic interest.

Apps that respect the resource constraints of mobile devices don't just avoid draining the battery, they also don't fill the disk with unnecessary files that can't easily be deleted, and don't prevent other apps from making use of all the sensors and capabilities of the device. Chapter 14 will help you better understand and consider how to use resources within an app and what can be done to prevent unnecessary power usage. This will help you ensure that the value your app brings to the person using it isn't canceled out by negative consequences of preventing that person from doing other tasks.

1.3 How considering all six components can make apps better

The six components are designed as a structure for thinking about the experience of using a mobile app. By considering how each component impacts the app that you're building, you can ensure you're creating something that meets the needs and expectations of the people using it, works well on the devices it runs on, and overcomes the challenges of being mobile.

Right now, you're probably thinking this all sounds good in theory, but how does it work in practice? Let me walk you through three examples to show you how the six components can help highlight ways of improving users' experiences.

1.3.1 Example 1: an email client

Let me start with something familiar and that happens every day—an email client (figure 1.3). You may think email clients have been around long enough and are so well known and understood that there can't still be room for improvement. Not so. By using the six-component structure, in just a few minutes I came up with the following ideas on how to improve the experience.

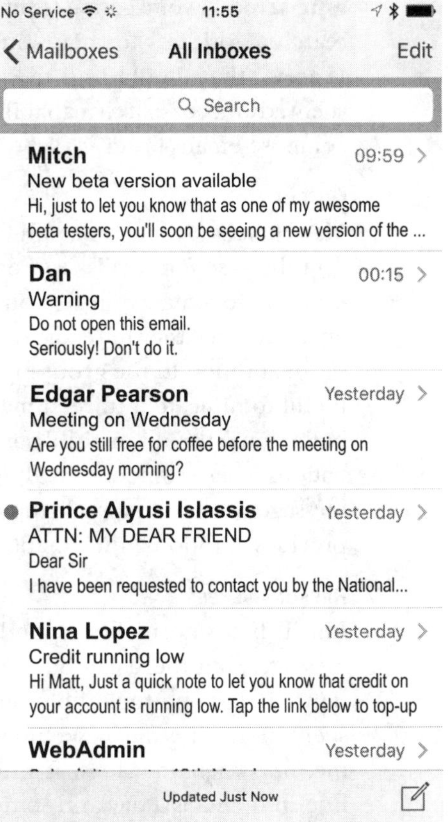

Figure 1.3 An email client

Context

Context covers a wide range of users, devices, and locations, as everyone uses email. Even if it isn't their primary method of communicating, it's almost impossible to use other services, including mobile phones, without an email account.

We know that on mobile devices people may not have a lot of time, and so a person using the device may get an idea for an email, but they don't have time to send it now. This suggests that the ability to start, save, and resume drafts of partially completed emails may be important, and so provides an area in which you can improve the experience.

Additionally, if a person is using email on multiple devices, it may be common that they read an email when it arrives on a phone but want to respond from a different device. There may be an opportunity to make this easier for people by adding a simple way to affix a specific flag for such messages. The benefit would be to distinguish any message for follow-up and any that will need to be on a specific device for responding.

Input

Email found popularity on the desktop, where messages are primarily text-based and entered via a keyboard. On mobile, this isn't always the case. Adding attachments or embedding content from other apps is desirable, but is hidden by some mobile mail clients deep inside a multilevel menu. Making this easier would help users who want to compose rich emails, some with multiple attachments, on a mobile device. Related to this is looking for easier ways of integrating with other apps.

Selecting who to send to should have a smart search that doesn't just rely on names, but also uses parts of domains. You can send me an email via me@mrlacey.com. If this were saved in your contacts without my name, it'd be hard to find (based on common search algorithms for name matching). But if you started to search for my surname (Lacey), that should find the address. Unfortunately, many email clients don't have such advanced search capabilities. Adding this ability will help make it possible to compose emails faster.

OUTPUT

Many emails are still sent with formatting, assuming they display on a large screen. This isn't the case for emails read on mobile. Being smart about reformatting or adding an easy way to switch to a text-only view if reformatting isn't possible could make many emails much easier to read, compared with manually zooming to view and navigate.

In addition to the grouping of threaded or otherwise related emails, it may also be useful to indicate if unread mail from the same sender has been received, even if not in the same thread or visible among the messages onscreen. This would help avoid situations where someone reading messages in the order they were received replies to a message without first realizing they've received another email that nullifies the first or provides additional information that would be useful when replying.

RESPONSIVENESS

Email clients normally respond to the receipt of new emails in a way that applies to all messages, but there can be times when this isn't desirable. Just as it's possible to configure my phone to audibly ring when certain people call me, even if the phone's in silent mode, there may be times when the same is true for email. My wife rarely emails me, but when she does, it's normally about something important. I receive several hundred emails a day and so don't want notifications about all of them, but any from my wife, I'd prefer to be notified about regardless.

When sending a message, it's often a case of pressing Send and hoping everything goes through OK. After pressing Send, a person may move on to doing something else while the app sends the email in the background. If something goes wrong and it's not possible to send the message, or a delivery failure response is received, the app should notify the person accordingly. It's not helpful for the email to remain in an outbox only for the person to discover this when returning to the app later. It's better to aid the process and help the person achieve their goal rather than being a passive bystander in failure.

CONNECTIVITY

If a person tries to send an email when they don't have a data connection available, the app could store that message and automatically send it when a suitable connection is available. The person who sent the email wouldn't have to concern themselves with whether they have connectivity and with manually triggering a send.

If people try to send emails with large attachments when using costly or slow network connections, they might appreciate a prompt to confirm the desired action. Doing so may help them avoid an unnecessarily large bill or a message not being sent, as they expected it to go quickly.

RESOURCES

Mail clients are generally good at managing resources related to data network connections, but there isn't always the same consideration paid to local resources on the device. When attaching a large file to an email, some clients create additional copies of the file, which can impact disk space and I/O. This should be avoided. Also, loading the contents of any attached file into memory before sending is an extravagant action that can slow the performance of the app and unnecessarily consume resources.

1.3.2 Example 2: a news app

As a second example, we'll consider a simple news app, like the one in figure 1.4. You'll find many apps like this in all the stores.

This news app shows a list of stories, grouped by categories. After selecting a headline, it's possible to read the story and see one or more related images.

Figure 1.4 A generic news app

CONTEXT

Because there's lots of competition in general-purpose news apps, specific targeting of content would provide a way to make the app unique and help appeal to and meet the needs of a particular audience. Short, text-based stories are good when a person has limited time, but it'd be beneficial to find ways to provide or link to more or related information if desired.

INPUT

Rather than show the same news to everyone, it may be possible to use the location of the device to identify and highlight relevant local news. This may be of greater interest and importance to the person using the app. Other information and apps on the device may also make it possible to identify stories more likely to be of benefit to the targeted audience.

Instead of showing the same stories, in the same order, to every person using the app, it's also possible to use a record of the stories the person has viewed previously to prioritize new stories. Working on the assumption and expectation that people will continue to be interested in the same topics they were interested in previously can be a way to highlight relevant stories a person would miss if otherwise sorting stories based on mass appeal. By tailoring the content without the person needing to do anything other than use the app, the quality of the experience and potential value grows over time with increased usage.

NOTE In this example, it's also important to be aware of the potential risks of any activity that filters news so you don't create a news bubble or reinforce a bias by only showing one side of a story.

Output

If people have little time to catch up on the news, they'll benefit from the display of easy-to-read summaries. They can also read the full version if they have more time available.

When people don't have the time or inclination to read a story, they may appreciate other ways to keep track of current affairs. This could be a pictorial view of images relating to stories, or a way for the story to be read aloud by the app so they can listen to the stories of interest while also performing another task. Formatting or presenting content in these ways achieves a better experience by ensuring that a person gets the news they want in a way that matches their needs.

Responsiveness

For an app based on providing information quickly, it's essential that the person who wants to use the app doesn't spend time waiting for content. To ensure that the reader can get the latest stories quickly, it could be beneficial to preload any recent stories in the background before the app launches. This works well if the use of the app occurs at predictable times or intervals, such as in the morning and evening. For example, the app could load new content in the early hours of the morning or late afternoon, ready to delight the reader by always having the latest content waiting for them when they launch it at breakfast or on the train for their commute home. Preloading images relating to stories would also allow content to load faster.

Building on the idea of using analytics from past usage as a heuristic for the stories that are likely to be of most interest to the person using the app, this data could be used to filter breaking news notifications. Rather than treating everything new as breaking news, filtering content would allow the app to notify people of the latest updates only on topics that interest them. This would mean the app's always there with relevant content and that it could preempt a person's desire to hear about what's most important to them.

Connectivity

Preloading content would also serve to ensure that there's content to display even while launching the app when there's no way of reaching the server to get the latest stories. As long as the age of the stories is made clear to the person using it, it's preferable to have some content to show the reader, so they can always read something regardless of network connectivity.

Loading data in the background can also be expensive, based on the location, type, and cost of connection available. Making this functionality configurable would be desirable for some people who'll use the app.

Resources

If the app takes input from other local sources, such as location or other data stores, you should consider the frequency of such checks and the cost of available computing power and battery resources. If preloading content and pre-caching images or videos, you need to

- Be careful of consequences to disk space usage
- Ensure an adequate process is in place to remove older files when no longer needed
- Make certain that the device maintains an adequate amount of free disk space

People are seldom impressed when improvements to the experience of using a single app come at a cost that prevents using the device for anything else.

1.3.3 Example 3: a tower defense game

As a final example, we'll look at something different—a tower defense game. Figure 1.5 shows an example of this.

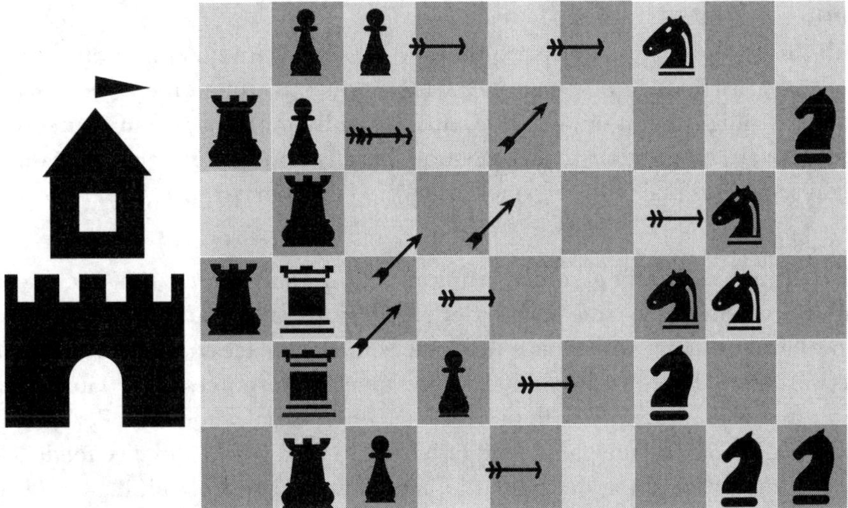

Figure 1.5 In this chess-inspired tower defense game, rooks and pawns are placed on the board to stop the knights advancing from the right as they try to storm the castle.

This is a popular strategy game where the aim is to position resources (towers) on a playing space to defend against approaching enemies. When successful, this earns a form of currency to obtain more towers to help guard against more formidable opponents.

CONTEXT

You'll find lots of competition for this type of game. To stand out, you'll need to find a way to differentiate your app from the alternatives and target a specific audience for it. Games like this often require playing for several minutes at a time. This contrasts with the common desire for short game play on a mobile device. The ability to have short as well long games may be appealing to players and will remove barriers to playing.

The size of the screen the game runs on impacts how much is visible or the level of detail, and may make play easier on devices with larger screens. You'll need to decide if this matters. In a single-player mode, this won't make a big difference, but it can create a disparity between players on different-sized devices who are playing against each other.

INPUT

With finger-based input, the hand obscures much of the screen and playing area on smaller devices. This makes it easy to accidentally position a tower in the wrong place. Having the ability to undo or modify such actions aids players' confidence; they won't suffer as the result of an accidental action or make a mistake from which they can't recover.

OUTPUT

With this style of game, there are times when things are quiet and other times when there's a great deal going on at once. During the busy times, the players may appreciate the highlighting of important events through appropriate sound effects and haptic feedback, in addition to information visually appearing onscreen. Some players might see this as making the game easier, but others may appreciate the assistance.

RESPONSIVENESS

With a graphically rich game targeting many different devices, it's necessary to have multiple copies of the visual assets used in the game, adjusted for different screens. An app will be faster if it only loads the images that are necessary and optimized for the specific device. There's no point taking the time and resources to load images the game won't use or that are bigger than necessary when equally good smaller assets are also available. By making the game load faster and providing informative feedback during the loading process, the delay for the person waiting will be minimal, and they'll be confident in what the app is doing while they wait.

CONNECTIVITY

A single player-mode means that the game can be playable offline. Having this would be in addition to an online mode that allows people to play against each other.

With an online mode, there'll be a need to handle connections lost part way through a game, without penalizing a person for network conditions beyond their control. Balance this with the need to consider players deliberately breaking the connection with the server and leaving the app when they're losing. The best behavior for this scenario will be dependent on the specific rewards and penalties the game employs for winning and losing. The key point is to ensure a player isn't penalized due to factors beyond their control. An online game would also need extra considerations for backend security to prevent other forms of cheating or misuse by unscrupulous players.

RESOURCES

Because what happens onscreen varies greatly between times when little is happening and times when there will be lots going on, this presents an opportunity to save resources when updating the screen. If nothing's changing or moving onscreen, there's no need to repaint the entire screen at a rate of 60 frames per second. By adjusting the refresh rate of the drawing algorithms used at different points in the game, it's possible to reduce overall battery consumption by not wasting processor cycles.

1.4 Why you need to consider the six components in your apps

Lots of apps have been built without knowledge of the six components and have still gone on to be successful. But to rely on luck instead of striving to make your app the best it can be to optimize your chance of success is a fool's errand. Considering each component will lead to improvements in every area of your mobile app.

You won't make a better app by tricking people into prolonged and continued use; that's not the aim. The goal is to create something that keeps people using the app because of what it provides or enables them to do. You'll better meet the needs of the user by first understanding what those needs are. You can help a person make better use of their time by making the app faster and easier to use. You can remove barriers that hinder comprehension and use by adopting common conventions and tailoring the app to the user. And, you can also create real value and grow by word of mouth through a best-in-class user experience. These points are important because of your competition and the expectations of those who are using or will use the app.

1.4.1 Experience is an important differentiator

Competition between apps can be fierce. Depending on the platform (or platforms) you build apps for, you'll be competing in the store with as many as several million other apps that all are vying for attention and installation. And, once installed on a device, you'll be competing with several dozen other apps for use. But it isn't that simplistic. You aren't competing against all other apps in the store or all the apps installed on a specific device. Few people will think, "Hey, I need a new app. I'll go to the store and see what's there."

Retail therapy through apps doesn't work the same way as purchasing physical products. The people who do browse the store looking for new apps for fun are part of a small minority. Similarly, people don't typically take their phone and choose from all the installed apps to find one they want to use at that time, unless they're bored.

Boredom

Boredom is a valid use case for many mobile apps, like games and social media apps that let a person browse through an endless stream of content. Solo journeys on public transportation and the period in the coffee shop while you're waiting for your drink: these are the times for which such boredom-busting apps were built.

Creating an app that people can use when bored or have a few spare minutes and want to pass the time isn't, on its own, an opportunity to compete. Any game that's playable for a few minutes or even a few seconds at a time meets this criterion, and they aren't all competition for your app. If the reason to install an app is that people might use it when they're bored, it's no different from myriad other apps. In turn, this makes it hard to persuade people to install the app.

Also consider the moral and ethical implications for creating something designed for use when bored. While people may use your app when they're bored, you'll make the world a better place by not creating something purely to help people waste time.

People get and use apps for specific reasons. If they want to access a specific service, they'll look for an app that provides that. If they want entertainment, they'll look for an app that provides their preferred types or sources. If they want to stay informed about a certain subject, they'll look to apps that focus on that specific area. In all these cases, it isn't the app that the person desires but the information, functionality, content, or value to which the app gives access.

ALTERNATIVE APPS ARE ONLY A FEW CLICKS AWAY

With millions of apps available, they can't be, and aren't, all completely different. For almost any task imaginable, several apps are available that will let you do some variation of the task. Do you want to edit your photos, record progress of important tasks, track your fitness routine, find somewhere to eat dinner, communicate with friends, meet new people, listen to music, track the latest fashion trends, monitor the status of an upcoming flight, discover new products, see the forecast for tomorrow's weather, or read a book? If so, you'll find many apps providing different ways to do all these things, more than you ever imagined possible.

The ready availability of alternatives means that you can't rely on your app's mere existence for success. With so many options, it's necessary to distinguish what you provide to separate yourself from the competition. Uniqueness isn't enough. To truly compete, your app should have meaningful differences that make it more desirable.

Even if there isn't an alternative or competitor to an app right now, you can't rely on this always being the case. Every day sees the release of thousands of new apps. If you've based your app on a new or novel idea, there's little to stop someone else from coming up with the same idea. If you've spotted an opportunity for an app, others may also see the same opportunity. In fact, the existence of your app in the store may show others who have the same idea that it's valid and serves a need that people want to solve. Furthermore, if you create an entirely new app and it becomes popular, your success will attract competitors who'll look to benefit from your success. You can't stop people from trying alternatives, but you can ensure that the experience of using your app is such that people come back after trying alternatives.

COMPETITION ISN'T LIMITED TO OTHER APPS

Many apps are created as alternatives to a website or other computer system, or as an alternative to a manual or paper-based system. Imagine going back to using the website of your social media network of choice rather than a third-party client that doesn't have every feature you require. Or consider remote workers who find it easier to record information on paper and later enter it into a terminal because it's easier than struggling to enter the details on the mobile device they carry with them.

Switching to any of these alternatives may be simpler for some people than changing apps. It's important to be aware of alternatives and ensure that the experience of your app is sufficiently preferable so that people start, and keep, using it.

EXPERIENCE STILL MATTERS, EVEN WHEN THERE'S NO COMPETITION

Two scenarios exist in which there are no alternatives to your app. These aren't an excuse or reason to ignore the experience of the person using the app, and a full consideration of the six components is still important in these scenarios, as it's good for the person using the app and ultimately the business providing the app. The two scenarios without alternatives are

- The official app of a service for which third-party apps aren't available
- Internal enterprise apps (also known as line-of-business apps)

For an app that's tied to a specific service, in the mind of the user, the experience of using the app is directly tied to the service. Consider an online movie-streaming service. No matter how good the backend servers or the range of titles available, if the only way to watch the movies is via a slow, clumsy app, it's an unpleasant experience. The user isn't going to think, "The service is good, but the app is poor." The user is going to think that the whole service is bad. In such a scenario, the concern shouldn't be that a person will start using an alternative app; the concern is that the person stops using and paying for the entire service and they'll go to a competitor.

Within a business, the incentives for a high-quality experience when using an app are different but just as important. For a long time, and in many situations, there's been an argument that the experience of enterprise apps doesn't have to be good; people will use them as they are because they have no choice in the matter. Here are some of the reasons why this shouldn't be the case:

- *Such apps are typically tied to productivity.* If an app's causing someone to do their job slower, it can have a financial impact on the business. On one app I worked on, I made changes to optimize algorithms and use caching such that doing an often-repeated task was now one second faster. The consequence of the time saved when multiplied by the number of times the task was performed and the number of people using the app resulted in a change that was worth the equivalent of around $15,000 per day (approximately $4 million per year) to the business.

- *Apps that are difficult to use frustrate or annoy the user.* It's generally accepted that you don't want to annoy or upset your staff if they'll be representing the business to customers; they may project their negative feelings on the customer or potential customer. I've seen, first hand, the implications of a staff member complaining about the app they must work with in front of a potential client and the cost that had to the business when they didn't win that customer's business.
- *Unduly complex and complicated apps require training.* Not only does this have an initial cost to the business, but it also adds to the cost of onboarding new staff and ensuring temporary and cover staff are able to use the app correctly.
- *Repeatedly having to use a tool that frustrates the user can be bad for morale.* Many studies indicate that a happier staff works harder and is more productive. Giving people tools (apps) that make them less productive doesn't make good business sense. Additionally, studies also show that unhappy workers end up taking more time off work due to illness. Again, this has a financial impact on a business.

Hopefully, these examples demonstrate the importance of creating apps that fully consider the experience of the user, and that it's insufficient to have an app that's merely functional.

1.4.2 Meet the expectations of those who'll use your app

It's rare for any app you build to be the first-ever app that a person uses. People will compare your app with other experiences, including the operating system (OS) and other apps that come with a device.

People are spoiled. They've seen and used a wide variety of high-quality apps and other software. In light of this, any app you create won't just be judged on what it does, or on how it compares to other apps in direct competition with yours, but with every positive experience they've had. You might create an app that's a million times better than your competition, but if it isn't easy to understand in comparison to other apps used on a regular basis, it still won't be seen favorably. Being the best of a bad bunch isn't good enough. You should strive to be one of the best. Period.

People have learned to expect more over time. Go back a relatively short time to the start of the millennium—the majority of software wasn't great. PC software was mostly the same, a series of battleship gray forms. The rise of mobile phone apps over the last few years has changed all that. People want and expect something fast, beautiful, and easy to use. It should help them achieve their desired task and get out of the way. It should improve their life or at least make it simpler or easier, and it must never frustrate or prevent a person from doing what they want. It's also the case that what was once the high-quality exception soon became the norm, and people want better still. Consumer expectations are high and likely only to increase. A desire for continuous improvement exists in people's minds.

These comparisons and level of expectations aren't limited to the consumer app space. The experiences people have outside of work inform their opinions relating to work too. It shouldn't be the case that people bemoan the fact that the apps they use at home or on their own devices are easier to use, faster, better, or in other ways preferable to those provided as part of their jobs. As mentioned earlier, when looking at alternatives, such negative app experiences can be financially bad for business.

1.4.3 Planning for success

The software business is more like all other kinds of businesses than many people wanting to create apps realize. At some point in time, it gained a place in the mind of the population as being a special case. I suspect this was due to the early stories of the success of a few developers. That anybody can have an idea, build an app, and make their fortune overnight is appealing. It's led to the idea that anyone who can write some code can build an app and be a success. Ultimately, this is unrealistic for all but a few "lucky" exceptions.

If you assume that you just need to write some code to be successful, now might be a good time for a reality check. To achieve success without doing the work to help achieve it is like buying a lottery ticket for a retirement plan. There's a tiny chance it may pay off, but that isn't something I've ever heard anyone recommend.

Beware of treating a mobile app differently than other products

The idea that a mobile app is special has thrown up some curious assumptions by those creating them. Compare an app with a website. The technical knowledge and skills to create the two are roughly similar, but you wouldn't hear the developer of a website blaming a search engine if no one comes to a new website they had built but not promoted. Oddly, however, many people creating apps seem justified in blaming the store if few people download an app they've made but not promoted.

Or, imagine a friend told you they wanted to leave their current job in a bank and start a business making and selling loaves of bread. You'd probably have lots of questions for them. "Lots of companies are already making and selling bread. How will you compete with such large, established competitors? Many types of bread exist. Which will you make? How will you persuade people to buy your bread? How and where will you sell it? How much will you charge? Will you be able to make enough money to pay your bills?" And so on. These are all reasonable and sensible questions to ask when starting an endeavor with financial considerations. If you were the friend, hopefully, you'd ask these questions of yourself too.

Now consider building a mobile app. A lot of similarities exist here. They're both low-cost, low-margin products with lots of competition. Both will require making something remarkable or sufficiently different from what already exists to be successful. Both will also require lots of effort to tell people about the new product, and persuade

(continued)

them of the benefits of purchasing. The questions you'd ask your friend are equally valid for both scenarios. Do you consider such questions before creating a mobile app or game? Treat a mobile app like any other product. Expect that making money and being a success with it requires as much effort.

"Failing to plan is planning to fail" is a modern-day proverb attributed to the well-known author on time management, Alan Lakein. It's a phrase that's often used in a variety of situations, and, I believe, it's appropriate to the business of mobile apps. There's also a corollary that is even more relevant, and that's that success which isn't defined in advance is harder to achieve. If you don't define success at the start of a project, when you come to measure it, you're making a judgment call based on what happened. This is the same as waiting to see what happens and then deciding if you want to call it a success or not. If you define what success looks like for you, you can do things that will help you work toward achieving it.

At the start of this chapter, I gave you the formula for app success, but I didn't define success in and of itself. What you consider a success might be different from what someone else would consider a success. That's perfectly fine. What you consider a success today may be different from your idea of it next year and will also likely vary between projects. Whatever your metric for success, you can achieve it in your apps if you provide value, use the six components to create an excellent experience, and do all you can to maximize your chance of luck.

It's time to delve deeper into the individual components. Context lies at the heart of any app experience, so we start there in the next chapter.

Summary

- App success comes from providing value, the experience of obtaining that value, and an element of luck.
- Experience is the most important factor to focus on when striving for success, as it's the one you have the greatest influence over and the one that can more easily set you apart from the competition.
- The six components of an intuitive app experience are context, input, output, responsiveness, connectivity, and resources.
- Context covers all the circumstances of use, and that knowledge lets you tailor the app for where, when, why, how, and who uses it.
- Input is about all the ways that data and instructions get into the app. Covering more than touch, understanding input lets you enable the people using your app to achieve their ultimate goals easily and as quickly as possible.
- Output needs to consider more than a miniaturized version of what's shown on a larger screen. Create visual output specifically for the mobile context in use. This may also include audio, haptic, or digital output.

- The perceived responsiveness of the app matters more than the time it takes to perform a function. Apps should be made to feel as fast as possible.
- Communication requires connectivity. Connectivity isn't universally available and can have different speeds, costs, and reliability. Apps need to tolerate all the different network conditions they'll encounter.
- Portable devices run under constraints that impact resources. The most important resource to manage is power.
- Businesses benefit when the experience of using internal apps is positive.
- Creating a high-quality experience helps you stand out from your competition and meet the expectations of the people using your app.

Part 1

Context

Think of context as the *environment and circumstances of use* for your app. To understand context is to understand everything around your app that isn't the app itself, but can impact interaction with it. Context is the who, where, when, which, why, what, and how of your app:

- Who is using the app? What's special, unique, or different about them?
- Where is the app used? Are there different uses in different countries or rooms?
- When is the app used? Is it used differently at different times of the day or year?
- Which tasks is the app used to help with? What alternatives are there?
- Why is the app used? What are people actually trying to achieve?
- What parts of the app are used? What do the people using it want the app to do?
- How is the app used? Is it the way that was originally intended?

Having answers to such questions provides a knowledge of context. In turn, it allows for the creation of apps that can provide an experience better suited to the people and circumstances in which they're using it. Without this knowledge, there's a risk of creating an app that's too generic and all-encompassing. This provides no distinct benefits to the people using it. Or, worse still, it's an app that no one wants or needs. Sadly, such apps make up the majority of what's available in app stores today. You don't want your app to join them.

Over the next three chapters, this part of the book will help you consider context by exploring three broad questions. You'll be asked to think about the device an app is running on, where and when it's used, and who's using it.

2 Who's using the app?

This chapter covers

- Seeing yourself as different
- Knowing who the app is for
- Understanding how people differ
- Appreciating how people use the app

You're unique. There's no one in the world who's exactly like you. That's a fantastic thing. You get to bring something unique to the apps that you create. The downside of your uniqueness is that the people who use the apps you create can be vastly different from you. If you're creating apps for yourself, that doesn't matter. If, as I suspect, you want more people using your app than just yourself, then it'll pay to consider who those people are. The consequences of not doing so can include a lot of wasted effort in creating something that doesn't meet the expectations of the people using the app, or that doesn't work the way they want, need, or expect. It's hard to create something that's intuitive for a person if you don't know anything about that person. Worse still, you may create something that they didn't want at all.

In this chapter, I'll introduce you to Mitch and share some of his experiences learning about the differences between himself and the people he builds apps for.

Let's begin by focusing on the most important thing to remember—the people who'll use your app aren't like you.

2.1 You aren't your users

Although there may be philosophical debates about what it truly means to know yourself, it should be easy to recognize that as the person creating an app, you'll have different ideas, thoughts, and feelings about the app than the people who use it. To create an app that allows for these differences, it's important that you

- Recognize how you're different
- Recognize that you're not average
- Be aware of how your situation affects your thinking

Your goals for using the app, the needs you want it to satisfy, and even your motivations for using it will differ wildly from the people who'll use the app. The following sections expand on those differences.

2.1.1 How you're different from your users

You can build something that exactly meets your needs, and easily justify or tolerate any rough edges. Not so with other people. Other people are an unknown, and it's much harder to meet the needs of another person if you don't know what they want. They'll also have an expectation of a level of quality you can't ignore.

KNOWING WHAT OTHER PEOPLE WANT FROM THE APP

Mitch did something that may seem strange to people with a business, research, or marketing background, but is common among developers, as it allows them to focus on what they know best. He built an app he wanted and then hoped others would want it too, without doing any research to test this. Mitch's app tracks a person's status and score on a popular gaming platform. It then creates an automatically updated wallpaper image displayed on a phone or a connected smart watch.

This wasn't Mitch's first idea for an app. Some of his friends were expecting their first child, and Mitch thought about creating something for them. As apps about infant and child development are popular, he found lots of information online he could use to build it. Creating apps this way is common. A developer has some information or access to an API, and so they turn it into an app. Fortunately, before Mitch went down this route, he did a quick evaluation of his options (figure 2.1).

It's possible to build a successful app without any knowledge of the subject or that isn't something you'd use. The latter scenario is a lot harder, and it means that you'll need to spend a lot more time talking to the people who might use the app. Although Mitch's friends who were expecting children could give him feedback on the app, he decided against this. This was the right decision. He'd have to spend a lot of time talking with them about what they wanted and needed from the app, and, although his friends wanted to be encouraging and liked the idea, they were more interested in preparing for the arrival of their child than in testing an app.

An example of using some simple questions to help evaluate app ideas

Factors	Baby/child app (idea 1)	Game info app (idea 2)
Have access to data/information	✓	✓
Know about the subject		✓
Interested in the subject		✓
Likely to use it		✓
Know or have access to users & beta testers	~	✓

Figure 2.1 Evaluating app ideas based on their relevance to a sole developer is important.

If you're building an app for a subject you're not familiar with, you need to start by finding out about it from the people who'll use the app. Don't rely on guesswork, but take the time to understand the domain and the people who'll use the app. With knowledge of the subject to which your app relates, you can be confident of using correct terminology. But more than that, it lets you use and test the app realistically. For personal projects, a level of knowledge also helps maintain interest and enthusiasm in the app. In enterprise scenarios, having knowledge about the business you're building apps for will help in various aspects of your job, not just in creating apps for your colleagues to use.

TOLERATING ROUGH EDGES

Although it's easy to be tolerant of any rough edges, imperfections, or other factors that compromise the experience of using the app when you build it for yourself, other people are far less accepting of any defect or inadequacy. This is especially true when alternatives are available (and there are almost always alternatives).

Getting back to the gamer info app, because Mitch originally built the app for himself, he added some features only for him. He hid these features behind an Advanced Features menu and assumed that no one else would use them. Although Mitch may appear to have recognized that he's different than the people who'll use the app, he made a dangerous mistake. He guessed at what people wanted and based his assumptions about what to build on these untested guesses (figure 2.2).

There's a popular variation of the Pareto Principle (or 80/20 rule) that's often applied to software: 80% of people use only 20% of the features, and it's not always the same 20%. This highlights the need for you to verify what people want and use, and then focus your efforts there.

Because Mitch didn't think other people would use the features he built for himself, he paid less attention to them than he did to other parts of the app, and spent less time on getting the interface and exception handling right. Mitch was happy to live with these "rough edges." He could easily improve the app in these areas, but he

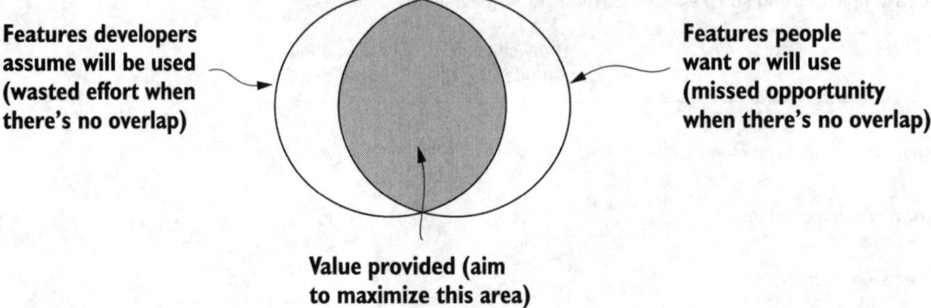
Features developers assume will be used (wasted effort when there's no overlap)
Features people want or will use (missed opportunity when there's no overlap)
Value provided (aim to maximize this area)

Figure 2.2 To avoid wasted effort and missed opportunities, match the features an app provides with what people want.

thought that no one else would benefit from them or was affected by them. Mitch was imagining a graph like that in figure 2.3, assuming the features of his app were down in the bottom-left corner.

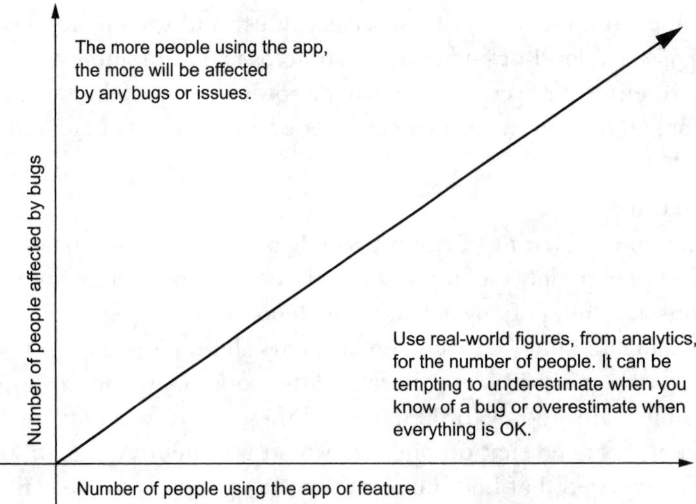
The more people using the app, the more will be affected by any bugs or issues.
Number of people affected by bugs
Use real-world figures, from analytics, for the number of people. It can be tempting to underestimate when you know of a bug or overestimate when everything is OK.
Number of people using the app or feature

Figure 2.3 As the number of people using an app goes up, so does the number of people affected by bugs.

Although a graph like the one in figure 2.3 can be useful in helping to inform priorities in the development and maintenance of an app, it can be dangerous to use this as an excuse to not fix a specific issue. People often feel a sense of entitlement to a high-quality app that you won't feel with something you've created for yourself. This expectation is influenced by other apps on the device. With few exceptions, the apps that come with a device are normally of high quality, and people expect the same from your apps, too.

NOTE The typical response to bugs found in apps downloaded from an app store is to leave a negative rating or review, and then look for an alternative app that, hopefully, will be better.

2.1.2 *You're not an average user*

When creating an app, you'll likely need to consider all aspects and scenarios of the app to a level far greater than anyone using the app. You, hopefully, know more about what's happening within the app and the device itself. Beyond that, you also know more about the wider ecosystem that the app and device are part of.

Mitch had to learn about all the different statuses and largest scores possible on the gaming platform, not just the ones that he had or had seen. He also needed to know about the entire range of devices his app would have to create images for. Creating an intuitive app experience requires that knowledge. He, like the creators of most apps, was like the developer in figure 2.4. When it comes to knowledge, information, and abilities related to the app, Mitch was atypical. This isn't a bad thing. What's important is recognizing being in such a position and that it's uncommon.

When creating an app, you need to be aware of the differences between yourself and all the people who'll use it. The people at the right of the graph are like you: the

Figure 2.4 The overconfidence and false consensus effects can easily lead to overestimating a typical user.

super-users of your software. They're the experts of the domain and will be the people who can teach you about the world in which your software lives.

Remember that such a group doesn't reflect most of the people who'll use the app. To focus on a small subset of the people who will or could potentially use the app is doing a disservice to them and hurts yourself by creating a poorer app experience: it won't be what most people want or need.

2.1.3 Be aware of the effects on your thinking

Be aware of two effects when considering your experiences. Together these can combine to create a negative synergistic effect, such that you presume that other people are a better version of yourself:

- *The overconfidence effect*—The inclination to overestimate what you know or what you're capable of doing.
- *The false consensus effect*—The presumption that your ways and beliefs are "the norm" and so will reflect the thoughts and behaviors of other people, too.

In the last section, I highlighted the importance of recognizing that as the developer, you have more knowledge and skills related to the app than a typical person. These effects emphasize the importance of recognizing that you're not like most people who'll use the app.

It's important to think about your app from the perspective of the people to the left of the developer in figure 2.4. These are the people who are choosing to use the app or need it as part of their job. If you focus on how you think the app will work and will be used, you increase the chances that what you create will be hard for people to use and not meet their needs in the ways they expect. This will be bad for both them (as they're frustrated by trying to use it) and you (when they stop using it and find an alternative).

Regarding figure 2.4, Mitch didn't think everyone was like him; he thought he was an exception. He had himself out on the far right as the only person using the advanced features and then everyone else far to the left. He was missing out by not offering the advanced features to others who may have wanted them, and he ignored the differences among the people using the app. Mitch would have benefited by asking early in the app's development, "Who is the app really for?"

It's important that you do the research before you start building any app to ensure that what you create is something that people want to use and will pay for. This may mean that you don't create some apps, or you iterate and evolve an idea with potential customers so you'll build something suitable for the people who'll use it.

Exercise: know that you're different

Check your understanding of how you're different from the people who'll use your app by saying whether the following are true or false:

1. You should always plan and research the people who'll use an app and what they'll want before you start building it.
2. People don't care about apps containing bugs.
3. You don't need to know about a subject to make an app for it.
4. As the developer of an app, you're like a typical user of that app.
5. Because you've built an app, you'll have a good understanding of who uses the app and how they use it.

2.2 Who's the app for?

One of my all-time favorite lines from a movie is by Jeff Goldblum in *Jurassic Park*. His character, Doctor Ian Malcolm, laments that, "Your scientists were so preoccupied with whether or not they could, they didn't stop to think if they should." In the film, he was talking about trying to bring dinosaurs back to life, but I think there's a strong parallel with app development.

Far too many people build apps to satisfy their curiosity, or because they feel they should have an app. They want to create an app without first considering whether they should, where *should* means whether anyone wants or needs the app. As in figure 2.5, ask a developer who's just released an app, "Who it's for?" They'll pause before finally responding with, "Everybody." What they mean is they don't know.

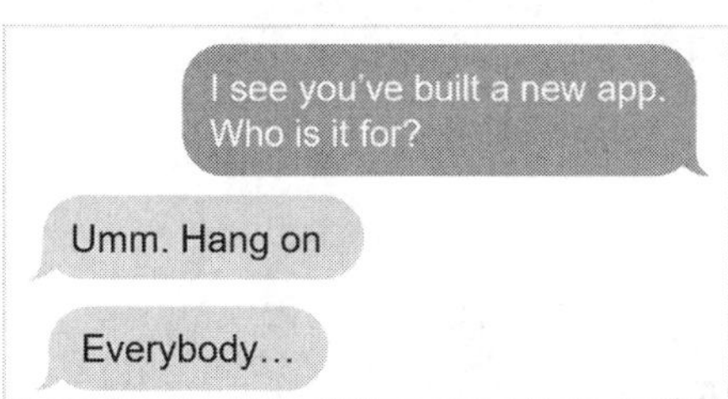

Figure 2.5 The belief that an app is for everyone is often a sign of not knowing who it's for.

In the film *Jurassic Park*, the consequences of making dinosaurs were complex and far-reaching. The consequences of making an app that nobody wants or needs aren't nearly as serious, but can extend beyond the time, money, and effort consumed in its creation. If you don't know who an app is for, or who'll use it, how can you know if they'll want it?

When there are many apps you could be working on, you'll want to work on something that might be a success. You'll have assumptions about the likelihood of success and what people want, but without identifying the consumer, you can't verify your beliefs. And, if you don't verify your assumptions, you risk building the wrong thing and wasting a lot of time, money, and effort in the process.

A poorly constructed app doesn't consider the needs and desires of the people who'll use it, doesn't give them value, wastes their time, and may frustrate them or inhibit them from achieving their desired goals or doing their job. That's if they download it at all. Such experiences also reflect badly on the companies and services related to the app.

To create an app that meets the wants, needs, and desires of consumers requires that you know who those people are. In the last section, I highlighted the importance of understanding that the people who'll use the app you create are different from you, but there are also many ways in which they can be different from each other.

People vary in many, many ways that include, but aren't limited to, age, gender, race, beliefs, education, language(s), physical size, health, income, employment, country, and the size of their immediate family or household. When you see such a list, it's easy to dismiss it as unhelpful. You could look at that list and say that people vary so much that it can't be possible to build something for everyone. That's true, but it's also not the point. The aim isn't to build for everyone. The goal is to highlight that there are lots of important ways that people differ, and so it's crucial that you don't create an app for a different group of people than those who'll end up using it.

2.2.1 Who'll get value from your app?

People use apps or play games because they get some value from doing so. You saw in the last chapter that value might come in one of many forms:

- It makes a task possible.
- It makes a task simpler.
- It earns a person money.
- It saves a person money.
- It entertains.
- It informs.
- It educates.
- It helps a person practice a task or skill.
- It may serve as a distraction or way to pass the time.

In all these instances, a person is trading the utility they gain from using the app against some alternative. That alternative could be another app, something in the real world, or something else entirely.

The consumers who'll be getting value from your app are real people, not vague concepts. Knowing they're real people with feelings should affect your perspective. They aren't some nondescript, unknown users somewhere outside of the room you're working in. They have hopes and dreams, wants and desires. They can be happy or sad, relaxed or stressed, and they have other things to do. With so much going on in the lives of people, you need to understand their motivations and reasons for using your app. This should be your primary classification for people using the app.

Categorizing the people using your app by traditional means (such as age, gender, location, and socioeconomic grouping) can reveal other benefits, but these factors are secondary. If you make an app for fans of a specific pop band, it might well be that a large proportion of your users are teenage girls in a certain part of the world, but it isn't these factors that make them your audience. The band that they're fans of matters most. As fans, there'll be things they'll want to do with the app.

The functionality that your app must provide isn't primarily defined by the age or gender of the people using it, but by what value the app provides them. Specific demographics can play a part in influencing the app to a secondary degree, but it's more important to focus on what value the app can provide. In the case of Mitch, the people his app can offer value to are those for whom their status and score on the gaming platform are important.

2.2.2 Understanding the potential user base

After Mitch released his app, he looked at the number of downloads and was disappointed. He had identified the people who'd use the app, and geared some promotions toward them, but they weren't downloading it in the numbers he'd hoped. The unique feature of Mitch's app was the smart watch integration, but the use of this was particularly low. Rather than focus on the disappointing usage numbers, Mitch decided to try to apply some context to these numbers and find out who might be interested in the app.

As an extreme case, he began by thinking of all the people in the world. It was clear that he could never get all the people in the world using his app because it only existed on a single platform. In an absolute best-case scenario, he'd never have more users than there were people using that platform. His app also worked with a specific smart watch. As not everyone had a device that could run the app, even fewer had the smart watch. And, although available in app stores worldwide, the app was only available in English, so this ruled out anyone who couldn't speak or at least get by with that language. Additionally, as the app related to data from a gaming platform, the value of the app was specific to those who used the platform.

The value the app provided also came at a cost. Because it was the default image displayed on the smart watch, the person wearing it couldn't display something else. This became an additional limiting factor on the number of people who might use the app.

After doing the analysis, Mitch could visualize who might use his app (figure 2.6). Considering this analysis, Mitch could view his download numbers in the context of an estimated total number of downloads the app might ever achieve (the shaded area). Although he was using an approximation, compared to this figure, his download number was much better than he originally thought.

There's a lot to learn from Mitch's experience. Although he'd identified the people who might get value from the app, this wasn't automatically the same as those who might use it. It wasn't merely a case of looking at all the people with a particular

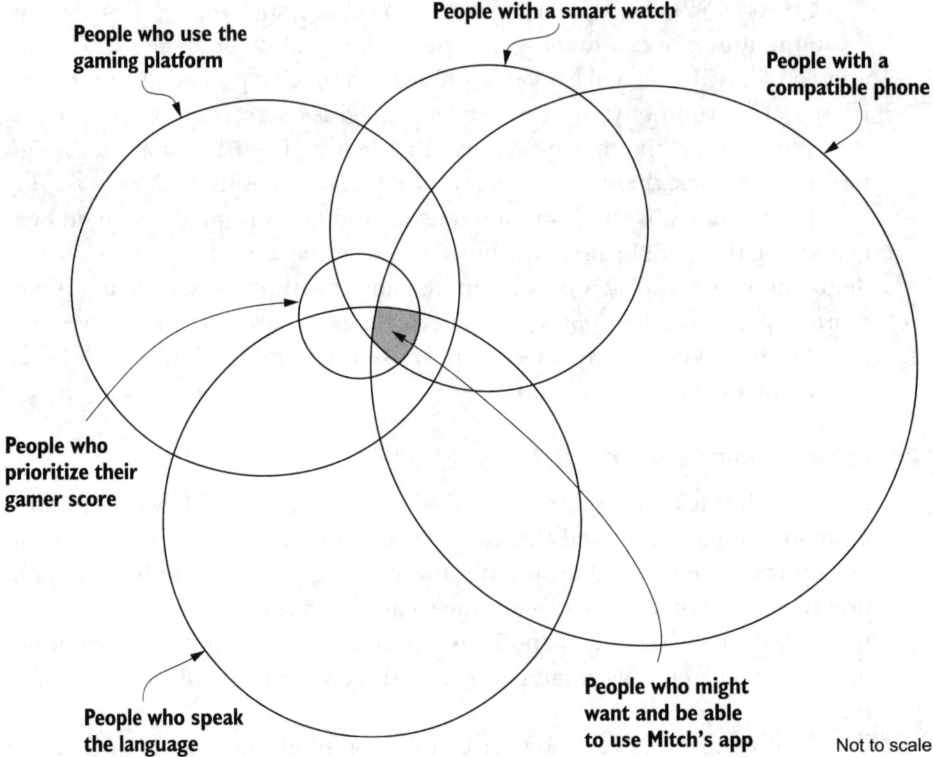

Figure 2.6 Venn diagram of potential users for Mitch's app

interest, who used a particular service, or had a device running the operating system (OS) that the app ran on and assuming they could potentially be a user.

Mitch's case was unusual as it relied on extra hardware, but the process of focusing on the factors that show who might use the app can be extremely valuable. Just looking at the size of an install base of an OS doesn't tell you much. It's rare that an app can provide value to every person with a device capable of running it. It's more relevant to consider the people an app can bring benefit to.

Mitch had made his app as an experiment and for the learning experience. Getting lots of users was nice, but if he wanted to make money from the app, it wouldn't be enough to know how many people could potentially use it. He needed to know if enough people were using it to be profitable.

2.2.3 Are there enough people who want the app?

"I want as many people using my app as possible." I've heard this statement many times, but it's naïve to want this and not do anything to achieve it. More importantly, it misses many essential points and raises lots of questions:

- What counts as "using [the] app"?
- Does the number of times people will use the app matter? Or is once enough?
- Do you want people to use the app regularly? If so, how do you define *regularly*?
- Do you care either way if they pay for it?
- Does it matter what the people who use the app do with it?
- Is it more important if people only use certain features or give specific information (such as creating an account)?
- What's required to get people to start using the app?

It's always possible to pay (either directly with incentives or indirectly by advertising) to get more people to use an app, but it won't always make economic sense to do so. Having lots of people wanting to use an app can be a good start, but if there's no way to make money from them, then it may not be wise to build and release the app. Similarly, having only a small number of people interested may not be a bad thing if they're each willing to pay a lot for the app.

It wasn't Mitch's original goal to make money from the app, but when he started charging for it, he only received a small payout from the app store. Out of curiosity, Mitch decided to do some calculations to see how profitable, or not, his efforts would have been as a business, and how many people he'd need to have using the app to make money.

If financial considerations are helping to drive your app, the number of potential users and the income they generate aren't the only factors. Development costs must be considered in any calculations about the potential viability of an app. Many ongoing costs also need to be considered:

- What will it cost to create updates?
- How much will it cost to support the people using the app and to maintain any ongoing services?
- How much will need to be or can be spent promoting the app?

Once you have an idea of these costs (even if they are zero), you can assess the viability of an app from a financial basis against an estimated return from each person using the app or playing the game. Figure 2.7 shows a simple formula for such an assessment.

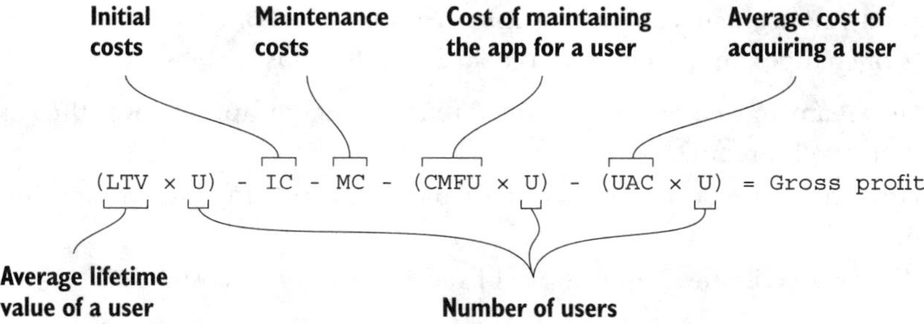

Figure 2.7 A formula for assessing the potential financial viability of an app

Initially, Mitch focused on two figures: how many downloads the app received (4,000) and how much money he got from the store ($278.60). It was at once clear from these numbers that his efforts weren't profitable, and he'd need to look at more figures. For each download, he was getting less than 7 cents (278.60/4,000). As Mitch was asking for $1.99 to keep using the app after a trial period, this didn't tally up. There were two types of people who were using the app: those who paid and those who didn't. The total number of downloads didn't matter. The number of people who paid was much more important. Of course, people must download before they can pay, but it doesn't automatically follow that a percentage will consistently convert to paying customers.

To help Mitch understand how profitable his app may have been, let's put the figures into the formula (figure 2.7). To do this, we first need some more numbers. Mitch estimated that he had spent 40 hours building the app and would spend half as much again working on bug fixes and new features in the future. Regarding valuing his time, he heard that a typical hourly rate for app developers was $100 per hour and so chose to use that figure. (It also helps make the math easier.) Finally, he estimated that he had spent four hours on support emails.

His initial development cost was $4,000 (40 × $100), ongoing costs would be $2,000 (20 × $100), and the maintenance cost per user was $0.10 (4 × $100 / 4,000). Putting these figures into the formula, Mitch got quite a shock. Had he built the app to make money, he would have lost more than $6,000:

(0.07 × 4,000) – 4,000 – 2,000 – (0.1 × 4,000) – (0 × 4,000) = -6,120

By experimenting with the figures, he discovered he'd need a lifetime value of $1.60 from each person who downloaded the app to break even. Potentially more worryingly, he realized that it cost him more to handle support for each person than he received in value. If Mitch wanted his app to make him money, a serious rethink was in order.

The value of using this formula isn't in the accuracy of the figures it produces, but in the lessons gained from understanding what's involved in creating a profitable app and the consequences of changes to your financial model. It's not a yardstick by which to measure your predictions. It's a tool to assess the perceived realism of your predictions, and a way for you to show that you've thought about all that's involved in making your app a financial success. Using this formula, it becomes easy to see the consequences of changes and it allows you to answer questions such as

- How many more people will I need to get using my app to cover the costs of further development?
- How much more can I afford to pay for acquiring new users and still be profitable?
- What would be the implications of reducing support costs?

Having answers to such questions can help after launching an app. More importantly, it gives you an idea of the level of work ahead of you before you start working on something, and the number of people you'll need to be profitable. This may result in not building something you'd like because the numbers don't make sense. Even though it doesn't look like it'll be a financial success, there are many reasons you may still want to build an app. At least you won't be surprised when you receive your financial statements.

2.2.4 Targeting groups of individuals

Individuals download (and buy) apps, but they need to know about them to do so. You know all about your app, but it's likely that most of the people who may be interested in using it have never heard of it. Targeting individuals can be difficult and expensive. Targeting groups of similar people is easier and cheaper.

Here's how Mitch used targeting to promote his app. He started out by promoting his app on social media and online forums relating to the gaming platform his app interacted with. He chose these options as they're free. After thinking about how the app could be profitable, he decided to spend some money on advertising to attract more people to download and eventually pay for his app.

Most advertising is bought based on demographic targeting. I mentioned earlier that traditional demographics of the people who may use an app might only have limited use in showing who may get value from an app, but they can be useful to know when advertising to those who may be interested in the app. By targeting your advertising to those who are more likely to become paying users of the app, you can be more effective in acquiring new users. To continue with Mitch, using his knowledge of the people active on the gaming platform, he knew where to target his advertising (figure 2.8).

If the demographic information hadn't been available to Mitch, he'd still have been better off by making an informed guess about the types of people most likely to be interested in the app, rather than displaying ads to anybody. Regardless of whether

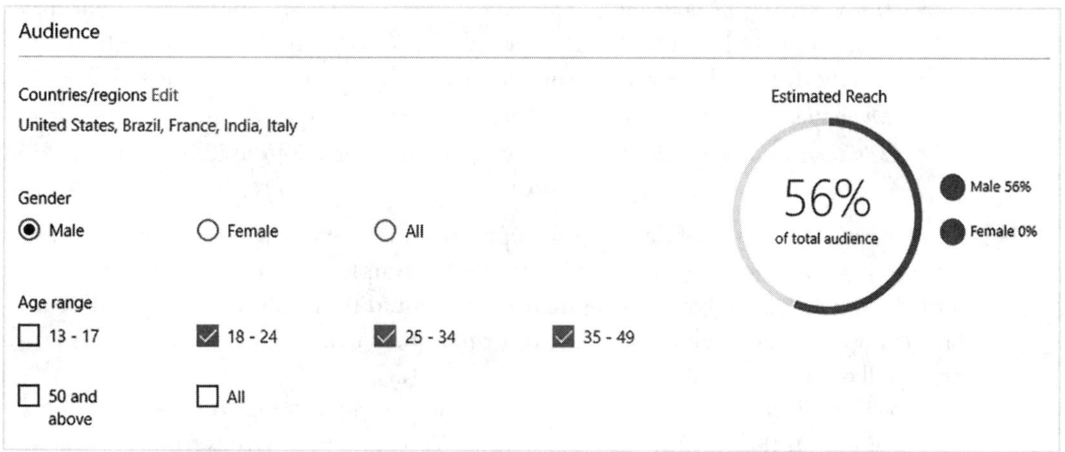

Figure 2.8 Targeted advertising is still typically based on traditional demographics.

the targeting is based on data or guesswork, it's still important to test both the ads you display and how they're targeted to ensure they're as effective as possible.

There are other reasons to understand the demographics of the people the app is intended for. For example, it'd be important to know if an app was intended for use by children or the elderly, as this would influence many aspects of the app's interface and functionality. Whatever the groups of individuals you define as the target audience for your app, it can be tricky to think of them in abstract terms, especially when you need to communicate about them within your team or company. For this reason, it can be useful to create personas for the targeted audience and what they'll be looking to get from using the app.

2.2.5 Putting on a persona, or several

Personas are a popular UX tool that helps you think about and relate to the people who'll use the app. A *persona* is a definition of a fictional person you can use to represent the needs of your targeted audience. The purpose of a persona is to help you think about the app from the perspective of a person who'll use it, rather than from your own. The aim is to help you avoid thoughts such as "I want it to do X," but rather, "It'll help Betty if the app does X," presuming Betty is one of your personas.

The amount of information in a persona can vary. Some people like to have rich personas with a detailed backstory. If you're just starting out with using them, then this is probably unnecessary. Start simple and add more details as you find helpful. The specific information needed for a persona can vary, but some essentials are always required:

- *A name*—This should be a real name to remind you that personas represent real people.
- *An image*—Use a photo of a real person. Stock images are fine for this, as the aim is to remind you that the persona represents real people.
- *Demographic and personality information*—Personas that represent people differ from the people using them, and so you'll need more details, enough to allow everybody who'll use the persona to imagine things from their perspective.
- *Motivation and value*—Prioritize these if there's more than one.
- *Additional information*—Include any specific notes about abilities, expectations, or goals (see section 2.3 for more).

Mitch created a couple of personas to represent the people his app was aimed at. You can see one of them in figure 2.9. Although a simple persona, it contains enough information to enable you to imagine how Ben would think about the app. This example also uses symbols for some of the information, which is optional but avoids creating a wall of text.

If you already have an app in the market, and people using it, you can create personas to represent the existing user population. You can use analytics from the app and related services, combined with the responses from any interviews or surveys, to help

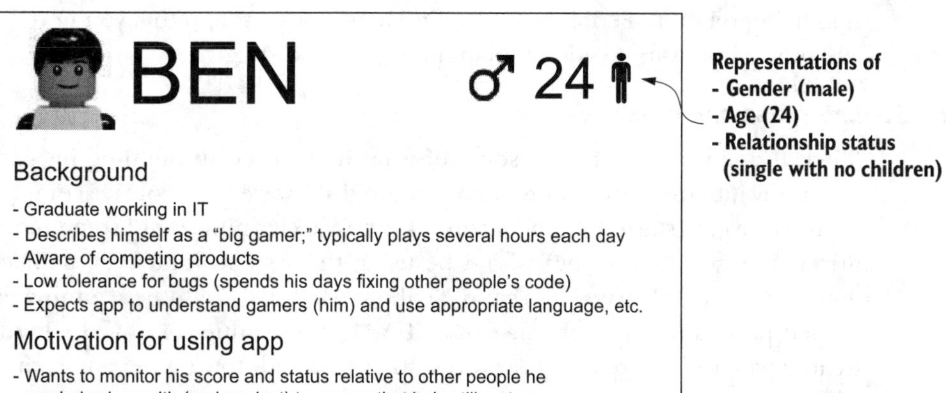

Figure 2.9 An example persona: with it, you can get an idea of someone the app is intended for.

with this. For enterprise apps, look to create personas for each of the job roles that use the app. In this scenario, it helps if your personas represent real people in those roles.

> **TIP** Once you've created your personas, it's often helpful to print them out and put them somewhere that you'll regularly see them to help you become familiar with them.

When starting to define personas, the question that often arises is about how many different personas you should make. Like all good technology-related questions, there's no single answer. A small, simple app with a few strictly defined features targeted at a narrow audience may only need one or two personas. A larger and more broadly featured app intended for use by a variety of people will need more. Four or five is the practical limit. Beyond this, it can be hard to remember them all, and there begins to be overlap among the personas.

There can be cases where you'll need more personas. Be sure they are all genuinely different. If you have more than four personas when creating the first version of an app, it may also be a good indication that what you're creating is overly complicated. In this scenario, you'll benefit from reducing the initial scope of the app so you can be sure you create something that people will use.

Once you have an established app, you can add further features to extend the value and usefulness it offers, and to make it relevant to a wider collection of people. When enhancing an existing app and adding more functionality, the number of personas can start to grow. If creating new functionality for different people, create new personas. Existing personas will still be relevant, as, presumably, you don't want any new features or functionality to negatively impact the people currently using the app.

You may need to update existing personas over time and as new features are added. Competition and other changes in the marketplace may mean some personas stop being relevant. People may also find a use for your app that you never intended, and so you may want to add or adapt personas accordingly.

2.2.6 Enterprise app usage

Mitch thought he could take some of what he learned in building his gaming app and apply it to his day job of building internal software for a courier company. When his next project started, he persuaded his boss to let him spend some time with the drivers and warehouse staff who'd be using the systems he'd eventually create. By doing this, Mitch learned a great deal about what it's like to be scanning awkwardly shaped parcels in the back of a van at 4 A.M., the realities of how the hardware was treated when it's cold, and how the software slowed down a person at the end of a 14-hour shift. These lessons were important and weren't things he'd learn while sitting at his office desk. Nor would he appreciate them as much if a colleague had told him.

Just as important as the technical insights were the things he learned in the break room over a cup of coffee or chatting in the van between deliveries. By spending time with the people who needed the software as part of their jobs, he gained special insight into what it was like to live with the software he was making. He learned how they felt at different times of the day, what was important to them, and what motivated them. These were valuable lessons that he could apply to the software he was building for the company. In this instance, Mitch wasn't building a mobile app, but it was clear that this information would be equally valuable if he were. It works the other way too, as shown in figure 2.10.

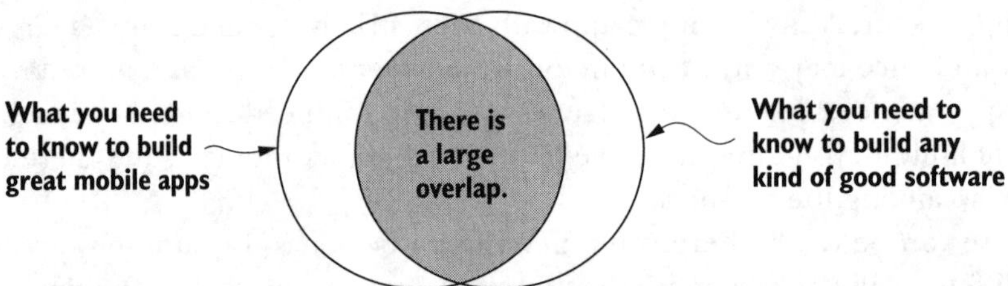

Figure 2.10 Learning to build great mobile apps can help with other types of software, too.

If you're building enterprise or line-of-business apps, then identifying and accessing the people who are, or will be, using the app should be easy, as it'll probably be based on their job. Go and talk to them. Watch as they use the app and perform their tasks. Ask them how they feel about the software. Ask how the software makes them feel. Understand what they find easy and what they find hard. Watch what they do with the software while they use it. Don't just listen to them describe using it, try using it yourself to perform the task.

To be able to build something and to understand the impact it'd have on Karen, who worked in the warehouse, and a hundred other people like her, at the busiest part of the day, meant that Mitch knew how what he was doing with the code would directly affect people in the real world. Plus, he could be confident he was making something that would help and not hinder business. He'd know where to focus on improving application performance so it would most help drivers like Andy. He came to understand how the realities of doing a job could sometimes conflict with official operational procedures. With that knowledge, it was easy to implement the updated procedures in the software to help both the people doing the work and the business.

The benefit came from a focus on people, rather than technology, and that focus translated into a benefit for the business. A similar focus on people over the technological side of your app can help you too, whether it's for use in an enterprise or not.

Put it into practice: know your users

- Answer these questions (there may be multiple answers, but be specific):
  - Why are you making this app?
  - Who's it for?
  - What are these people trying to do that the app will enable? (What's the value they'll get from the app?)
- Create personas to represent the different people who'll use the app. Where the people who may use the app are different from you, pay attention to any particular abilities, expectations, or goals they may have.
- Identify the targeted audience. If the eventual number of people who'll use the app matters, estimate how many people could potentially use the app. This is important if there are prerequisites or other requirements for using the app, or it may have a niche appeal.
- Understand your possible finances relating to the app. If the app is expected to make money, do some calculations to see how many people you'll need using it for it to be profitable. Then see how changes in lifetime value and user-acquisition costs cause these figures to vary.

2.3 People aren't all the same

I've covered a lot of details about how the people who use your app are different from you, and how to categorize their differences to think about them in groups. You should also consider differences in their

- Abilities
- Expectations
- Goals

Many people creating apps ignore these differences, but that isn't a reason for you to do the same. Don't copy what others have done before in other apps. Instead, focus on what's right for the people using your app.

> **Person vs. user**
>
> It's common to refer to the people who use an app as *users*. In other scenarios, calling someone a user has negative connotations. When thinking about software, there are reasons not to use this term.
>
> By using the abstract term *users*, it's easy to dehumanize the people who use your app and think of them as an anonymous and homogenous group, where they're all the same and aren't important. Instead, by talking about the people or a person who uses an app, you can more easily think about how the app is designed and behaves. This impacts its usability for real people rather than theoretical ones.
>
> As I have throughout this book, I encourage you to talk about the people who'll use the app rather than the users when not discussing an abstract concept. This helps you think about the consequences of your decisions and actions in terms of how those affect real people.

2.3.1 Consider people's differing abilities

Disability is a term that has many connotations. It covers physical, mental, emotional, and developmental impairments that affect people from birth or as the result of an event during a person's life. It can also have negative implications and result in discrimination. Rather than use the term *disability*, it may be more helpful to think about *inclusivity* or *universal accessibility*. Using these terms can help you think about how you'd create something that's useful to and usable by more people, instead of concentrating on their differences or limitations.

By being fully inclusive, you can avoid discriminating on a wide range of factors that extend beyond an individual's abilities but also include knowledge, education, culture, location, gender, and age. It may not be possible to make something that'll work for absolutely everybody all the time. But by considering all people, you can make something for the broadest spectrum of people. If an app doesn't have any capability for accessible use, then no one will be able to use it all the time.

To make your development task simpler, you may try to argue that those with disabilities are beyond your targeted audience. There are three potential issues with this argument:

- Many countries have laws preventing such discrimination. Similarly, many large companies and governments also have policies about only using suppliers and services (including apps) that are usable by all.
- There's a moral argument against discrimination.
- Not all disabilities and limitations are permanent. Some apply to people at certain times or in certain circumstances.

Table 2.1 shows temporary situations that could potentially affect anyone and comparable permanent situations. Even though these can differently affect a person's ability to perform a task, the consequences for handling them can be the same.

Table 2.1 Examples of temporary and permanent situations affecting app usage and the consequences for handling them

Temporary situation	Permanent situation	Consequence
Having a cold or the flu	Limited speech capability or speech affectation	Limits the ability to rely on the accuracy of speech-to-text interpretation for input into the app.
Using the app in a noisy environment	Deaf or hard of hearing	The audible output from the app can be missed. It shouldn't be the sole mechanism for communicating from the app.
Using the app in bright sunlight	Blind or visually impaired	You can't rely solely on communicating information through displaying it onscreen.
Broken finger or sprained wrist	Arthritis or other condition affecting fine motor control	Limited ability to interact with items onscreen or perform precise gestures.
App in an unknown language	Learning difficulties	Complicated text may not be understood. Avoid having complicated text as the only way you communicate something.

Inclusivity should form part of the discussions around the context of your app, as it can have fundamental and conceptual implications for how you build it. Your aim should be to focus on creating something that more people can use from the start, rather than adding considerations for those who are in some way different toward the end. It's harder to add such support to an app that already exists. Providing this support at the beginning is also normally faster and cheaper.

NOTE Meet the expectations and needs that more people will have for your app by building in accessibility from the start.

Mitch overlooked making any special considerations for people who need them because he didn't have any such requirements when initially building the gaming app for himself. Based on feedback he received after launching, he went back and changed some of the colors in the app, because some people with color blindness (or color vision deficiency) had difficulty reading parts of the screen. He also added support for the text in the app to reflect the system text-size settings on the device; some people needed the text to be larger to be able to read it comfortably.

2.3.2 Consider people's differing expectations

Like the person who expected Mitch's app to respect the system setting for the size of displayed text, we all have expectations about how things work. We expect that the things we use now will work like the things we've used previously. And when using something again, we expect that it'll work in the same way on each later occasion. To provide an intuitive experience for the people using your app, it's important to understand expectations.

You'll recognize the leftmost icon in figure 2.11 and understand that it shows an action for saving something. The image represents a floppy diskette and is still used in

PC apps. Although apps that ran on PCs informed much of what happened in the early periods of mobile app development, the evolution of apps over the last few years means that many such influences are no longer relevant—but they persist. The other icons in figure 2.11 also show real-world items that may not be familiar to all mobile users outside of apps.

Figure 2.11 Traditional and common icons don't make immediate sense, or may seem out of place, to many people in a mobile app–first world.

A Save icon makes little sense for people who came straight to mobile apps and never used a PC (such as in parts of Asia, Africa, and South America, or younger people the world over). The need for the icon can even break some expectations. For many people, it isn't unreasonable to expect the app to save information automatically. Why should a smart device need instruction to save something? If it's smart, why wouldn't it know to do this automatically? And, why the image of a physical disk when saving in the cloud? The device and the other apps that come with it set expectations for all subsequently installed apps. Expectations extend to the content of an app, too.

Consider a game about managing a farm. No one would expect the inclusion of all the different animals pictured in figure 2.12. The inclusion of some is appropriate to different people, based on religious and cultural reasons. Similarly, the reason for having some animals on the farm for food rather than as working animals may be as out of place as having rice as a crop in some countries.

People will have different expectations about which of these animals might be seen on a farm.
This is similar to how different people will have different expectations about your apps.

Figure 2.12 Do all of these animals belong on a farm? In every place your app is used?

The enterprise is a special case when it comes to managing expectations. There's often a necessity to balance a consistency with existing software and the expectations of staff, based on their use of apps outside of work. Unfortunately, the creation of existing enterprise software focuses on functionality over usability. This focus contrasts with popular consumer apps that typically make usability a much higher priority. There's a growing expectation among people using enterprise apps that they offer an experience comparable to that which they get from the consumer-focused apps they use outside the enterprise.

Our experiences have taught us that most of the time things work, but they've also shown us that sometimes things don't work, or don't work the way we expect. When it comes to failures, bugs in software, or other exceptional circumstances, we need to consider expectations here, too.

Your actions when things go wrong can leave a lasting impression on the people using your software. If you know what to expect when a person reacts if something goes wrong, you'll gain insight into how to prioritize, ensuring that you meet those expectations. And even though you should always look to minimize bugs in an app, there are times when this is more important because of what the person using it expects. Having had to deal with scenarios like the one in figure 2.13, I'm keenly aware of this.

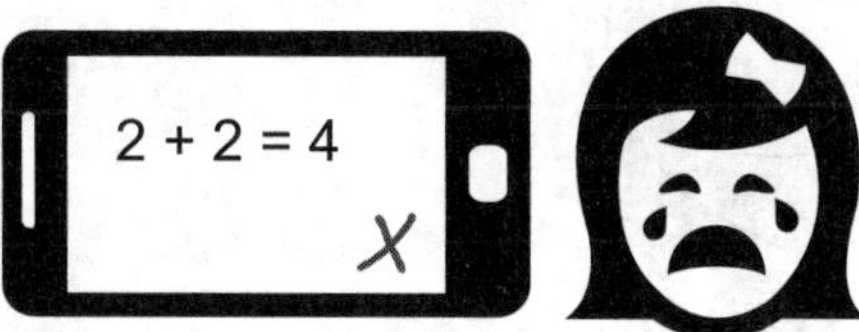
"But, [sniff] it said I got it wrong [sniff] when I didn't, Daddy [sniff]!"
2 + 2 = 4
X

Figure 2.13 As well as showing other problems, errors in code can cause negative emotional reactions.

Our expectations influence what we want from an app in many ways. As a developer, it's wise to remember the biggest presumption—the people using the app expect to achieve their desired goal.

2.3.3 *Consider people's differing goals*

Just as different apps provide different value, different people can also have different goals for using an app. Although the definition of value is broad, goals are more targeted. A game can give value by entertaining and helping people pass the time, but different players can have different goals. Some may want to complete it as quickly as possible and then move on to another. Others may want to be as good at the game as they can be, while still others may want to achieve a feeling of satisfaction from completing a challenge. A great game allows people to achieve these different goals.

As another example, where the value of a social networking app is defined as being able to help connect with friends and acquaintances, this translates into many different goals. A person using the app may want to keep up with everything done by a specific person, find out what's been happening in the lives of people they haven't been in contact with, or keep in touch with family in another part of the world. In each case, the architecture of the app affects how easy it is to meet a specific goal. It could have a generic interface that allows the person using it to achieve each of these goals.

But the generic nature can make it harder to achieve a specific goal when compared to an app created specifically to accomplish an individual goal.

With many different potential goals for using an app, it's important to define the goals the app is trying to help people achieve. It may not be possible to design for all specific goals, and so you'll have to decide which ones the app will help people achieve. Figure 2.14 gives a simple way to visualize this.

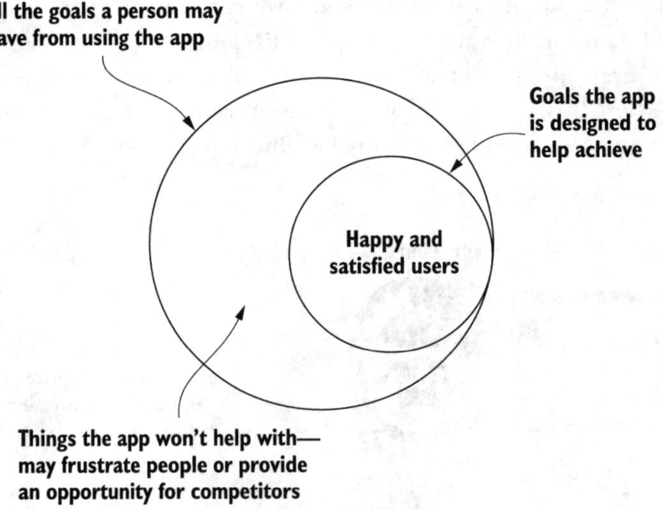

Figure 2.14 Design your app to achieve the goals of the people using it.

You can identify goals with which the app doesn't help. Knowing this is important because it identifies limits and helps define whom to target when promoting the app. Alternatively, you could create an app that might not target a specific goal, but serves people broadly by providing value in a generic way. Such broad functionality can give value to more people, but people who have specific goals may get more from an app that focuses on helping to achieve their objectives.

As with Mitch, there may be times when you might not want to provide support for certain goals. A person who used his app contacted Mitch and asked for the ability to work with another gaming platform. The person's goal was to visualize all their gaming scores in one place. Because the other gaming platform didn't have an officially supported API to get the data the app needed, Mitch chose not to do this. There was an unsupported, unofficial way to get the data, but Mitch decided the risk of this changing or going away in the future outweighed any potential benefit.

Exercise: being aware of people's differences

Fill in the blanks in the following paragraph to confirm your understanding of the last section:

Differences in abilities that affect how people interact with your app can be ______ or permanent and can potentially affect ______. Make your apps inclusive and accessible, to avoid ______ and to meet moral and ______ responsibilities. The expectations people have for your app will be based on other ______ they've used and other ______ on the same device. By defining and communicating the goals the app will help with, you make it easier to ensure you help people ______ what they want and make them ______.

2.4 *What are people doing?*

Despite all the planning, research, preparation, and theorizing you may do about your app before it's released, there are certain to be disparities once it's released and in use. Two you need to consider include

- What people do with the app
- What else people are doing while using the app

This knowledge lets you verify assumptions made about the use of the app so you can adjust and make changes if they don't reflect reality. To help your understanding of these considerations, I go into greater detail about them in the following sections.

2.4.1 *What are people doing with the app?*

Mitch wanted to better understand the people who were using his app, and the ways they were using it. He wanted to understand what worked and what needed changing or improving. He also wanted to confirm the expectations and assumptions he had about what people do with the app and how they use it.

To get details about how people are using an app, watch them or ask them. Because people don't always do what they say they do, intentionally or otherwise, it's normally smart to do both. This is the approach Mitch took.

AUTOMATED MONITORING

Automated tools provide the easiest means of monitoring crashes and errors. For simplicity, Mitch started by using the analytics data from the store. (He knew he could switch to a third-party solution in the future if needed.) The first time he did this he discovered some issues that he hadn't been aware of, or even considered previously. The situation wasn't as bad as for the app shown in figure 2.15, but it was certainly a task worth doing.

Monitoring feature usage is also important because it can show where people are getting value from the app. Unused features may not be wanted or may not be discoverable. Such features can highlight areas where you need to invest more effort to make them easier for people to use. They can also indicate something that isn't providing any

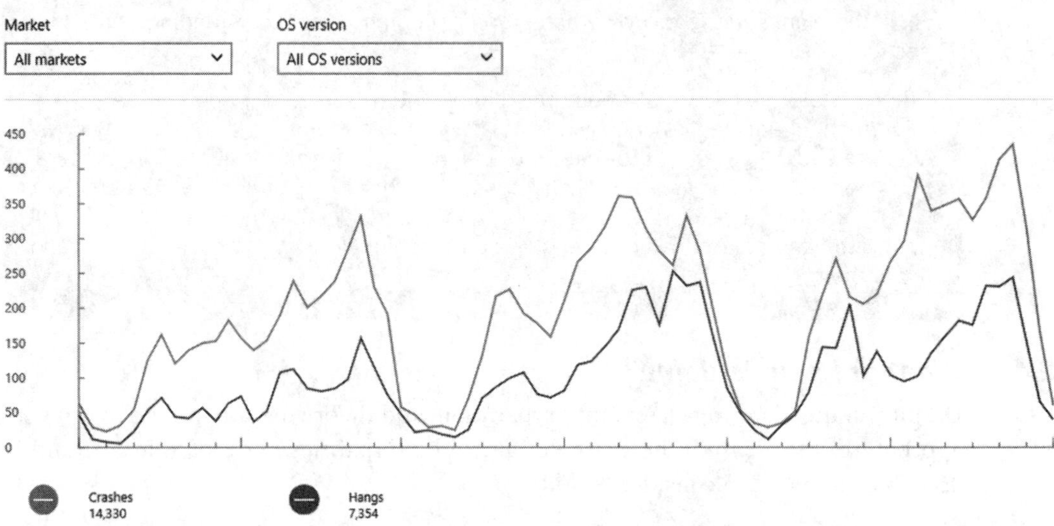

Figure 2.15 An example crash report showing many crashes and hangs. The value doesn't come from capturing data, but from acting on the information revealed.

value to the user, and so could be removed from the app. This was how Mitch learned that the use of the smart watch integration in his app was particularly low.

Tracking feature usage is particularly important when testing new features. It can be crucial to verify that any testers do check new features or functionality before you release them to a wider audience.

> **Privacy considerations and analytics data**
>
> Any information you capture about a person has potential implications for privacy, and you shouldn't do anything with a person's data without their permission. When people use an app and enter their information into it, they put a level of trust in the app and the people who produce and support it. It's important to respect their trust. Where in the world you and the person using the app are can have different legal requirements regarding the need for and contents of a privacy policy.
>
> You can also include an End User License Agreement (EULA) with your app. But EULAs have gained a bad reputation due to their length and because the legal language they use is hard for those who aren't in the legal profession to understand. Because of this, many people have become accustomed to not reading these and just click Accept. This behavior has, in turn, raised questions about whether people are giving their *informed consent* to the agreement and what's in it.
>
> You're also responsible for any data captured through third-party services, libraries, or SDKs you include with your app, as they may have their own privacy, data collection, and retention policies. Include references to these in your apps.

> To avoid any legal consequences, always store personal data in line with the laws of the territories where both you and the person using the app live. You should also be transparent about the data you capture and store, and take reasonable steps to keep it secure. The security of data is an important topic, but its size and scope make it too big a subject to include in this book.

As well as the information you specifically capture, third-party analytics providers may offer additional information about the people using the app. This information can include demographic details that may be useful in profiling and grouping the people using the app, and in helping to identify common traits among them. Some stores provide demographic information about the people downloading and using apps, but this is provided at a high level and cannot be tied to individual user sessions, so it has less value.

Every app should include some level of instrumentation and automated monitoring, and many free solutions are available. Even basic information about crashes and actual usage can be invaluable in addressing problems and knowing what people are doing with the app.

MANUAL OBSERVATION

Don't overlook physically observing what people are doing with your app. Mitch wanted to see what he could learn from manually seeing people using the app, especially after the insights he gained from the automated monitoring of app usage. So he performed some "guerilla" usability testing.

While talking with some people at a local developer meetup, he told them about his app. He noticed that someone got out their phone, downloaded his app, and tried using it. He watched carefully from a distance and then asked them some questions to understand what they were trying to do and why they did what they did. Many of the answers were as expected, but he did get one surprising answer that's making him reconsider some of the wording in the app.

Such a basic usability study is available to anyone, not only to those with access to dedicated labs and experienced researchers as part of the development team. For basic usability testing, you need to follow three simple steps:

1. Find someone using the app.
2. Watch them use the app (preferably without them realizing you're watching).
3. Ask questions about what you see.

It may seem a trivially simple process, but it can be effective. There are some subtleties and clarifications, however, of which to be aware:

- It's OK to ask someone to use the app or show you how they perform a specific task. It isn't necessary for you to wait until someone next to you happens to start using the app as you happen to watch over their shoulder.

- People may modify their behavior if they know someone's watching them. Therefore, it can be preferable to observe people who don't know you're watching. When this isn't possible, one good alternative to this is to ask people to recreate how they've done something in the past, or ask them to show you how to perform a task. If they make comments about the possibility of other ways of doing things, you can ask them about these, too.
- Ask questions about why the person performed the actions they did. What was their goal in doing so? Ask if there are alternative ways to achieve the same thing (whether there are or not) and how they compare. Were these considered?
- Also ask general questions about the app if they've used it before. Why do they use it? How did they hear about it? What alternatives have they tried? What do they particularly like about it? Have they had any problems with it? Is there anything they'd like it to do that it doesn't?

You'll get value from every person you talk to about your app, but you'll start to hear the same things repeated after you talk to more than five or six. That makes this a good number of people to start with and is something that anyone can achieve.

Usability testing is a complex task and can be daunting when you first approach it. To learn more about usability testing, I recommend the book *Rocket Surgery Made Easy* by Steve Krug (New Riders, 2009). It's an introduction to usability testing for websites, but most of what it covers is also applicable to mobile apps.

SOLICITING FEEDBACK

Mitch wanted to get input and feedback from more people than he could reach physically, but many of the people who use his app live in different countries. The app didn't need the creation of an account to use it, nor did it ask for any contact information. This meant that he couldn't ask people directly for feedback outside the app, so he added a Send Feedback option to the menu in the app so people could contact him at any time. He also added a prompt for feedback (figure 2.16) every five times someone used the app. Mitch was also careful not to ask for feedback if someone had already submitted some or indicated they didn't want to be asked again.

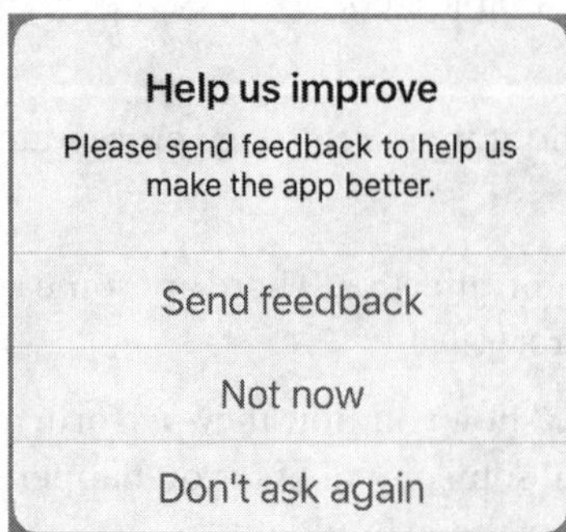

Figure 2.16 Let the people who're using your app know you want their feedback by asking for it.

The feedback options in Mitch's case produced a few useful pieces of information, and he was able to reply to the emails for more information when needed. But the number of responses has been lower than he hoped for. So Mitch is considering changing the approach to ask specific questions, and offering to extend the trial period for people who provide useful feedback as a way of indicating his appreciation for their responses.

You may also want to add feedback prompts or links in areas that are new, or you feel possess opportunities for improvement. This can be particularly useful as part of beta testing as it draws attention to what's new and focuses responses on the specific areas you want to hear about. But be aware that there may be biases in the feedback that people give. Try to understand the motivation that people have for giving the responses they do, and remember that you don't always have to do everything that people ask for. What someone asks for and what they want aren't always the same thing.

MONITORING SUPPORT AND REVIEWS

As a solo developer, Mitch handled all the support requests and emails for the app. He also carefully read every review in the store to know what people were saying about it. He wanted to find out more about common requests the support team received so he could do more about the issues. After he started asking for feedback, he noticed some duplication between what people were saying in the feedback and in the contents of support email and reviews.

Providing support to customers wasn't a favorite way for Mitch to spend his time, but he found it highly beneficial. Mitch realized that he knew a lot more about what was going on with his app and the people who used it, compared to the software he built for his employer. He also recognized that this knowledge allowed him to make a better product for the people using it.

2.4.2 What else are people doing?

Few apps are used in isolation. A person may use multiple apps in combination to achieve their task. Knowledge of such larger tasks offers some opportunities to improve an app to help people achieve their goals and make the app more desirable. It can be difficult to identify the other things people are doing by looking at their usage of your app, so cover this as part of any conversations you have with the people using the app.

If a wider task involves using multiple apps, this can indicate an opportunity to incorporate extra functionality into your app. If people are using multiple apps that each present content from different sources, they may prefer a single app that has content from all sources. Functionality can also be combined in similar ways. For example, standalone image-editing apps used to be popular until individual components became widely available. That meant that any app could incorporate basic image editing and customization without the need for a separate app.

Mitch discovered that the images his app created were popular, and some people were going to extraordinary lengths to share them with other people on social media. To encourage this activity and make it easier for the people who want it, Mitch added the ability to share the images using native sharing capabilities, like the ones shown in figure 2.17.

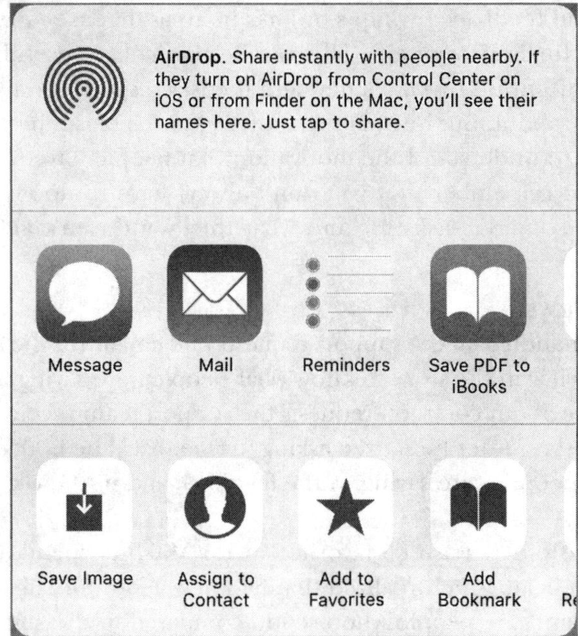

Figure 2.17 Sharing content between apps and services is a popular requirement and should be done through the native platform capabilities.

Where an app provides content can be a great sign of wider interests and opportunities. Focusing on the specific content that a person looks at may indicate ways the app can better meet their needs. Mitch saw such behavior with his app. He noticed that although his app dealt with a gaming platform, there was one game that was particularly popular with the people using his app. Based on this knowledge he created a separate version of his original app targeted toward fans of the popular game. Where he could, he added some specific extensions related to it. This second app became popular with fans of the game, who treated it like a companion app to the game.

This chapter has been about the people using your app and how knowledge of them can help you create a better experience for them, making your app more desirable. In the next chapter, I'll build on this to show you how knowledge of where, when, and how people are using the app can help, too.

Put it into practice: analyze app usage

- Add analytics to the app.

  Capture exceptions and page views. You can start by looking at the information you get from the store(s) where the app is available or look to a third-party service. You can always build your own system if you have special requirements or want to easily relate the analytics to other information you're capturing as part of the app. Spending time building your own tools for this at the start, however, risks becoming a distraction from building and improving the app.

  Avoid trying to capture analytics about everything, as you risk becoming overwhelmed by the volume of data. Instead, identify the things you're most interested in and add analytics to allow you to understand those first. Add more over time as the need arises.

  Update or add a privacy policy about the data collection and retention of analytics information.

- Monitor feedback.

  Have everyone involved in the app regularly read reviews and support requests relating to the app so they can see what the people who're using it think and gain insight into their perspectives. Ways you do this can be a weekly appointment in everyone's diary to look at reviews, regular time spent answering support requests, or having reviews automatically added to your internal group chat system (if you have one).

- Conduct a simple guerrilla user research study.

  Find someone who uses the app and ask them to show you how to (they) use it. Receive extra credit for any other (stealth) user observations or interviews you can implement.

Exercise: learn about and from the people using the app

Fill in the blanks with these terms:

analytics   support requests   details from the store

automatic exception reporting   store reviews

1. Add ______ to your app to see which features or parts of the app are used.
2. Use ______ so you can be proactive about addressing any errors or crashes.
3. Monitor ______ and ______ to learn what changes to the app people want.
4. Look at ________ to learn about user demographics.

Summary

- Do research before you start building an app to ensure you're going to make something people want.
- Recognize that you're different from the people who'll be using the app.
- Understand who the people who'll use the app are and what their aims are for using it, the value they're trying to achieve, and the goals they're trying to accomplish.
- It's important to understand the number of people who may be interested in and get benefit from the app before you start building it if it's going to matter once you have.
- Documenting details about the people who'll use the app and what they want, need, and expect in a persona can help you remember, then talk about these requirements.
- Appreciate that people have different abilities, capabilities, and skills that change and affect different people in different ways at different times.
- Building an app that's inclusive for all people is beneficial to people with short-term or circumstantial impairments, as well as those with long-term or permanent afflictions.
- People will have expectations about your app and how it'll work. If you can be aware of these in advance, you can avoid any negative experiences felt by breaking them.
- You'll gain lots of useful information to help improve the app by monitoring and watching what people do with it.
- Once released, verify that your assumptions and expectations of app usage are correct, and make any changes based on what's seen.

3 Where and when is the app used?

> ***This chapter covers***
> - Considering location on a macro and micro scale
> - Thinking about the time when an app is used
> - Thinking about how much time the app is used
> - Appreciating how other activities affect the app

The circumstances of use for your app extend beyond the person who's using it. Where and when people use an app can be as important, or, in some cases, even more significant. The place and time of use can impact who'll use your app. Who's using it can influence when and where they do so. Understand how the location and time of use can affect what people experience when using an app so you can apply this to your apps.

In this chapter, I'll introduce you to Harriet. She's an app and game developer. Harriet used analytics about where and when her apps were used to enhance their success by improving the experience of the people using them.

3.1 Where is the app used?

We know that people use apps everywhere, but what about your app specifically? Location can affect what people can and want to do. You could build an app that looks and behaves the same in all locations, but this might lead to a sub-optimal experience in some locations, or even to the app becoming unusable in others. Location can cover a broad range of places with varying levels of specificity. To help you think about how this can affect your app, this section looks at location from the macro and micro perspectives. Let's begin with Harriet.

3.1.1 App usage at a macro-geographic level

Harriet had a game that was only in English but was available worldwide. She had set aside some money and resources for improving the app for non-English speakers, but she didn't know which languages or locations to focus on. Rather than relying on guesswork or general guidelines, she added some analytics to the app to track which parts of the game were popular in different countries. Once she'd gathered a few weeks' worth of this information, she was able to act upon her discoveries.

First, she discovered that the game was unexpectedly popular in Thailand. She hadn't translated the app to Thai, and she hadn't done any specific promotion in that country. Knowing it was popular there encouraged her to create some modifications for people in Thailand. She then promoted it there so that it grew further in popularity (and profitability).

Second, she noticed that players in Romania spent 50% more time playing one of the mini-games than players in other countries. There was nothing specific about the mini-game that should have made it popular among Romanians, but it happened to correspond to a local trend at the time. In reaction to this, Harriet created a standalone version of the mini-game specifically for that market. The standalone mini-game gained popularity on its own and became a good driver of players to what was originally the main game.

Thinking about location on a macro level means thinking about regions, countries, and even continents. Location at this level can affect

- The types of apps that are appropriate
- The services that may be available
- Monetization and distribution approaches

Macro location isn't a proxy for context. You can't always be sure that when using an app in a specific country, certain other things are always true. But location can inform you about the people who are using the app and how they may differ.

> **Remember your data obligations**
> As mentioned in the last chapter, consider the implications of privacy, data capture, and retention of all information you obtain when identifying a location. There may be legal implications for you and your business relating to this.

It's easy to have broad views and expectations about people in a specific location. Such stereotypes can be largely true, but they never apply to everyone. That's OK, as it's unrealistic to expect to reach everybody in a market. A stereotype, if true, can help identify the appropriateness of an app or service, how well an app may function, and the viability of the intended monetization strategy.

In a country or region where people earn, on average, the equivalent of a few dollars a day, they may not have money to pay for content that people in other markets can. This means that you may need to price an app differently in different parts of the world. Or, you may need to use different monetization techniques in different regions (for example, charging in some countries while using in-app advertising in others). App stores and ad networks make this easy to do and are regularly improving, but the main app stores are still heavily reliant on credit card billing in most of the world. For large numbers of people in many parts of the world, this isn't realistic, but carrier-based billing is. To reach people in many growing countries, it's necessary to distribute your app through multiple app stores where the OS allows this.

Average income in a country also affects how much people can spend on services. As figure 3.1 shows, this is a part of the reason that people in countries where wages are lower also have slower internet connection speeds. If you're about to launch an app featuring streaming video content to a country where wages are low, now might be a good time to reconsider.

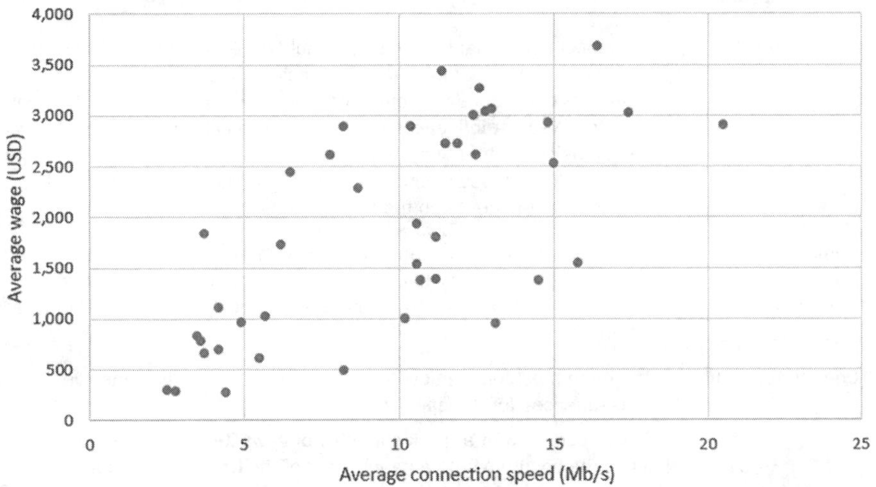

Figure 3.1 Data from the UN and Akamai shows there's a correlation between average wage and internet connection speed. Relying on fast connections where wages are poor may, therefore, be unwise.

The devices people use in different locations can also vary greatly, as income affects the ability to afford the newest devices. In parts of Asia, Africa, and South America, the secondhand device market is hugely popular. Such devices may be of a lower specification or only able to run older versions of an OS. If you want people in these locations to use your app, it's important that you verify it'll work on the devices that these people have.

Many third-party analytics tools exist that are easy to integrate and will let you track macro-level usage information. If you can't track this yourself, then use a free service to do this, as you never know what useful insights you may uncover. It's much harder to use analytics to identify information about location usage at the micro level.

3.1.2 App usage at a micro-geographic level

As with macro-level location information, usage at the micro level doesn't always serve as a proxy for context or for telling you what a person wants to do. But it can provide insights that help create a better experience for the person using the app.

The immediate environment may impact how the app can help or hinder the task at hand. For many consumer-based apps, people want to do different things with them in different locations. Throughout the day, a person may choose or be required to be in many places. This can lead them to want numerous things from an app. Table 3.1 shows considerations for these differences.

Table 3.1 Considerations for consumer apps based on micro-geographic location

Comparison	Considerations
Inside/Outside	Is connectivity available and, if so, what type? A person may be connecting to Wi-Fi when inside, but have a slower, paid data connection when outside. Outside there may be environmental conditions to consider and potentially optimize for. Weather influences how your app can give the best experience to the person using it. There may be bright sunlight or rain affecting screen visibility. When cold, the person using the app may be wearing gloves and so can't hold or interact with the device in the usual way.
Home/Work	At home, a person may want a quick summary of new information that they'll review in detail when next in the office and in "work mode." When in the office, a person may not be able to give as detailed a reply to a personal message as they would when at home.
One room/another	The room a person is in can indicate other activities they may be doing and the consequences for the app. A person may want a quick summary of news items if checking them while dressing in the bedroom before heading out of the house in the morning. If reading the news while relaxing in a favorite armchair, they're likely to have more time for the task and may want more information. If watching video content in the lounge, it's reasonable to assume the full attention of the viewer. But if watching video content while in the kitchen, the viewer may be busy with other things and just listening to the content. That they're busy and distracted by other tasks can mean people may need to pause or go back to content more often. This, in turn, can change the control people will need with the app.

Within the enterprise, the location of a person often gives a good indicator of what they need to do at that time. Field service agents will do different things when on a visit, compared to what they'll do when back at the depot, and so may benefit from different ways of presenting functionality in the app accordingly. Salespeople may want something different when with customers, compared to when they're alone at their desks. A supervisor may want a differently tailored experience when in a busy warehouse, rather than when in the site's office. All these circumstances suggest different tasks based on location.

For many of the previous examples, it isn't always possible to automatically detect or identify the specific location of the person using the app. Despite this, there's still a benefit to considering and designing for usage in specific locations so that you can provide a better experience for the person using the app.

Put it into practice: location of app usage

Answer these questions:

1. Where in the world will people use your app? Be careful about saying "everywhere" if you mean that nothing in the app would prevent it from being used by a particular group of people based on their location. Even if you do make your app available in all countries, it's often more helpful to first think about people in a few parts of the world. Keep this in mind as you answer the next question, too.
2. What are the differences and similarities between people and their circumstances in different countries?
3. What types of buildings or locations are people likely to be in when using the app?
4. Are there any special considerations you must make for these locations?

3.2 *The regional impact on an app*

Often related to the person's location is regionalization. This also provides an opportunity to customize an app to improve the experience of the person using it. Specifically, it lets you support multiple languages with different formatting for words, numbers, and dates.

3.2.1 *Considering support for multiple languages*

When looking to create an app that's used in multiple countries, one of the first things to consider is region: people speak different languages depending upon their locality. Supporting multiple languages is an obvious way to tailor your app to the people who use it. It's often overlooked, or dismissed as too complicated or something that the developer can't do because they aren't a native speaker of the language. This section should help you overcome those hurdles.

Structuring your code base and resources to support more than a single language is much easier if done at the start of development. Extracting all the text used in an app is complicated and error-prone. By building this in at the start, it's easier to spot the use of untranslated text and to avoid future problems when you add support for more languages.

When creating an app that supports translation, you should start with supporting two languages. This provides a way to verify that you've implemented the support for multiple languages correctly. With almost anything, it's harder to go from one version of something to two than it is to go from n to $n+1$, where n is greater than 1. Additionally, by creating a fake or pseudo language translation (or *pseudo-loc*), you can easily see any text that isn't localized. Figure 3.2 shows an example of this.

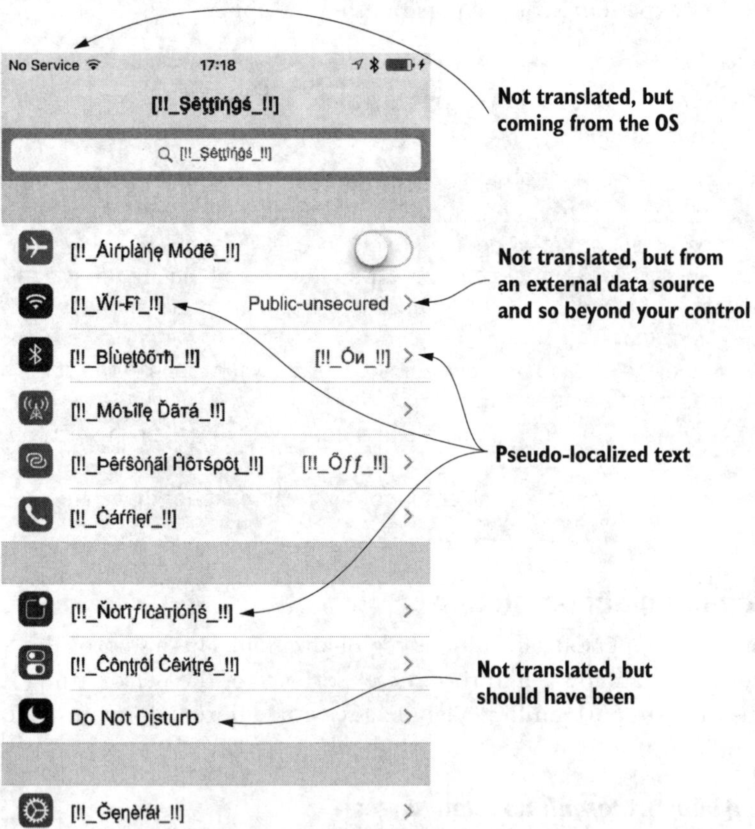

Figure 3.2 An app configured to use a pseudo-loc translation makes it easy to spot any words that aren't coming from a correctly translated language resource.

Table 3.2 shows examples of different ways for creating a pseudo-localized translation and how each can be useful. Adding translations to an app using one or a combination of these methods is useful for testing.

Table 3.2 Some approaches to pseudo-localizing text

Name	Example	Notes
All Caps	MENU	Leaves the app easy to use as the text is readable. Doesn't work when displaying text in the app that's normally in all caps. Also unnecessarily increases the amount of space needed to ensure that all text is visible.
Added Diacritics	M̳eȟŭ	Easily usable while testing, but it's also easy to miss any words not translated, especially short words.
Top and Tail	##Menu##	Stands out easily and highlights words that will be clipped or truncated when replaced with something longer.
L337 Speak	M3nu	Usable, as you can still read what's displayed and interacted with, but it may not be clear if implemented for all words.
Reversed	uneM	App is fairly usable, but it's easy to spot when not done for everything except palindromes. Of limited use when the UI has mixed left-to-right and right-to-left content.
Censored (all Xs)	XXXX	Easy to spot anything not translated, but it can make it harder to use the app while testing.

Additionally, it may also be useful to have a pseudo-loc translation that allows for the translated version to be much longer than in the language you develop with. It's a common joke in Kung Fu movies dubbed or translated into English that a long piece of dialog is a single short word when translated in the subtitles (figure 3.3).

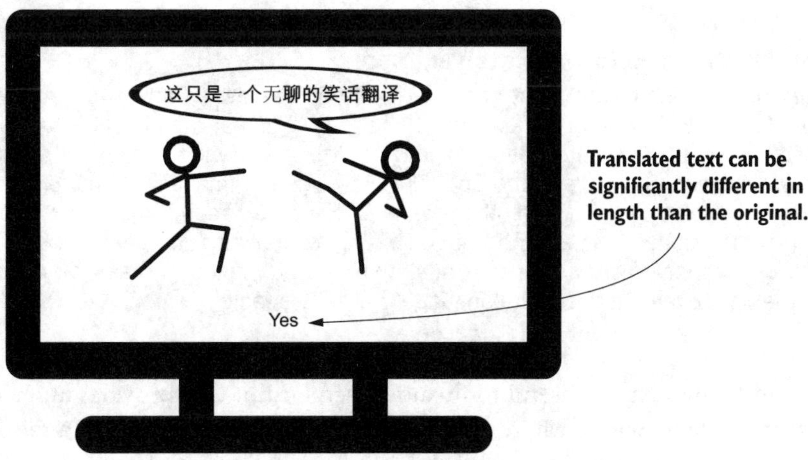

Figure 3.3 As in real life, text in one language can be much shorter or longer when translated into another.

On a more directly applicable basis, the German language typically has longer words than their English equivalents. To account for this, create a custom pseudo-loc translation that increases the length of the text by 40%. Add a specific final character to ensure that everything is visible.

Apps that display text in multiple languages at the same time need extra consideration. Supporting languages written from right-to-left is more complex than supporting multiple languages written left-to-right. Platform and tooling vendors have guidance for this, but you'll need to test and verify this with fluent speakers of such languages. You must also consider many nuances and exceptions that are easy to miss if you don't speak the language.

> **TIP** Many tools are available for creating pseudo-loc translations. These include open source projects, tools from companies that specialize in translations, and manufacturers. You can use these on their own, but because translations are stored in plain text files, it's easy to develop a tool to create them yourself if what's available doesn't meet your specific requirements.

Another advantage to building in support for multiple languages from the start is that you have a single place to see all the text. This makes it easier to spot inconsistencies in abbreviation, capitalization, punctuation, and so forth. It can also highlight differences in the wording and tone or voice. When pieces of text are displayed infrequently, it may not be clear that they're different than other text used more frequently. For example, when prompts are side by side, more formal or different terminology will stand out, making it easier to bring those in line with the rest of the application. Seeing all the text at once is useful, even if you aren't translating the app into different languages.

Avoiding the need to translate your app

Angry Birds is one of the most popular mobile games ever. Part of that success is attributed to its universal appeal. But there was, at least initially, little translation done to support this. The reason for having little translation is that there are few words displayed anywhere in the app. The clever use of images, animation, and following conventions common in other apps removed the need for most text within the app (the credits being an exception). Converting a small amount of text makes it easier (and cheaper) to create a new translation. It also makes it easier for anyone to use the app, even if it isn't in a language that they speak.

When translating text, it's useful to include a screenshot that provides an example of the text in context. Seeing where and how the text is used can lead to a more appropriate translation. It can also show if the text is used in multiple places, as the same translation may not be appropriate for all. And, any images that include text should also be translated.

Ideally, the person providing a translation should be a native speaker of the language. Although hiring a specialist can be expensive, it may be possible to recruit people using the app to do this for free. Fans of your app can often be persuaded to provide translations, as it's beneficial to them to have the app in their language. This is something Harriet did. She added a request for translators in the About page of her game. She was able to add translations for multiple new languages that were provided and verified by people who were previously playing the game in their second language.

> **NOTE** Translating an app using free, automated tools can be appealing. But use these with care, because they don't make translations based on the context of where the text is used.

Knowing which languages to translate to, or which to prioritize, can often be determined by using analytics. This lets you see the language specified on the devices people are using. This approach limits the languages you can support at launch, but avoids any unnecessary effort and expense in obtaining translations that people using the app don't need.

Three other considerations matter when using analytics to determine which languages to support. First, it limits the languages to those supported by the operating system. Apps aren't limited to only supporting these languages, but doing so means the app must provide a way of specifying the language to use.

Second, it doesn't account for people who keep their devices set to English even though it isn't their first language. They do this because it provides access to additional features in the OS or other apps that are controlled by the configured language. For such people, it's necessary to listen to their feedback or suggestions to determine if providing a translation for them would be suitably beneficial, and worth the effort it requires.

Finally, it may be that people prefer that the app is in another language. I've heard of one game where the developers spent a year adding French and German localizations only to discover that the people playing the game in France and Germany did so because it helped them practice their English. The lesson here is that you mustn't rely on assumptions from analytics data, but instead verify your plans with real people.

3.2.2 How culture and locale can impact an app

Adjusting your app to support people in different countries with different regional settings requires more than having translations for different languages. You must also consider and account for the manipulation of words, numbers, and dates. You can think of these considerations as relating to formatting, but there are some important subtleties to be aware of when handling words and sentences in different languages. This also includes the formatting of numbers, dates, and times for transmission between different systems, as well as for display. We'll look at those subtleties in this section.

FORMATTING WORDS

Words should be capitalized, compared, and pluralized in different ways for different languages. German is an example of a language that has different rules for capitalization than does English. In English, we only capitalize proper nouns. In German, all nouns are capitalized. In English, we capitalize adjectives describing nationality, ethnicity, and religion. In German, they don't.

Turkish is another example of a language that demonstrates potential issues if you apply capitalization rules and conventions from other languages to it. The Turkish alphabet includes both a dotless and a dotted *i*. On its own, that may not seem problematic, but the uppercase version of the Turkish dotless *i* looks the same as the uppercase version of the English letter *I* (table 3.3). Given the similarity, you shouldn't be surprised to hear that many bugs have been created as the result of comparing text that looks the same visually due to the glyphs that are used, but actually contains different letters.

Table 3.3 Comparing letters from different languages

Language	Letter	Lowercase glyph	Uppercase glyph
English	i	i	I
Turkish	Dotted i	i	İ
Turkish	Dotless ı	ı	I

Examples of edge cases like the Turkish *i* may lead you to think that we have it easy with English. Pluralization rules may catch you out, though. I'm sure you've seen, if not created, software that displays something like `1 minute(s) remaining`. It's easy to look at this and think the person was lazy, as improving it requires appending the *s* to the end of *minute* if the number is greater than one. In this case, you're correct. But that doesn't apply to every word you may want to pluralize: there are exceptions.

In other languages, pluralization is done based on more than if an object is singular or plural. Table 3.4 shows examples of a few of the complications pluralization presents in different languages. There may be no difference between the singular and plural (also true for some languages such as Japanese). The plural form may require the addition of a single letter or multiple letters; or it may be an irregular plural, where in English the final vowel is replaced with the letter *i* before adding the plural ending. In some languages, pluralization can also vary based on whether the quantity is few or many.

Table 3.4 The pluralization of words differs in different languages

Animal	Quantity	English	Polish
Pig	1	1 pig	1 świnia
Pig	2 (few)	2 pigs	2 świnie
Pig	5 (many)	5 pigs	5 świń
Sheep	1	1 sheep	1 owiec

Table 3.4 The pluralization of words differs in different languages *(continued)*

Animal	Quantity	English	Polish
Sheep	2 (few)	2 sheep	2 owce
Sheep	5 (many)	5 sheep	5 owiec
Octopus	1	1 octopus	1 ośmiornicy
Octopus	2 (few)	2 octopuses	2 ośmiornice
Octopus	5 (many)	5 octopuses	5 ośmiornice
Mouse	1	1 mouse	1 mysz
Mouse	2 (few)	2 mice	2 myszy
Mouse	5 (many)	5 mice	5 myszy

This is a small example of how plurals vary in different languages. Even though there are many things to consider, it's important to be aware of anything programmatic that the app does based on rules for one language. Both Android and iOS have good native support for handling most pluralizations. And, open source projects (like Humanizer) mean that you shouldn't need to create your own solution.

FORMATTING NUMBERS

The formatting of numbers used as decimal indicators and thousand separators varies in different cultures. In fact, in some cultures, numbers aren't grouped in a way that calling it a thousand separator is appropriate. Table 3.5 shows some examples of number formatting in different locales.

Table 3.5 Comparing different number formats and groupings for various countries

Number format	Country where used
10,000,000,000.00	USA
10 000 000 000,00	France
10.000.000.000,00	Germany
10'000'000'000.00	Switzerland
10,0000,0000.00	China
10,00,00,00,000.00	India

> **NOTE** Use the functionality built into platform SDKs to format numbers; never hard code the formats.

Beyond the formatting of numbers, different languages and cultures use symbols to give added information about a number. A percentage sign (%) can be placed before or after the number, so you can't always append a character onto the end. Even showing a negative number isn't straightforward, as there are four different ways of doing this:

- Place a minus sign before the number.
- Place a minus sign after the number.
- Place the number in parentheses.
- Show the number in a different color (typically red).

To always display a negative number the way the person using the app expects can take more thought than you may have previously considered. Here's where you can use the formatting functionality built into each platform's SDK.

These may appear to be small issues, but when it comes to experience, the small things matter. If you can't do something simple, such as format a number the way a person expects, why should they trust you with something more important, like their credit card information or all the details of their contacts?

FORMATTING DATES

Harriet once got reports from someone who was unable to get their app working on a newly released, top-of-the-line device. When the app started up, it would crash. Her concern was that the app didn't work on the latest device. After looking at the automatically generated crash logs (see how useful these can be?), she noted that a formatting exception was occurring. After some investigation and experimentation, she determined that the server was returning the US-formatted date when the app was expecting a Norwegian format (due to the device settings), and failing to convert it correctly. Using a standard format for date transmission, and not assuming dates are in the device's local format, would have avoided this.

Date formats also vary around the world. Consider the date 8/9/16. In some parts of the world, this represents the 9th of August, 2016 and, in others, the 8th of September in the same year. There's no right or wrong answer for this value. If you're in North America, you'd assume the August date, but if in the UK, the September one. If you're in the USA and looking at that date displayed in an app, and it's intended to be a date in September, that's where problems begin. A date should be displayed the way a person using the device expects. If you can't be sure what the person using the app would expect, use something that's unambiguous. For example, there's no doubt what the date September 8th, 2016 means.

How the date is displayed within the app is important, but how dates are stored internally and transmitted can be more significant. If the server sends the date 8/9/16, you'd have to know what each element means. You may know that the server returns the date in the format month/day/year, but someone else working with the data may not know that or may wrongly assume a different structure, or the format the server used could change.

I once had to help a company solve an intermittent problem with date formatting. I eventually identified the cause as one of the four load-balanced servers that hosted the API being set to a different locale. Because of that, it returned data in a different format than the other servers. The app developers weren't expecting this.

Details of the format can be sent (and stored) with the value, but this also increases the amount of data sent and stored. To avoid problems like this, there's an internationally recognized and accepted format for representing dates and times in the Gregorian calendar. It's defined by the International Organization of Standardization (ISO) as ISO-8601 and shown in figure 3.4.

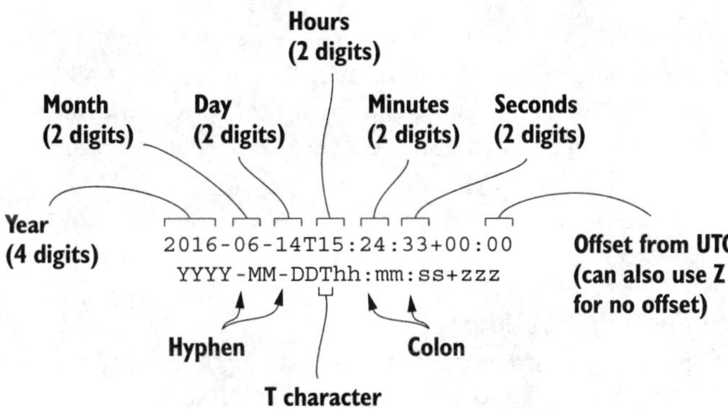

Figure 3.4 The structure of the ISO-8601 date format. Use this for sending and storing date and time values.

A date-related formatting gotcha relates to regional settings. Developers format a date with the formatting string of `yyyy MMM dd` and expect this to always return a four-figure year value, the month as a three-letter abbreviation, and the day of the month as two digits. In some cultures and for some months, however, a period (.) is added after the abbreviated month name, even though the provided formatting string doesn't include this.

Most platforms let you specify regional settings separately from the language used on a device. This affects date and number formatting. You'll need to allow for the formatting settings and language to be different and to use the formatting options specified. Don't assume based on the configured language.

It can also be useful to track these settings as part of your analytics data. This information can be particularly useful as part of any extra information captured with an exception. While this is often informational, if you find anomalies, they may lead to insight about the people using the app. Should you, for instance, notice that the language is set to English, but the date formatting is set to a value for a non-English-speaking country, it can indicate an opportunity for localization.

The formatting of time can also vary with differences arising from using a 24-hour clock or a 12-hour clock, and an indicator of the period (A.M. or P.M.). Additionally, as Harriet was localizing her app for use in Thailand, she discovered that it's traditional there to use a 6-hour clock. Handle variations in how time is transmitted, stored, and displayed in the same way as for dates. (You hopefully noticed this when looking at the ISO-8601 format in figure 3.4.) This format also allows for storing any offset from UTC, so you can account for differing time zones or daylight savings time.

Put it into practice: regional impact on your app

- Make plans to support multiple languages in your app if you don't already do so.
- Identify the places in the app where numbers, dates, and times are used:
  - Where they're stored or manipulated, ensure that these aren't dependent upon a specific regional format.
  - Where they're displayed in the app, be sure to format them appropriately based on the device's settings.

Exercise: regional and location impact

Test your understanding of the last two sections by deciding if the location where an app is used will or won't affect the app for the following situations:

- Appropriateness of the app and potential users
- Language to display the UI
- Which stores to use to distribute the app
- Third-party service integration
- Formatting dates, times, and numbers for display
- Formatting dates, times, and numbers for storage and transmission
- Data transfer speed and costs
- Pluralization of words

3.3 When is the app used?

Here are four ways that time can apply to the context in which people use your app:

- The time of day the app is used
- The day of the week the app is used
- The time of year the app is used
- The length of time that the app is used for

The following sections dive deeper into each of these. By building specifically for or adapting to these situations, you can improve the experience when using your app.

3.3.1 Consider the time of day

Harriet had an app that reported weather information. Because there are many apps like this, Harriet looked at the analytics she captured about usage at different times of day to help differentiate her app. The analytics highlighted a common behavior tied to the time of day when people used the app.

When opened, the app would default to the current day's weather. When people used the app in the morning, they would rarely go beyond the first page of information. But when they used the app in the evening, they would typically swipe across to see the weather for the next day. Harriet inferred that when looking at the app in the evening, people were more interested in what the weather would be the next day. Based on this, she changed the app. When opening the app after 8 P.M., it defaulted to showing the weather for the next day.

On its own, this may seem like a small change, but great experiences come from many small optimizations and attention to even little details. The analytics data after the change supported her action. Few people would swipe back to the current day's information when the app displayed the data for the next day. She also experienced a small increase in user retention.

People use their phones throughout the day. Figures vary, but research (by organizations including Deloitte, Pew Research, Nottingham Trent University, Locket, and Gallup) shows that people look at or use their phones typically anywhere from between a few dozen to a few hundred times a day. Research also shows that people tend to use different devices more at different times of the day. Figure 3.5 shows how usage varies.

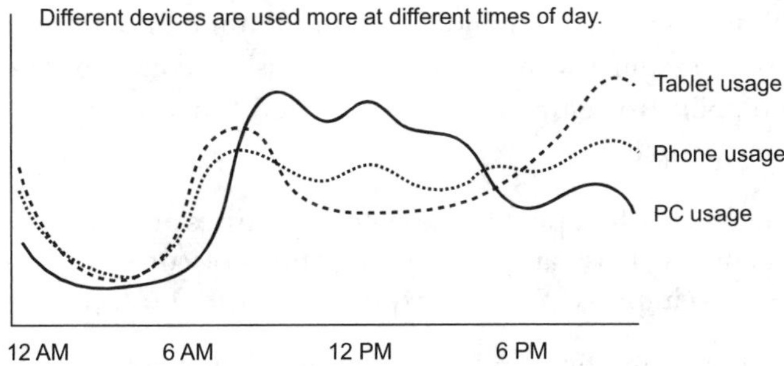

Figure 3.5 The usage of different device types at different times of day

Is your app used more at certain times of the day? Are different features used more at different times of the day? For many apps, there'll be no preferences, but for some, there could be. Most apps always present the same interface or the same type of information regardless of when they're used. But there are distinct times when an alternative view or dataset would be more helpful and easy to provide. If you can add such features, you can use them to differentiate your app from the competition.

Basing a decision on the time of day is simple but may be inappropriate in some circumstances. Edge cases and other factors may need accounting for, too. This could add significant complexity to your app. Although the complexity of code can be undesirable, it shouldn't be ruled out entirely. As figure 3.6 shows, what's easy to do doesn't always correspond with what'll be best for the person using the app. Everyone does the easy things. Doing the hard things can add real value, if they'll make a difference to the people using the app.

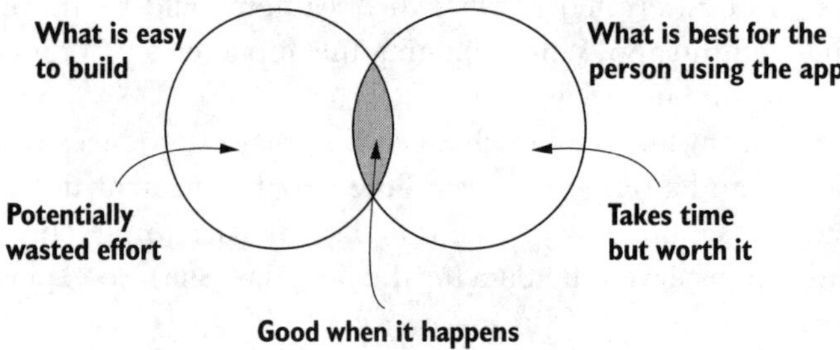

Figure 3.6 What's easiest to develop and what's best for the person using an app are rarely the same.

Adjusting the displayed content dependent upon the time of day has little risk of upsetting or confusing the person using the app. Moving functionality (such as menu items or other navigational controls) dependent upon the time of day and what you expect they'll want, however, comes with a much greater risk of confusion for the person using the app. The ability to remember where desired functionality is within an app is important to many people.

> **TIP** Record the time of day when people use specific features and functionality as part of your analytics. This can provide indications of common behaviors that may allow you to improve people's experiences with the app.

Although analytics can show common trends, you may also be able to track patterns of usage among individuals. If a person regularly uses an app at approximately the same time each day, you could improve their experience by preloading the latest content shortly before that time. This means that the person using the app would see all the latest content or data when they open the app. If they happened to open the app at another time, the app would still behave as normal. In that case, you may have to load the latest data upon launch rather than having it readily available at startup. iOS includes the Background Fetch capability for such a scenario, but it's easy to create a simple version of this on any platform.

3.3.2 Consider the day of the week

As people's routines and activities vary between the days they are working and when they aren't, it's also common for their app usage to vary. In addition to usage variation at different times of day, there can be big changes on different days of the week. You may want to account for changes in the backend server load or support requests at different times of the week. This can be particularly important if those occur outside of your normal working hours.

For a smaller number of apps, it can also be necessary to consider variations in usage based on the day of the month. For example, apps relating to financial information, diaries, or tasks may naturally see more activity at the start or end of a month.

3.3.3 *Consider the time of year*

The time of year can impact apps in two ways:

- The data people use or the services they access can impact some apps.
- Other events throughout the year can impact all apps.

The scope of the impact varies between apps, but don't ignore it. Scheduling the release of or update to an app should be planned carefully, and not only based on when it's ready.

HOW SPECIALIZED APPS CAN BE IMPACTED BY THE TIME OF YEAR

Some apps are tied to a time of year—typically, those for a specific event or series of events. These events might be conferences, sporting events, religious holidays, a television series, or anything else along these lines. For apps related to events like these, there are some obvious hard deadlines and times when app usage will be higher. Ensuring the app and any related services are ready for such times should be obvious, but people often overlook the times before and after such events.

Consider an app for a conference. It might have content about the sessions and workshops during the conference, plus information about sponsors and exhibitors. This would allow those attending the conference to plan their time while there. That seems perfectly reasonable and a valuable thing to provide. But what about the times before and after the conference?

Before the conference, the app could offer added value by including directions and instructions on how to get there. It could include information about other things happening beforehand and after or about places to stay. It could also serve as a way of allowing delegates to connect and share thoughts during the build-up to the start. After the conference, it could point to resources mentioned by speakers or show recordings of sessions. It could also collect feedback and allow attendees to connect with speakers or other people they met during the event.

HOW ALL APPS CAN BE IMPACTED BY THE TIME OF YEAR

When people get new devices, and, to a lesser extent, receive a major upgrade to an existing device, they predominantly install apps. Holiday periods vary around the world, but those that involve gift giving mean lots of people are getting new devices and looking for apps to install on them. Given these scenarios, it's often better to release a new app or a major update before such times.

The release of a new update to an OS can also see a boost in downloads because consumers look for an app that takes advantage of new capabilities. Taking advantage of this opportunity means being able to provide additional value based on any new feature, and having it available in the app when the OS update is released. This means keeping up with OS updates and feature announcements. These happen at predictable times of the year, so you can easily plan for them.

Where appropriate to the brand, an app can use major events to add some customization and personality to the experience. Cheesy clichés can have a negative effect if implemented poorly, but it may be appropriate to adopt color themes based on the season or specific dates. The Google doodle and the Reddit mascot are well-known examples of such actions, but a small number of other apps do this too. Making the background pink on Valentine's Day, or green on St. Patrick's Day, or adding a snow effect or holly around the screen at Christmas, can also be appropriate. Major sporting events like the World Cup or the Olympics also offer an opportunity for doing something different. And it can be fun to see what special new features apps claim to have added on April 1.

Consider dates, holidays, and events as opportunities to stand out from the competition. This also reminds the person using the app that it has some characteristics others don't. If appropriate within your app, those little details could be a welcomed addition.

Having functionality that's dependent upon the time of year can make it harder to test in live environments or with beta testers. It isn't always practical to have them change the date on their devices to trigger the required app behavior. For this reason, it's even more important to test such features thoroughly before release. You don't want your app to stop working at a busy time of year or for a fun addition. It can create bad feelings in people who are using your app.

3.3.4 How long is the app used?

The final aspect of your app experience that's related to time is how long the app is used. This idea comes in two parts:

- What is the total amount of time someone spends between their first and final use of the app?
- How long does a person spend with the app each time they use it?

Knowing the answers to these questions can have a big impact on how you should design the app. Understanding how long the app is used is crucial to creating a great experience.

HOW MANY TIMES IS THE APP USED?

Harriet did some contract development work for a real estate agent who had an app that helped people find properties to buy or rent. Their app was popular, but once people had found a new property, they'd uninstall the app. To continue a relationship with their customers, the company wanted to find ways to encourage people to keep the app installed. The company owners particularly wanted the app to still be on a person's phone when they next looked for a new property. The solution to this was to add extra features to the app so that it continued to give value.

This targeting began by adding information about other properties around customers' locations. This information was along the lines of, "There's a property on the next street on sale for X." Or, "There's another apartment in your building available for only X per month." The functionality of the app was also extended to integrate with third parties to give information and provide services to renters and homeowners. These changes led to the desired effect: increased retention and engagement.

Some apps have a natural lifetime. For example, games can only be played until completed if not built with repeated play in mind. Apps tied to a specific event or task are rarely used once the event or task is completed. If a person only uses an app once or twice, it's important that it's easy for them to get up to speed with it immediately. There's no need for many complex features. People won't be around long enough to need or learn to use them.

Knowing how many times someone is expected to use an app lets you make something that's right for the people who'll use it, and how they'll use it. The reason that many games start with a few simple levels is to teach people how to play. It also lets them make some progress and build up a commitment to, and investment in, the game. If their first-time playing is overly challenging, they're much less likely to play again. The same is also true of apps.

If an app is intended to be used many times over a longer period of time, people will have the opportunity to learn more complex functionality. Not every app needs a tutorial when first used, but providing an easy way to learn more advanced features will keep them coming back. Alternatively, don't overwhelm people on their first use, or they won't come back.

How long is a session?

The idea that people want to use mobile apps for quick tasks, often during idle periods, is popularized and summarized by "The Starbucks Test." This test asks one question about an app or game: "Is it possible to have a meaningful interaction with an app in the time between placing an order and your drink being ready?" In this time, the person has nothing to do but wait for their drink, so they pull out their device and want to get some value from an app. Can your app do that in under a minute?

Not every interaction a person has with an app will be this short, but these are the most common. The person who sits on their couch all evening, watching television and simultaneously playing a game on their phone, and the person watching a film on a tablet, are exceptions. The underlying truism still stands. People want to be able to use mobile apps for short periods of time and still get things done (figure 3.7).

If people can't get value from using an app for a short period, they may stop using it. The ability to obtain value from a short interaction with an app doesn't remove the possibility of longer sessions; it removes the necessity for them. It's hard for a game to

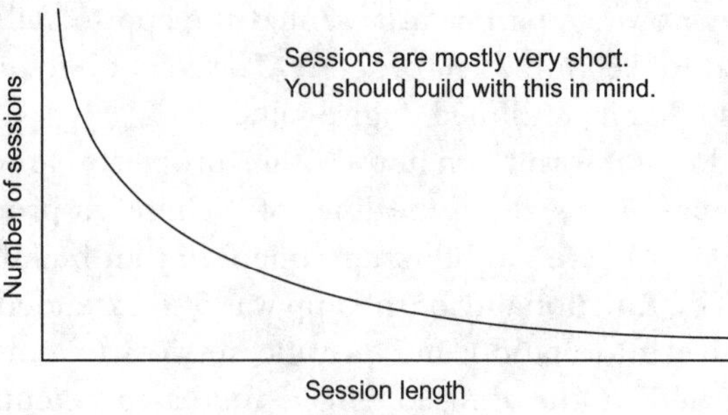

Figure 3.7 How session length relates to the number of sessions in mobile apps

get broad appeal if it's only possible to have success with it if you play for hours at a time. A game that can regularly be played for short periods of time is doing more to avoid discontent and failure. Longer play can still be beneficial, but by not punishing the player when they stop playing after a short time, you avoid discouraging them from returning.

The benefits of short session lengths apply to apps as well as games. Reducing the time needed to perform a task is always preferable. Optimizing tasks so they can be performed faster by the person using the app is preferable to building or designing the app so it's easier for the people creating it.

The number of times and for how long an app is used affect the appropriateness of different monetization options for that app. For example, an app that's only used once doesn't have a lot of time to make money from advertising. Table 3.6 shows how session length affects common monetization methods.

Table 3.6 How session length impacts monetization techniques

Monetization method	Impact by session length
Banner advertising	Best suited for long sessions.
Video advertising	Increases session length. Suited better to longer sessions or apps that provide value that outweighs the inconvenience of increased session length.
Paid-for features or content	Not impacted by session length.
Sponsorship	Depends on the sponsor. Some see the association as value; others will value longer sessions more.

The intended monetization strategy for an app should consider the number of times an app will be used. Lots of short sessions or a few long sessions can allow you the opportunity to monetize successfully. A small number of short sessions can make successfully monetizing an app much harder. It's better to identify any potential issues before you invest in the app's development and launch.

NOTE In case you're wondering, it's never a good idea to make a task longer, or an app perform slower, so you can show more ads.

Validating your assumptions about how often and for how long the app will be used is important in ensuring that you're creating the experience that people using the app want and deserve. When using analytics to track how often and for how long the app is used, there are two things to watch for. The first is when the person using the app frequently switches back and forth with another app. Depending on the app, this may or may not indicate separate sessions. The second consideration is that it's important to be aware of apps displayed on a device with multiple apps opened and displayed at the same time. In this scenario, just because the app is displayed doesn't mean it's providing value. Some apps provide value when open, even if a person isn't directly interacting with them, but not all.

Put it into practice: when the app is used

- Consider how time affects the use of the app, and identify how to adapt the app to those differences.
- Identify the common activities or scenarios a person may be involved with while simultaneously using the device. Identify the ones that make using the app harder. Consider alternative ways the app could behave or interact with the person using it in those situations.
- Add or update analytics for your app to track the following:
  - What country the people who use your app are in
  - Time of day or night (local to the person using the app)
  - How long the app is in use
  - Language and regional settings configured on the device
- Update or add a privacy policy about the data collection and retention of analytics information.

Exercise: when the app is used

Fill in the blanks in the following paragraph:

People may use an app differently or for different purposes and different times of the ______. Some apps are more relevant or will be used more at specific times of the ______. Adjusting the app based on the time of year or in relation to special ______ can be a simple way to create interest and show personality. Anything relating to specific times or dates should be ______ carefully before release. How ______ and for how long an app is used can impact many factors of its ______ and commercial viability.

3.4 What activities are being undertaken while using the app?

Considering the activities a person is undertaking while using the app makes it possible to identify ways to better meet their needs. This consideration also provides easier or more appropriate mechanisms for interacting with your app. I address activities in four ways:

- Is the person moving or stationary?
- Is the person using the app also doing something else? If so, what?
- Is the person using the app on its own on a single device or in combination with other apps, or on multiple devices?
- What position is the person in when using the app?

Knowing how the person using the app is likely to be interacting with their physical environment and any other activities they may be performing can all influence the experience of using the app. The following sections explore these ideas further.

3.4.1 Is the person using the app moving or stationary?

Whether a person is moving or stationary when using an app won't be relevant to some apps. For others, it can be critical to the functionality they provide and the way it's provided. Considering movement primarily affects three aspects of an application: location, connectivity, and interaction.

How location can impact movement

Apps typically use location either when first launched or in functionality throughout the app. If the latter, and if a person is moving, this affects how to track location. The type of movement (whether on foot, in a vehicle, and the type of vehicle) also impacts if and how you need to think about appropriately tracking changes to location. You'll find more details on the use of location while moving in chapter 14. For now, an understanding of how important this is to the people using the app is necessary for the context of use.

How connectivity can change while moving

If constant server connectivity is necessary for an app to function, you may need to give special consideration to this if you expect that people will be moving while using the app. Small amounts of movement within a room or a building rarely have an impact on connectivity. Usually this isn't enough to make a difference to an app. Movement described as "travel" or "going on a journey" is, however, and that's the type to consider.

Although walking between rooms is unlikely to result in a loss of connectivity, walking between buildings could. As well, use of an app while on a train or plane is likely to result in encountering a lack of connectivity. Car journeys to remote areas or through valleys and tunnels can also create connectivity issues. I'll go into more detail about connectivity in chapter 13, but to understand context, you need to know what's expected of the activity of a person while they use the app.

HOW MOVEMENT AFFECTS INTERACTION WITH AN APP

Movement can affect a person's interaction with an app in terms of both input and output. Parts 2 and 3 of this book explore this in more detail, but it's important to be aware that not considering if the people using the app will be moving or stationary runs the risk of creating an app that doesn't adequately provide for their needs.

The first challenge of interaction is that movement can make precision activities harder. Activities like typing and accurately tapping a small target become harder while walking or if swaying on a crowded bus or subway. The second challenge is that while moving, a person is often distracted or has additional things to concentrate on. Whether walking, a passenger, or in control of a vehicle, the need to navigate and be responsible for their own and others' safety restricts if and how they can use an app. Legal considerations may also apply if in control of a vehicle.

To overcome these challenges, there are two approaches. First is the use of alternative communication methods for input and output. Speech-based input and output remove the need to touch or look at the screen, so hands and eyes can focus elsewhere. Second, where alternatives aren't possible, reducing the amount shown onscreen and increasing its size focuses attention, while making text easier to read. And, it reduces the consequences of less precise screen contact.

3.4.2 *Is the user dedicated or distracted?*

Apps used in environments with many distractions make it unreasonable to expect the people using them to complete highly detailed or complex processes within the app. Such scenarios are more common for enterprise apps, but this can apply to consumer apps and games, too. If you could guarantee the people using an app will always be able to focus only on their task, you might argue for creating something that needs a lot of concentration. Such scenarios are rare. So you must allow for distractions by letting the people using the app switch between apps and tasks at different times.

When an app doesn't have a person's sole focus, they may leave it at any time. If an app involves completing a long process or series of steps, it's often simpler (from a development perspective) to have the person start the process over again when returning to the app. This is seldom desirable for the person using the app. It's a rare personality type that enjoys repeating tasks unnecessarily. It would be much better to allow the person to resume the process where they left off, with the ability to review what they've already done and see a clear sign of the progress they've made. In some instances, it may be beneficial to respond to this with a prompt like that shown in figure 3.8.

It may not be possible to identify inactivity if the content from the app is passively consumed. Reacting to idleness in this way may not always be appropriate. For example, consider an app that plays video or audio content. It's reasonable to assume that the app should stop if no one is watching or listening, as a way of preserving battery life and bandwidth. The problem here is how to tell if anyone's watching or listening. At the time of writing, there are few devices in use that make it easy to tell if a person

Are you still there?
Playback automatically paused due to inactivity.
We don't want you to miss anything or waste your battery or data.
I'm still here

Figure 3.8 Detecting inactivity can be tricky, but it's better to respond to it rather than let an app run indefinitely.

is actively looking at the screen. Even with the ones that are capable of this, there are limitations you can't easily work around.

In such scenarios, it's better to let the person using the app stop playback when they're finished. The alternative of periodically asking the person to confirm they're still there and watching or listening typically frustrates people. It's a rare occasion where people leave content playing on their device when they aren't there to consume it.

Games can have similar behavior. On one occasion, I was playing a popular strategy war game. I had built my army and was attacking another camp with a large opposing force to overcome. Having fully deployed my troops, I sat back to watch the unfolding melee when a minute or so later a message flashed onscreen: "It looks like you've gone away, so we've ended the battle." Just like that, I lost all my troops and got none of the rewards for my efforts. All because I hadn't touched the screen, even when there was no need to do so. There may have been some negative consequences if I had kept the battle running indefinitely with no troops deployed, but I felt I was punished for doing nothing wrong. This isn't a feeling you want to give anyone using your app. Detecting inactivity can be tricky, and you should do so tentatively if you have a compelling reason.

3.4.3 *Is use isolated or in conjunction with something else?*

It's common for people to have multiple devices and to use multiple apps. They may even use versions of the same app across different devices. Can the tasks that your app helps with be performed on multiple devices or in combination with other apps? If so, enabling your app to do this can improve the experience people have, and they'll experience less anxiety while completing those.

If people would receive help from using versions of your app on multiple devices, it's valuable to know if they're performing the same or different tasks. This could include the ability to start a task on one device and finish it on another. This will affect

- Requirements for data synchronization and whether to synchronize settings across devices
- How and if you should remember state and data entered in sessions on different devices

The sharing of data or functionality is becoming increasingly important, as it can have a synergistic impact on all parties involved. New apps are continually adding support for this. If common or popular usage of your app also includes data from, usage with, or sharing to other specific apps, investigate opportunities to interact with those apps on a deeper level. Not only can such integrations aid the people who are using your app now, but it may make your app more appealing to people who are using the app you're integrating with.

3.4.4 Are they standing, sitting, or lying down?

Posture can influence the number of hands they use to hold and interact with the device and the orientation of the device. Although it's uncommon to use an app in a single position, it's important to understand common scenarios. For example, for apps frequently used while reclining in a chair, the device is more likely to be in a landscape orientation and held with two hands. If standing, single-handed use in a portrait orientation will be more common.

Understanding a person's posture for common use cases can highlight scenarios that are important to design and test for. Although it's simpler to develop an app for use in one orientation, this isn't what's ideal for all the people all the time. Having an app that works in the ways people want to use it makes it more intuitive.

Even though the position a person can be in may influence the app, this is often in combination with the physical size of the device the app is running on. I'll cover the impact of understanding the device an app runs on in the next chapter.

Exercise: activities influencing the app

Check your understanding of how different activities and environments can affect your app by stating whether the following are true or false:

1. What a person is doing while using the app affects how they hold it. This influences whether you should support the use of the app in landscape and portrait orientations.
2. It's OK to capture location and connectivity status when the app is launched and use that information for the whole session.
3. Adding integration between your app and another should be avoided, because it may encourage a person to spend more time in the other app, rather than in yours.
4. If an app is used on different types of devices, it may be used in different ways or for different tasks.
5. The needs of someone using an app while sitting at a desk might be different from someone walking in a field.

Summary

- The region, country, or even continent that the person who's using the app is physically in can influence how you'll be able to monetize an app.
- Getting your app to people in some countries will require distribution through multiple and different app stores.
- People in different countries often use different features of an app or parts of a game more than others. Treating everyone the same can result in missed opportunities.
- Translate your application to support the languages of the people who are using or want to use your app.
- Even if you don't want to start with support for more than one language, there are benefits to building with this capability, and it'll make adding new languages in the future much easier.
- Supporting people in other countries, cultures, and those who speak different languages also means treating numbers and dates in the different ways they expect.
- Use standardized formats for transferring and storing numbers, dates, and times, so you don't have issues when converting them to different regional formats.
- People often want different things from apps at different times of day and at different times of the year. You can delight the people using the app by preempting this and defaulting to show them what's most appropriate for the current situation.
- Ensure that the person using the app can get value from the app even if they only use it for a short amount of time.
- Appreciating how long a person can spend on a task with an app allows you to create something that'll fit in the available time.
- Knowing what a person is likely to be doing at the same time as using the app can help you create something that better meets their needs in those circumstances.
- Apps that are used in distracting circumstances or in combination with other apps or systems can also benefit by being designed to meet the specific requirements of those situations.
- If and how a person is moving or their position when stationary can influence requirements from the app.
- The building a person is in, or if they're inside at all, can dictate what they want or are able to do with an app.
- Use analytics to monitor where, when, and how the app is used to track any changes in these, and adjust the app in response to those variables when appropriate.

4 What device is the app running on?

This chapter covers

- Understanding how devices influence app functionality
- Balancing development for multiple platform support
- Considering OS differences
- Handling variations in device capabilities

The final aspect of context is the device the app runs on. While often a final thought in the development process, the device can be crucial to the person who owns or uses it. Other than specialist medical devices, mobile phones are the most personal piece of technology in use. People are rarely more than a few meters away from their phones, even when sleeping, proving the relationship between owner and phone can be deep. For your app to integrate well into this relationship, you need to understand the device.

App developers often want to create apps that run on all devices that use a specific operating system. This can be thousands of different models, and there can be many differences between these devices that you can't always ignore. But, increasingly, people want to build apps for more than a single OS.

I'll start this chapter by considering how you might support building an app for multiple platforms with minimal duplicated effort. I'll then look at the specifics of supporting multiple operating systems and balancing the need for a consistent visual identity (branding) while meeting the needs of supporting the different conventions of the UI on different operating systems. Finally, I'll explain how to handle differences in the varying hardware that the app will run on.

I'll also introduce you to Gerry. He's the head designer at a company with a website and an iPhone app. I'll tell you about the challenges he encountered and overcame as the company redesigned its iPhone app and added an Android version.

4.1 Write once, run everywhere?

In principle, it makes sense that building an app that works on multiple devices takes the same amount of effort as building an app that works on one. But having an app run on every (or any) device can be difficult when you start pushing the boundaries of what defines a device. When you say *device*, do you include phones, tablets, wearables, PCs, servers, bespoke-embedded devices, or more? As you start to push the definition of every device, the challenge becomes even harder.

When developers talk about a *write once, run everywhere* (WORE) solution, they usually mean building for multiple operating systems used on similar devices. This typically means an app that will run on iPhones, Android phones, and, occasionally, Windows. Many people extend the definition of WORE to also include equivalent tablets or PC-style devices.

When building for more than one platform, different people often work on entirely different code bases for each platform. It was once necessary to take this approach of having separate silos of development for each platform. With modern tooling, this is no longer the case. Whether using web-based tooling and a common UI on all platforms (with a tool like PhoneGap/Cordova), or a native UI and a shared codebase behind the UI (with tools like React Native and Xamarin), the ability to remove duplication of effort by writing equivalent code for each target platform means developers can devote more time to improving the app's value and experience.

NOTE The value and experience created are greater factors in the success of an app than the programming language or tools used to write the code. Focus on what's important.

I've worked with many organizations that had different teams building versions of the same app for different platforms. Such projects have been fun to work on and allowed a deeper focus on the specifics of each platform, but the app-specific work often consisted of porting code from one language and platform to another. As a developer, it's tempting to feel sad that such work is going away, but there are some key points to remember:

- Even with a WORE-based solution, creating a great experience still requires knowledge of the individual platform.

- By removing duplicated effort, companies can lower costs and thereby increase the likelihood they and the app will survive longer.
- Without the need to spend time on duplicated effort, there are more resources to invest in improving the app, adding innovative and exciting new features.
- There's a large demand for skilled app developers.

A WORE-based solution doesn't need a single build for all targets (compile once, run everywhere) and shouldn't result in the use of a *lowest common denominator* approach, which only uses what's available on all platforms. Good cross-platform tooling allows for the creation of WORE solutions that produce sophisticated apps, which take advantage of the unique features and capabilities of each platform.

Table 4.1 shows the positives and negatives of taking a WORE approach. Even though the number of negatives outweighs the positives, the value of the positives is far greater.

Table 4.1 The positives and negatives of building an app with a WORE solution

Positives	Negatives
■ Quicker to write ■ Simpler maintenance, as developers only need to make changes in one place ■ Able to adapt to different devices as necessary ■ Useful when the app has a fully custom UI (often common in games)	■ Developers must be familiar with the platform. ■ Developers must have greater discipline about the code structure to simplify managing any platform variations. It can be challenging to ensure that the benefits of a single code base aren't lost in one that's more complicated. ■ Visual assets and resources must be customized for each targeted platform. ■ Developers need to be knowledgeable of both native and cross-platform toolings. ■ Fewer developers are familiar with cross-platform tools, so hiring them may be more difficult. ■ Although there may be less code to test, the app still needs to be tested on all targeted platforms/devices. More retesting may also be required. When the code is changed to address an issue on one platform, it must be tested again on all platforms.

The choice to use a technology to simplify building a version of an app on multiple platforms is a business decision. You can consider many factors, and it can be a fine balance between ease and speed of development versus the level of control and polish in the UI (and the level of customization needed) to meet device/platform-specific requirements.

Sharing a UI across multiple platforms is often a compromise that results in a substandard experience. The speed and responsiveness of the UI and the richness of the graphics often suffer. Highly complex and performant games or apps created with wrappers around web technologies are exceptions because they require lots of optimization. A high-quality experience take a lot of effort, and most developers are willing to compromise in this area. Once you start compromising, it can be hard to know when to stop.

The competitive difference gained from a high-quality user experience comes from being much better than the alternatives. People prefer (and pay for) a better experience. Compromises for the sake of cheaper or simpler development are unlikely to be worth it.

You may only be interested in building apps for a single platform. Regardless of your reasons, there are lessons to learn from considering the device people are using to run your app. Unless you have complete control over the devices people will use to run the app, it's inevitable the app will run on different devices and different versions of the OS.

4.2 Supporting multiple operating systems

In this book, I offer principles and advice that apply to all mobile platforms. This doesn't mean you can ignore the OS on the device your app will be running on. You'll notice sizeable differences between mobile operating systems, and their capabilities and requirements will impact what your app can do. When thinking about an OS, consider these four areas:

- Imposed limitations and restrictions
- Visual expectations
- Variations between versions of an OS
- OS-related expectations and business requirements

Most modern operating systems have a lot of functionality and include many utility and service apps in the box. For many people, these are perfectly satisfactory. If your app is similar in functionality to any of these apps, it's vital that you're aware of those apps and the need for yours to be much better, or offer considerable advantages over what a person will get from the others. There's little competitive advantage to being only slightly better.

4.2.1 OS-imposed restrictions

The differences between operating systems impact what's possible and what's allowed. The consequences of what's allowed particularly extend to apps distributed through a store. Each store has its own rules about what's allowed. Some of the reasons Apple may reject an app from its iOS App Store include

- Portraying realistic images of people or animals being killed, maimed, shot, stabbed, tortured, or injured
- Depicting violence against or abuse of children
- Having "enemies" that target a specific race or culture, a real government, a real corporation, or any other real entity
- Realistically depicting weapons in such a way as to encourage illegal or reckless use of such weapons

- Including games of Russian roulette
- Presenting excessively objectionable or crude content
- Being primarily designed to upset or disgust users

NOTE Each store updates its own lists from time to time, so make sure you check for changes regularly.

It's crucial to be aware of any restrictions that can affect an app before you begin developing it. To spend a lot of time and effort creating something only to later find it isn't permitted in the store can be frustrating.

4.2.2 *Looking like you belong on the OS*

As I mentioned back in section 2.3.2, it's important that your app meets the expectations of the people who use it. This includes making sure the app works, looks, and behaves like the other apps on the device. Some apps existing on more than one platform look the same on all platforms. This can cause confusion for some users and outright frustration in others.

Gerry was the head of design but hadn't previously been involved with the company's iPhone app. When it came time to redesign it and add an Android version, he received negative feedback on his first attempt from prospective users; they said it looked like an iOS app. Using this feedback, he designed an app for both platforms, which didn't look like either OS and yet still followed what he knew to be good design principles. The feedback from this version was that users of devices on both operating systems didn't feel it was obvious how to use it on either. The version he ended up with and that users found best was similar on both platforms, but varied on each to reflect the styling and layout conventions of the different operating systems.

It's understandable that a company may want its app to be the same everywhere, especially if the company is creating the app with a tool that allows the same UI to be used on all platforms. But this is rarely what the people using the app want. Consider this question:

> *What's more important: that an app looks, works, and behaves like the same app on a different device/OS; or that the app looks, works, and behaves like the other apps a person uses on the same device?*

Although a company can benefit if its app looks the same on all devices, because the app needs to be designed only once, the company will typically design it to match one particular OS. Anyone using the app on a different OS doesn't see the consistency of the app across multiple platforms; they only see it as different than the other apps they use. Likewise, if a person typically only uses a single device, they can't appreciate any benefits of the app being the same on different platforms. They only see an app that doesn't follow the conventions of the OS and other apps they use.

Consider the screenshot in figure 4.1. It should be clear that it follows Android's material design guidelines. Now imagine this app running on an iOS or Windows device. At best, it'll look out of place. At worst, it'll look wrong. This was the opinion of many users after the YouTube app was updated on iOS to look like it does on Android, and when the Instagram app was released on Windows looking like an iOS app. The response to both was a backlash of negative reviews and a lot of upset users.

Figure 4.1 The design of this app matches the visual style of Android, and so would look perfectly natural there. But it looks odd to people running it on a device with a different OS.

For apps on more than one platform, there's a design challenge between adjusting the app to follow the styles, patterns, and conventions of each platform, or creating a single design, and, where the app doesn't match the platform of the device people are using, relying on them to learn the differences. Like Gerry's second design, you can argue that following good general design principles is sufficient, and that the app gives enough value to encourage people to learn how to use it, rather than using intuition gained from other apps on the same device. If you take this approach, you must verify your assumptions and make sure that people using the app also believe the same.

The quality of the experience is an essential aspect of the success of an app. Creating an app that looks like it belongs on a different OS compromises the experience for people using the app on a platform it wasn't designed for. Not looking and behaving like a native app risks competition from other apps that look like they belong, and risks setting a precedent that the people using that app on one platform aren't as important as those on another. Such people may not be as valuable as customers, but that can be a dangerous train of thought to start down.

4.2.3 Belonging on a version of the OS

Looking like an app belongs isn't tied to a specific OS, but can also have consequences when new versions of operating systems are released. Both iOS 7 and Android L made changes in their design languages to a flat or material design aesthetic. Apps that weren't updated to reflect the new style quickly looked dated and stood out when running on the newer versions of the operating systems.

Look at the icons in figure 4.2. You'll notice the older-style icon stands out. Don't have your app stand out like this. Instead, you should want it to stand out for the value and experience it provides.

Figure 4.2 An icon built for an older version of an OS stands out and looks like it doesn't belong when placed next to icons designed for a newer version of an OS.

In the fast-moving world of mobile apps, looking old and out-of-date can reflect badly. This can also lead to negative reviews, because the people using the app question the commitment to its support and its long-term future. To avoid this happening to your app, monitor and be aware of releases of new versions of the operating systems that the app runs on so you can plan, prepare, and be ready for any such changes in the future.

4.2.4 Belonging in the enterprise

Internal enterprise and line-of-business apps are a place where the rules can often be bent. In these scenarios, there can be arguments for completely ignoring the OS of the device the app is running on. This is true for devices used for a single purpose, when the person using the app never uses other apps on the device. Having an app that anyone in an organization can use on any device, even if running a different OS, is more beneficial than the app looking and behaving like other apps.

In enterprise scenarios, all internal apps can use a single visual style. For customer-facing apps, there's still the need to reflect a sense of belonging on the OS on which the app is running. Even if it follows the platform conventions for a device, an app can still differentiate visually from competing apps and maintain the identity of the brand offering the app or service.

Put it into practice: knowing the OS your app runs on

Complete the following tasks to solidify your understanding of the devices people are or will be using to run your app, and to help you make plans for applying this to the apps you work on.

- Answer these two questions as precisely as possible:
  - On which devices do, or will, people use your app?
  - Which versions of which operating systems are on those devices?

  If you don't already have it in place, add analytics to monitor this in the future.
- Review all the features of the operating systems (and related development SDKs) that your app runs on. Identify any features or functionality that could add extra value to the users of your app or improve the experience of using it. Then make plans to add them.
- Add details of planned announcements and events by all major OS and device manufacturers to your calendar. You may have to make plans for changes to your apps in response to anything that's announced. The announcement can also provide information about new opportunities or ways to enhance your app. Even if your app doesn't currently run on that device or OS, what you can learn could help you in the future or provide ideas for your app anyway. Not being prepared for a potentially major change or opportunity can have a big impact on your plans. It's therefore wise to at least prepare for the need to do something.

Exercise: understanding different operating systems

Fill in the blanks to test your understanding of the section you've just read.

It's important to know about the OS your app will run on so you can take __________ of unique capabilities it may offer to your app. The OS can also impose _______ on what's possible. The different stores you use to distribute your app can also _______ your app from doing some things. Your app will _______ if it looks like it was designed for the version of the OS it's running on. Matching the conventions of the OS the app is running on is _______ in making an app easy to use. It's _______ important to match OS conventions for internal business apps.

4.3 Maintaining brand identity and differentiation

As mentioned in section 4.2.2, when Gerry first designed the Android version of his company's mobile app, it had a strong visual resemblance to the iPhone version. The company had only an iPhone version for a long time and had grown to think that was the way the app should look. Without experience with different platforms, the company wasn't aware of the aspects of the app's design that were due to the app being on iOS and that were unique to the app. With feedback from Android users and by spending time using Android devices, Gerry began to see the differences.

It's common for a company to build a version of an app for one platform and then expand to other operating systems. When a company already has a version of an app on one platform, it can often be difficult to separate the aspects of the app that are the company's from those that are reflective of the OS.

On many occasions, I've heard people make claims along the lines of, "How our iPhone app looks is part of our mobile brand." This was particularly true of Gerry's company. By living with their app for so long, the company had confused elements of its brand and visual identity with the visual identity of the OS.

4.3.1 Branding vs. visual identity

Branding is a term that's misused and misunderstood. Branding, like design and marketing, relates to all parts of the app, but is sometimes thought of as only relating to parts of the UI. Fonts, icons, logos, and color schemes (or anything else) can help the person using the app associate it with a product, service, business, or organization, but those aren't the brand. They're the *visual identity*. If you're a cattle farmer, you might put a mark on your animals to show they're yours and call that process *branding*. For your apps and your business, branding is much more than a mark of identity or ownership.

The *brand* is all the things you associate with an entity. It's the feelings, status, and attributes you project onto the products and services associated with that entity. You wouldn't buy a can of cola just because it's red with a certain style of writing on it. You would choose it because of many conscious and subconscious factors:

- How you expect it to taste
- How you feel when choosing it
- How you feel once you've drunk it
- What it might say about you to others who see you drinking it

All these factors and many more come from the brand. To constantly evaluate all our decisions based on so many factors would be overwhelming, so we use a brand's name or visual identity as a proxy for those thoughts and emotions.

The value assigned to a brand isn't because of the right to a name, trademark, or visual appearance. The value comes from the fact that consumers buy products or services that use those elements because of the expectations and status they associate with them. Visual identity is a means to an end. It's the end that you should focus on, as it can impact the experience for the person using your app.

4.3.2 Separating your brand from the OS

The companies behind the operating systems and devices on which your app runs have brands they want to maintain. They want people to make positive associations with their products and to keep using them. Each OS has its own set of design guidelines that it encourages developers to follow. Having a consistent visual style and set of behaviors helps the people using the apps and creates a reliable experience.

When apps look and behave differently, the people using them are more likely to blame the platform they're on, rather than the individual apps. It's in the interest of the OS that there's a similarity between the apps that run on it. But unfortunately, like Gerry and his company, many app creators have confused the visual identity of their app with that of an OS. When an app has been on a single OS for a long time, the distinguishing elements of the brand become lost in a UI that's also reflective of the tailoring for the OS.

When expanding to a new platform, you may need to separate the brand from the visuals. That way you can be sure you consistently separate platform specifics and maintain the consistency of the brand across each OS. Finding the elements of an app's design and visuals that aren't unique to the app is easy: follow the chart in figure 4.3.

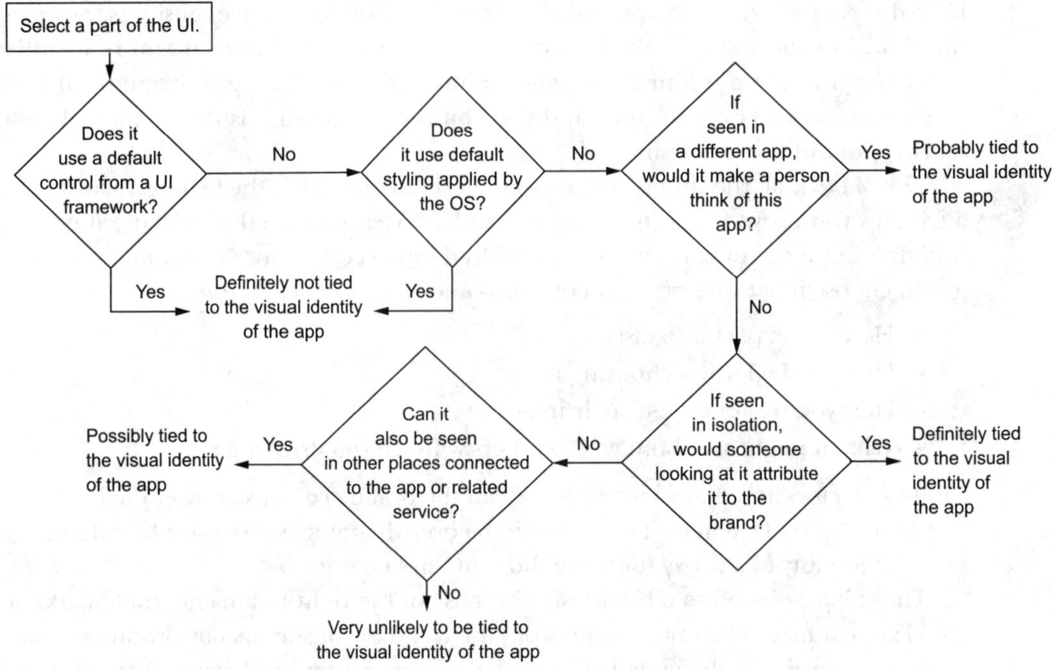

Figure 4.3 How to identify if a part of an app is unique to the brand or part of the OS on which it's running

People who use your app expect the developers to take the time to ensure that an app has its own identity, while still looking like it belongs on each platform it runs on. If that's not the case, the app won't gain a lot of positive feedback. Although this may seem like a lot of effort for little gain, not doing so reflects badly.

4.3.3 Maintaining OS conventions while still reflecting a brand

Identifying parts of an app that aren't unique to a brand is one thing, but applying the visual identity of a brand to the app on a different OS can be a challenge. Regardless of the OS the app is running on, here are some simple ways to reflect the essence of branding in your app:

- *Use the brand's assets*—Icons, logos, images, and other visual assets can normally be reused on multiple platforms with minimal difficulty (beyond adjusting for different size requirements).

  If you're using custom fonts, do so sparingly. The default fonts on each of the major phone operating systems were designed to aid readability. Overuse of custom fonts not only makes the text harder to read, but can also make the app look out of place on the device. It's best to stick to using your own fonts for headers.

  It's not necessary to have a large logo on every page. You want the positive experience of using the app to imprint on the person using it. If a person using the app doesn't remember who made it unless you force them to repeatedly view a large logo, that's an indication of a poor or neutral experience, providing limited or questionable value.
- *Use the brand's color scheme*—Using the same colors everywhere is a simple and non-intrusive way of subtly giving an indication of a brand. This is true if the colors involved aren't used in any competitive apps and aren't part of the standard system color set.
- *Use the brand's copy*—Use the same language, tone, and words in the app, regardless of the OS. Let the personality of the brand be consistent across all versions of the app so people always know what to expect.

Exercise: brand identity and differentiation

Check your understanding of brand identity and differentiation by stating whether the following are true or false:

1. Internal business apps should always look the same even if running on different operating systems.
2. A brand is about more than colors, fonts, and logos.
3. Feelings and emotions toward a company or app are a valuable part of its brand.
4. The quality of a company's app reflects on the company's brand.
5. You should sacrifice brand identity to make your app look like it belongs to a specific OS.

4.4 Supporting different device capabilities

In many ways, all iPhones are alike, but there are some big differences between an iPhone 5c and an iPhone 7 Plus. There's also a lot in common for all phones running

Android. But a device from a lesser-known manufacturer running Cyanogen has many differences from the latest Pixel device. This section explains the key differences to be aware of between devices:

- Physical size
- Hardware capabilities
- Software variations

Whether you're building an app that must work on specific devices, or the requirements of the app dictate the devices it can run on, you should consider the capabilities available and how they can be incorporated, or not, into an app. Don't incorporate any functionality just for the sake of it, or because it's possible. Do it because it can add something valuable or useful to the experience.

4.4.1 Handling multiple physical device sizes

Mobile devices come in a wide variety of sizes, and you'll need to build your app to work on most, if not all, of them. You must consider many factors to provide a high-quality experience across that range. Don't take the dismissive attitude of "just make it work everywhere." Instead, consider the different sizes on which you need the app to work.

SIZE CAN IMPACT WHO USES A DEVICE

The physical size of a device may dictate who can or who wants to use it. Combine this with what you know of the people likely to use your app and the environments and times when they'll do so. This can mean that an app will rarely, if at all, be used on devices of a certain size. This knowledge can be helpful in prioritizing the screen sizes you spend more time optimizing and testing. As figure 4.4 shows, getting this wrong can lead to wasted effort.

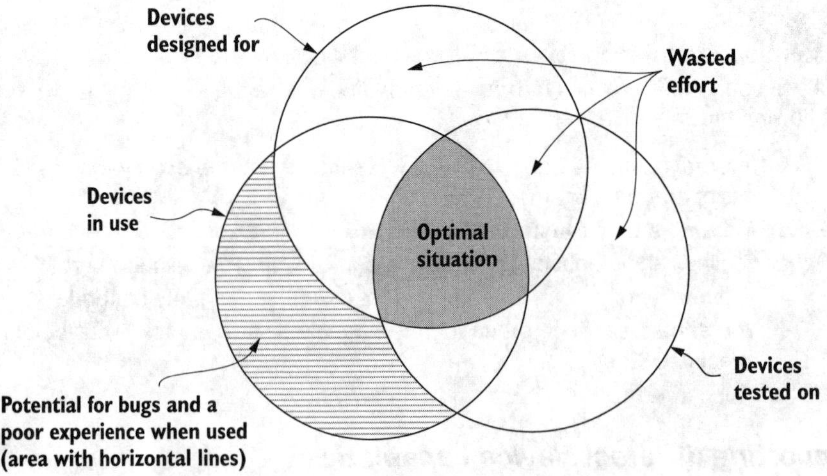

Figure 4.4 Ensure the best use of your time by designing for and testing on the devices people will use your app.

Size also impacts how a device is held and what can be displayed onscreen. The following sections elaborate on those considerations to aid in the optimization and success of your app.

SIZE CAN IMPACT HOW A DEVICE IS HELD

The size of a device affects how it's held and interacted with. Modern operating systems have ways to make it easier to use a large screen with one hand. Although this can be useful, an app may still be cumbersome to use if a person must invoke such aids repeatedly. Instead, it's better to have common functionality easily accessible. As figure 4.5 shows, this depends on both the physical size of the device and the physical size of the hand of the person using the app.

The top of the screen is harder to reach.
With a larger device, more of the screen is difficult to reach.
Darker areas are easier to touch with a thumb during one-handed use when the device is held in the right hand.

Figure 4.5 The parts of the screen that can be most easily reached with one hand relate to the size of the hand and the screen.

It's common for high-level navigation to be at the top of the screen. Although this functionality may be needed, it isn't where a person will spend most of their time in the app. I'm not saying that you should never put content at the top of the screen, but that the content that's most interacted with should be in the easily reachable area.

> **Fitts's law**
>
> Closely related to the impact of the physical size of the device and the hands holding it is the position of content. Fitts's law shows that the ease of interacting with an item onscreen is a factor of its size and the distance traveled to reach it.
>
> The consequence for app designers is that anything onscreen that you want to be easy to interact with should be large and close to the natural positions of the thumb or fingers holding the device. Smaller items that are further away are harder to touch.

Fitts's law *(continued)*

This can have both good and bad implications. It's harder to touch smaller elements accidentally, but a need to touch such elements frequently can become uncomfortable and frustrating.

The physical size of the screen can also influence how a person holds it. Larger devices are more likely to be

- Held in a landscape orientation
- Held with two hands
- Placed on a surface to interact with

If the predominant usage for an app is in one of these large-device scenarios, then to optimize for something else would be a mistake.

SIZE AFFECTS WHAT CAN BE DISPLAYED

At a simplistic level, the size of a screen affects how much the app can display. It isn't always the case, however, that because a screen has more pixels, it's capable of displaying more content. There's little advantage in displaying more if the pixels are smaller and harder to read, or it becomes harder to touch the desired element.

Not only are different size devices available, but items onscreen can be resized, and you must account for both scenarios. When these features are optional, it's still important to support them in your app, because they make the app accessible to more people. When they're not optional, it's even more important to design for and test these scenarios.

Figure 4.6 shows an example of how an app can change when scaled differently on a single device and the consequences of not accounting for this. *Scaling fallacy* is the idea that everything that works in one scale works in another. As figure 4.6 shows, this

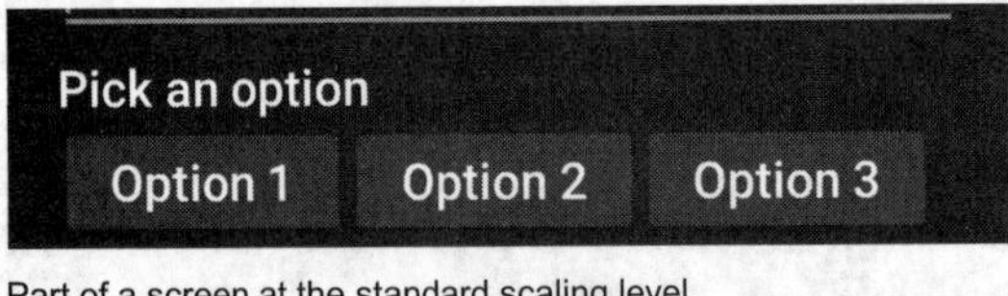

Part of a screen at the standard scaling level.

The position and alignment of the buttons don't allow for all of them to be seen when the content of the app is scaled up by an OS-level setting.

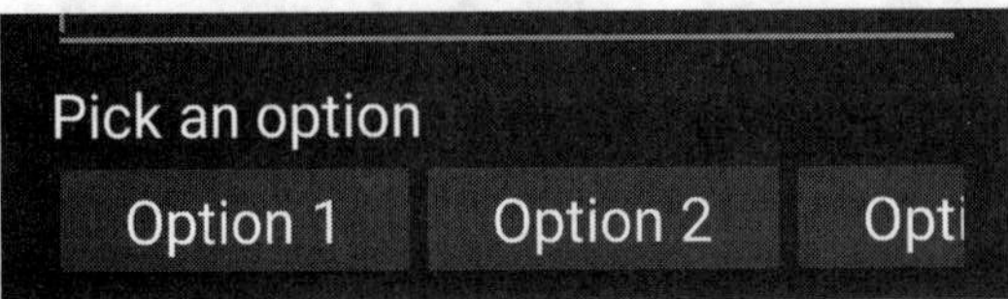

The same part of the screen, scaled up by the OS. Not only is the text larger, but controls are, too.

Figure 4.6 Scaling of screen elements can impact both how an app looks as well as interaction with it if parts of the screen become unreadable or inaccessible.

isn't true. One of the buttons isn't fully visible when increasing the size of screen items. Issues like this can also affect devices of different physical sizes.

Regardless of whether constraints on screen space result from the physical size of the device or due to DPI or scaling settings, if it's important that functionality is always accessible, then you must ensure that it is. If it doesn't matter if something isn't visible in some scenarios, it's worth evaluating if you need that functionality on any device.

4.4.2 Variations in internal hardware capability

Although Gerry's company's mobile app was popular, it suffered some criticism. People felt that it didn't do anything that wasn't also possible on the same device via the website. Gerry took the redesign of the app as an opportunity to address this. By adding functionality to the app that used device settings, the user's location, and the address book on the device, he was able to simplify and speed up some of the app's capabilities.

Many apps are little more than a highly specialized browser for a specific service, or provide other functionality that's also available via a website. If your app provides the same functionality as a website, you'll miss out on many of the unique opportunities and possibilities of a modern mobile device. A typical mobile device has far more sensors and other hardware-related capabilities than a computer. If you ignore this, you risk not creating as rich, simple, or valuable an experience as possible.

> **Using analytics to track device details**
> As mentioned in the previous two chapters, it's important to use analytics to monitor how the devices of the people using the app match your initial expectations and how they change over time. Any changes in use or differences from expectations may mean that you need to change the app to better meet the needs and expectations of the people using it and provide a better experience.
>
> Also, consider the privacy and legal implications of any data captured. Reflect the details in a privacy policy and include any terms of use. You could also use a licensing agreement for this. See chapter 2 for more on privacy considerations.

SUPPORTING THE INCLUSION OR ABSENCE OF PHYSICAL BUTTONS

Other than the physical size of a device and its screen, the next biggest difference between devices is the inclusion or lack of hardware buttons. Having software buttons in the app that perform the same functionality as hardware buttons on the device is at best redundant, and at worst confusing. Figure 4.7 shows an extreme example of such a case. In the figure, you can see the bottom of a Windows Phone app with a physical button as well as two onscreen back buttons for navigating back through the app and its content.

When an app's running on a platform that's guaranteed to have a physical button or an OS-provided software button, there's no reason to have a software button in

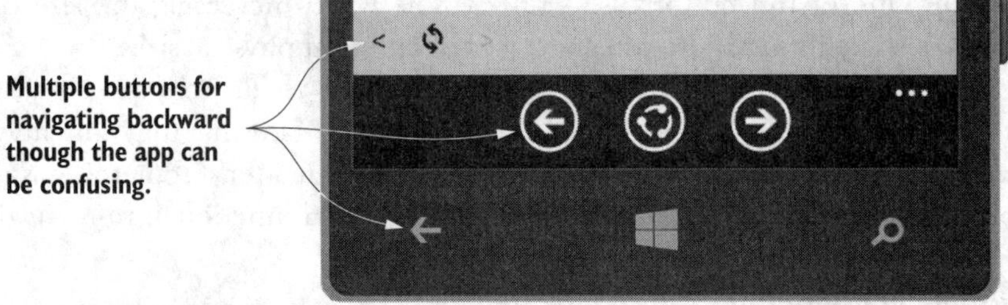

Multiple buttons for navigating backward though the app can be confusing.

Figure 4.7 Having software buttons in an app that match the behavior of hardware buttons is not only redundant but can also be confusing.

your app that performs the same action. Controls for manipulating media playback (play, pause, and so forth) are probably the most common exception to this, but you should start with the assumption that you shouldn't duplicate functionality. Only add it when testing, and if feedback says it'll be valuable.

When your app runs on a platform where devices may have a hardware key equivalent to functionality displayed in the app, then test for the existence of such a key. Don't display the onscreen version if the physical key exists. Consider building an app that takes photos, for example. Whether you need a virtual Take Photo button depends on whether the device it's running on has a dedicated hardware button for this.

Including software buttons that mimic hardware buttons has been problematic in the past. There have been mobile platforms that included dedicated buttons for search and menu functionality. Inconsistent use of these buttons led to confusion among users. In the worst scenarios, apps added their own duplicate buttons, but the system buttons and the app's versions behaved differently.

Follow the guidance and design directions of the platforms you're building for, but watch and test for what the people using your app want and are doing. Then adjust as needed. Platform guidance and the expectations of the people using the app will normally match, but if they don't, give people what they want.

Testing on devices

As the number and range of devices you need to test on increases, you may also experience issues with the cost of obtaining and accessing such devices. Simulators and emulators are great up to a point, but they can't give an exact representation of all aspects of using a device. This includes what it feels like when held.

When you're buying devices for testing, be sure to focus on the devices that are used by the most people using the app. Even if you have infinite resources to buy devices, you could end up with hundreds of devices that are more of a burden than a benefit. The ideal is to test the largest representative sample of the devices used to run the app, but with the smallest number of devices possible.

Borrowing devices from friends, family, or a device lab or library can be a cost-effective way to see how an app runs and looks on devices beyond those you own. It isn't a solution for every situation and can be difficult to scale, but it's a good start. Using other people's devices also encourages you to use them in different environments. Using devices this way can help you test an app in a location that can be closer to the environment where the app is used. It can also teach you more about how other people use their devices, providing a better understanding of people and their circumstances, which, in turn, can help you optimize your design.

Be sure to start testing on devices early in the process, and avoid underestimating the time and effort needed for testing. When an app is released that provides a poor experience due to a lack of testing, it's a waste of resources and raises doubts about the credibility of your company.

USING AVAILABLE SENSORS

Devices come with an increasing number of internal sensors. By being aware of the sensors in the device the app is running on, you can identify potential ways of extending or adding useful functionality in the app.

Even if a sensor isn't available on every device, by detecting when it is and then using it, you can improve the experience of people whose devices enable the sensor. Table 4.2 includes several sensors that may be possible to use in your app.

Table 4.2 Some of the sensors available in modern mobile devices

Motion sensors	Environmental sensors	Position sensors
Accelerometer	Light	Orientation
Gravity	Thermometer	Compass
Step counter	Humidity	Magnetometer
Gyroscope	Barometer	Proximity

With any sensor or potentially sensitive capability, always verify its existence and get permission before using it. When requesting permission to use a sensor, show a useful message that explains why the app needs it rather than have your app crash or give no explanation for why functionality is missing or disabled when permission isn't granted. Chapter 7 includes details and examples of how to use input from sensors to improve your app experience.

OTHER HARDWARE DIFFERENCES

You'll find many other potential differences in the devices on which your app can run. These include both more common items and those that are added by manufacturers to differentiate their devices. By using these capabilities when they're available, you can add extra functionality to your app or make a task simpler. In addition to size, screens can differ in their support for the types of touch detection, the number of concurrent touch points, the use of different pointing devices, and detecting the amount of pressure applied when touching the screen.

The inclusion of cameras on devices has become increasingly popular, but still isn't guaranteed on all devices. Even if the device has a camera, there are variations to consider: Is the camera on the front or back of the device, or both? How large is the image it can take? Can it capture video or only still images? Is it capable of other functionalities like biometric identification and iris recognition?

Fingerprint scanners are also increasingly included on devices. Compared with entering a password, these can be much more convenient for people to use as a form of authentication. If a person uses their fingerprint to unlock a device and sign in to other apps they use, but yours requires typing in a username and password, it may feel like a step backward, and reflect negatively on your app.

The CPU (and GPU, if included) can also vary in their capabilities. The most obvious difference is in speed and the number of cores available. This can be important to check if your app needs to do lots of parallel, processor-intensive tasks. Less obvious are differences in media codec support across devices. Similar devices may have the same OS, but not all will be able to play the same video. It's much better to know this in advance than to discover that due to a video's format, some people using the app won't be able to watch it.

The final hardware difference to be aware of relates to the ability of a device to connect to other networks or devices. Radio and networking support can vary between versions of operating systems and individual devices. (The inclusion, or not, of GPS may affect location accuracy.) Not all devices include both Wi-Fi and GSM radios. If you're developing an app that depends on those, you may need to consider how to handle this. Bluetooth and NFC radios can also enable extra value and functionality when included, but they aren't in every device.

4.4.3 Accounting for software variations

Just as hardware functionality can differ across devices, software can also vary. The biggest software-related variation is found in the OS on the device. It may seem obvious to consider the OS, but a mobile OS includes so many features that it can be difficult to familiarize yourself with all of them. New versions of operating systems consistently offer new ways for apps to integrate and extend functionality. From extending search results to being a target for other apps to share data with, the opportunities are numerous. You should explore the options available to you in the versions of the operating systems your app runs on.

Beyond the OS, consider the other apps installed on the device. Many offer other opportunities for integration. This can be a simple integration, such as sharing data, or a deeper level of integration, where functionality is shared or exposed via the other app. As the importance of the services that underlie apps grows, so does the desire for them to integrate more extensively into people's lives. This often takes the form of exposing APIs and other functionality that third-party apps can use and drives greater usage of the service.

Put it into practice: device differences

- Review the capabilities of the devices that your app is used on. Identify anything that could improve or extend the usefulness of your app, and make plans to add it.
- Ensure that your designs and test plans correspond with the devices that people are using to run your app. If they don't, change them so they do.
- Ensure that your app is at least usable with the different scaling and text size settings that are available on the devices that people use with your app. Any improvements beyond just being usable will likely be appreciated by the people using such settings.

Exercise: varying hardware and software capabilities

Test your understanding of the last section by filling in the blanks in the following sentences with either *hardware*, *software*, or *hardware and software*:

1. It's important to know about the ______ that your app runs on.
2. The ______ can influence who uses a device and how it's held.
3. When displaying content onscreen, you need to think about ______.
4. Test for the presence of specific ______ before trying to interact with it in your app.
5. The ______ of a device can change over time, and you must allow for this.

Now that you have a full appreciation for the circumstances in which people will use your app (the context), it's time to move on to look at the next dimension—input.

Summary

- Even if you're building an app that runs on a single OS, you must understand that OS and the devices the app can run on.
- Cross-platform solutions that support a native UI can bring the benefits of shared code without compromising the user experience. If you're using a cross-platform solution, you need a thorough understanding of the platforms on which the app will run.
- Choosing to build with a cross-platform solution should be a business decision, not a purely technical one.
- The OS of the device that an app will run on impacts what's possible and what's allowed. Differences between versions of an OS can be as large as the differences between operating systems.

- To meet the expectations of the people using an app, it's important for the app to follow the conventions of the layout and behavior of the operating systems it's on.
- A brand and its visual identity aren't the same. Use a brand's assets, color schemes, and copy as a basis for visually communicating a brand's identity, while still respecting the conventions of an OS.
- The physical size of a device can influence where and when it's used. It also affects how it's held and which parts of the screen are easier to touch and interact with.
- Consider physical size along with screen pixel density and any user-configured scaling to understand how much you can display onscreen at any time.
- Beyond the physical size, the other big differences between devices are buttons and sensors. If a device may not include a specific hardware feature, you should test for its existence before trying to use it.
- Different operating systems offer varying ways of integrating with an app or allowing apps to work together. Focus on designing for and testing on the devices that people use the app.
- Use analytics to track the devices people are using and the versions of the operating systems on those devices.

Part 2

Input

While the first part of this book was mostly theoretical, in this part things get more practical. For many people, mobile devices started out as consumption-focused devices, but due to their ubiquity and the rich input capabilities they contain, they soon evolved to be considered equally as creation devices. The ability to capture and create data has been the source of a revolution in publishing and has changed many industries forever. Whether it's part of the increase in written personal communication or the capturing of videos or pictures, input drives the apps that enable this.

Should you consider input before or after output? You may argue that until the app outputs guidance on where, when, and how input should be provided, the person using it won't be able to provide suitable input. This way of thinking is app focused, but to create an app that provides the best experience for the people using it, you need to put the user first. That's why I spent the last three chapters talking about context. It's important to focus on the value the person will get from using the app before considering how it looks or what's asked of the person using the app.

Your app may have a clear purpose, but it's essential that you understand the goals of the person using it. Unless an app is highly specialized, the way a person obtains value from it requires first providing some input. Such input may be as simple as choosing an item from a list, or it may require the entry of complex data. Whatever the situation, by making the capturing of the input as easy and painless as possible, it becomes quicker and easier for people to start getting the value they desire.

A person may go to a hardware store and buy a spade. But do they want the spade for the hole it can be used to create or to enjoy the experience of working in the garden? Similarly, a person may have different reasons for using a messaging app. They may just want the outlet to say something. They may want to read what other people have written. Or, they may want the experience of connecting with other people through the messages they exchange. There can be good reasons to use an app for any or all of these scenarios. There can also be apps that specifically provide for just one such scenario.

It's appropriate that the tool (or app) that's being used to achieve the desired goal be able to perform the task well. Our person with the spade would struggle to create a hole or get satisfaction from their work if the input mechanism for the spade (the handle) was loose, uncomfortable, or a strange shape. It's the same with an app containing substandard input facilities.

Input drives the interfaces of almost all apps. That is, the app only does something in response to the input. Mobile devices are considered to have both limited input mechanisms available and also rich and varied input capabilities. This highlights how mixed the experiences and thoughts are of people who use the apps that run on their mobile devices. It's in light of these mixed opinions that I'll now get you to think about the input of data and information in your mobile apps. Over the next three chapters, we'll look at the three key aspects of input: touch, data entry, and input that doesn't come directly from the people using it.

5 How people interact with the app

This chapter covers

- Providing the best experience with input devices
- Using gestures in appropriate and accessible ways
- Handling low-level touch events

This chapter explains the different ways people can interact with your app, and why it's important that you consider these. If your app uses only system-provided controls and has little customization, this is a relatively simple subject with few core issues to be aware of. But if you're customizing visuals and interactions, you can do many things to impact a person's experience. You'll benefit from understanding the differences.

The most frequent approach to giving input and interacting with an app on a mobile device is touching the screen. Many such devices are referred to as *touch-screen devices*. This ubiquity of use can lead to complacency when creating apps for these devices. People touch the screen of devices a lot, but there's value in taking a metaphorical step back and asking why and how they're doing so. Assuming people touch the screen because they must interact with your app risks overlooking the understanding or intention behind the interaction. By not thinking about what you're asking them to touch, you may also overlook considerations for alternative input methods.

Whereas a finger (or thumb) is the most common implement used to touch a screen, other things can be used as an alternative or in combination with a finger. Development tools and SDKs do a good job of abstracting the device that's used. But if you need to optimize for specific input tools, use something other than raw input events or define your own gestures.

Throughout this chapter, I'll also tell you about Linda and some of the challenges she had while working on an app used by sales people within her company. The app included many custom controls and needed to support many types of input.

5.1 Supporting different pointing devices

This section looks at the different pointing devices people use to interact with what's onscreen. A finger, mouse, and digital stylus have much in common, but there's more you can bring to your app when you know the differences and variations between those.

Different input devices can be more suited to various tasks or to differences in the type or size of the screen. They can also provide additional information. The key differences between the primary input mechanisms relate to

- Precision
- Pressure sensitivity
- Screen technologies
- How their use obscures the screen

An intuitive UX is one that meets the expectations of the people using the app, and this extends to input devices too. How do you allow for numerous input devices and account for the differences? Table 5.1 shows a summary of the differences between the three pointing devices.

Table 5.1 Comparison of different pointing devices

	Finger	Stylus	Mouse
Precision	Low	Medium to high	High
Popularity	High	Medium	Low (but growing)
Screen technology works with	Capacitive best Resistive ok	Any (but not all work with a capacitive screen)	Any
Can obscure other content	Yes	Yes	No
Pressure sensitivity	Limited	High	None
Other notes	Not good if person is wearing gloves	Can be easily lost	Often requires use while sitting

Because using a finger is the most common way of interacting with a mobile device, the next section focuses on what's special about that way of input. Then we'll look at input with a stylus and with a mouse or keyboard.

5.1.1 Providing input with a finger

Let's begin by considering an example. Linda's app needed some specialized input. As none of the built-in keyboard configurations were appropriate for this, she decided to build her own keyboard. This wasn't an actual custom keyboard, just buttons onscreen that resembled one. She wanted to place more buttons in the same space than normally appear on a keyboard; this meant that the buttons were small. Early users of the app reported difficulties with pressing the buttons they wanted. The solution to this was twofold. She increased the space used by the keyboard so the keys would be larger, and she added some logic to automatically correct common mistakes.

Although a thumb (or finger) is usually available to touch a screen, using it as an input method isn't without its downsides. The biggest downside is the limit of precision and accuracy that it affords on a small screen. Consider figure 5.1. Estimate which key the finger is pressing. It's probably *G*, but could conceivably be any of those covered. This is one of the reasons why accurately typing without looking on a small touch screen is harder than on a physical keyboard.

Figure 5.1 It's hard to tell what key is being pressed when a finger (or thumb) covers multiple targets.

Because typing with an onscreen keyboard is such a common task, much has been done to address this issue. This takes the form of predictive analysis of the likelihood of the desired key being touched and automatic correction of mistakes and misspellings.

When controls are placed close together, modern frameworks are good at figuring out which was the intended target when both are touched at once. Where possible, avoid this issue in the first place by using adequate spacing between the items. It's also important to be aware of this if you're not relying on a UI framework and are processing touch events directly. Deciding which point onscreen a person intended to touch is further complicated by variations in the size of the digits on a person's hand. Figure 5.2 shows how great the difference can be.

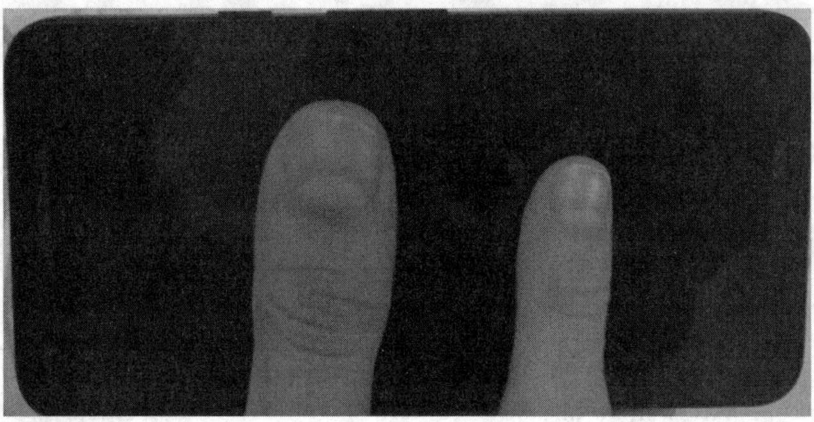

Figure 5.2 Two thumbs on a screen that show how hands come in a range of sizes. Your app must cope with all of them.

Rubber fingertips

If you've ever licked your finger to improve the grip when flicking through a stack of papers, you'll appreciate that this might get frustrating, especially if you need to flip through large quantities of paper every day. If you've worked in an office where this was an issue, you may know that there are companies that make rubber fingertips for just this situation. These rubber thimbles provide extra grip, and so make working with paper easier. A few years ago, Linda found another use for them.

Linda had small hands and struggled to grasp that although she could easily use the interfaces she was creating, people with larger hands couldn't. The solution was to have her test her designs while wearing one of those rubber fingertips. The layer of rubber served to increase the size of her finger, soon giving her an appreciation of the challenges faced by some of the people who'd use her app. Regardless of the size of your fingers, equally creative ways exist to help you appreciate any differences between you and the people who'll use your app.

Because all apps must allow for varying sizes of fingers, you'll find official guidelines for handling this on each of the major platforms. Table 5.2 shows how each platform uses its own measurement and the approximate equivalent in millimeters.

Table 5.2 Recommended smallest touch target sizes on the three major platforms

Platform	Recommended minimum touch target size
iOS	44 points (approx. 11mm)
Android	48dip (approx. 7–10mm)
Windows	7–9mm (where 9mm = 48px at 135 PPI)

If the item to be touched in your app is smaller than the recommended size, accept touches in the area around it as if they were on the item itself. When increasing the size of the touchable area, do this evenly around all sides of the item, unless this leads to areas touching or overlapping. If touching a point would be ambiguous as to which item was the intended target, don't extend the touch area there. See figure 5.3.

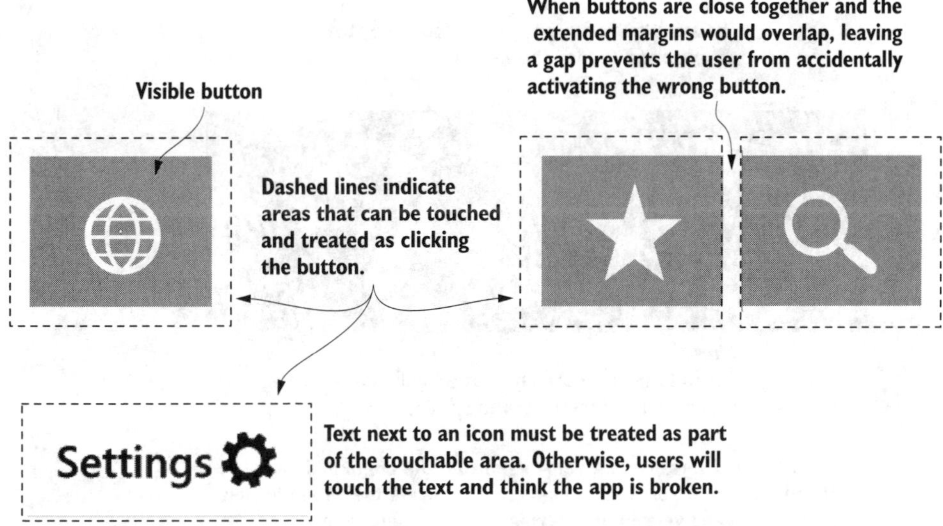

Figure 5.3 Add a margin to a button to increase the size of the area that can be tapped. Spacing needs to be left between items to avoid accidentally tapping the wrong one.

The need to allow space between touchable items often contrasts with the requirements for the desired visuals. Figure 5.4 shows speech bubbles and phone symbols that are buttons for sending a message or for making a call to the numbers they're next to.

In figure 5.4, the version on top shows an early design. Here the items are so close together that people regularly pressed the wrong one. This led to the creation of the variation beneath to avoid the problem, but it used a visual layout that wasn't deemed as visually appealing by the designer of the app.

As discussed in chapter 4, many variations exist in the physical screens of devices. Screen size, pixel density, and screen scaling all impact how the display size of an item onscreen varies. Good UI frameworks can handle this for you, but this requires that you don't use absolute values for pixels. You may need to consider this if drawing the contents of the screen yourself, or when doing other calculations or manipulations based on pixels.

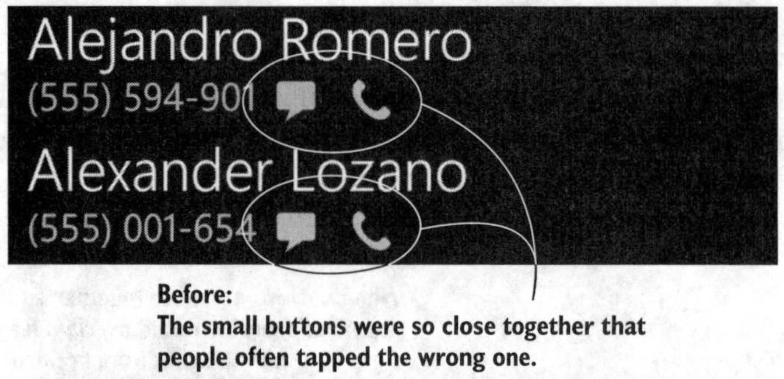
Alejandro Romero
(555) 594-901
Alexander Lozano
(555) 001-654
Before:
The small buttons were so close together that people often tapped the wrong one.

Alejandro Romero
(555) 594-901
Alexander Lozano
(555) 001-654
After:
The buttons have been moved to make it harder to accidentally tap the wrong one.

Figure 5.4 Two versions of a screen showing the original, designer-preferred version, which resulted in people pressing the wrong button, and the redesigned version, which was easier for people to use.

All this concern with the size of items and the space they take up can present challenges in creating the desired design. I've had many conversations like the one shown in figure 5.5. A typical response to such a conversation is for the app developer to decide they don't need all six buttons. They then move or remove one or more of the

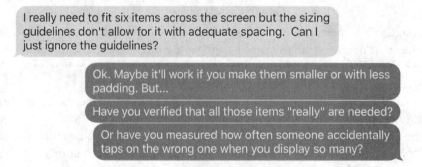

I really need to fit six items across the screen but the sizing guidelines don't allow for it with adequate spacing. Can I just ignore the guidelines?

Ok. Maybe it'll work if you make them smaller or with less padding. But...

Have you verified that all those items "really" are needed?

Or have you measured how often someone accidentally taps on the wrong one when you display so many?

Figure 5.5 A common conversation with a developer, where they want to break with guidelines to make their life easier. It's better to verify assumptions and test the implications of breaking them.

buttons so number isn't an issue. This may seem an easy win: a potential usability issue goes away, and there can be a little bit less code to write and test.

Taking this approach can be risky. Before you do so, avoid making assumptions about which buttons are less important and so can be [re]moved. Originally, they were all important. Did the developer learn something that gave new insight, or was the decision based on guessing about the importance of each choice? Whatever happened, this type of situation isn't what leads to the best experiences for people using the app.

Instead of relying on guesswork or a gut feeling, undertake analysis and testing to ensure the app provides what's best for the people using it. Use analytics to track which functionality to use within your app and with what frequency. This allows you to remove items with the confidence that they're not used. Or, it'll let you know which are the least often used and so would cause the least impact when placed in a More Options menu.

Another consideration relating to using a finger as a touch input device is the size of the hand it's attached to. The hand can obscure a large part of the screen. Although it's a potentially interesting contribution to the mechanics of some games, obscuring part of the screen isn't a desirable side-effect for most apps. Avoid any negative consequences by placing anything important at the top of the screen, or directly above the item to be touched. As shown in figure 5.6, a hand is most likely to obscure anything in the bottom corners of the screen.

Animals
Horses
Frogs
Squirrels
Important information is better displayed at the top of the screen, where it's less likely to be obscured.
Important information at the bottom of the screen can easily be missed when obscured by a thumb or fingers.
A user's right hand is holding the device and obscuring the bottom-right part of the screen. If the device was being held in a person's left hand, then the other side of the screen would be obscured.
Allow for people to use either hand without obscuring anything that, as a result, prevents them from using the app.

Figure 5.6 A thumb covering part of the screen and obscuring what's beneath

There's often a balance to be found between what's onscreen and where or how large it is. Lean toward the way a person uses the app as the deciding factor when weighing options.

It isn't only the size of a hand that varies between people; dexterity and range of motion also vary. If you've found that the people using the app are more likely to be affected in this way, you can make the app more accessible to them with simple actions like increasing the size of the touch targets and removing the need for complex movement gestures or repetitive actions like double tapping.

Supporting both single and double tapping is something you should avoid. You can't immediately respond to the first click because it's necessary to wait for a possible second click, making the app less responsive. It also increases the likelihood of accidental double taps, single taps, or slow double taps. You don't normally want to trigger both the single and double tap actions when making a double tap.

Although a finger is the most common "device" used to interact with a mobile app, its use isn't always possible or appropriate. In this case, the input is commonly provided with a stylus. The next section looks at the second most common form of input: a stylus (a digital pen or pencil), which is popular on larger devices and for certain types of apps.

5.1.2 Providing input with a stylus

A stylus is often treated like a finger, but it's the preferred input device when a high level of precision is required, such as when selecting a specific item or point onscreen. Or the level of precision might be in the input that's provided, such as when providing a signature.

In our case study, Linda's app captured a signature onscreen as part of an ordering process. To ensure the highest quality of the captured signature, she spent time researching different controls and styli to use. Sadly, much of this effort was wasted. No matter what the company tried, including physically securing the stylus to the device, styli would repeatedly become lost and spares misplaced, leading to the use of whatever suitable substitute was available. The app had to be modified to capture the signature as well as possible, regardless of the implement used.

If you were using Linda's app, you could have signed for a delivery with a thin piece of plastic or biro, probably leaving a mark that bears little resemblance to your signature. Such implements are the simplest type of stylus. Styli are also available in a variety of form factors and sizes, and with varying capabilities, including multiple buttons and pressure and movement sensors capturing data they send to the paired device.

A simple piece of plastic can be used on a device with a resistive screen, as it detects contact based on pressure, causing layers in the screen to touch. The more common alternative is a capacitive screen, which relies on the ability of what's touching it to conduct electricity. Not all styli have this ability the way a human finger does. A modern stylus on a capacitive screen, however, can do a significantly better job than a piece of plastic on a resistive screen.

NOTE Your app needs to work regardless of the pointing device used. Avoid requiring a specific type of stylus.

Figure 5.7 shows the size of touch contact points for different input devices. Smaller points of contact mean a person is less likely to touch multiple items simultaneously, thereby accidentally interacting with the wrong one.

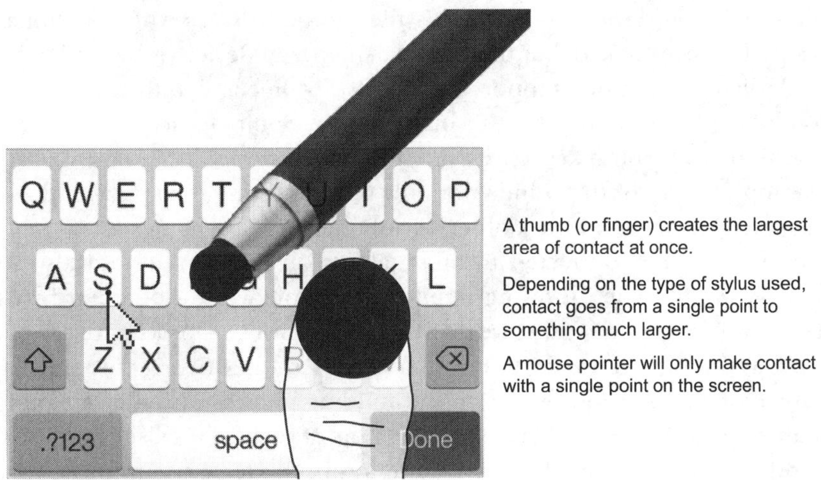

Q W E R T Y U I O P
A S D F G H J K L
Z X C V B N M
.?123
space
Done
A thumb (or finger) creates the largest area of contact at once.
Depending on the type of stylus used, contact goes from a single point to something much larger.
A mouse pointer will only make contact with a single point on the screen.

Figure 5.7 The size of the point of contact varies when using different input devices.

A stylus not only enables greater precision than a finger, it also enables extra functionality and is better suited for different interactions. The styli now available are becoming increasingly sophisticated and often include the ability to detect pressure on the device's screen. The amount of pressure applied can be combined with, or used instead of, the duration of a touch event to effect different actions in an app. Or, you can use pressure as a substitute for other settings like size or value. Imagine pressing harder to make a value increase faster, or to change size or color. This allows complex input with a single tap of the screen, when otherwise multiple taps, selections, or gestures would have to be made.

Pressure sensitivity in a stylus is measured by the stylus, but screens with the ability to detect pressure directly are also being introduced. Although pressure detection is becoming more widespread, there's still a lot of variation in how this is reported to an app. It can also be hard for people to learn to use accurately, and so, even where it can be used, you'll need to provide an extra way to provide fine adjustments to data gathered.

You can also combine the use of a stylus with a finger. Depending on the task being performed, it may be appropriate to have different devices perform different actions. Consider a large piece of text. A finger might default to scrolling the text, while a stylus, if present, may default to highlighting or annotating the text. This removes the need for manually switching between modes and could eliminate accidentally invoking the wrong behavior and being unsure what happened or how to undo it. The aim is to enhance the experience of using an app for anyone with hardware, without taking anything away from someone just using their finger.

5.1.3 Providing input with a mouse and the keyboard

The final pointing device to consider is the mouse. It's use with traditional mobile devices is often overlooked, but the boundary between devices is becoming blurred.

Linda had to consider support for the use of her app with a mouse when she received a bug report that it didn't work with one. Some of the people using the app had connected Bluetooth keyboards and mice to the device, as it was easier to use as a mini laptop. In light of this, Linda not only started testing the app with these devices but also added analytics to track other peripherals.

A mouse can be connected to most tablets on the market and also to a wide number of phones. For a growing number of people worldwide, their first computing device will be a phone; they're unlikely to own a PC. On occasion, these people may have tasks that are easier to do on a large screen with a mouse and keyboard. Several companies are addressing this by building phones with the capability to connect a mouse, keyboard, and large display. Lots of scenarios exist where this is desirable, and it's set to become far more common in the future, but for now, you need to consider the use of a mouse with a tablet. The specific considerations you need to make are

- Optimizations
- Precision
- A permanent cursor onscreen
- Multiple buttons
- Use of a mouse combined with a separate physical keyboard

I've seen attempts to optimize tablet apps based on whether a mouse is connected. The theory was that if a mouse is connected, the items onscreen can be made smaller, as it's easier to select something small with a mouse. When the mouse wasn't connected, onscreen items were made bigger for easier selection with a finger, and with more accuracy. The problem with this theory is that people still touch the screen with their fingers, even when a mouse is connected. In an attempt to be helpful, the designer ended up making things harder in some scenarios. It would have been more helpful to all users to have a single layout that worked with all input types.

People switch between input devices without removing hardware. Unless an app needs to work on a variety of devices, including those with touch screens and those without, there's rarely a need to allow for different input methods. Instead, create an app that works with all input types.

A mouse has a unique benefit that isn't possible with a finger or stylus. Figure 5.8 shows how it's possible to be more precise with mouse input, as the cursor can only be

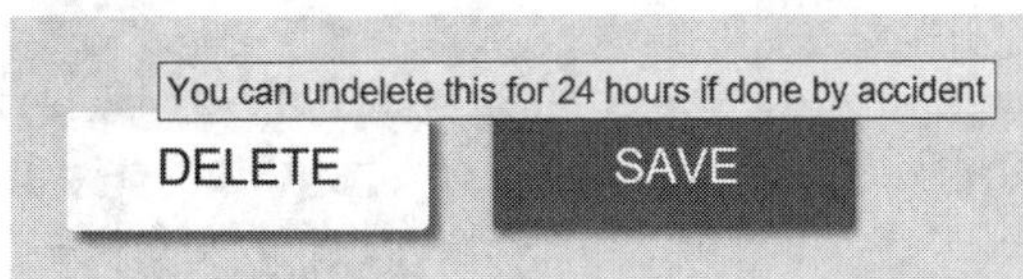

Figure 5.8 When a mouse is connected, the cursor can be used to highlight the item to select and display more information too.

over a single pixel. This makes it impossible to think you're selecting one item while invoking another.

Because a mouse's cursor is permanently onscreen, it can be used to interact with content instead of tapping. A cursor onscreen can also show information or hints without the need to click or tap an item. As shown in figure 5.8, tooltips or flyovers can be a nice added extra when a mouse is connected. A mouse's cursor shouldn't be the only way to access content or information, however, or to enable navigation through an app.

It's unlikely you'll want to design a mobile app with a mouse as the primary input method, but do support it if it's used. Also, if using a mouse to interact with your app, people expect the same behavior as they have in other apps where they also use a mouse, so you must respect standard conventions of mouse use in a mobile app:

- Left clicking with a mouse should have the same behavior as tapping with a finger.
- Double left-clicking with a mouse should be treated as a double tap with a finger. It should also select any text that's double clicked.
- Right clicking with a mouse should be the same as a long press or tap-and-hold gesture with a finger.
- Moving the scroll wheel on a mouse should move any content under the cursor.

Although some mobile devices support working with a mouse, more support external, physical keyboards. When testing your app for compatibility with mouse conventions, also do the same for keyboard support. Pay special attention to the Tab and Enter keys. Onscreen keyboards rarely include the Tab key, but don't overlook it as a way of moving focus. You can work around a lack of a soft Tab button by overloading this functionality on the Enter button. Be sure the Enter key behaves as expected in terms of shifting focus and submitting form data.

Put it into practice: different input devices

- Find a small device and someone with large fingers and watch them use your app. Are there any parts they find hard to use or places where items are too close for them to tap correctly with confidence? Adjust any layouts to increase sizes and spacing as appropriate.
- Verify that all parts of your app can be fully used with different input devices. Make plans to address any issues you discover.

> **Put it into practice: different input devices *(continued)***
> - Add analytics to detect if people are using different input devices with your app, assuming your app runs on an OS that lets you detect this. Ensure you update your test plans to include the devices people are using with your app. Consider any enhancements you could make for specific devices, and implement them as appropriate.
> - Ensure that any important information displayed in the app isn't obscured by normal use, such as a thumb hovering over the lower part of the screen.

5.2 Using a pointing device to provide input

Older definitions of mobile devices included single-handed operation. As devices have developed and user requirements have grown, this no longer is the case. It's now necessary to look beyond simple, single interactions with your apps and consider the rich interactions and input possibilities available through gestures and multi-touch input. In this section, we'll go beyond considering the use of input devices to think about how they're used.

5.2.1 Supporting gesture-based input

Everything done with any of the input devices mentioned so far is a *gesture*. Some, such as a tap or click, are simple gestures, while others are more complex. This section covers the standard gestures and then looks at more complex ones and those that need more than one point of touch.

Because Linda's app was complex, some of the people who use it asked for shortcuts to make things faster. Although the use of gestures can be a good way to offer shortcuts to less accessible functionality, the users of Linda's app had some problems with those. The gestures that were added were not obvious and were easily mistaken for other things. While people tried to remember and use them, the gestures were too awkward to consistently get right.

Following is a list of six standard gestures along with their expected uses. Using these gestures in other ways can lead to confusion for the person using the app, because preconceived expectations are not met:

- *Tap*—Place a single finger on an item and then remove the finger without moving to select or invoke the item.
- *Double tap*—Tap the same item twice in quick succession to invoke a different action from tapping once.
- *Swipe/slide/drag/flick*—Place a finger on an item and move the finger over the screen to move the item with it. Moving a finger quickly and then removing it from the screen should cause the item to continue to move for a short time as if it had inertia.
- *Tap and hold/long press*—Place a finger on an item and don't move or remove it for a short time (typically 1–2 sec), to trigger more actions or options relating to

the item. The common options are a change of mode or the display of a context menu.

- *Pinch/stretch*—Place two fingers on an item and move the fingers toward or away from each other to make the item smaller or larger, respectively.
- *Rotate*—Place two fingers on an item at once and rotate one or more fingers to cause the item to move accordingly.

A few other gestures are gaining in usage. It's in your long-term interest to maintain an awareness of them and to be ready for when their use becomes standardized:

- Multi-finger versions of single finger gestures (tapping, double tapping, long pressing, or swiping with two or more fingers at once)
- Press and tap (pressing down on an item with one finger and then tapping with another)
- Multi-finger spread and contract (like pinch/stretch but with all five digits on a hand)

As these gestures become more widely used, people will expect to use them within your app, as well as support for these actions. It's therefore necessary to monitor trends across other apps, particularly the widely used ones. As an example, pulling down a list to cause it to refresh (pull-to-refresh) was once novel. It started in a single app, but now is expected of all apps displaying lists. Popular platforms currently include a built-in implementation of this. When this was new, however, many developers built their own versions of this gesture, and they were often poorly done. Many people using these apps felt like they were wasting time and became frustrated by repeatedly pulling down on the top of a list to get it to refresh. Adding a button to enable refreshing data would have been easier for the developer and the person using the app.

The lesson here is that when a gesture becomes common, the people using your app expect it be available (if appropriate), and it needs to work the same way as elsewhere. For you as a developer, this'll probably mean using a standard, shared implementation of gesture detection rather than trying to create it yourself.

NOTE Although it can vary, depending on who's using your app, tapping an item and scrolling a list are probably the only gestures you can take for granted.

More complex gestures can serve as shortcuts for people who have lots of experience with your app. Because they can be hard to discover, people may need to be shown or taught how to use complex gestures. Even standard gestures can be hard for people to find if they aren't what they expect. Figure 5.9 shows the app from chapter 4. Notice that some of the gestures it supports and the ways to interact with them are more predictable than others.

Where gestures aren't immediately obvious, it's necessary to let the person using the app know they're there, so reveal them in another way. Animation is a popular way

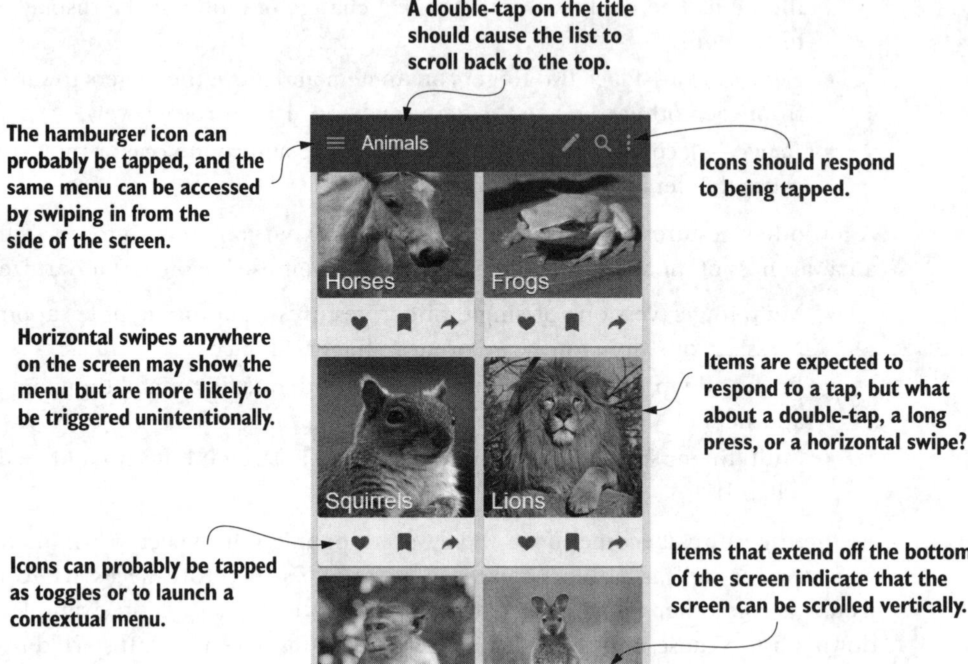

A double-tap on the title should cause the list to scroll back to the top.
The hamburger icon can probably be tapped, and the same menu can be accessed by swiping in from the side of the screen.
Animals
Icons should respond to being tapped.
Horses
Frogs
Horizontal swipes anywhere on the screen may show the menu but are more likely to be triggered unintentionally.
Items are expected to respond to a tap, but what about a double-tap, a long press, or a horizontal swipe?
Squirrels
Lions
Items that extend off the bottom of the screen indicate that the screen can be scrolled vertically.
Icons can probably be tapped as toggles or to launch a contextual menu.

Figure 5.9 An app and available gestures. Some are more obvious or predictable than others.

to draw attention to an item and to encourage a person to touch it, but adding an icon or instructional text can work as well. Having a walkthrough of features and non-obvious gestures when people use your app for the first time is another solution, but such lessons are easily forgotten.

Known gestures will be performed accidentally at some point. Never punish a person for this or leave them wondering what happened. And, don't have a gesture trigger an action that can't be undone easily. At least for the first few times when invoking gestures, clearly indicate what's happening. This is particularly true if you treat the shaking of the device as a gesture.

Many novel uses of a shake gesture exist, but few standard ones. Refreshing of data, prompting for feedback, or accessing advanced settings are the most popular uses. My experience is that, unless core to the use of an app, this gesture is triggered accidentally more than intentionally. You may consider the shake gesture a clever addition to your app, but it's more likely to confuse the person invoking it unintentionally. Unless you have a good reason to need such a gesture, it's best avoided.

Even with all the standard options available, you may need to create your own gestures. If you do, keep those simple, memorable, and recognizable. They also shouldn't be easily confused with any of the standard gestures used by the OS. The most common gestures handled by the OS involve swiping from the edges of the screen, but some platforms also support less well-known ones (like the four-finger swipe on the iPad to switch between apps).

Be aware of all the gestures you may be competing with on a device. I have used apps that use a swipe from the top of the screen to show the app's main menu on platforms where a swipe from the top of the screen is also used by the OS to trigger unseen notifications. As a result, some of the time a swipe from the top showed the app's menu and sometimes the list of notifications. This inconsistency and unpredictability meant I stopped using the app. This isn't something you want the people using your app to experience.

Finally, people can make gestures by rotating, twisting, and moving the device, as detected by sensors within the device. You'll find more on this in chapter 7.

5.2.2 Supporting multi-touch input

It's common for developers to think of single-point touch input to be comparable with mouse input on a PC. The comparison between mouse and touch breaks down when it comes to considering multi-touch. There are additional considerations as well. Let's look at those now.

Linda's app had little specific multi-touch input, but suffered another consequence of handling touch input and the use of multiple hands. Many people would use the app on tablets with small bezels around the screen. They'd hold the device in one hand and provide input with the other. Because the screen on the device reached almost to the physical edge, many people found they were touching items on the edge of the screen with the hand they were using to hold the device. The solution was to move interactive content away from the sides of the screen.

Handling or needing multi-touch input is common in apps and a key component in some games, but there are limits and variations to be aware of. The biggest difference is that the number of multiple concurrent touches supported can vary, even among devices from the same manufacturer or with the same OS. Needing a specific number can be limiting. Capacitive screens cope with at least two points of contact, and many support up to at least five. Even if your app will only be used on devices that support 10 simultaneous points of contact, don't feel compelled to require the use of them all. Unless crucial to a game, the use of two or three concurrent touches is plenty.

NOTE The multi-handed operation of a device and multi-touch input isn't always possible due to permanent or temporary circumstances. One-handed operation of a mobile device is common for general use. Aim to make this the default for your app.

Multi-touch operation can also be limited by how a device is positioned or being held. So some people will struggle with time-based and movement-based actions because of the coordination and control needed for some multi-touch gestures. If you must use a multi-finger gesture, ensure that a single finger equivalent is available, even if it isn't as prominent.

If your app responds to multiple touch points, treat each touch point equally in terms of the action and visual display of the action. It's odd to see an app responding to multiple touch points but only observing one of those. For example, if swiping with one finger causes a visual trail from that finger, then multiple fingers should display multiple trails. Or, if tapping on a single item displays an animation, then touching multiple items should display multiple animations.

If dealing with multiple touch inputs, for processing directly or converting into your own gestures, attention must be paid to how you handle them. Many edge cases must be considered too. These include multiple conflicting actions being invoked at the same time, or one gesture being completed while another is still in progress. The action to take in these scenarios is dependent on what's best for your app and the people using it. You may need to consult with the people using the app to determine this and ensure there aren't possible negative consequences from such input. Having to handle the complex behaviors of multi-touch input can be difficult, but there are other aspects of handling input that are harder. The next section looks at some of those scenarios.

Put it into practice: gestures and multi-touch input

- Ensure that any gestures in the app that involve more than a single tap or swipe are discoverable.
- Identify functionality that requires using more than a single finger. Monitor usage of this functionality (with analytics, support requests, and feedback), and provide an alternative way of using or accessing it if needed.
- Consider adding gestures for functionality that's often used (based on your analytics) but not easily accessible.

Exercise: appropriate gestures

Match the following activities that could be performed with a long press gesture, but that should be done with something else:

1. Access a shortcut to actions on an item in a list (without having to open a separate view of that item).
2. Make large and small changes to a value with a single button.
3. Access a single common operation on an item in a list that isn't the primary (tap) action.
4. Repeat an action multiple times without needing multiple taps.
5. Select an item without adding any specific selection UI.

5.3 When pointing and touch input become difficult

In this section, I'll cover how events can sometimes do what the people using the app don't want. If your app does little more with touch than supporting scrolling and tapping buttons, then it's easy to dismiss the complexities and subtleties that can arise. If you're not using complex gestures or handling multi-touch input, supporting touch input will still be more difficult than you may like. This includes the edge cases in the built-in control events and when you need to handle raw input events yourself.

In terms of touch events not doing what a person expects, this means minimizing accidental selections and double taps and making them easy to recover from when they do happen. When handling raw input events, be sure what you create behaves and responds like the built-in controls. The next section includes common issues relating to touch and what you can do to avoid them.

5.3.1 Touch events don't always do what the user wants

Linda needed a list in her app but wanted some minor variations to its behavior. Rather than modifying the standard control, she decided to build her own. After all, she thought, "How hard can it be?" She soon learned it was much harder than it originally seemed. Issues such as distinguishing between a small accidental movement and scrolling, and accidentally selecting items when touching to start scrolling soon persuaded her to build on what worked in the existing control.

When thinking about input, what's touching the screen isn't as important as the desire of the person interacting with the app. A person isn't using their app because they want to tap a screen, but because they want to access information or get other value from doing so. Understanding the underlying motivation becomes important when you need to handle raw input events. There's value in separating how a developer implements a user interface, what's represented, and how to interact with what's represented.

Consider the apps in figure 5.10. Each shows what could be considered as lists; both were implemented using the same controls. When an item is selected from the list in the app on the left, the app opens the related view. Selecting an item from the list on the right causes the information to be loaded into the main part of the screen. Both lists respond to selecting an item, but one does it by triggering navigation and the other by displaying data.

Some list controls make it hard for the person to get what they want when touching an item in a list. If the control interprets making contact as a selection and then triggers an action, and if it's a long list, the person may not be able to scroll through the list to get to something that isn't visible. This is particularly problematic to test and allow for if selection is determined in separate ways for different input types, or if it's only on some devices or configurations where scrolling is necessary.

Touch events can also be complicated in simple ways. People sometimes accidentally perform a double tap when they only intended a single tap. It's rare for this to be

Tapping an item in this list invokes the display of another page/view in the app.

But in this app, tapping an item selects the item and displays full details to the right of the list.

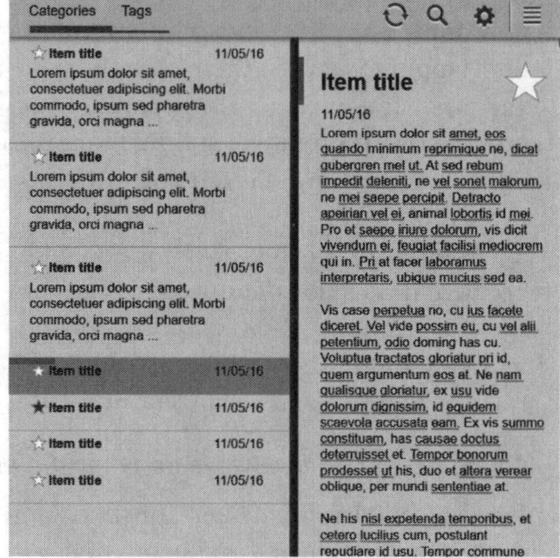

Figure 5.10 Tapping an item in a list has different effects, depending on whether you are selecting an item or invoking an action.

a problem, but if the second tap reverses the action of the first tap, then you may need to prevent the second action from being performed too quickly after the first. This might mean delaying the reversal of a toggle value or ensuring a Cancel button doesn't appear in the same place as the originally tapped button.

Tapping the wrong item can be worse than incorrectly reverting an action. Consider a person about to tap the Delete Current Item button, only for the current item to be automatically changed as the app loads something new in the fraction of a second before the tap occurs. A similar thing can happen if a person accidentally double taps the Delete Current Item button when they only meant to tap it once. To prevent such unintended negative consequences, there are several things you can do:

- Don't put options that revert an action in the same place as the action.
- Don't do anything with potentially negative consequences if something hasn't been onscreen long enough for people to see it.
- Make actions easy to reverse or undo.

Allow people to experiment without fear of negative consequences. People have been conditioned to think it's their fault when things go wrong, though it's more often a lack of consideration in the design or implementation of the app they're using.

5.3.2 Raw input events need special attention

In this final section on touch, we'll look at some areas that need special attention when working with raw touch events. There's a lot of nuance in the way these are combined to make the standard gestures and more common control-level events, which are used more often.

Linda had an issue with this when she wanted to create her own version of a button for her app. She soon reverted to a standard control after discovering how challenging it was. She needed to

- Cope with the timing on when to trigger the tap event.
- Handle multiple movement events over the button and other items without breaking contact.
- Avoid triggering events on other controls beneath the button when the button was dismissed.
- Handle multiple buttons being tapped at the same time.

When you trigger a tap event (or similar) on a control, the development SDK you're using normally hides a lot of other (raw) events and calculations. To trigger a tap event, several things need to happen:

- Contact is made with the screen over an item.
- There's little movement when contact is made, and the point of contact doesn't move from the original item.
- Within a brief time (normally under 300 ms), contact is broken with the screen.

Any variation from these, either in duration or movement, won't be registered as a tap event. A variation of the tap event, Touch Up Inside, may be of interest in the last part of the tap event. But if you contact one item and then move the point of contact to another and let go, you almost certainly don't want the event to be triggered on the item you were in contact with when you let go. Such an event won't be fired, even if that was the item you are "inside" when contact with the screen is broken. It's this level of abstraction you need to consider when handling raw touch events.

> **NOTE** Having a way of canceling a tap event is useful in some instances. For example, you make contact with the screen over an item. Then, realizing it isn't the item you want, you move your finger before letting go.

The people using the app will notice the slightest of differences from the behavior of standard controls. They may not notice what the specifics are, but only that something isn't right. This is enough to make them question their confidence in the app, how it works, and how well they can trust you with their data. A far worse scenario can be with greater deviations from normal behavior. If you need to implement your own version of a button or other onscreen control or image, ensure that your implementation covers all scenarios and behaviors in the same way as the standard controls.

Using any raw or low-level touch event like down, up, drag, started, delta, or completed is a signal you need to be careful in matching the experience you create with the built-in ones. Always verify that you aren't creating any unexpected consequences or differences in behavior.

Exercise: the truth about challenging touch input

Test your understanding of the last section by stating whether the following are true or false:

1. If you only use standard control events, you don't need to think about touch-related input.
2. There's a semantic difference between touching something onscreen to trigger navigating to another part of the app and displaying more information on the same screen.
3. You should always consider what happens if someone taps something twice in quick succession.
4. You should always consider what happens if someone taps something to make it disappear and then taps the same point on the screen.
5. As soon as someone makes contact with something onscreen, it can be treated as an action on that item.

Touching the screen is one of the simplest forms of input a person can provide, and it's easy to overlook the subtleties and complexities of how people do that to interact with your app. But, when they do, you now know how to provide the best touch experiences. Things can get far more complicated when you ask people to complete a form, which is what I'll cover in the next chapter.

Summary

- Different pointing/input devices are better suited to different tasks and environments.
- Fingers (and thumbs) come in lots of shapes and sizes and can be used with different levels of precision. Your app needs to account for all of them.
- Items that a person will touch onscreen need to be large enough and not too close together so that the person can be confident in engaging with the desired item.
- Guidelines can be broken, but you need to ensure you and the people using the app can cope with the consequences.
- Allow for part of the screen being obscured by whatever will be touching it.
- A stylus provides greater precision of input than a finger, as well as offering additional options for capturing more information.
- Mouse input for mobile devices, especially tablets, is increasing in popularity, and there are simple ways apps can be enhanced to take advantage of the differences in input this way.

- Multiple input devices may be used at one time to remove the need to switch between modes and enable richer interactions.
- Standardized gestures exist for all common input actions. Use these for standard tasks to aid discovery, avoid confusion, and prevent betrayed expectations.
- Complex and multi-touch gestures can be hard to learn, discover, and perform. Provide simpler alternatives to these, even if that means including them on a secondary menu.
- If building your own controls or handling raw touch events directly, ensure that you're doing so in a way that's comparable to the native controls in the platform SDKs and with the other apps on the device.

6 User-entered data

This chapter covers

- The principles behind good form design
- Alternatives to typed entry
- Optimizing form entry
- Handling validation and reporting errors

In this chapter, we look deeper at some of the specifics of capturing data from the people using the app. Few apps are simple enough that the only input they need is from the intent to launch the app and basic touch events. The usefulness of such apps is dwindling. Your apps will need to do more than this, as the level of sophistication demanded by consumers continues to grow.

Capturing complex information of differing types takes more than just putting controls onscreen. A great experience requires you to execute the basics perfectly and then add sophisticated refinement. Just doing the basics isn't enough to be remarkable. This means going beyond the triviality of what's required and adding a level of smart logic to the app. Then, you'll create an app that people will find effortless and love to use. To help you create such an app, we'll dive into

- Understanding the goals of the people using the app
- Tailoring forms within the app to aid ease of use

In this chapter, you'll also hear about the experiences of Sam, who developed an app for his company that required lots of data entry. His app went through many changes to improve the experience of providing data, making it easier for people to provide accurate information.

6.1 The goals of the people using the app

In this section, I'll focus on ways to improve how you provide information as part of meeting the goals of the people using the app. If you remember figure 1.2 in chapter 1, you'll recognize figure 6.1 as a part of it. Here you see the interaction between the person and the app. The actions start with the person, their expression of intent, and subsequent input.

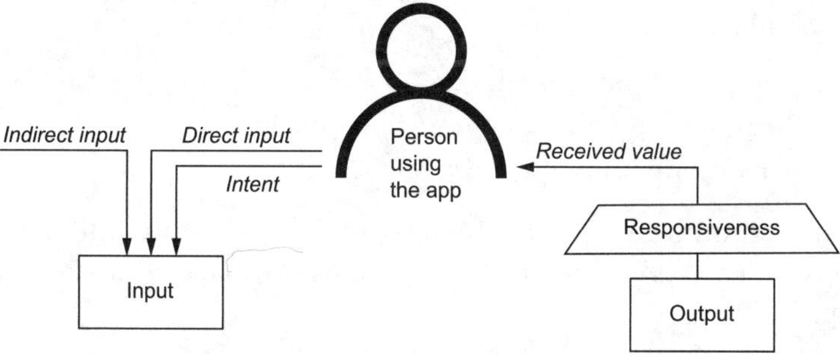

Figure 6.1 Apps get input in many ways, but the aim of each is to give value to the people using the app.

The primary goal of the people using your app is to obtain value. Whether this is finding out the latest news, listening to music, making a purchase, or being entertained, your app needs to meet their desires. Having people provide input and any work performed by the app stand between the person and getting that value. You have the power to reduce both.

Beyond a primary goal, your app and the people using it will have many secondary goals. The primary goal in using an app for a social network could be to keep up with what friends and family are doing. Secondary goals may include sharing their own updates, responding to what they're sharing, and gaining an awareness of relevant wider news. When using a music and podcasting app, the primary goal is to receive entertainment or information. Secondary goals might include the ability to record and track what's listened to or to share and comment on what's heard.

Secondary goals vary based on who uses the app, where and when it's used, and the device it's used on. But the primary goals of everyone using the app are for it to be as easy to use as possible and quick to respond. This may seem obvious to you, but it's something that often goes unstated. Because people rarely verbalize their desire for these goals, many apps overlook this. This provides an opportunity for you to set your app apart from others.

Jef Raskin worked at Apple and was a key player on the team that developed the Macintosh. He had strong views about software. In his book *The Humane Interface* (Addison Wesley, 2000), he defined two rules of interface design. His first rule, inspired by Asimov's first law of robotics, is an idea I'll cover later in this chapter; it's the second I'll focus on now:

1. A computer shall not harm your work or, through inaction, allow your work to come to harm.
2. A computer shall not waste your time or require you to do more work than is strictly necessary.

Consider the computer he speaks of as your app running on a device. The *time and work* referred to are what's required to input data by the people using it. To reduce the input required by an app

- Avoid requiring the input altogether
- Minimize the input requirement as much as possible
- Use an alternative input method

I'll explain how to minimize input in the next section. Then we'll look at defaults and suggestions as a way to improve the experience of data input for the people using your app.

6.1.1 Improve tasks by minimizing input

A general (and universal) rule of form completion is that the longer a form, the less likely it is that a person will complete it. Correspondingly, by making something easier for a person, they're more likely to do it. If you're asking for information in your app, there should be a good reason for doing so. If it makes the form longer, you risk not getting anything. This section describes three approaches to minimize the amount of time and effort needed to enter required input:

- Make it easier to provide the input.
- Reduce the amount of input by not asking for things you don't need.
- Remove duplication by not asking for the same thing more than once.

The simplest way to minimize required input is to only ask for something when it's needed or when you're able to do something with it. If you don't need to send a person something via email just yet, wait until you do before asking for their address. If a person gets value from an app without registering, don't force them to do so before using the app.

Sam's app had a long registration form that needed to be completed when someone first used the app. That's when the company assumed they had a captive audience. It saw this as an opportunity to gather as much information as possible. To do that, the marketing department added lots of fields to the registration process. The length of the registration form was highlighted when Sam began investigating why the number of people who registered and used the app was so much lower than the number who downloaded it.

The volume of information requested in the registration form was seen by many as unnecessary, and raised uncertainty about what the app would do with all that information or how it related to the app. After receiving this feedback, Sam reduced the amount of information requested when registering, and the registration rate soared.

Like some of the people in Sam's company, you might think it's better to ask for more information earlier, so you have it when it's needed. This ignores two important points:

- You may never need it. In this case, you've asked someone to do something for no reason and wasted their time.
- You degrade the experience for the people using the app by asking for more than is necessary at the current time. This can decrease the likelihood they'll still be using the app when you do need the data.

Don't worry; people will provide the information you need at a time that's relevant and provides value to them. And, using the approaches mentioned in this book, you can improve the experience further.

MINIMIZE THE EFFORT INVOLVED IN PROVIDING INPUT

It's useful to have a measure of the effort involved in providing input. One way to do that is to count the number of taps or touches needed to provide the desired information. This means how many times a person has to tap or swipe the screen, press a button, or click a mouse. It's not a perfect measure, but it's quick to calculate, easy to understand, and simple to compare results (lower is better). The following shows some approaches to reducing effort when providing required input:

- *Select instead of type*—If you need a piece of information that's one of a small number of options, provide buttons for each selection. A person only needs to make a single touch for any input, rather than several touches, depending on the length of the word.
- *Shortcuts*—Scrolling through long lists to find the desired value requires some touches impacted by the number of swipes that must be made to scroll to the value, based on its position in the list. Using a sorted list combined with fast scrolling, indexes, or jump lists gets a person much closer to the desired value with a single swipe or a couple of taps.
- *Auto-suggest/auto-complete*—Instead of typing a whole value (one or more words) or scrolling through long lists, you can reduce the total number of required touches if the app displays a shortened list of values. These can be filtered to those starting with (or containing) what's been entered. This allows a person to type the first few letters and then tap the desired value. It's usually shorter than typing the complete value.
- *Combine inputs*—Where two related values are needed, it's simpler to capture them both with a single control. For example, consider a need to provide starting

and ending dates. It's easy to have one calendar control for the start date and another for the end date. A simpler alternative is to have a single calendar that displays both dates: the earlier date would be the start and the later, the end. Ignore the order of selection, and there's no potential for the start date to come before the end date.

In another example, consider the need to specify a range between two values. A slider can represent the entire range. Using a slider control with two handles to select the start and end values within the range is simpler than selecting from two lists.

- *Auto-focus*—If an app presents a series of input controls for a person to provide data, and nothing else is on the page, it's unnecessary to first tap the field. Instead, set focus appropriately so a person can just start typing.
- *Auto advance*—If the app requires multiple values to be entered, once any values of a specific length are entered, automatically advance the focus to the next field. A word of caution: use this approach with care. Test its usefulness with the people using the app. If you're moving the focus when they don't expect it, or not moving it quickly enough, the confusion you introduce will outweigh the benefit of saving a keystroke.
- *Advance until submit*—When focus can't be advanced automatically, a person should still be able to move it from the keyboard. Consider a form containing three mandatory fields and a Submit button. In a worst-case scenario, a person

  1. Moves their finger to the first field to set focus
  2. Moves to the keyboard to enter the value
  3. Moves their hand to set focus on the next field
  4. Goes back to the keyboard for the second value
  5. Moves again to set a final focus
  6. Uses the keyboard to enter the last value
  7. Moves to tap the Submit button

  On a desktop, such a scenario is exacerbated by transitioning between mouse and keyboard. But even on small, handheld touch screens, changing hand positions for holding and typing on a soft keyboard at the bottom of the screen and tapping fields at the top of the screen is unnecessary. As a better alternative, use the Enter key to move from the first to second fields and then again to the third. When pressed while the focus is in the third field, it should perform the same action as tapping the Submit button directly. The worst thing for an app doing this is when a person can't set focus by tapping on a field directly. For the increasing number of people who expect such functionality, your app will meet their expectations and not frustrate them.

MINIMIZE INPUT BY REDUCING WHAT'S ASKED FOR

If less input is better, it follows that no input is best. Although it's rare for apps to require no direct input, this doesn't mean individual components for input can be avoided. If you were to avoid input entirely, you could prevent people from achieving their goals and severely limit the functionality of your app.

The value of data to business has grown in recent years. Advances in data science and machine learning have increased what's possible and have made those prospects more widely available. Because of this, it's become desirable for businesses like Sam's to capture, store, and use as much information as they can gather. This can lead to apps like the one in figure 6.2, where unreasonably large amounts of data are requested and extend far beyond what's relevant to the app.

Figure 6.2 is an example of the conflict between what's best for the business creating an app and what's best for the person using it. Like Sam's app, the business wants as much information as possible, and the person using it wants to provide only what's necessary. Focusing on what's best for the person and not the business can be the

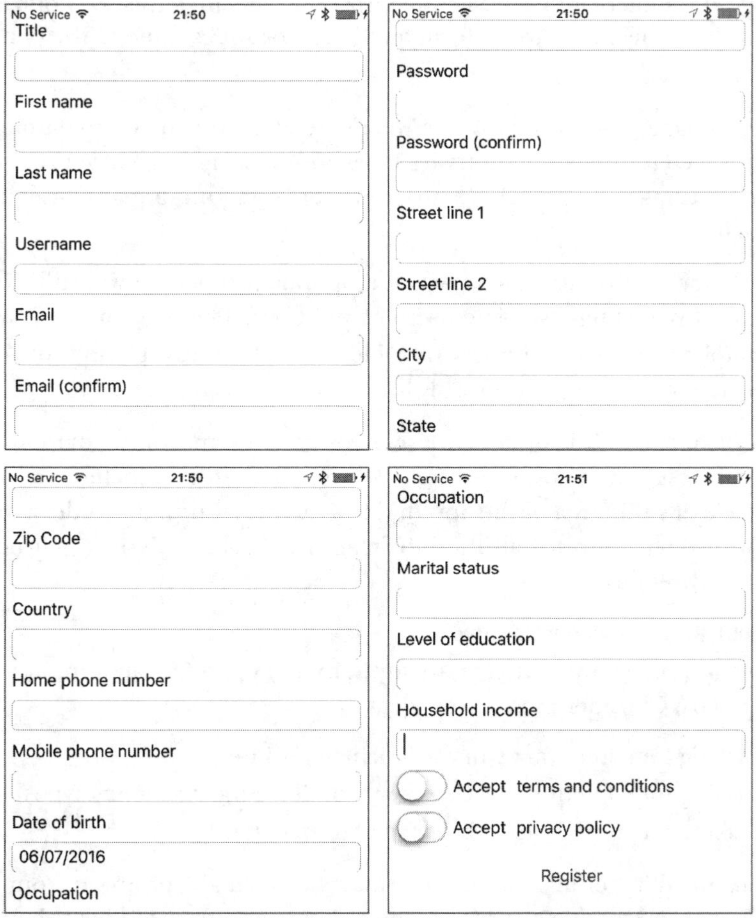

Figure 6.2 A large form spread over many screens is hard to use. Including fields not directly relevant to the app's immediate needs creates more work for the person using it and stands as a barrier to their goals.

difference between lots of contented customers or a smaller, less happy number whom you know more about.

There'll be times when the requirements of a business or the opinions of a stakeholder demand gathering specific input. In such scenarios, ensure that the business or stakeholder is aware of the potential negative consequences of increasing the amount of information that's asked for. The best way to make this clear is by providing data for your app. If you're able, test this by having versions with and without extra required fields (an A/B test). See how the inclusion of extra required fields affects how many people complete the form and the number of validation errors they experience. Once you're clear you want to avoid as much input as possible, you'll have to decide which input you do ask for.

> **NOTE** When all data is potentially useful, decide what to ask for based on what will add immediate value. I summarize the guidance this way: only ask for input that is necessary to perform a task that provides value to the person using it.

Notice the guidance is to only ask for what's needed. You may be tempted to use optionality as a compromise when trying to avoid imposing large input requirements on the people using the app. There are, however, some unwanted consequences to this approach:

- It isn't always obvious which parts are optional, so people will still experience the negative feelings associated with being shown a large form.
- Incomplete forms may be less valuable to the business. Having lots of partial information provides significantly less insight and is harder to work with.

Regardless of how much is optional, larger forms are significantly harder to create and accurately test. On almost every app I've encountered that includes a long registration process, it's this area of the app that has the most bugs. It's understandable to argue for providing input for all the information a business desires, but only make what's necessary required.

MINIMIZE INPUT BY AVOIDING DUPLICATION

As you strive to remove the unnecessary input in an app, duplicated input is an obvious place to start. Consider these three ideas:

- Not asking for something you can calculate or infer
- Not asking for something twice as a way of detecting accidental typos
- Not asking for something to be retyped unnecessarily

Remove the need to enter something you can calculate or infer from another response. For example, don't ask for a person's age and date of birth when you can calculate one from the other. Or, don't ask if a person is employed and for the name of their employer when "none" for an employer's name shows they're not employed.

Asking for the same data twice is also an obvious candidate for unnecessary input to remove, but doing so requires addressing the reason the duplication exists. The most common reasons are to avoid accidental mistakes or typos when entering email addresses and passwords. It's important these values are entered correctly, but asking for them twice has issues:

- Many people copy the first value they enter, including any mistakes, and paste it into the second field.
- It can be an excuse to not provide more sophisticated analysis of the value entered or to address common mistakes. Telling someone they haven't typed the same thing twice isn't as helpful as pointing out or automatically correcting:
  - Common domain misspellings
  - Use of a comma instead of a dot
  - Commonly confused symbols (quotes, apostrophes, or the number 2 instead of the at [@] symbol)

  You can also identify possible errors based on other information, such as highlighting if I entered `mtt@example.com` (note the missing *a* from the local part), when I've already said my name is Matt.
- If used with passwords that are obscured when entered, duplication doesn't address the issue of not being able to see what was incorrectly entered. (More on this later in the chapter in section 6.2.5.) Avoiding the entry of incorrect credentials can be an excuse for not optimizing the recovery process. Even if previously entered correctly, data can still be lost or input forgotten, so recovery handling is essential.
- Having two fields takes up more space. Having a single, larger display of the entered value makes mistakes easier to spot and to correct without prompting.
- Duplicate entry tends not to work well with platforms that support the automatic completion of forms. The app ends up working against the platform's attempts to make input easier.

If you want to know if having duplicate entries makes things easier for the people who use your app, track

- How often errors are encountered during validation
- How often people edit what they're entering
- The number of invalid or unusable email addresses you receive

The most impactful issue with duplicate content is with apps that lose or forget what's entered. It's normally easier for people to correct a minor error than to retype the whole thing. Avoid the following:

- Clearing previously entered data when people set focus on a text input control
- Automatically removing data that fails validation

Save all data entry, including partially completed forms, so the same data doesn't need entering again. For example, if a person is part way through typing a message to someone but leaves the app to answer a phone call, on completing the call and returning to the app, they'd expect to be able to complete the message. Have the input there when they return.

NOTE Passwords can be an exception to saving all data, depending on the security requirements of the app.

It's possible the person may not want the saved data. If so, give them a way to clear it (figure 6.3). This is better than forcing them to enter it again.

Welcome back
Do you want to carry on from before?
Carry on
Start again
When a user may not want to continue from where they left off, make it easy for them to start over. In this example, the prompt is useful, but one that lets the user see the content while making the decision would be better.
If someone leaves an app part way through completing a form, remember where they were and what they entered previously so that they can resume in the same place and not have to re-enter information.

Figure 6.3 Prompt people on returning to an app in which they'd previously entered data rather than assuming they want to keep or delete it. This keeps them in control and avoids unnecessary duplication.

In our example, if the person using the app chooses to save the partially completed message, you must make it obvious how to access and retrieve the draft. If the app is used by the same person on multiple devices, having drafts roam so they can be started on one device and then finished on another is an added way to help the people using your apps.

6.1.2 Improve tasks with defaults and suggestions

You'll want to avoid unnecessary input, as that's desirable and preferable for the people using the app. By requesting unnecessary information, you increase the chances the people you're asking will be put off by the volume of data, decide not to provide any, and go elsewhere.

Even if a person has no choice but to use the app and must provide the information that's asked for, the request to provide what they see as unnecessary or irrelevant creates frustration and disappointment. The key word here is *unnecessary*. You don't want to, and probably can't, remove everything. If it doesn't contribute directly to the functionality of the app or service, it's not needed. Be careful, however, that you don't remove the ability for people to provide the information they want to give you or the business needs.

> **NOTE** The more you ask of a person, the less likely they are to do it successfully. Any such failures reflect poorly on the app because it makes the person using it feel bad about themselves for not being able to use it successfully.

You can avoid input by not asking for things you can make an informed guess about. Here are two common scenarios:

- Configuring default settings when first using an app
- Making suggestions for what to search for

Sam's app has many configurable options affecting how it behaves and how it structures what's displayed. Some of the people at Sam's company had strong but differing opinions about which options should be the defaults. The compromise was to ask the people using the app which options they wanted when they used the app for the first time. Many people who used the app didn't have the knowledge to know which choice was best for their needs, and so ended up choosing sub-optimal options.

This issue became apparent when Sam looked at the support requests and negative store reviews the app was getting. Many issues were due to the configuration options people selected. The app was changed to remove the requirement to select configuration options on startup. Sam selected default settings based on the most common usage scenarios as indicated in the analytics data. This not only made it easier for people to get the desired behavior from the app; it also removed the delay in getting value from the app on first use.

Making an app customizable or allowing personalization of the way an app looks or performs is often a desirable feature. Some people like to change color schemes, control the frequency with which new content is loaded, or arrange the order in which items are listed. Forcing a person to make decisions about every setting when they use an app for the first time is unlikely to be valuable or useful.

Rather than having the person using the app specify settings they don't have sufficient knowledge or experience to answer, provide sensible defaults and inform the person that settings can be changed if desired. Many people choose not to customize or personalize the apps they use. Presenting options they'll skip is an avoidable obstacle to obtaining value from the app.

Search is another common feature easily improved with a zero-input approach. Where identical searches are often performed, either by other people or the same person, you can save them from having to type or retype a term by automatically displaying recent searches, as well as popular or trending terms.

6.1.3 Improve tasks with alternative inputs

Faster experiences lead to happier users because they get the value they want sooner. Measuring how long it takes to get a desired result and the number of clicks/taps/touches taken to get there and minimizing both is great. You must also consider how conditions vary and the specific contexts of use for your app. For this, look at

- Alternatives to typing
- Manually and automatically correcting mistakes

Here's what Sam did. Sam introduced support for alternative input in his app in two ways: autocompletion and speech-to-text input. Sam used text fields for entering one of a large, but fixed, number of options, such as country. These were changed to provide suggestions after a few characters were entered. Whereas typing was seen as preferable to selecting from a large list, only having to type some of the text was better still.

In Sam's app, fields for capturing potentially large amounts of text, such as the app's feedback-gathering system, were also changed to support spoken entry on devices that had microphones. This was captured if speech to text was available. Otherwise, an audio file was submitted instead of the text, and it was converted to text on the backend.

Even when touching the screen is the quickest way to enter data into an app, it isn't always possible or practical. Cold and wet conditions or a small screen make it hard to type accurately. In these scenarios (and more) and where the device permits, you improve the experience with the app by supporting text entry in these ways:

- *Typed with keyboard*—Supported by all devices, but it's not always the most practical. This is normally the best choice for fine-grained alterations and editing.
- *Dictation (voice input)*—Can be faster and more accurate than typing. But it produces mixed or no results with some languages and accents, or in noisy environments. Potentially limited by the network connectivity needed for translation and is hard to edit.
- *Handwriting (with stylus)*—Can work with a finger but normally works better with a stylus. Accurate interpretation of input can vary greatly, and editing input is often easier with a keyboard. Works well if already using a stylus with the app or when entering text that's hard to input with a standard keyboard, such as mathematical formulas.
- *Optical character recognition (from image or camera)*—Requires a network connection and good lighting if using a camera. It's most effective for large or complex text entry.

Whatever method people use, it's necessary to be able to correct any mistakes. Even better than making it easier for people to correct invalid entries is for your app to cope with errors. Also, people expect support for partial matches and intelligent suggestions for alternatives from web-based searches. There's no reason your app, like the one in figure 6.4, can't do this.

Incorrect spelling in a search term
●●○○○ 3
21:22
Usability marters
usability matters
A suggestion based on the most likely alternative, even though it doesn't match exactly, is more helpful than no result.

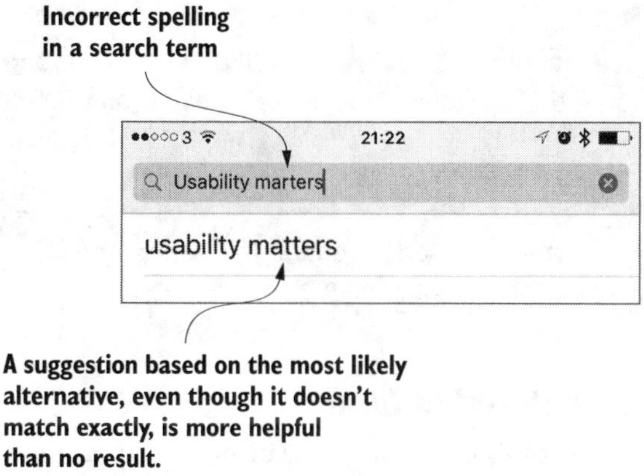

Figure 6.4 Make searching for something easier by being smart about incorrect entries and providing results based on likely or common misspellings.

Sometimes the best alternative input is an entirely different approach. The most common example of this is in capturing a location. The text-based approach is to type an address or location name, but alternatives also exist. You can

- Use a geographic lookup based on the public IP address of the device.
- Use the location settings on the device to provide the location.
- Allow a person to specify a location on a map.
- Select an address from a contact in the device's address book.

Put it into practice: align your form with user goals

Do the following to ensure you make your forms as intuitive and easy to use as possible:

- Identify everywhere data is entered or changed in your app.
- Understand the business implications of removing any optional or unneeded fields. Remove all that the business doesn't need, and then remove anything that's duplicated or can be combined.
- Don't ask for what you can get automatically or from the device.
- Auto-advance the focus on any fields that have a fixed length when that length is reached.
- Support use of the Enter key to advance focus through a multi-text-field form.
- For any pages, screens, or views in which the only task is to enter text, set the focus appropriately on accessing the page.

Exercise: minimizing input

Test your understanding of the last section by stating whether the following are true or false:

1. Prefer shorter forms to improve the likelihood they'll be completed correctly.
2. Ask for important information to be entered twice to avoid and identify any typos during entry.
3. Only include default selections from a list if there's a strong likelihood that they'll be correct.
4. Avoid asking for information you can easily obtain from other sources.
5. Allow text entry for all information required.

6.2 How to ask for data to be entered in forms

This section shows how to ensure you'll create a good, intuitive experience with the forms in your app. These include forms for login, registration, search, data capture, sharing content, and settings. I use this broad definition for a *form*—anywhere data or values are entered or adjusted in the app.

It's common for people to blame themselves when filling out a registration form or completing a purchase that is hard or goes wrong, but human error is often the result of design failure. Whether accidental errors or mistakes are due to something being misread or misunderstood, your actions can prevent this. To make the entry of data into your app significantly more intuitive

- Optimize the layout of the form.
- Capture text.
- Capture and process passwords.
- Specify a value in a range or set.
- Indicate and validate optional and mandatory data.

I've yet to meet a single person who's never complained about a website's registration process, or struggled to check out when buying something online. It's not only websites that have such issues; traditional desktop applications can be just as bad. Even if you ignore the differences between platforms, I'm sure you appreciate the idea that building mobile apps like desktop apps and websites isn't a smart move.

6.2.1 Optimizing how the form is arranged

In the first version of Sam's app, all form fields were the same size onscreen. The simplicity of this was considered visually pleasing, but it caused some issues that affected usability. It made it hard to view or edit all the entered text if it was longer than would fit in the space provided. This led to the frequent entry of incorrect and incomplete information. To address this, Sam provided appropriately sized fields so people could see the information they entered.

If all things were equal, being able to fit all parts of a form onscreen at once is best, but this is rarely practical. Consider three areas key to an optimal arrangement of the elements in a form:

- Support for scrolling and different orientations
- The ordering of fields
- The position and inclusion of labels and hints

Without the need to scroll, all parts of a form must be visible. Trying to squeeze a lot into a screen in a way that scrolling is never necessary is tempting; doing so often compromises both aesthetics and usability. On a portrait screen, it's impractical or unrealistic to do so without the need to scroll. With the device in a landscape orientation, space is further reduced (figure 6.5).

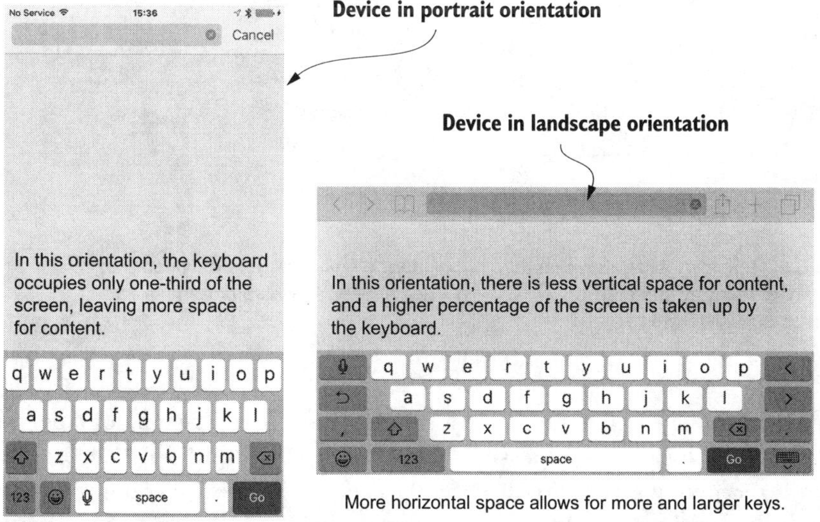

Figure 6.5 Screens displayed in portrait and landscape orientations show the differences in keyboards and available space for content.

Don't use the limited space on a landscape screen as an excuse to not support it. Landscape orientation offers the following benefits:

- Space for larger keys means fewer typing mistakes.
- More space allows for extra keys, making it easier to edit or change the text.
- Holding the device in this way can be more comfortable if using two thumbs to type.

Whichever orientation you use, ensure that it's possible to navigate and understand the position within the form. Keep the label of the focused control in view, and show the next field too. You don't want the person using the app to be unaware there's another field they haven't gotten to yet, or to be unable to get to a button that's behind a keyboard. To require a person to tap another part of the screen to dismiss the keyboard so they can get to the next field or a Submit button is frustrating and unnecessary.

Arrange the contents of a form in a single vertical column. Position clear, simple labels above each field. As shown in figure 6.6, having the label beside a control limits the space for the control, making it harder to see or select all that's been entered.

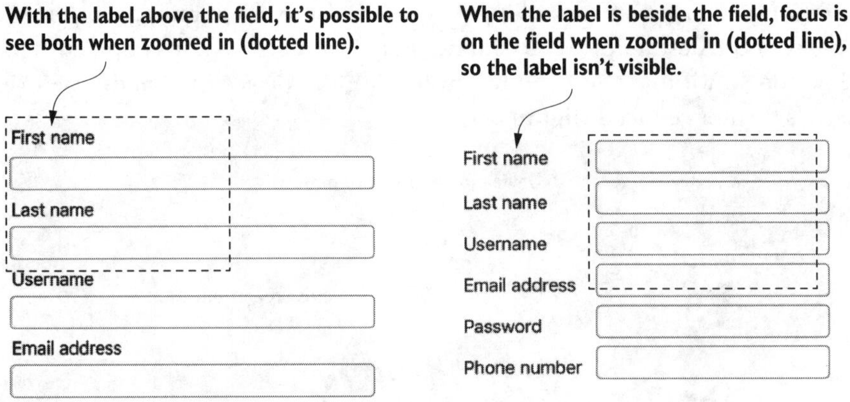

With the label above the field, it's possible to see both when zoomed in (dotted line).

First name
Last name
Username
Email address

When the label is beside the field, focus is on the field when zoomed in (dotted line), so the label isn't visible.

First name
Last name
Username
Email address
Password
Phone number

Figure 6.6 Placing labels above instead of beside the input controls to which they relate leaves more room for the control and improves usability with assistive tools or with increased text display size.

Even when displayed on a much wider screen, the vertical stacking of labels and fields is preferable. This makes it possible to see both labels and fields at once when the screen is zoomed in or the text size is enlarged. Using a single column also avoids any issues or confusion about the order in which fields are expected to be completed, and how the focus is advanced. Also, ensure that the field with focus is indicated clearly so people know where the data they'll enter will appear and what the app is expecting them to enter. Use a flashing cursor and a change in the border of the focused control to make this clear.

Placeholder or hint text can also be used as an addition to a label for a specific field. It needs to be styled so that it's distinguishable from actual values. People need to be able to easily differentiate between the fields they must enter data in and those already populated. This is important if the app or OS can automatically fill in part of the form for the person using it.

Using a placeholder instead of a label reduces the amount of space needed and is appealing on a device with limited space. But this not only loses the benefits of having labels, it also requires more concentration when entering data. It negatively affects accessibility by reducing the size of the area that can be touched to set focus (as touching a label should set focus on the associated field), and requires more effort to work with screen readers. The top example in figure 6.7 shows how useful information is hidden when placeholders are used in place of labels.

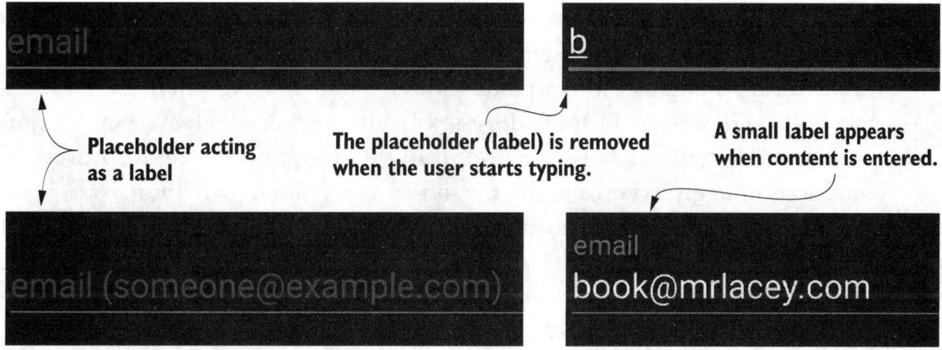
If a placeholder is used instead of a label, then as soon as a person begins to type, they lose the label.
This can be problematic if they're distracted while entering a value or when reviewing what's been entered.
email
b
Placeholder acting as a label
The placeholder (label) is removed when the user starts typing.
A small label appears when content is entered.
email (someone@example.com)
email
book@mrlacey.com
Here, a placeholder is used instead of a label, but when information is entered, a small label is placed above it.
This way, it's clear what the entered value represents.

Figure 6.7 Using placeholders instead of labels makes it unclear what a value represents once entered. Adding a small label above is one way to address this.

The lower example in figure 6.7 uses the *float label pattern* to provide samples or additional information. Then the placeholder becomes a small label once the field has focus or content. This is increasingly popular as a compromise between requiring labels and the space saved by not displaying a label. When using this technique, consider these questions:

- Are you providing useful information in the hint?
- Is a hint the best way to provide information?

Showing an example of an email address may be useful to some people, but it can seem patronizing to others. What information or example to give depends on what's appropriate for the people the app is intended for. Remember, not everyone is like you. Some people require that everything is spelled out and made as simple as possible. In general, doing something that benefits some but not others is still worth doing.

The second consideration is whether a hint is the best way to provide information. Hints are often used to indicate that formatted data must be entered. If you need information in a specific format, such as formatting characters around parts of a phone number, the use of input masking or automatic formatting ensures that you get these values as you want.

Removing a hint while data is being entered makes it harder for the person entering the data to know they're doing so correctly. This means you must redisplay the information from the original hint when showing something has been entered incorrectly. Keeping the hint constantly displayed as part of, or next to, the label avoids this issue.

> **NOTE** There's a simple rule for defining the order in which information should be asked for: ask for information in the order it's traditionally given, unless a different order will make it easier.

Asking for a person's last name before their first name can cause them to pause and wonder about the order. You should avoid even such small amounts of friction, as it's unnecessary. In another example, a zip code is normally entered at the end of an address. If an app can look up addresses from a zip code, then you could ask for the zip code and present a list of addresses for the person to select from. It's quicker than typing a full address. This variation from the normal order of an address is common and so is unlikely to confuse the person entering the information.

In addition to the judicious use of hints and the order of fields in a form, the wording used is important too. Use clear terminology and language appropriate to the people using the app. Use terminology consistently within the app and any associated website. Don't, for example, ask someone to define a password during registration and then ask them for a PIN code when logging in. And, don't require different credentials for the same account on different platforms. Avoid jargon or complicated and inconsistent language that won't be understood by the people using the app. Figure 6.8 highlights some of these issues.

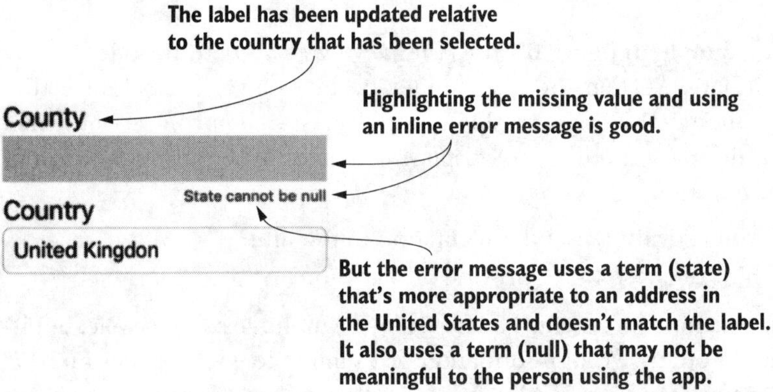

Figure 6.8 Part of a form showing inappropriate jargon and inconsistency in an error message, both of which are to be avoided.

Consideration for the people using your app shouldn't stop with the language used. To not allow for variation in the accessibility requirements of the people using your app is to do them a disservice. Make your app fully usable with common accessibility tools, including screen readers, color-blindness settings, and enhanced zoom.

The transit test

One way to evaluate how practical it is to use your app and particularly any forms is with the *transit test*. This simple and unscientific test asks one question: "Can the app be used on a crowded bus or train?" Although this isn't the only environment where your app is used, it's a challenging one. If the app is usable there, it'll be usable almost anywhere.

This test serves as a loose proxy for general usability. If a more advanced or capable user can successfully use the app in difficult circumstances, anyone with additional requirements should be able to use it in a less challenging environment.

6.2.2 *Simplify how text is entered*

This section looks at three ways to improve the accuracy, speed, and simplicity of entering text. I'll cover how to

- Make it easy to enter correct data.
- Make it hard to enter incorrect data.
- Make it simple to provide multiple pieces of data.

Typing on a mobile device isn't fun. It's much easier to type on a full size keyboard than a small one. This doesn't mean that people don't type on mobile devices, but they do so differently. I've written parts of this book on a phone and a tablet, but I wrote most of it on a laptop because doing so is easier. Correctly formatting the text on the phone is hard, and so I avoided doing this as much as possible.

I once had to make a series of complex annotations and modifications to a presentation while on holiday, with access to only a phone. Doing this took a lot longer than if I had access to my laptop, and it repeatedly felt like an exercise in frustration. What this means is that we cannot argue that people don't or shouldn't use a specific type of device for a task. People will use whatever devices they have available, even if it's not best suited to the task. So it's in your interest to provide apps that make it as easy as possible for people to complete the tasks they're trying to do.

MAKE IT EASY TO ENTER CORRECT DATA

Small devices don't have the space to show as many keys on a keyboard as a larger device, and so can show one of many onscreen keyboards comprised of different options. By choosing the keyboard most appropriate to the information that's being asked for, you reduce the number of touches needed to enter a value. Figure 6.9 shows this.

Exposing all the required keys on the soft keyboard prevents the person using the app from wondering how to access a specific key or enter a specific character. Such a pause is small, but you should avoid any barrier to a person getting the value they're after—no matter how trivial.

In addition to the keyboard displayed, use other options as necessary for text entry. Facilitate the capitalization of the first letter, no letters, or all letters as appropriate for the field. For example, proper names and sentences should start with capital letters,

When entering the email address book@mrlacey.com, different keyboard options affect the number of touches required.

This keyboard requires 20 touches.

This keyboard includes buttons for @ and the period (.), so 16 touches are required.

A long press on the period (.) launches a menu of top-level domains, so only 13 touches are needed.

Hiding the top-level domains (TLDs) behind a long press makes them difficult to discover. Some platforms have a separate button for the TLD, to aid discovery.

Figure 6.9 Different keyboards make it possible to enter the same value with fewer taps. Use the one that enables the fewest touches for each field in your app.

so have this enabled. Disable this if requiring case-sensitive input. Also, enabling auto-correction, auto-completion, and spell checking are useful additions if the entered text is likely to comprise common words or proper sentences. Conversely, if the entry doesn't contain common words, such as a username, then this isn't helpful.

MAKE IT HARD TO ENTER INCORRECT DATA

If only certain values or characters are acceptable, prevent the entry of anything invalid with an input mask or by handling events when the entered value changes. Avoid trying to do this with key-based events; these won't work as expected if pasting text into a field. For long or complicated values, such as phone numbers or credit card numbers, specific formatting makes those easier to read, and, therefore, spot errors. Controlling formatting and limiting the characters accepted makes entry easier and still benefits readability.

If you're unable to use controls with built-in capabilities for masking input, you can re-create something similar by doing the following:

- Automatically adjust capitalization as appropriate. If you want all letters uppercase, accept any case but change anything entered in lowercase.
- Automatically correct common errors or substitutes. This might be the letter *O* instead of the number zero (*0*) or a hyphen instead of an underscore.
- Ignore any characters that are definitely invalid by doing nothing when they're typed.
- Add formatting automatically. If you want a space between the third and fourth characters, add one even if it's not typed.

To the people entering data, aim to provide the freedom to do so as they wish, yet consistently display correctly entered information. This will provide yet another reason for people to continue to use your app.

Make it simple to provide multiple pieces of data

As mentioned earlier, using the Enter key to advance the focus through multiple fields on a form can make the process faster. Better still is when you combine multiple separate controls into one. For example, don't have separate fields for the different parts of a phone number or an address; use a single field, and decompose the respective parts as needed. Likewise, you shouldn't need the country or area code for a phone number to be entered in separate fields. Instead, allow the person to enter the phone number as needed, and then use some simple processing to break up the number and reformat it as necessary when saved. By ignoring any spaces or formatting characters, it's easy to tell if the entry is valid based on the length of the entry and optional inclusion of a country code. Figure 6.10 shows a comparison of these two entry possibilities.

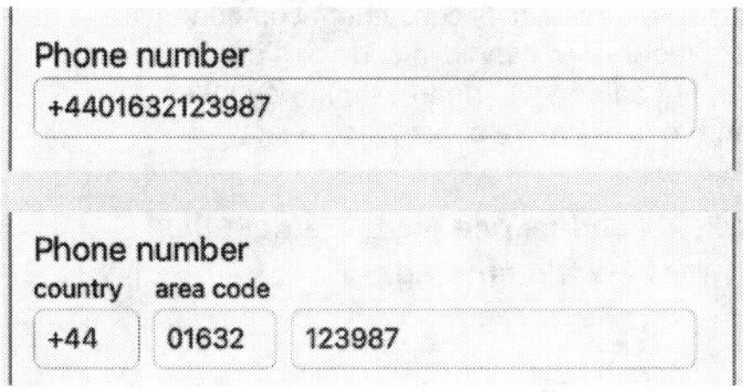

Phone number
+4401632123987

Letting people enter their phone number in the way that's easiest for them will lead to fewer mistakes. Because phone numbers have specific lengths and structures, you can decompose them into their component parts if needed.

Phone number
country area code
+44 01632 123987

Forcing people to enter their phone number in a specific format causes them to have to think more about what they're doing and takes longer. It also requires more work to support variations for different countries.

Figure 6.10 Phone number input as single and multiple fields. A single field makes entry simpler, without losing any ability to validate what's entered.

Addresses are another common example of multiple fields that you can combine to make data entry easier. For the parts of the world with structured address systems, an address can contain many optional components. This leads to many unused, and, therefore, unnecessary, fields, or to people having to think about how to enter an address in the fields presented. Showing a simple, multiline text field as in figure 6.11 is a simpler alternative. Any address validation or lookup tool should be equally capable of coping with addresses provided this way, too.

The ability to cope with semi-structured data given as freeform text is also beneficial for data entered through a speech-to-text interface. With that functionality, it's simpler and preferable to dictate an address all at once, which is hard when the UI requires that each line be entered separately. The ability to accept even more complicated, semi-structured data allows for further possibilities.

Imagine an app that allows people to create reminders. The app needs to know what to remind the user about, and the date and time to do so. Rather than display a text box for the reminder and separate controls to select date and time, allow a single piece of text entry such as, "Remind me about Bob's party at 7 P.M. next Tuesday." Then you can extract and convert the appropriate parts and act on them. Not only would this make speech-based entry easier and more powerful, but it'd also make it

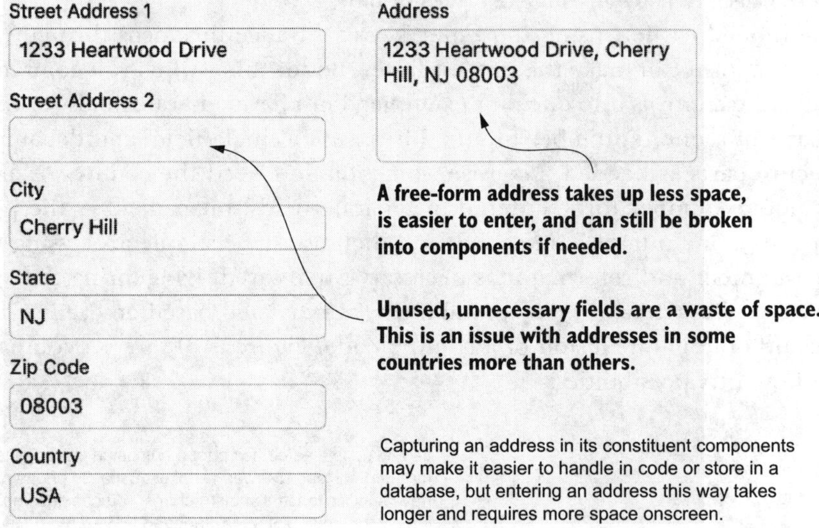

Street Address 1
1233 Heartwood Drive
Street Address 2
City
Cherry Hill
State
NJ
Zip Code
08003
Country
USA
Address
1233 Heartwood Drive, Cherry Hill, NJ 08003
A free-form address takes up less space, is easier to enter, and can still be broken into components if needed.
Unused, unnecessary fields are a waste of space. This is an issue with addresses in some countries more than others.
Capturing an address in its constituent components may make it easier to handle in code or store in a database, but entering an address this way takes longer and requires more space onscreen.

Figure 6.11 Comparing address entry as many fields and as one field. A single field uses less space onscreen and provides flexibility for how it's entered.

simpler to integrate with voice-based input via the OS or with text-based input from a chat interface—both of which are popular areas for future app growth.

6.2.3 Password entry requires special consideration

Every time someone wanted to use Sam's app, they were required to sign in with the same credentials as on the website, which had strict rules about password complexity. Correctly entering complex passwords was an issue for many users of the app, so the company allowed the creation of a numeric PIN value that could be used instead of a password. The PIN was tied to individual devices to prevent its use elsewhere.

When it comes to entering them, passwords are a special form of text entry. They suffer from all the same challenges of accurate typing as regular text, but with the added challenges of being unable to verify what's been typed and a need to meet arbitrary added restrictions. Mobile security is a massive subject and more than enough for a book on its own, so this section focuses only on the entering of passwords.

The entry of a password is as much about perception as it's about security. Past use of computers has taught people passwords shouldn't be displayed onscreen, where someone could be looking over your shoulder to see what you've entered. But if someone was looking over your shoulder, they could see which keys you pressed on the keyboard, so there's little to be gained by hiding the entered text. Think of it like an ATM, where you're reminded to "cover the keypad while entering your PIN."

This doesn't mean you shouldn't obscure the entered password. You'll make people using your app question its security by breaking their expectations if you don't obscure it in some way. What you do need to do is address the issue of not being able to easily verify the entered values.

As it's so easy to make a mistake when typing on a mobile device, add a way to view a password while it's being entered. This allows a person to check what they've entered without the round trip of submitting the form. Without this, a person who suspects they've entered it incorrectly must delete it and start again, or guess how many characters to delete and then re-enter those. Figure 6.12 shows ways of doing this.

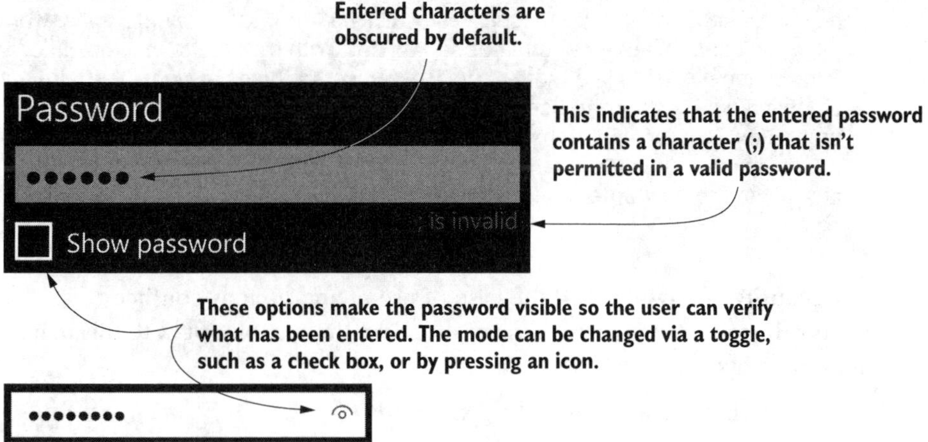

Figure 6.12 Password entry is made easier by providing a way to view what's entered and indicating if what's entered is invalid.

Making the password briefly visible does lessen security a bit, but the password is already visible if someone is watching you type. The benefit of improved usability far outweighs the small drop in security. But, as is often the case, you must find a compromise between security and usability that's right for your app.

You also make it easier for a person to accurately enter their password by verifying the entered value against any basic rules enforced when creating a password. People use different approaches to manage their passwords, but these don't always correspond with the constraints an app, site, or service imposes on what can be used for a password. If a person enters a password containing a character that's unacceptable, or because they thought it was part of the password, tell them so.

There's a misconception that this compromises the security of your system and makes it easier for someone trying to guess passwords. If there's a public registration process for the app/site/service, and this enforces rules about what's acceptable, then make public what those constraints are. Using this information to help people avoid accidentally entering an invalid value doesn't affect the security of the system in any way.

Similarly, when asking for a password as part of a registration process, show any rules that exist for the format of the password as or before it's entered. Don't wait for a person to submit all their registration data and then tell them their password must contain (or not) certain characters, symbols, or combinations thereof.

App vs. device security

Should a person have to re-enter a password every time they launch your app? If the app has highly sensitive information or makes it possible to perform irreversible, highly consequential actions, such as a banking app, then repeated password entry might be needed. For most other apps, it's not. With the wealth of capabilities on and information available in a modern device, far worse things are possible with a stolen, unlocked device than the use of an app. If you feel it's necessary to have password protection for each use of the app, consider only doing this if the device doesn't have a PIN lock or passcode enabled. This gives your app the extra protection you want, but without forcing a person to sign in twice.

The security of a system and the ease of use of an app may conflict. If you lower security for the sake of increasing ease of use, have the person opt-in to this behavior. Here are some ways to increase the ease of use:

- Allowing gestures instead of passwords
- Using biometric alternatives to passwords, like facial recognition, iris scanning, and fingerprint readers
- Supporting integration with third-party password managers
- Allowing the pasting of password values from the clipboard
- Advising on what makes a strong password without forcing its use

Forcing someone to use a password more complicated than they want will cause them to write it down and compromise its security, or it'll mean it's forgotten more often, and so the person must use the forgotten password process many times.

Forgotten passwords

When someone must reset or recover a forgotten password, they're already far from the golden path that leads to the value they're after. Because the process has become more than just logging in, it's more complicated than desired, so it's important that this experience be as easy and simple as possible. Sadly, most developers pay little attention to this process. Spend time on this functionality to try to help the person who must use it. They're likely already frustrated by having forgotten their password, so don't make things worse with the experience you provide.

Security recommendations are frequently updated, making it inappropriate and impractical for me to try to give you specific advice on how to fully manage passwords and security in your apps. That said, the following are universal points and should be observed:

- Passwords shouldn't be recoverable.
- Never store a password in plain text. If you must store a password, combine it with a unique salt value and encrypt it with a one-way hashing algorithm.
- Encourage the use of strong passwords or passphrases.
- Use multi-factor authentication where possible.
- Don't write your own encryption algorithms, and use the strongest algorithms available.

When it comes to entering passwords, allow for future changes to the encryption algorithm you use. You don't want to become tied to something that, in the future, can be compromised.

6.2.4 *Simplifying entry from a fixed set of options*

Forms will often need to capture more than text. As mentioned earlier, when looking at minimizing input, it's often easier to select from a list rather than type the desired value. It's not enough just to present a list of options. Make choosing from a list easier by

- Making intelligent use of defaults
- Simplifying the list
- Making the most likely options easiest to find

Although these ideas are simple, each can make a big difference. We'll look at these in more detail, beginning with defaults.

SIMPLIFY ENTRY WITH DEFAULT VALUES

Where a selected value impacts how an app behaves and the experience a person will have, the opportunity to set a default value is a privilege. The privilege is to control the experience that people will have with the app and how they'll interact with it.

Keep track of the values people choose. If you don't have a default but a majority of people choose a particular value, make that the default. Or, if you do have a default but people are regularly changing it, you may need to consider changing the default.

Many companies assume a large section of their user population work as accountants, live in Afghanistan, and were born on January 1st, 1970. These are all the default values or first in the list for occupation, country of residence, and date of birth in those apps. That these values are so popular highlights factors to be aware of when considering default values:

- If they don't matter to the person completing the form, default values will be used regardless of their appropriateness.
- People can overlook automatically populated data and the need to change it.
- Because data is submitted doesn't mean it's correct. Validate the input, especially if multiple defaults are submitted.
- If no value is provided (such as for date of birth), don't assume a default.

Automatically selecting a default is one way to help people avoid needing to evaluate the options in a long list. Another way is to simplify the process.

SIMPLIFYING SELECTION BY REDUCING OPTIONS

With many options for a person to select from, you make it harder for them to choose one. People need to evaluate all the options and choose the most appropriate, which takes time. This is defined by Hick's law: with more choices, it takes longer to come to a decision. To simplify selection, keep these points in mind:

- For some selectable values, common options exist that are chosen far more often than others.
- Provide quick access to the most recently used options to aid faster and more convenient selection, especially if a list will be selected from multiple times.
- If displaying a long list of options, track which are selected and remove any that are never chosen.

To remove unnecessary options, only ask for the needed level of specificity. If you don't need a fine-grained level of precision, don't ask for it. If you want an approximation of the industries people work in, you could have them choose from a small number of industries rather than a much larger number of possible job titles. If you want to know roughly where in the world people are based, you could ask them to choose from a list of five (or six) continents rather than from 200+ country names.

When it comes to estimating time, people gravitate to the "time anchors" of 1, 2, 3, 5, 10, 15, 20, and 30. If your app requires the selection of a time duration, having these 8 options will satisfy most people and will be easier to use than a list of 30 (or more) durations. When precision isn't needed, having a small number of values in a range will be easier to use than a large list of specific values.

MAKE LIKELY OPTIONS EASY TO FIND

The final factor that impacts the ease with which people can find their desired option in a list is the order in which the items are arranged. The most appropriate ordering will be dependent on the items in the list, but is likely to be one of these:

- Alphabetical (from A to Z is normal)
- Numerical (from smallest to largest or vice versa, with most common nearer the top)
- Time sequence (from shortest to longest or vice versa, with most common at the top)
- Hierarchical (arranged with most appropriate nearer the top)

Figure 6.13 shows an example of multiple factors combined to make selecting from a list as fast and simple as possible.

When selecting from a list, it shouldn't be possible to select an invalid option. And it's possible that no item will be selected when one must be. In the next section, we'll look at how to verify what is entered and how to indicate if it's missing or invalid.

Common options are near the top of the list, to make selection easier for more people.
select
Australia (based on your IP address)
- common ------------------
Canada
United Kingdom
United States of America
- all ------------------
Afghanistan
Albania
Algeria
The most-likely option is at the top of the list so that it's the easiest to select. It also indicates how the prediction was made.
Indicators separate the groupings and explain what might appear to be an unusual order.
All the options appear in alphabetical order, to help people easily find the option they're looking for. This section includes the values that appear at the top of the list so that anyone who overlooks the common items at the top will still find the item they're looking for lower down.

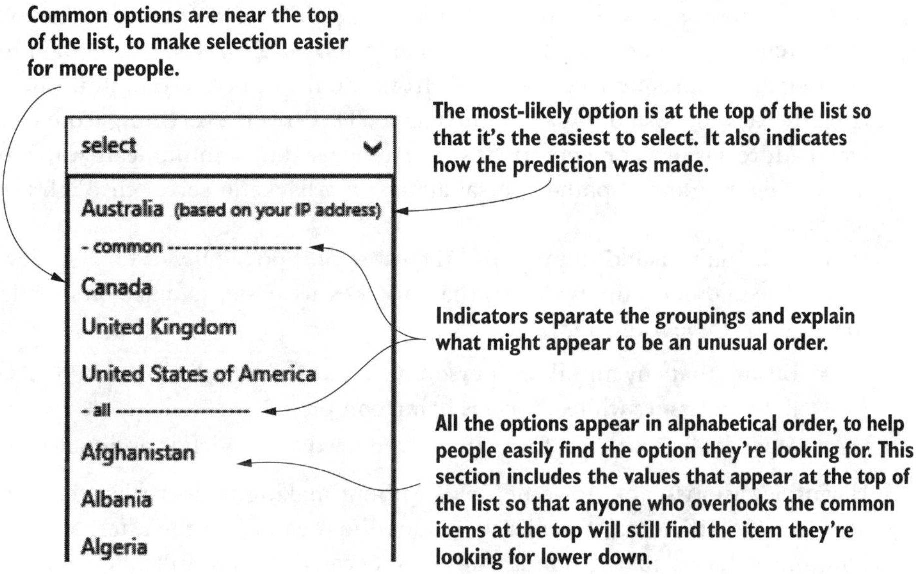

Figure 6.13 An optimized drop-down list for selecting country. It includes the use of external information to highlight the most likely option and common options. It also sorts all options to make the desired value easier to find, if not one of those called out at the top of the list.

6.2.5 Validation and required fields

The main data-capture form in Sam's app had many complex validation and requirement rules. Because it was only possible to do some of the validation on the server, it was decided to do all of it there. Missing or incorrectly formatted entries wouldn't be reported until after a round trip to the server had been made.

The consequence of this was that less than half of people were able to complete the form on the first attempt. Also, a large percentage of those who failed on the first attempt didn't try again and so never used the app, causing the company concern. The first-submit success rate was greatly improved when the indication of missing but required fields was added to the form by Sam, along with the addition of all the validation that could be duplicated in the app.

> **Postel's law**
>
> You may be aware of and follow the guidance of Postel's law:
>
> > Be conservative in what you do; be liberal in what you accept from others.
>
> But it often leads to more work for you and your app. To provide a robust experience for those using the app, this approach must be combined with Raskin's first rule of interface design (which you saw at the beginning of this chapter).

Because your app may receive a wide range of potential values, it's necessary that you verify that what's been provided is acceptable and advise if it isn't. You want to prevent any negative consequences that result from the data provided, both in the app itself and any backend system it passes the data to. This covers everything from ensuring an email address is in a correct format so it can be used to communicate with a person to preventing a potential path-traversal attack on a backend server through the submitted data.

Even if you've acted to minimize the cause and possibility of errors, they may still occur. I've said many times already that mistakes are easier to make on mobile devices, so you need to be forgiving:

- Ensure that any mistakes a person makes are easy to discover and correct. Highlight any issues while a form is being completed.
- Make it clear which information is required and which is optional.

Having an asterisk next to some fields without making it clear what the asterisk represents isn't sufficient. At the least, include the meaning of the asterisk and make it a different color so that it stands out. Also, because people will often want to do the minimum required to get the value they seek, not showing required fields creates a poor, unintuitive experience. You shouldn't leave them guessing which data they must provide and which is optional.

If a field has been skipped or populated with invalid data, indicate this when advancing to the next field. Don't wait for them to get to the end of the form before pointing out the issue. If the data entered into the form will be submitted to an external service for validation, do as much of that validation on the device as possible. This lets you inform the person using the app of any issue without the expense and delay of making the server call.

When a problem is identified, report it inline with a clear indication of the mishap and what's required to address it. Although a summary of issues may seem appealing, it makes the problem and its resolution less obvious. This is more noticeable where the form is larger than fits onscreen. A summary error message at the top of the form when the bottom of the form is visible is of no help. It may not be clear any issue exists at all. Equally unhelpful are error messages displayed in a dialog, like the one in figure 6.14.

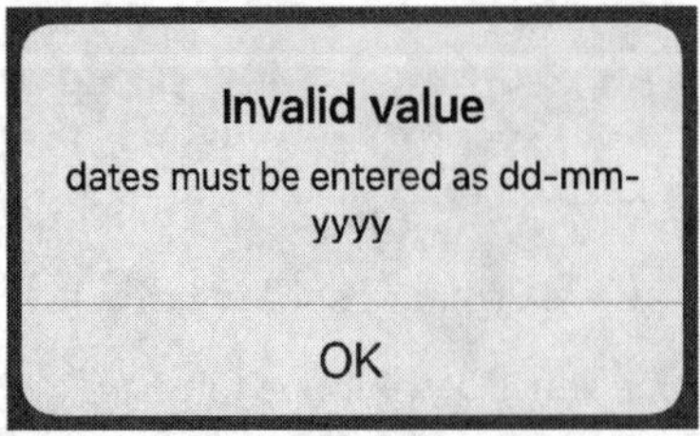
Invalid value
dates must be entered as dd-mm-yyyy
OK
This is a great example of what not to do.
It doesn't indicate which date is invalid or whether a single value or multiple values are affected.
It also requires people to remember the correct format once the dialog box has been dismissed.

Figure 6.14 A dialog is a poor way of showing a message about invalid data that's been entered. It's shown out of context and requires the person viewing it to remember what needs changing once dismissed.

Once this message is dismissed, the person using the app must remember what's required. With multiple issues, or as in the figure, it's not specific about which entry is incorrect, this can be very confusing. A person may have to submit the form multiple times to be reminded of what needs correcting. Also, that many people ignore prompts makes this a poor choice for reporting actions they must take.

Put it into practice: optimize your forms

Do the following to ensure you make your forms as intuitive and easy to use as possible:

- Ensure that lists of options are ordered appropriately for the information you're asking for. For large lists, if a few options are selected significantly more than others, include a copy of those options at the top of the list.
- Allow a person to type to filter the list or jump to the options starting with the typed character(s).
- Position labels above the fields they relate to.
- Ensure that any hints about the required formatting of data are visible when the text box has the focus or is partially complete.
- Set all keyboards appropriate to the data being asked for.
- Add masking to input where appropriate.
- Ensure that default values are used appropriately. Add any you can; adjust any you must.
- Add smart validation to email addresses. But beware of using simple regular expressions, due to the large number of edge cases and international/Unicode domains to consider.
- Add tracking to analyze what's selected from large lists to keep common summaries up to date.
- Analyze validation failures to see what issues are being encountered, and address them.
- Indicate errors inline and not in a summary at the top or the bottom of the form, where they may be scrolled out of view.

Capturing information from the person using the app is necessary to provide the value they're using the app for, but can be complicated and covers many varied scenarios. This chapter presented some fundamental issues to be aware of and common approaches available to make the process simple and intuitive for the people providing the data. While this chapter was about data that's provided directly by the person using the app, in the next chapter, I'll discuss data that comes from elsewhere.

Exercise: evaluate this login form

Test your understanding of the last section by stating whether the following statements about this partial screenshot are true:

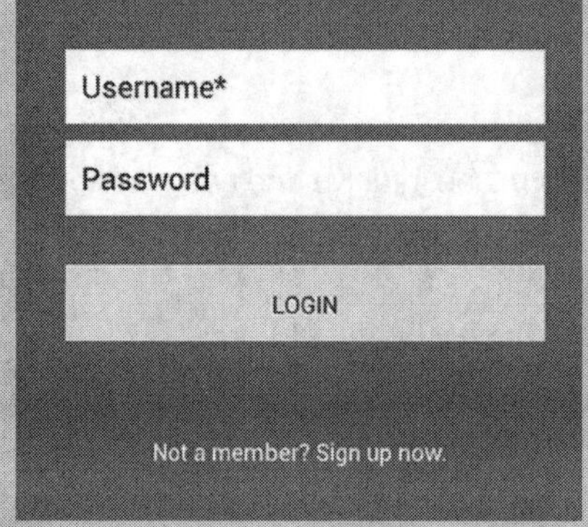

1. The username may be an email address.
2. The username is mandatory.
3. The password is optional.
4. No special restrictions on the contents of the password apply.
5. It's clear what to do if someone has forgotten their username or password.

Summary

- When it comes to entering data into forms, less is better; none is best.
- Typing accurately is difficult. Avoid the need for it where possible.
- Adjust keyboards for the type of information you're asking for, and don't ask for things you don't need. Ask for things when you need them.
- Selecting is easier than typing.
- Passwords are harder to type accurately and impossible to verify when you can't see them.
- Getting information for the business and doing what's easiest for the person using the app aren't always the same thing. You must find a balance.
- Make required fields and error messages clear.
- Give feedback as quickly as possible. Do this without calling a remote server when you can.
- Don't rely on just typed text input. Consider the many alternatives available, some of which are simpler and easier to use than typing.

7 Data not from a user

This chapter covers

- Working with data from the internet
- Working with data from the device and other apps
- Working with data from sensors
- Using heuristics and analysis to infer input

In this chapter, I discuss ways of working with data that isn't inputted directly by the person using the app. Many developers and companies overlook the opportunity to use this data. But it allows you to make a more intuitive experience and create processes that are faster and more pleasant to use. Common sources of input for your app that don't come directly from the person using it include the following:

- *Data from the internet*—It's the most common source of data in mobile apps.
- *Data already on the device*—Because apps often need to work offline, there's no need to obtain data from a remote source if it already exists on the device.
- *Data from sensors and device hardware*—These sources allow your app to take advantage of some of the benefits of being on a mobile device.
- *Data obtained by watching how people use the app and their device*—This allows you to tailor your app and to offer the best experience possible.

In this chapter, I also tell you about some of the challenges Rachel had with the app she built and helps maintain. It's a sports news app containing news and statistics about several popular sports. We'll look at how she used multiple data sources to improve the app, and the challenges she had with this.

7.1 Data from web-based resources

Beyond utilities like a flashlight or calculator, apps rarely exist in isolation. The majority connect and interact with internet-based services. In this section, I'll focus specifically on treating this data as input and consider how the app obtains this input:

- Is it requested from the app on the device?
- Is it pushed from the backend?

Whether created by the same organization or from a third party, connecting to services, just as communicating with other people, is part of the DNA of mobile apps.

7.1.1 Dealing with the data you directly request

Requesting data is easy. When returned successfully, the app can function as desired. It's when the app doesn't receive the data as expected that you need to consider because this can affect the experience a person has with your app. We'll look at these scenarios in this section:

- You may not receive what you requested.
- What's requested may not come back in the format you expect.

Rachel encountered both issues. She worked at a large company, and her team was separate from the group who managed access to the data via web APIs. The APIs created by the data team and used in Rachel's app would change regularly. This meant the app had to allow for URI endpoints that might move or change, and the information and structure of the data the app used would also change. Having to work in this way is far from ideal, but it's common to use APIs that evolve and change separately from the apps that use them.

Rachel dealt with this situation by having the app load configuration data from a separate URI that she could control and ensure wouldn't change. The configuration data contained the details of the current URIs to use to retrieve data and any extra transformations that the app would need to convert the returned data to the expected format. Use of a loaded configuration file removed the need to update the app every time the data changed. It was also preferable to creating a proxy API for the app to connect to. It did require that Rachel monitor changes in the backend APIs, but she created tooling to do this automatically.

ALLOW FOR INPUT NOT BEING RECEIVED

The occasionally connected nature of mobile means that there will be times when it's not possible to connect to the server for the app to retrieve the desired input. If your app is waiting for the person using it to provide the input directly, that's rarely a problem. If the person is waiting for your app to display data or content, they'll perceive any delay negatively, which reflects badly on the app experience.

Having an app with no content isn't good for anybody. After an app's first use, it's better to display the same data than to show nothing. It's also appropriate to indicate the age of data so the person using the app is clear when older content is shown. You want to avoid confusion between old and current data. Even if the app's data constantly changes (such as the price of stocks, current queue lengths, or product availability), it's better to be able to tell the person using the app, "Unable to get the current data, but here's what it was [a specific period of time] ago," rather than, "Unable to display data."

For apps that don't have connectivity when launched for the first time, you can avoid showing no content by shipping some with the app. This could include instructional text on how to use the app or some of the most popular content previously shown in the app. Even other entertaining placeholders or dummy content are more interesting than showing an empty screen the first time people use the app.

Additionally, your app mustn't leave a person wondering what's happening while it tries to obtain data from the internet. Show activity as appropriate for the app and the people who use it. Use a language and level of technical detail that's appropriate, and explain any problem and how to correct it or retry the request. Figure 7.1 shows an example of this.

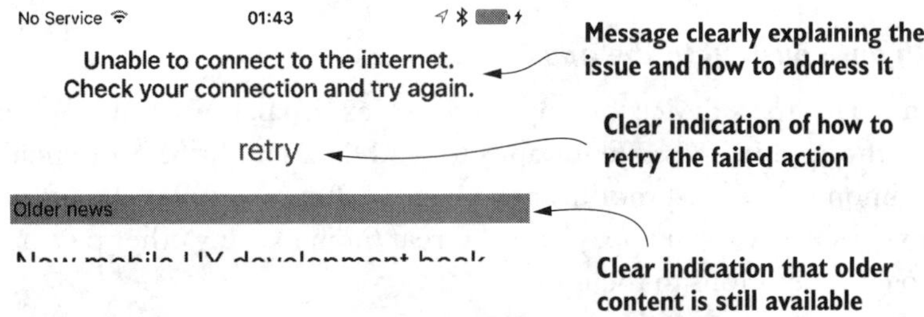

Figure 7.1 Handling an inability to load new data from a remote source should still give some content and information about why data couldn't be retrieved.

ALLOW FOR MALFORMED OR UNEXPECTED INPUT

Even when the app does receive a response for its request for remote content, things can still go wrong. Just because you get a response to a request for data, it doesn't mean it's in the expected format or structure, and hasn't suffered any corruption or modification in transit. Your app must tolerate such issues, and you must test this behavior to ensure its resilience.

Treat the handling of errors from a web request as seriously as you would handle data directly entered by a person. The way you architect your app plays a large part in how easy this is. Common issues you need to prepare for include the following:

- *Unexpected content*—Before attempting to process any received content, check that it's in the format you expect. For instance, the service you connect to may always return JSON, but your app may not always get JSON back from a successful request. A common scenario for this situation involves a person using a public Wi-Fi network that requires logging in or providing registration details before use. Such networks assume all requests come from a browser, and so return the HTML for a login page before it allows connecting to the desired server.
- *Corruption*—Your app may occasionally receive data that becomes corrupt while in transit. For example, HTTP is a simple protocol with no built-in checking for the corruption of its body content. Even if the content appears to be of the expected type, it can contain variations you've never considered. Your app must be able to handle any data corruption gracefully, and it must not crash.
- *Unexpected formatting*—Web-based resources don't stay the same forever. Your app must cope with specific versions of responses or with changes not accompanied by a new version number for the service or data format.

As far as possible, have all your remote resource access done by a single piece of code. (Some background process restrictions and the handling of large uploads and downloads may require their own handling, but make these an exception.) If you only have a single place in the code that's making and trying to handle requests for internet-based content, it's much easier to test and modify this code when necessary.

7.1.2 Dealing with data pushed to the app

You can send data to a device or app from an external source at any time after enabling it in the app. It's possible for apps to read data sent by SMS or email, but it's far more common to use push notifications instead. Because any such messages form part of the experience with an app, you must treat them like any other part of the app. Here are two considerations to focus on:

- What does the person viewing the message see?
- How is the content of the message used by the app?

Rachel's app would send push notifications with the results of matches, games, and events involving teams and sports that users expressed interest in. Some devices receiving the notifications couldn't display the entire content. This can result in losing important information. (To know the score of one team and not see the score of the other can be more frustrating than not knowing anything.) On becoming aware of this issue, Rachel changed the structure of the content of the messages so the most important details were first, and used abbreviated names to keep messages as short as possible.

There's a subset of push notifications that provide value without requiring people to start the app. Their value comes from displaying information or from responding to the notification without launching the app. A background process connected to the app handles the receipt and display of the message and any response. It also stores the activity for later reference by the app on the device or sends it to a backend server.

Figure 7.2 shows an example of input from a push notification. Having such "rich notifications" that don't require launching the app allows people to get value from the app in a faster and more convenient manner.

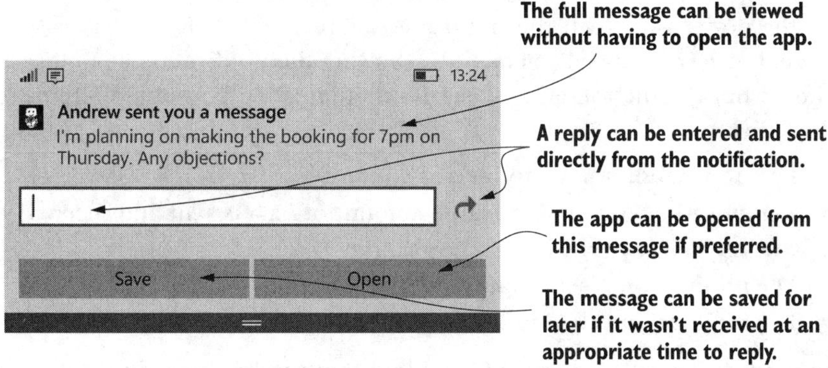
The full message can be viewed without having to open the app.
13:24
Andrew sent you a message
I'm planning on making the booking for 7pm on Thursday. Any objections?
A reply can be entered and sent directly from the notification.
The app can be opened from this message if preferred.
Save
Open
The message can be saved for later if it wasn't received at an appropriate time to reply.

Figure 7.2 Push notifications can be a form of input and allow the capturing of input from a person without launching the app.

A typical use of push notifications is as a trigger for people to open the app and engage with new content, such as breaking news or a change in circumstances (like something happening in a game). When a person launches the app from a notification, you should treat this differently than when launching an app normally. Go straight to the content or activity directly related to the notification. Invoking the app from a notification is equivalent to saying, "I want to see what this notification relates to." That's different from, "I want to use this app or see what's new in it."

NOTE Launching an app from a notification and seeing something unrelated is confusing and leads to feelings of frustration or a belief the app is broken.

If a person doesn't respond to a notification within a sufficient timeframe, they'll end up with messages that when tapped won't lead to the app showing relevant content. Remove any notifications like this from the list of displayed messages. You can do this in three ways:

- Send an expiry value with the notification so the OS removes it after the configured period of time.
- Send subsequent messages to remove or update the older notification.

- Have a background process on the device that periodically handles any notifications that haven't been dismissed or acted on.

Notifications don't just get old; receiving too many can be overwhelming and frustrating. The most common reaction by a person receiving what they consider to be too many notifications is to disable them. This is often quickly followed by a negative store review. To reduce such feelings from a person receiving too many or unwanted push notifications, intercept the notifications when the device receives them and don't display them until a later time.

A background task running on the device will have access to more information about the device on which the notification is received than the server sending the message. It can increase engagement by showing the notification at a more appropriate time. Consider the following scenarios that impact the display of input from push notifications:

- The notification relates to specific content.
- A notification containing a large amount of data is sent and received over specific types of networks.
- The notification is sent while a device is "silent."
- The notification is tied to a date.

If the notification relates to specific content that will be shown in the app, the background task that intercepts the notification could download (pre-fetch) and cache the relevant content before displaying the notification. When the person later invokes the app from the notification, the content is immediately available. In this scenario, the person doesn't have to wait for the content to download, or worry about being online.

If a notification is received over a mobile network connection, and if acting on it requires the app to download large amounts of data, or the app has been configured to only request data over a specific type of network (typically Wi-Fi), then it's better to wait for such a connection before displaying the notification. That way you avoid asking a person to open the app for a task that they've previously said they don't want to do.

Displaying a notification when a device is set to silent, or the person using it is asleep, leads to less effective notifications. Because the sending server doesn't know the volume or local time setting on the device, have the app be responsible for silently receiving the notification and showing it at an appropriate time.

In addition to volume and time settings, the app may also have been granted access to the calendar on the device. In this scenario, using this information also enables more effective delivery of notifications that are acted on: it avoids showing a message when a person is in a private meeting or has another appointment, which may make engaging with the notification and app inappropriate.

As with other input, it's necessary for any process that handles input via notifications to be tolerant of receiving unexpected or differently formatted content. You don't want such a process crashing due to a formatting error. Notifications can also be an important way for an app to provide output. This is discussed in detail in chapter 9.

Put it into practice: data from the web

- If your app relies on remote content, identify and add placeholder content to ensure that there's data that can be displayed on the first use of the app, even if the remote content source cannot be accessed.
- Ensure that the app handles cases where no content, unexpected content, or corrupt content is received.
- Ensure that the messages displayed when there are problems provide advice specific to the issue. Include actionable instructions on how, if possible, they can be addressed.
- If old or cached data is displayed in the app when new content can't be obtained, confirm that this is indicated as such.
- Look to identify options for moving functionality into any notifications sent, to minimize the need for people to open the app to access functionality.
- If sending notifications about specific items or contents, ensure that the app will open on these if accessed from the notification.
- If notifications you send have a natural lifetime, remove them from a person's device if they aren't acted on in that time frame.

Exercise: data from the web

Test your understanding of the last section by using the following words to fill in the blanks in the paragraph:

old activity corrupt explanations

ships retrieved format request unexpected

It's important to consider both how you _____ data and what the app should do when it can't be _____. It's normally better to show _____ data rather than no data, as long as this is clearly indicated. Include data with the app when it _____ so that it'll always have something to show. Show _____ when the app is doing something. Provide clear _____ when something fails and what, if anything, can be done to address the problem. Test how your app copes with _____ data or data in an _____ format. Ensure that you _____ content so it displays appropriately for the space available.

7.2 Getting data from the device

In this section, I look at the three broad categories of on-device data:

- Data available from the device
- Data stored on the filesystem
- Data available from other apps

Mobile devices have so much information that it's often unnecessary to ask people to enter it manually. It's faster and more accurate to reuse what's already on the device.

7.2.1 Input from the operating system

A device's operating system (OS) provides access to a common set of data via the Personal Identification Manager (PIM), which can be used instead of requesting data directly from the people using the app. PIM data includes the information stored on the device relating to known contacts, accounts, messages (sent and received), and appointments (from connected calendars). The OS can also serve as a source of input to an app when triggered as the result of integration with OS extensions and integrations.

Rachel's app created reminders about upcoming events. A person would say they were interested in a specific event, and the app would trigger an alarm a few minutes before the game or match as a reminder to watch it. The theory behind this feature was good, but the implementation had two issues: it wasn't possible to see which events had reminders set or to see what else was happening at the same time.

The revised version allowed a person to see what else was on their calendar at around the same time and added a reminder directly to their calendar. That way, people could still see the events they were interested in when not in the app and planning other events in their diary.

USING PIM DATA

A primary feature of mobile devices has traditionally been communication with other people. As such, mobile devices have their own central repository of PIM data for information about contacts and their details. Examples and how to handle the use of this data follows:

- *Detail lookups*—Instead of, or in addition to, having a person manually enter details that may be stored in a PIM database, add the ability to retrieve these details. For example, if your app requires entry of email addresses, phone numbers, names, or postal addresses, having the ability to select these from a list can be faster, simpler, and more accurate than typing these values. Filtering the list based on the type of information required is also appropriate, so that if the app requires an email address, only the contacts for which an email address is known are displayed.
- *Finding contacts*—For apps that allow sharing information or communicating with other people using the service, the ability to identify personal contacts who also have accounts on the service to which the app relates is useful. This makes it much easier for people to communicate, and helps build the value of the app by increasing the number of people the app allows communication with.
- *Checking for errors*—If names or other contact details are manually entered, checking for differences between what's stored in the PIM database can help identify and highlight any errors that can otherwise negatively impact a person's experience with your app.

- *Finding appointments*—If your app includes any time- or date-specific content, it may be appropriate to automatically cross-reference this with events in a person's calendar. This can also provide additional income opportunities.

  For example, "We have a sale tomorrow, which could be an opportunity to get a present for Fred's birthday next month." Or it can provide an opportunity to give additional context. For example, "The announcement is set for 3 P.M. tomorrow—after your meeting with Mary."

As with all uses of personal data, it's essential that you have appropriate policies in place to govern and explain how you use and store this information. I also advise that you test how appropriate and useful this is for the people using your app. It's easy to become carried away with trying to use all the data that's available without first confirming its value to the people using the app.

Verify data from a PIM source in the same way as with any other data. Just because you're retrieving an email address or phone number doesn't mean that it'll automatically meet your rules for the formatting of those values, or even be a valid value. The differences may be small, like a phone number that includes an extension, and those which you haven't thought of or allowed. Or, the value could be completely invalid from your perspective, such as an email address that just contains the local part of a corporate address, because that's acceptable in the data source from which the value was originally obtained.

INPUT FROM OS INTEGRATION

Modern operating systems are providing an ever-growing number of opportunities for third-party apps to surface content or act as extensions. Being aware of the opportunities for each platform your app will run on gives you ways to identify and tailor the value your app provides and to improve the experience for the people using it.

With the release of new versions of platforms, new possibilities and opportunities appropriate to your app may become available. This allows the OS to expose your content or functionality, or for you to enhance apps, like maps or messaging, that come preinstalled with an OS.

7.2.2 Data from the filesystem

Some data common to the OS and many apps is stored in the filesystem. The most commonly used examples are photos and videos. This also includes music and files downloaded from the web. Whether you're using files inside the app's sandboxed area of the filesystem or accessing files in a shared location, there are some potential issues to be aware of and allow for in your apps. This section covers the challenges and potential issues you may encounter when working with the filesystem.

To begin, you can't guarantee that a file won't have changed since the last time you accessed it. Don't assume that because you read a file without issue previously, subsequent reads will be OK. Files do become corrupt and can be changed by other apps, processes, or sneaky testers. Add appropriate error handling to all file access.

Some platforms allow the moving of content between removable storage cards. If storing the path to a file, be aware that the file may not be in the same location or even still exist when the app is next run. Also use appropriate file extensions for the app's content. This not only helps with identifying files in the app and when debugging, but avoids some issues with specific content types. Media files are susceptible to issues here.

As an example, for one music-streaming app I was asked to help debug, I discovered an issue that was the result of variations in different MP3 encodings. The files were saved without any file extensions. When the app tried to play them, the OS attempted to determine the format based on the contents of the files. This led to some tracks not playing. When the .mp3 extension was added to the files, the OS used this as an indication of the file's contents and allowed all tracks to be played without issue.

How data is stored across multiple files impacts the speed with which it can be accessed. Storing a large amount of data in a single file means the whole file must be read and loaded into memory to access even a part of it. If only a small part of a larger dataset is needed, or part of a larger dataset can be used while the rest is being loaded from disk, use multiple files to store the data. Breaking data across multiple files also increases resiliency, as the corruption of one file doesn't mean the loss of all data.

Store any files you create in appropriate directories. Storing files or other data in places deleted by a person trying to free up space on a device could lead to them losing important data, or at least wondering where something has gone or why it's been lost. Regardless of the cause of such an issue, if your app is perceived to have lost important data, it'll reflect negatively on the experience. You must also ensure that nothing that's intended to stay on one device is incorrectly shared. This has the potential to affect data security.

When it comes to choosing where to store files, another consideration is using locations that are copied to and synchronized with cloud storage. Doing this enables a synchronized experience with the app across multiple devices, but you'll need to allow for the potential of synchronization issues if doing so. If one or more devices is offline when used, data won't be synchronized as expected, and a person may think data was lost.

7.2.3 Data from other apps

The final way to avoid having a person enter information directly is to get it from other apps on the device. Isolated, standalone apps are on their way out—a decreasing number of apps have value when used on their own. Check with the people using your app, but the general trend is for people to want to use multiple apps in collaboration, and share and copy information among them.

By not having data locked in a single app, you make it easier for people to do what they want and to achieve the outcome or value they're using the app for. This might be as simple as sharing data from one app with another, or it could be the apps serve as different steps in a larger process. They could also be from a single company and use the same database. The following are different ways that your app can receive input from other apps:

- *Common local data*—Data can be in a shared location on the filesystem and can be anything from a custom file format to a shared database. Avoid locking these files or changing a format to one that isn't supported by all apps that use the data.
- *Native sharing*—Every mobile OS has a built-in way of sharing common data types. Support sending and receiving data in this way if relevant to your app and the needs of the people using it.
- *Deep linking*—Exposing specific functionality via extensions, public intents, and app links enables customized ways of sharing between specific apps. This allows for greater control over what's shared between apps and a closer integration between different apps. If you enable this in your app, document this thoroughly to make it easy for other app developers to use.
- *File extensions and MIME types*—If your app works with data in specific, common formats, register the app with the device as a handler for them. This will allow the app to open these files automatically.
- *Copy and paste*—Allow the cutting and pasting of data from and to your app as a simple way of extending input and supporting the sharing of data. Don't rely on plain text; support different data types and formatting as appropriate to the data.

Consider it a failure on the part of your app if a person must think about how to get data from one app to another. It's even worse if they can't work it out or it's not possible.

Put it into practice: data from the device

- If the app requires the entry of PIM data, consider adding the ability to obtain this directly from the device, in addition to allowing it to be manually entered.
- Review the extensions and advanced integration options available from the operating systems that your app runs on.
- If you're using the filesystem for data storage and retrieval, ensure that you're adequately testing for and handling changes, corruption, and missing files.
- Confirm that files are stored in appropriate locations on disk so that a person using the app won't lose anything important if temporary files are deleted, and that non-essential files aren't kept longer than they need to be.
- Enable the sharing of data with and the receipt of data from other apps as appropriate.

Exercise: data from the device

Test your understanding of the last two sections by stating whether the following are false or true:

1. PIM data can be an appropriate source of data for apps that involve contacting other people or appointments.
2. Files your app writes are guaranteed to still be there and unchanged the next time your app needs them.
3. You should treat the contents of a file in the same way as you would data typed into the app.
4. Your app should make it easy to share data.
5. It's not necessary to allow your app to support copying and pasting of data.

7.3 Getting data from sensors

Mobile devices are highly sophisticated computers that allow your app to gain input from many different built-in sensors. In chapter 4, I introduced some of the environmental, positional, and movement sensors that can be available in a device. In this section, I cover two factors relating to the use of these sensors you can't ignore if you want to create a great experience for people using your app. These are how getting permission to access the data impacts the experience with the app and how sensor responses can vary.

7.3.1 Transparency and permission when using sensor data

Sensors have access to information that will either make an app possible or provide an enhanced experience. In either situation, and whether using sensors in the background (location tracking, for example), actively in the foreground (a fingerprint reader, for example), or a combination of scenarios (accelerometer, or other movement sensors), you must ensure that the person using the app allows you to access data from the sensor and any implications are clear. You want to avoid asking the person using the app for permission to access a resource or sensor without telling them what will be done with the data it provides.

Rachel's app had a targeted audience of sports fans. Based on preferences in the app, it was possible to identify the team or teams a person supported. By combining this knowledge with location information from the device, the app could provide targeted advertising to the people using the app when visiting as away-team fans at sports events. The challenge Rachel had was that people attended home games more often than away games. When first using the app, people were asked about enabling access to their location for local information. Permission was frequently not granted, and research indicated this was because people didn't see a benefit in getting local information about their home town or city. The benefits of doing so weren't communicated clearly to the user.

Rachel addressed this problem with a more well-defined value proposition. By asking, "Allow access to your location when attending the game at {venue} for discounts and local tips?" more people granted permission. Because visiting fans would be in a town or city they weren't familiar with, they were open to trying suggested restaurants, and so forth. Users of the app also liked what they saw as helpful suggestions when away from home. This form of referral advertising was profitable because location tracking could also verify if the person visited the promoted location.

If your app uses sensors that return what may be considered sensitive data or need explicit user consent before being used, you must ask for it in an appropriate manner. Different platforms enforce this in different ways, and there are variations between the use of different sensors. Before you use any sensor, you should

- Make it clear how the app will use data from the sensor.
- Explain why it's needed and any alternatives or implications if not used.
- Highlight any potential privacy policy issues.

Figure 7.3 shows examples of good and bad ways of asking for permission.

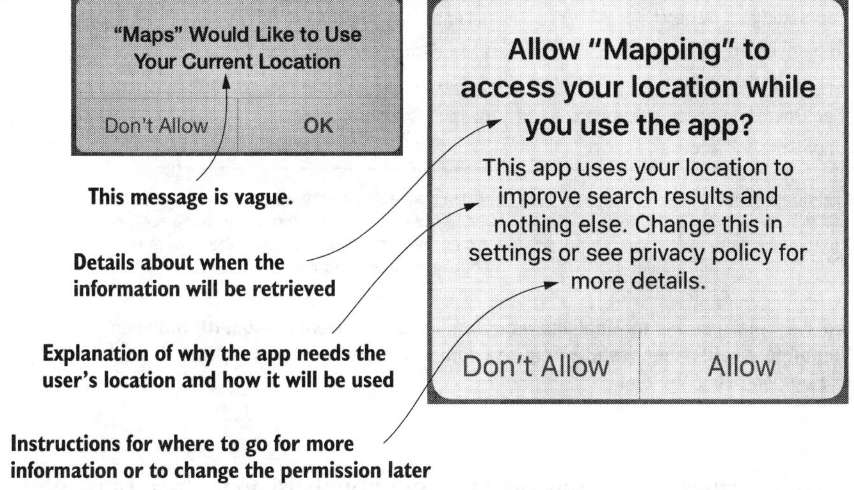

Figure 7.3 Explain why and how a sensor will be used to avoid questions and uncertainty from the people using the app.

People tend to assume the worst if it isn't clear what data is captured, why it's needed, and how it'll be used. Whether enabled or not, there will be times when a person using your app will want to change their mind about the granted permission. It's not enough for your app to preempt questions about the use of sensors and related data, you also need to avoid the need for a person to ask how to change a previous answer.

Some platforms encourage or require a distinction and separation between settings and configurations: *settings* are handled centrally by the OS, and *configurations* are controlled by the app. Although some people find this separation helpful, for others the difference isn't clear. It leads to confusion and uncertainty about where they should go to make a change. Because an app that creates such adverse feelings isn't intuitive and negatively impacts the experience of the person using it, Rachel carefully tested the way this was controlled and labeled in her app.

Just as a retailer may take the approach of assuming their customer is always right, if the person looking for a setting does so in a particular place, then that's where your app should have the setting. As a rule, this means having settings within the app itself. Even if the platform dictates that settings must be handled centrally, the Settings option in the app should redirect to the central one.

This is also true of any settings-related instructions or other configurations that must be changed outside of the app itself. Figure 7.4 shows an example of doing this for an app that enables the use of a custom keyboard and the consequences of making this unnecessarily complex.

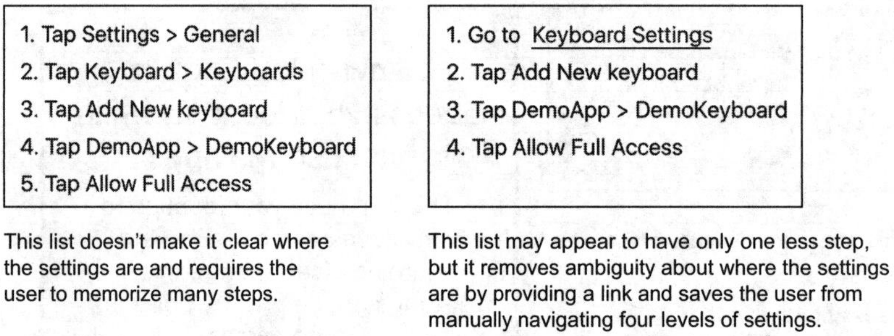

1. Tap Settings > General
2. Tap Keyboard > Keyboards
3. Tap Add New keyboard
4. Tap DemoApp > DemoKeyboard
5. Tap Allow Full Access

This list doesn't make it clear where the settings are and requires the user to memorize many steps.

1. Go to Keyboard Settings
2. Tap Add New keyboard
3. Tap DemoApp > DemoKeyboard
4. Tap Allow Full Access

This list may appear to have only one less step, but it removes ambiguity about where the settings are by providing a link and saves the user from manually navigating four levels of settings.

Figure 7.4 Instructions for enabling a custom keyboard (DemoKeyboard) provided by DemoApp. Avoid unnecessarily long and complex guidelines, as they aren't good for the person using the app.

It doesn't create a great impression for your app to ask to use a sensor and then fail to do so. The negative feelings felt toward your app will be further amplified if other apps on the device can use the sensor successfully, thereby demonstrating that the fault is actually with your app.

7.3.2 Allow for variations in sensor input

It's not just the location of settings or the ways of controlling permission to a sensor that can change. The input your app receives from sensors won't always be the same across different devices and platforms, and your app must handle this. In this section, I look at the potential variations your app must allow for and be able to handle.

ALLOW FOR VARIATIONS IN FORMATTING

The data you receive from a sensor can be formatted in a hard-coded fashion or can be affected by the settings on the device. Common variations you're likely to encounter are the differing formats mentioned in chapter 3. The most frequent of these are the decimal and separator characters when working with numbers, and the format of dates and times. These may or may not match system settings or even be consistent on the same model of device used in different countries. The uses of varying date epochs and custom date formats are two scenarios that I believe exist to keep developers on their toes.

As your app is used on devices with different operating systems and from multiple manufacturers (of components, as well as the assembled device), then your chances of encountering such issues increase. Failing to retrieve or parse the correct value from a sensor isn't good. This is yet another reason to test your apps on a wide variety of devices and to include the devices used by the people using (or who will use) your app.

ALLOW FOR VARIATIONS IN ACCURACY

The same types of sensors can return data in different ways. It's important to be aware of this if you're creating a cross-platform solution, and you write a single piece of code to handle the returned data from all platforms.

If a sensor returns data without a scale, ensure that it's the expected scale. You don't want to assume a distance is in meters because that's what's on one platform, when the sensor is returning kilometers. Similar to variations in scale are variations in rounding. For example, assuming a figure will always be rounded to a whole number can cause problems if running on a device with a sensor that returns a value with precision to several decimal places. Likewise, confusing output can be the result of similar sensors that output time in milliseconds or seconds depending on the version of the SDK being used.

Your app must allow for all the possible variations it can receive. Failing to do so will result in data being displayed incorrectly or not at all. You can catch most of these issues by checking that values are within expected ranges. This also highlights the need to test that your app works consistently on different devices.

ALLOW FOR VARIATIONS IN AVAILABILITY

Whether disabled in settings or not physically included as part of a device, there'll be times when your app will run on devices that don't allow you to access a required sensor. In some instances, an app store will prevent the installation of an app on a device that doesn't include the required hardware.

Always check directly for the existence of a sensor and don't assume its presence based on the type of device or another factor. Because the functionality in a specific type of sensor can vary, even among devices of the same make and model, it's necessary to test not just for the existence of a sensor, but also for the capabilities it exposes and supports. Additionally, it's necessary to check if you have permission from the person using the app to access a sensor or that it hasn't been revoked since the app was last run.

Even when checking for the inclusion of a sensor and permission to use it, you'll still need to handle occasions when it's not available. Here are some approaches you can take to cope with missing sensors or hardware capabilities:

- *Required only*—The app or piece of functionality won't work without the required sensor. If this is the case, be sure to provide a clear explanation to the person using the app. Use this approach only if there's no way of offering the functionality without the sensor.
- *Fallback when missing*—If the desired sensor isn't available, the app resorts to a limited feature set that doesn't use the sensor, or relies on the manual input of the data instead.
- *Enhance when available*—Develop the app to provide the best possible experience without the sensor and then extend the functionality when the sensor is available. This is the preferred approach to dealing with potentially optional hardware as it ensures that every person using the app has the best experience possible.

Keeping track of which combinations of device and OS versions include the ability to use specific sensors can be a lot of work. It will mean regularly updating the app as new devices and OS updates are released.

Put it into practice: using sensors for input

- Explain why and how any data or device resource will be used before asking for permission to access it.
- Ensure that the use of all data from the device and sensors is covered by the app's privacy policy.
- If you can, make it possible to use the app without the use of any sensors or data that require additional permissions from the person using it.

Exercise: data from sensors

Test your understanding of the last section by stating which of the options in the square brackets should be used to correctly complete the sentence:

1. It's [better|unnecessary] to get user consent before using a sensor.
2. A prompt to ask to use a sensor should be [short|clear].
3. The format of the response from sensors on different devices [will|won't] always be the same.
4. Different makes of a sensor [are|aren't] guaranteed to provide the same level of accuracy.
5. Access to a sensor [can|won't] change between sessions.

7.4 Using heuristics and inferring input

This section looks at the final type of input that doesn't come directly from the person using it—that which you predict or infer. This extra input can enhance and supplement what's input directly. I'll look at inferring data based on the usage of an app by an individual and by all users collectively.

7.4.1 Enhancing the app experience based on an individual's usage

You can improve the experience a person has with your app by doing things just for them. This doesn't mean building an app just for them, but one that adapts to the needs, habits, behaviors, and context of the people using it.

The first page of Rachel's app displayed a list of top news stories from a range of sports. Originally, the content editors defined the order of stories in the list, and it was the same for everyone. When Rachel changed the app to prioritize the order of stories based on which sections of the app a person looked at, this increased the number of stories people read. Like Rachel, by tracking the features and different parts of the app that a person uses, you can adapt what's displayed in the app to reflect this. I'll highlight three approaches; each requires increasingly more work, but also adds more value and enhances the UX:

- The simplest enhancement is to track the most recently used or accessed files or areas of the app and present these as a special list within the app.
- Combining details of the most recently used items with the frequency of which they're used creates a list of automatic favorites. This is useful for larger lists of items of which a few are accessed significantly more often.
- More advanced recommendations can be provided by incorporating extra factors in the monitoring of different activities within the app. This includes variations based on time, location, and connectivity.

To be able to provide suggestions based on observations can be enormously powerful and helpful. These observations can include "When the app is launched between 8 and 9 A.M., the person normally does X" or, "When they're at home, the user normally does Y," and so forth. Such observations can also be used as a basis for optimistically preloading remote data that the person is most likely to want before they next use the app. iOS includes something similar with its background fetch capability, but the logic needed to implement this yourself on any platform is relatively simple.

Beyond the actions of an individual, you can use information from the device as a form of input that will help enhance the experience. Automatically obtaining details about the device's power and connectivity allows for implementing behavior such as

- If offline, saving data and automatically submitting it when next online
- Disabling automatic refreshing of data when power is low
- Reducing the frequency of background polling when on a slower or more expensive connection

If implementing such behaviors doesn't apply unilaterally, offer those as a hint or suggestion. No matter how smart your logic, there's no way to be 100% confident that it will be what's wanted. Figure 7.5 shows an example of the IP address of the device used as a way to estimate location. (You also saw something similar in the last chapter.)

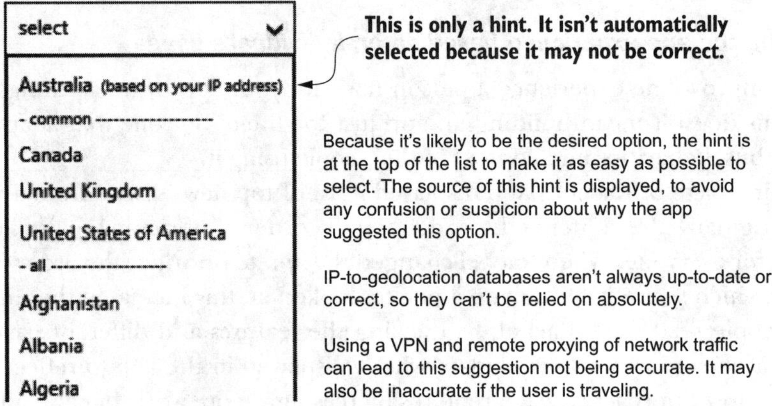

Figure 7.5 Information captured from the device can be used to provide hints and suggestions, but you must allow a person to change or correct this.

As with the data in figure 7.5, don't force people to use your hints, suggestions, and recommendations. Allow the person using the app to refine or correct any value you may suggest. In a few cases, it can also be useful to track and learn from any corrections that are made, but this is beyond the needs of most apps. A simpler alternative is to support keyboard input that allows for the suggestion of alternative spellings and their automatic correction.

7.4.2 *Enhancing the app experience based on the usage of all people*

In addition to using information about how a person uses the app to help that individual, information about how all people use the app can be combined to improve the experience for some or all of the people using the app. Examples of improvements made to apps based on this type of analysis include the following:

- Introduce common corrections and alternatives to search terms to remove a disparity between what people were searching for and how content and functionality was classified and, therefore, displayed in the app.
- Enhance in-app search functionality based on what people searched for and what they eventually did.
- Group different pieces of functionality in the app based on features that are regularly used together, rather than what was perceived to be the best order.

- Optimize the out-of-the-box experience based on what people do with the app on their first few uses, rather than the features that the company wants to emphasize.
- Emphasize different functionality and options based on the time of day and day of the week that a person first uses the app.
- Prioritize different types of content based on the time of day a person uses the app.

Any improvements you bring to the app based on consensus use won't benefit all the people who use it, but they can bring a substantial improvement to some.

Put it into practice: giving people what they want without asking
Identify analytics that could help you understand how the app is used and improve the experience of using it for the people who use it. Then start recording the data.

With this, you've come to the end of the part of the book that focuses on input. In the next part, I'll move on to talk about the third component of mobile app experiences—output.

Summary

- Input comes from many more sources than what's directly typed by the user.
- You may not be able to get the input desired, so you need to allow for and handle this.
- You may be able to handle input without opening the app.
- You don't always have to act on input when it's received, and may be able to offer a better experience if you wait for a more appropriate time or circumstance.
- People have a lot of information on their devices available for use as input.
- Integration with and communication between apps is growing in importance and is increasingly expected and required by people using apps.
- Regardless of where it comes from, you must allow for possible variations in formatting, completeness, and accuracy of data.
- Rules for handling and processing input without making assumptions about its accuracy or completeness must be followed and applied.
- Tracking what individuals do with the app and how they use it provides indications of ways to make it easier for both them and all people who use the app.

Part 3

Output

What an app displays onscreen, its styling and the organization of content, are the most obvious aspects of an app's output. Your initial reaction may be to consider this as simply relating to the user interface, but the output of an app comprises much more. The output from an app should also consider information architecture, visual design, interaction, copywriting, and accessibility, as much as the UI.

For a sighted person, the visuals in an app will have an immediate impact and set the tone, expectations, and association with the app and its usage. With very few exceptions, popular, successful apps have a polished, high-quality interface that both takes and shows focus and attention to detail. It isn't that you can't have success without a well-designed visual output, or that visuals alone will be enough for you to have success, but that the visual part of your app's output is as important as the other five components.

It's easy to focus on just the immediate visual parts of your app when considering output, but apps can take many actions to produce other forms of output, and these actions are just as important. Whether it's sound or haptic feedback, content, or instructions sent to other apps or systems, all forms of output contribute to the experience of using an app.

Over the next two chapters, I talk about each of these ideas in turn. In chapter 8, I discuss output with regard to what goes on the screen, and then in chapter 9, I look at the other output that your app may produce.

8 Displaying items in the app

This chapter covers

- The principles behind a good user interface
- How everyone can find and use what they're looking for
- Making visual elements clear and consistent

In this chapter, I cover one of the most obvious aspects of an app. It's what most people focus on, and it's the most visible—it's what you display onscreen. What you display and how you do it are crucial to your app's success. To not give people adequate consideration can leave you with an app that's confusing, misleading, or otherwise hard to use.

The creation of UIs is a large and complex topic. Many books focus solely on this topic, so for me to try to cover everything in this one chapter is unrealistic. Instead, this chapter focuses on the core aspects of UI design, which you can apply to any mobile app platform. With this knowledge, you'll be able to create an app with a good layout and logical navigation that people can easily use even if you don't consider yourself a designer.

At the core of creating a UI that contributes to an intuitive UX is the idea that what you display will preemptively answer questions people have before they ask them. It'll also avoid users asking questions not directly related to their task. A person shouldn't need to ask, "How do I do X?" This should be clear from what's onscreen. Similarly, don't cause someone to wonder why something looks the way it does or how to interact with it.

Throughout this chapter, you'll also read about Daryl's app-building experiences. Daryl's app gives a way for music lovers to discover and experience live shows. The most complex part of Daryl's app is the backend infrastructure needed to support it, but here we'll be focusing on what went into the UI.

In addition to this chapter, I encourage you to familiarize yourself with the specific design guidelines for the platforms you're developing for, so you can create apps with visual interfaces that are intuitive and easy to use. Also see the "Recommended Reading" and "Bibliography" listings in the appendixes.

8.1 The fundamentals of good visual output

It's easy to start thinking about the controls to put onscreen, but in this first section I want to highlight four factors to keep in mind. These factors will help ensure that you create a positive, intuitive experience for the people using your app.

8.1.1 Focus on the person using the app and their goals

As I've said many times already, the people using the app are a key part of the context and circumstances of use for your app. You need to focus on their abilities and what they'll need from the app, not what you want. Take Daryl, for example.

Daryl started with the approach taken by many developers who aren't business or user focused. He built an app with the features he thought he'd use or were most interesting to him. He spent lots of time showing animations when the app started. This meant it took longer for the people using the app to get to the information and functionality they were looking for.

For your apps, start by understanding the goals of the people using the app. If a person wants a weather app to tell them the temperature, don't fill the app with beautiful weather imagery and bury the temperature deep within the view hierarchy. Make the content people want most immediately available.

Or, consider a reporting app that shows summary business metrics and performance data. That an app displays elegant graphical summaries when all is well can be great. But, if things start to go awry, the person using the app is likely to need more detailed information and specific values. If the app only shows high-level graphical visualizations, it becomes much less useful at the time it's needed most.

Focus on the people using the app. Include the information they want and need in a way that's easy to use and understand. Refer to chapters 2 and 3 for more on this.

8.1.2 Meet the expectations of the people using the app

Daryl broke the expectations of the people using his app by adding all the animation when it opened. People weren't expecting this, and the majority didn't want it. After removing the unnecessary animations and presenting a more traditional opening screen, feedback about the app improved.

Your app should also meet the expectations people have based on other apps they've used. By using the same actions, gestures, layouts, navigation, paradigms, terminology, and icons, your app is at once intelligible, understandable, useful, and usable.

Consider an app that uses a picture of a spanner and screwdriver labeled Configuration, which gives access to the app's settings. Most people using that app are not only forced to remember that this app does things differently, but can also become distracted by wondering why it's different and what else may be different.

Apps used more than once should be consistent and predictable. Use a single navigational structure throughout your app, and apply a consistent layout across all parts of the app. Once a person knows how to use a part of the app, don't make them then learn something different for another segment of the app. Also, have the app look the same each time it's used. Don't have a first-use experience that's dramatically different from that of normal usage.

8.1.3 Account for the specific device being used

Your app's UI will appear on devices that vary widely. It's rare for a single design to be right for all sizes and aspect ratios of the screen. At its simplest, you must allow for variations in the size and alignment of elements onscreen. For more complicated scenarios, you may need multiple layouts to allow for different screen sizes and dimensions. A larger screen lets you include more information or combine what would otherwise be multiple smaller screens. But doing so isn't without risks:

- *If adding more content to a screen, don't do so at the expense of legibility.* This will make the app harder to use. And don't reduce the size or spacing of text to fit more in.
- *If adding more functionality to a single screen, be aware of causing confusion if you combine pages that have similar or different practicality.* When similar options are on the same page, small differences or what a function relates to can be unclear.

  One app I know merged two payment-related screens. On their own, it made sense that one page showed owed amounts as negative numbers and the other showed them as positive numbers. When combined into a single screen, it led to much confusion, as an owed amount that was previously shown as a negative number became a positive value to create consistency in the new screen.
- *If adding more to a screen, be careful to avoid negatively affecting the aesthetics of the app.* People perceive more aesthetically pleasing designs as easier to use, regardless of whether they are. The inverse is also true. People presume unappealing designs are difficult to use, and these create a negative feeling toward the app.

As a rule, small screens suit single tasks. When adding more to a screen that's larger, don't try to combine unrelated tasks or add more to a screen because there's more space available. It's OK not to fill every screen.

8.1.4 Respect standards and conventions

You may have noticed that most apps implement common functionality and page layouts in similar ways. They do this to help improve the intuitiveness of an app. When an app looks and behaves like other apps, people won't need to learn how to use another interface.

Daryl experimented with a few ideas early on in development. He wanted to use concepts from the world of music to give alternative ways of navigating the app. This included an image of instruments acting like a menu, where each represented a different area of the app. He remembered early websites taking a similar approach, but didn't get far with this idea for the same reasons the websites he remembered changed too—people want to use the app (or websites) to get to the information or functionality they need. They don't want to waste time working out how to use it.

Some behaviors have become the default, or de facto, standards. For example, it's now rare that anyone develops an app with a list that doesn't scroll vertically and with the most recent items at the top. When someone tries an alternative, feedback from the people using the app quickly stops this.

Pattern libraries are collections of common layouts and conventions. They show how many popular apps have solved the same design challenges and serve as a guide for your app. You'll find many online collections of such patterns, including www.mobile-patterns.com and http://pttrns.com. Unless you have good reasons for doing so, and you test variations thoroughly with the target audience for your app, you should avoid breaking such conventions. Even small variations can have negative effects. The person using your app might not be able to say what's wrong, but they'll notice when you do something different for no distinct benefit.

The final set of considerations for your app's visual output are those defined by the platforms on which your app will run. You can find online design guidelines at these sites:

- *Android*—https://developer.android.com/design
- *iOS*—https://developer.apple.com/design
- *Windows*—https://developer.microsoft.com/design

Each site has practical, specific guidance, as well as the principles that inform the style and design language. It isn't a requirement that every app follow the same visual style as the OS on which it runs. But if you do choose to follow a style with your app, you must follow it closely, or you'll end up with things that don't look or behave as the people using the app expect. This makes them unsure what the app might do.

Focus on the parts of design guidelines that also form part of the store's submission rules, so you don't waste time creating an app the store won't accept. For example, Apple will reject your app if the screens are poorly formatted, so the size and contrast of content make it hard to read. Other stores will let you have whatever UI you want, but this isn't an excuse for you to not care about it or to create something of low quality.

Put it into practice: visual fundamentals

- Understand and document the goals of the people using your app. These should be high-level goals of things they want to get from using the app and not how to use it. Evaluate your app against these goals, and address any inconsistencies.
- Verify consistency as part of your testing process. There should be no unexpected or unintended changes in the UI within the app or between releases.
- Familiarize yourself with the design guidelines and store submission rules for the platforms your app will run on.
- Regularly use devices like the ones your app will run on. Become familiar with the conventions and standards of the popular apps and platforms of those devices. You won't know if you're breaking expectations if you don't know what is "normal."

Exercise: visual fundamentals

Test your understanding of the last section by stating which of the options in the square brackets should be used to correctly complete the sentence:

1. Good visual output comes from focusing on [the person using the app|what's easiest to create].
2. The people using your app expect it to behave [like other apps they use|in new and innovative ways].
3. Handle different screen sizes by [always resizing the content|considering the impact on each view in the app and adjusting accordingly].
4. It's better for an app to look [the same on every device|like it matches the conventions of the device it's running on].
5. It's better to [follow common design patterns|not think about how the app looks|always try to invent something new].

8.2 Laying out controls on a screen

In this section, we move on from the theory of what should go in an app to the practice of positioning controls onscreen. The layout of controls can influence the intuitiveness of the UI by implying meaning and showing relationships. Four techniques available to do this are

- Alignment
- Hierarchy
- Consistency
- Proximity

The next sections delve into each of these techniques and show simple ways to make a big difference in your app's interface. Apply these techniques to give your app a more professional and refined appearance.

8.2.1 *Implying meaning and relationships through alignment and hierarchy*

Daryl originally had a single way of ordering information about events, but soon discovered this wasn't always best. Depending on the context, the details of the displayed item varied. Daryl used two simple ways to show the importance of an item onscreen:

- Positioning an item onscreen
- Adjusting its size and weight

If listing events by a single artist, it wasn't necessary for Daryl to repeat the artist's name in each entry, so the date and location of events were given priority by their positioning onscreen. Similarly, if listing events at a specific venue, then the venue name was omitted and the date and artist names were given prominence.

Hierarchy applies throughout the app, and not just on individual pages. Upon launching an app, important information and functionality should be easy to reach and not hidden behind several levels of navigation. People see items nearer the top first and assume them to be of higher importance. The same assumption applies to larger items. It therefore follows that the most important items should be larger and at the top of the screen.

It's a common mistake to try to indicate hierarchy with the use of alignment. A better use of alignment is to show a collective relationship. Figure 8.1 shows two versions

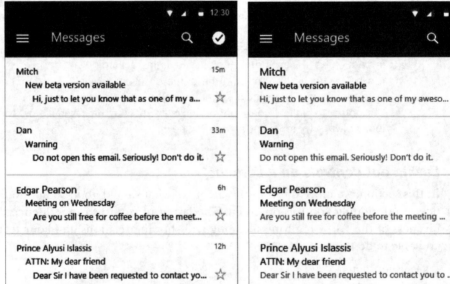

Here, indentation has been used to show hierarchy and associations between the different parts of each message.

Here, the size and weight of the text show the hierarchy of the parts of each message. Alignment indicates that each part is related. The left edge of each item is the same as the left edge of the title at the top of the page, to reinforce the relationship.

Figure 8.1 Avoid using indentation to show hierarchies. Instead, use a consistent alignment and variations in size and weight to indicate the order.

of part of an app displaying a list of messages. Both show the same information, but the way they present it is different.

In figure 8.1, the list on the left uses indentation to create a hierarchy between elements within an item. The sender is more important than the subject, which is more important than the message. The downside to using indentation is that it wastes space, makes scanning the list harder, and looks ragged and inconsistent. In contrast, the version on the right uses a consistent left alignment to show that each of the parts of the overall message (who sent it, what it says, and when it was sent) are related.

Rather than use indentation to reinforce the hierarchy of importance implied by the order, you can vary the size of the components to show this. In both examples, the name of the sender is the most important thing, so that comes first. That's because it's often enough for a person to know if they want to open an email from the sender. The same order won't always be appropriate for everything that's displayed, however.

Using a consistent left edge for all elements on the page reinforces the relationship between items, but it's also possible to use consistency to communicate more, as I discuss in the next section.

8.2.2 *Implying meaning and relationships through consistency*

If things look the same, it's natural to assume a similarity between them. Correspondingly, if something is visually different from its neighbors, there's an assumed difference in meaning or functionality, and it'll draw attention to itself. Your use of this knowledge will allow you to make content easier to scan and to direct the attention of the people using the app to anything new, important, or actionable.

Daryl used this principle in his app to change the styling of events that the user had indicated they were going to attend or of artists they had previously marked as favorites. This made it easier for the person using the app to identify the more important items in a list.

Figure 8.2 shows an app that aggregates messages from various systems. One of the messages from a system is visually different from the others, to draw the attention of the person using the app.

A consistent display of items ensures nothing stands out unintentionally, whereas deliberately making something different draws attention to it. In figure 8.2, although the basic styling of each message is similar, differences that show where the system message comes from help to indicate relationships between messages that aren't next to each other.

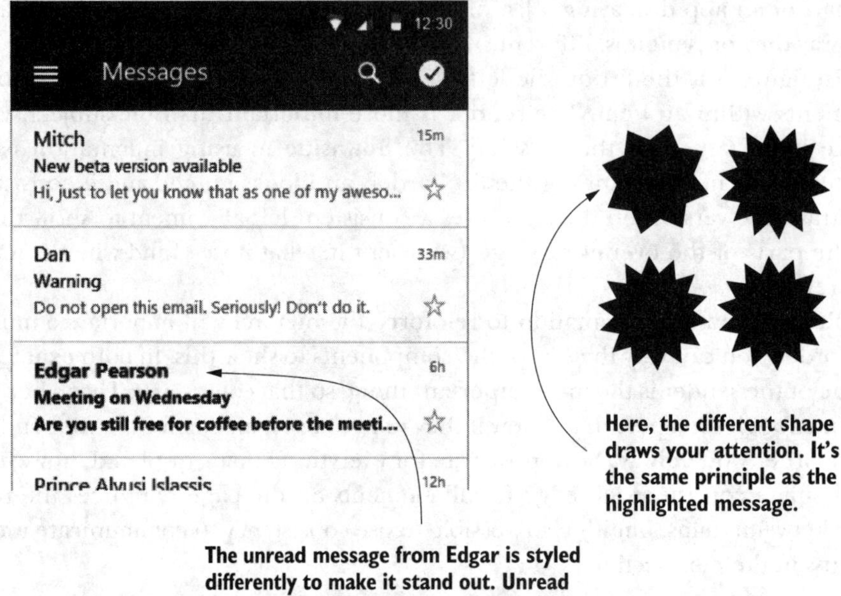

Here, the different shape draws your attention. It's the same principle as the highlighted message.
The unread message from Edgar is styled differently to make it stand out. Unread messages can be identified quickly.

Figure 8.2 Things stand out when visually different from the items around them.

8.2.3 Implying meaning and relationships through proximity

The final tool available for communicating meaning and relationships is based on the proximity of elements onscreen. People assume a relationship or similarity between items that are close together. A physical proximity implies a contextual proximity.

The image in figure 8.3 shows the options in an app that let a person interact with other people who use the app. This is an example of what not to do.

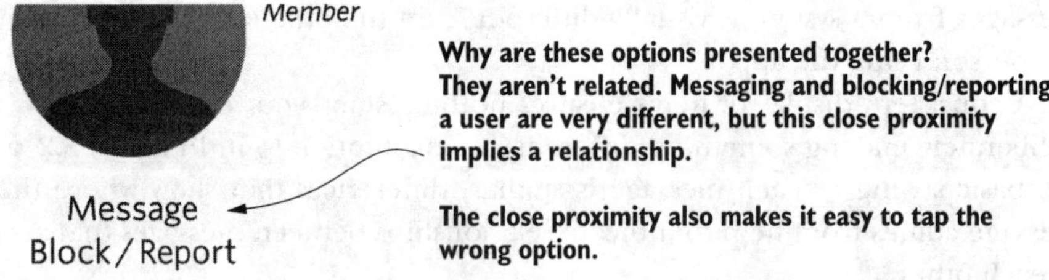

Member
Why are these options presented together? They aren't related. Messaging and blocking/reporting a user are very different, but this close proximity implies a relationship.
Message
Block / Report
The close proximity also makes it easy to tap the wrong option.

Figure 8.3 People assume items that are close together are related, even if they aren't.

As figure 8.3 shows, although the options available apply to a person who uses the system, they're fundamentally different in their actions. It's unusual for a person to look in the same place for options to send a message and to report or block a person for their misuse of the app. But by placing them close to each other in the app, the design implies they're related. Further, ignoring that the options are small or close together increases the likelihood of someone accidentally tapping something they didn't intend.

An unintentional, but unfortunately common, negative side effect of not considering proximity is when the space between items gives the appearance of groups of elements that don't exist. Figure 8.4 shows this.

The space between the picture and the name is larger than the space between other items on screen, suggesting little connection.
Kris Athi
Patrick Long
Pete Stensønes
Phil Trelford
Kris Athi
Patrick Long
Pete Stensønes
Phil Trelford
The images are closer to each other than they are to the names, giving the impression that the images are more closely related than the images and the names.
Putting the person's name close to the picture makes it clear that the two are related.

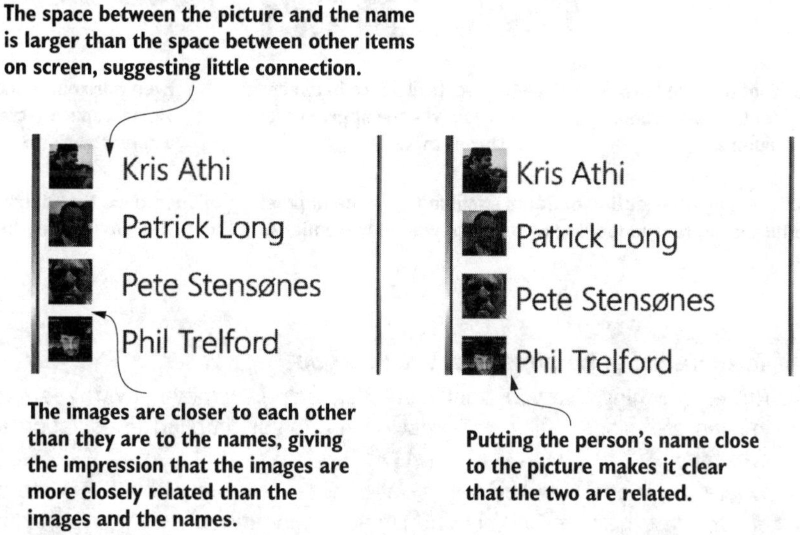

Figure 8.4 Part of a screen showing a list of people laid out in two ways. Differences in the spacing between the items and the parts of an item give the appearance of a column of images and another of names.

Association through proximity doesn't just apply to lists. Small differences in the horizontal and vertical spacing is another common issue. It can cause people to notice something is "off" with the display, but without being able to say what's wrong specifically.

The layouts in figure 8.5 each show images, but two layouts imply nonexistent grouping in the way they use whitespace. Larger differences can distract a person, who's trying to understand if there are subgroups in what they see. Or, it can cause them to wonder why there's so much whitespace between images rather than larger images.

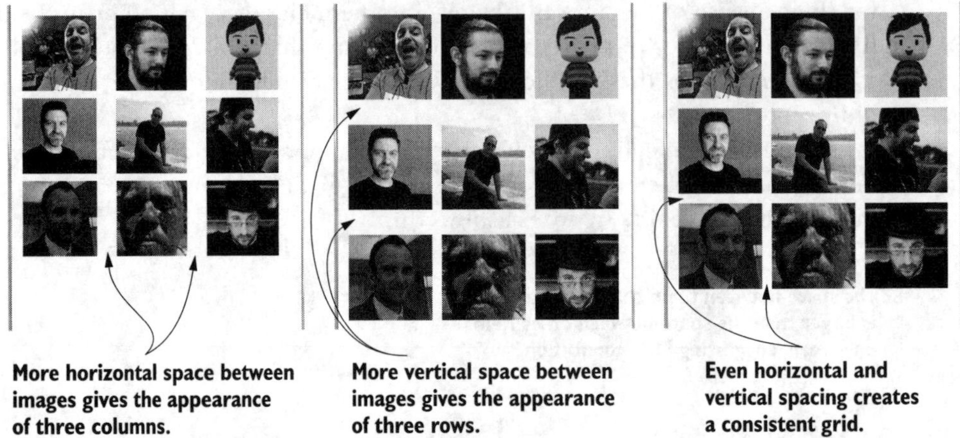

More horizontal space between images gives the appearance of three columns.
More vertical space between images gives the appearance of three rows.
Even horizontal and vertical spacing creates a consistent grid.

Figure 8.5 A single collection of items shouldn't give the impression of subgroups that don't exist. It risks confusing the person looking at the app, who may wonder why things are grouped as they are.

> **Put it into practice: be consistent with layout**
>
> - Review anything that you display in a list or grid. Remove any whitespace that implies groupings that don't exist or any falsely implied association due to proximity.
> - Where variations between items onscreen are shown with visual differences, ensure that the difference is enough so it's identifiable with a quick glance.
> - Use less whitespace within sub-elements of an item than between items. Ensure consistent spacing between groups to avoid the impression of subgroups that don't exist.

8.3 Navigating within the app

Few apps only have a single screen, so it's necessary to provide a way to navigate between them. In this section, I look at common patterns for navigating within an app and the special cases impacting navigation.

8.3.1 Common navigation patterns

When an app has multiple screens, it needs a way to navigate between them. In section 8.1.4, I mentioned how Daryl created an exploratory navigation pattern. He wanted people to tap on different items to see what would happen and what they would discover. If you remember, this was not a good navigational experience for people, because they found it uncertain and confusing.

Good navigation does two things: it aids discoverability and it provides signposting. *Discoverability* helps people find the content and functionality they need. *Signposting* helps people know where they're going and how to get back to where they've been. The following is a list of common patterns for structuring navigation within an app:

- *Stack*—A single page is shown at one time. People interact with content on the page to view related items sequentially. This pattern is also known as a *hub and spoke.*

  The main entry point for apps using this pattern is often a menu. If the app allows for navigating forward through multiple pages, a Back function enables return to a previous page. A stack pattern works well with pages that have a hierarchical relationship.
- *Tabs*—The screen is mostly filled with content, but a small horizontal area at the top or bottom of the screen (convention varies by platform) displays options for switching between different views of related items.

  A tab pattern works well for when there's a small number of options available, but the value of this layout declines when all options aren't visible. It's best used when people need to see the available options and functions, and need to switch between them quickly or frequently.
- *Drawer*—A menu for the app is hidden offscreen and only revealed by swiping from the edge, or, when requested, by tapping an icon (usually the hamburger menu icon). The contents of the drawer (so called because it slides out) can be fixed or can vary, based on who's using the app. Use this pattern when the app has many options and areas of functionality people may often switch between.
- *Master/Detail*—The screen is divided in two. On one side is a list of items and on the other is a detailed view of the selected item. The stack pattern is a fallback for this pattern when the screen isn't large enough to show both the list and the detail. This pattern is different from the drawer pattern; the drawer isn't permanently displayed and may hold dissimilar and unrelated items. Use the master/detail pattern for messaging and where a list has items viewable in more detail, but it won't lead to further navigation within the app.
- *Wizard*—Like stack navigation but used as a part of the functionality in an app when people won't want to go back through everything they've previously seen when they get to the end. Use a wizard for registration, tutorials, and payment/checkout processes.

By following common navigational patterns, you help people using the app easily find and access the information and functionality they want. You won't leave them wondering how they get to specific things, and you won't have to give instructions on how to use the app or explain where functionality is found.

TIP When providing text-based navigational options, use the language and terminology that the people using the app are familiar with, and do it in a consistent way.

If a person can't find the functionality they're looking for, it's as if it doesn't exist. As the number of features in an app grows, it's easy for specific items to become lost among all the options. Avoid scenarios like the one I experienced when trying to configure a podcast app on a new device in the same way it was configured on my previous device.

Because it was a highly configurable app, I wanted to keep all the various changes and tweaks I'd previously used. Unfortunately, the level of the configuration available came at the cost of navigation. After exploring the eight different submenus for the settings and reading through extensive help tips and documentation, I was starting to think what I wanted wasn't possible. At the same time, it was looking increasingly like I'd have to go and change them manually on the new device. Eventually, at the bottom of the Tools menu, I found options for Backup/Restore and Import/Export. With experimentation, I finally discovered I could import and export the list of podcasts from various locations, and I could back up and restore app-specific settings from a single connected cloud storage provider. I eventually achieved what I wanted with the app, but it was far from a simple process.

8.3.2 Special navigation considerations

Three navigation-related components need special consideration:

- Use of a Back button
- Use of a Home button
- How to handle a person returning to the app

As with the navigational patterns mentioned earlier, creating an intuitive experience that's easy to use depends on meeting the expectations of the people using the app. The following sections describe how a person's expectations relate to using these navigational components.

Use of a Back button

iOS is different from Android and Windows. iOS devices don't have a dedicated, built-in Back button. The other platforms have either a physical hardware button or a virtualized software button built into the UI provided by the OS.

On Windows, you don't need to create your own Back button, as one will already be available via a physical button or within the OS-provided UI. In an Android app, you can add a button for this. In an iOS app, you must add one where necessary. Regardless, the behavior of pressing your Back button should be identical to pressing the physical button if the device has one. If you do add a button to navigate backward within the app:

- Place the Back button in the top left of the screen.
- Display it only if it's possible to navigate back within the app itself.
- Don't allow it to close the app or switch between other open apps, and don't display it if pressing it does nothing.

It's also necessary to distinguish between Back, Cancel, and Save buttons (where Save is a positive action equivalent to Submit, Confirm, and so on). Moving backward is a purely navigational action and shouldn't trigger any other behavior or action. Save and Cancel are options that require an action be taken, but are often combined with navigation similar to going back. If using an app to edit some data

- The Save button will persist the changes and return to the non-editable version.
- The Cancel button will discard any changes and return to the non-editable version.
- With the Back button, it's not clear what will happen to any changes.

Fortunately, these simple rules will prevent logic from becoming complicated:

- Don't show a button for moving back if also showing Save and Cancel options, as it raises questions and potential confusion about how it's different from the other options.
- A multi-step process may need a Back button, but be sure to test if the meanings of all options are clear to the people using the app.
- If showing Save and Cancel options, treat the hardware Back button like Cancel.
- Don't put the Save button in a location otherwise occupied by the Back button.
- If putting the Cancel button in the same position as the Back button, make it visibly different to show the dissimilar functionality tapping it will invoke.

Use all buttons consistently, not just the one for moving back between screens. When a popular messaging app moved the position of the Send button, the reason for the change didn't matter. The fact that the button was no longer where it had been (a less common option was now in its place), and that the Send button wasn't in the same place as in other apps, led my wife, justifiably, to call the change "stupid." This told her something about the company that makes the app: it's willing to make what seemed like arbitrary changes to the app regardless of the consequences to the people using it. Few apps are indispensable enough to keep people from investigating alternatives when made to feel as though the company behind an app doesn't care about them or their experiences.

USE OF A HOME BUTTON

Website design had a strong influence on early mobile app design. The top-level navigation menu and the use of breadcrumbs to show the position within an app are unnecessary with the navigation patterns shown previously. But the idea of a top-level Home link that's available on each screen is still appealing to many. The idea of always having a simple way for a person to be able to get to any part of the app is likewise appealing, but flawed.

If people genuinely need to jump between disparate parts of an app, this shows the contents of the app aren't structured in a way that meets the needs of the people who'll use it. If you add a Home button because you don't know how people will use the app and which parts will be important to them or most often used together, this shows a need for more research with the people who'll use the app.

The common navigational patterns remove the need for a general-purpose Home button in an app, but a similar concept is necessary when the person using the app would otherwise be left at a dead end. Never leave the person using your app wondering, "What do I do now?" or, "Where do I go from here?" If your app includes a multistep process, such as payment/checkout or data submission, you may be tempted to end with a screen that shows the person has finished. What should they do when viewing such a screen?

Forcing someone to press a Back button to move forward with using the app is never a good idea. If there's no logical next step within the app or other, relevant functionality to display instead, only then is it permissible to present a way to take the person back to the main entry point of the app by using a Home button or equivalent. Another occasion when a Home button may be acceptable is as a way to handle someone returning to the app.

HANDLING A PERSON RETURNING TO THE APP

People often use multiple apps to complete a single task. They can be switching to access data they'll copy into another app or directly launching one app from another. When people are rapidly moving between apps as part of a single task, it's necessary to maintain the state of the app so the person can carry on from where they left off previously. When there's some time between a person leaving and returning to the app, what's right requires considering several factors:

- How long has it been since they last launched the app? The longer it's been, the less likely it is that maintaining context since the last launch is correct.
- Which part of the app were they viewing when they left?
- If content changes often, will what was being viewed previously still be relevant or appropriate?
- Were there changes in connectivity that prevented a person from continuing a task even if displayed?
- Were there changes in the availability of functionality in the app that can make it inappropriate to try to return to the state where the person last left? (An upgrade to the app between launches can change or even remove what was being accessed previously.)
- What is the context of launching the app on this occasion? If the app is being launched as the result of a deep link or to access specific functionality, this is more important than whatever was being viewed previously.
- How hard is it for a person to re-enter something if not saved by the app?

A hybrid approach here is the other time it's permissible to include a Home button: when you launch the app and return the person to deep within a complex navigational hierarchy. In that case, you can also add a shortcut option to return them to the main page in the app. It can be appealing to define a simple rule about always doing the same thing upon launching the app, but this isn't what's always best for the people using it, and will degrade the experience for some of the people who do use it.

Put it into practice: in-app navigation

- Pay special attention to devices that have a Back button provided by the platform and how that works in combination with a Back (or equivalent) button presented in the UI.
- Remove any unnecessary Home buttons from your apps.
- If you treat a person returning to the app in the same way as when launching it, review the analytics on what they do in each situation and gather feedback on which behavior they prefer.

Exercise: navigation

Test your understanding of the last section by filling in the blanks in the following paragraph:

Good navigation aids _____ and provides _____ to help the user know what's possible and where they are. By following common navigational _____, you'll help people find and access the information and functionality they want. Give special consideration to handling the _____ and _____ buttons, and when someone _____ to the app.

8.4 Avoiding discrimination with what you display

When creating the UI for your app, it's easy to get caught up in how it looks, but there are other considerations:

- Offering additional assistance for those who need it
- Communicating consistently around the world

Depending on where in the world your app is used, there may be legal requirements that affect the accessibility of your app. But that's not the only reason to avoid creating an app that can only be used by a subset of the potential user base.

8.4.1 Ensure your UI works for everybody

An awareness of the differences in physical abilities between people is important when considering the UI for your app. Here are four things to consider:

- *Do parts of the app rely solely on color to communicate information?* If they do, they shouldn't. This isn't only significant to anyone who suffers from an ability to distinguish between colors (often called *color blindness*); it also helps in poor lighting conditions. Communicating information in more than one way also helps make it more obvious and aids a person using the app while distracted.
- *Can the app be used with the screen covered and with a screen reader enabled?* Your app should be usable in this way. If you don't know how to enable and use a screen reader with your app, consider this the time to learn how.

- *Do the people using your app need high-contrast or high-DPI settings?* Your app should be usable with these settings. These settings aren't just for those with severe vision impairment, and you should provide support for them.
- *Are there potential health risks associated with your app?* More of an issue for games, but any app that uses flashing or flickering images risks causing seizures for anyone who has photosensitive epilepsy. If you can't remove them from the app, include a configurable setting to disable them for those affected. Include appropriate warnings when the app is first used, or disable affected functionality by default to avoid any unwanted lawsuits.

When creating an app that can be used by the widest range of people globally, these are all important factors. The one that developers often think of first is translation and localization. The translation of text is just a part of communicating with people in different languages and cultures, and that's what's covered next.

8.4.2 Saying the same thing to everybody who uses the app

When thinking about the way the UI communicates with the people who'll use it, consider these questions:

- Does it use the same terminology?
- Is it in a language spoken by the users?
- Do the colors and imagery match expectations?

If you don't use the same words, terminology, or jargon as the people who'll use the app, you risk confusing them. If an app is for a special purpose or for an industry, it must use the appropriate terms for those situations. This may mean that the developers of that app need to immerse themselves in that industry or special purpose and become familiar with it before they can create the app. Contrary to that, if an app is to be used by a broad range of people, it should avoid any jargon, complicated terms, or specialist language, so it's easy to use. And, if people who speak different languages will use your app, your design needs to allow for differences in the lengths of translations.

NOTE Exercise care when obtaining translations. The translation performed by an automated service may not allow for an implied meaning to be clear in the translation, and you could end up with something different in meaning.

The only way to be confident of translations is if the people who do them are familiar with the language and the culture where it's spoken. If not, you may end up with an app that talks about giving people a "gift" in German or a "kiss" in Sweden, where they mean "poison" and "pee," respectively. You'll find more on translations in chapter 3.

Beyond words, colors have meaning and associations that vary by culture. Purple is often associated with wealth and royalty, but in some cultures wearing purple is used to indicate mourning. In the West, mourning is shown by wearing black; in parts of Asia, the convention is to wear white; and in South Africa, people wear red. Red is the color of wedding dresses in Asia, although they're traditionally white in the rest of the world. This isn't a complete list, but if your app depicts people in distinctly colored clothing, it's important to be aware of the need to account for what this might suggest to the people using the app.

It's not just the color of clothing you need to account for. Use all colors carefully. For most of the world, pink has feminine and blue has masculine associations, but it's the reverse in parts of China with less influence from other parts of the world. Also of note is the use of the term *yellow books* to refer to all forms of pornography. This specific knowledge is particularly important if you're making an e-reader app, but the need to consider the possibility of different associations applies to all.

IMPORTANT Check for unintended meanings and cultural associations for all the places where your app will be available by testing with people in those places and with those who speak the local language/dialect.

Put it into practice: avoid discrimination

- Support system settings relating to DPI or color schemes (including high contrast).
- Try using the app with a screen reader. Ensure that all functionality is usable.
- Ensure that nothing in the app is only indicated by a change in color.
- When using color, check the meaning of that color in the countries where you'll distribute your app.

8.5 Many factors affect the display of images

In this section, I focus on images. After text, images are the second most common element to display in an app, and, therefore, justify special attention. The images you display in your app are important. They can improve aesthetics, communicate context, and provide information. Few apps include no images at all, and for all other apps, there are many factors to consider. When the images in an app look bad, it reflects badly on the app.

8.5.1 One size doesn't fit all

Images are often a key part of the content displayed in an app, but they're not always easy to work with. Daryl's app sourced content from a wide range of sources. Artist images were displayed prominently in many parts of the app, and those images could be up to 11 different sizes. The available sizes covered a variety of physical dimensions and aspect ratios depending on where they were from and their original intended use. Not all images were available in all sizes, and the design of the app called for the use of different sizes of images. Ensuring that the images always looked good was not a simple task.

If you're fortunate enough to be in the position where you have different versions of an image to choose from, use the version that most closely matches the size and aspect ratio where it will be displayed. Manipulating an image before displaying it takes time, wastes networking and processing resources, and often results in displaying something of low quality. Minimize these negative side effects by carefully considering how you scale, crop, and stretch images.

It's common that you won't have an image that matches the aspect ratio of the space where you want to display it. Figure 8.6 shows three ways of manipulating a rectangular image for display in a square space. But, on their own, none give a consistent approach you can automatically apply to every scenario.

This original image has an aspect ratio of 3:2, but a square version (aspect ratio 1:1) is required.

Adding padding to the original image to achieve the desired aspect ratio wastes space.

Stretching the image distorts it.

Cropping and centering may result in losing important information from the edges of the original.

Figure 8.6 Different approaches to change the aspect ratio of an image. No one method will always give the best result.

Never stretch an image to match a different aspect ratio, as this distorts what's displayed and makes it look unrealistic or hard to see the detail. Padding can waste a lot of space, depending on the differences in aspect ratios of the original and target image sizes. Even cropping can result in losing too much information from the original. Although cropping can result in the loss of crucial details, it's generally the best approach upon which to base an image manipulation solution, but you can't use arbitrary alignment rules. Even with the simple image of a single person, it isn't possible to guarantee the best results by centering or aligning to an edge, as seen in figure 8.7.

When the difference between the length of the sides is greater, more of the original image will be lost and the quality of the output is lower. Consider needing a square

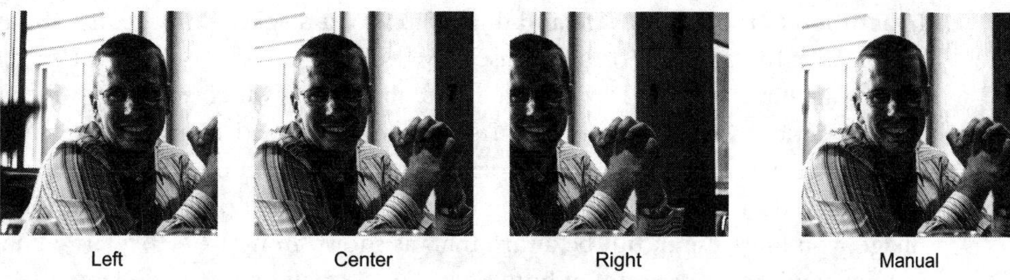

Cropping to the left, center, or right produces a different image and loses different parts of the original. The manually cropped version produces the most desirable result but requires more effort.

Figure 8.7 Automatically cropping an image regardless of the position of the key elements within won't consistently produce the best results.

version of a wide picture containing two people's faces. If you crop to either side, you only get one face, or if you use the middle you get half of each face. So, as far as possible, design the layout of an interface to display images in the same aspect ratios as the originals.

For images shown in a variety of sizes, manually resizing each is undesirable and unnecessary. Online services offering image processing, and powered by artificial intelligence, can now provide versions of a source image to meet your specific needs. They're also able to crop and resize images, keeping the most important elements in view. When needing a smaller image, this avoids cropping faces and makes them more prominent.

If your app allows people to upload or capture images at a different size or aspect ratio to what will be displayed, use one of the many SDKs and libraries available to resize and crop the image accordingly. This is a factor for images used as avatars or to otherwise represent the person to other people who use the app. Don't make people look bad without a way for them to change it.

If I wanted to show a small version of the square avatar created above, it wouldn't be clear. Instead, it's better to create a separate image that focuses on the most important element in the original image (in this case, my face) and crops the image differently, as shown in figure 8.8.

When you need a smaller version of an image, you'll get a clearer final image by focusing on the most important part of the original (in this case, the face).

Figure 8.8 Creating a clear, but smaller version of an image is unlikely to be achieved by scaling down the whole image; instead, reduce the amount that's shown, which produces a clearer image.

In addition to the relative size and dimensions of a displayed image, it's also necessary to consider the number of pixels used by the image and the screen. Use versions of images at all resolutions appropriate to the devices on which your app will run.

On devices with high-resolution screens, you'll need to use high-resolution versions of images. Development platforms for the common operating systems have simple ways to do this based on naming conventions. If you only have one version of an image, you must use it, but be aware that, as shown in figure 8.9, a large image made smaller tends to work better at both sizes than a small image made larger.

A large image scaled down works better at both sizes.
A small image made larger can look blocky or blurry.

Figure 8.9 Avoid using small images made larger as they look blurry or blocky. Large images made smaller are better, but it's best to have versions of images in different sizes.

8.5.2 Physical size isn't everything: consider formats and formatting too

Consider the format of an image as well as the number of pixels it's made up of. Different formats are more suitable for different types of images and are supported by different platforms. The format of an image impacts

- Clarity and the ability to display at different sizes
- The size on disk and in memory
- The speed with which it can be loaded
- How well it supports compression
- The number of colors it can include

Daryl's app ran on many platforms and devices. In order to do that, it needed eight different versions of all images to ensure satisfactory display across all the devices. By switching to a vector format for his graphics, he could use a single file that created a clear image regardless of the device it was on. Having one version of each image, instead of eight, meant that it was quicker to create and change images. It also reduced the overall size of the app package. Plus, the different image formats could be processed and loaded more quickly by the platform the app was running on. Having a smaller app that ran faster and was quicker to build and update was better for all involved.

Support for displaying different numbers of colors can also be an issue on some devices that are older and of a lower specification. The effect on complex images or images with gradients is also more noticeable. Figure 8.10 shows a simple gradient as seen when created with fewer colors or on a device that's only able to display less colors.

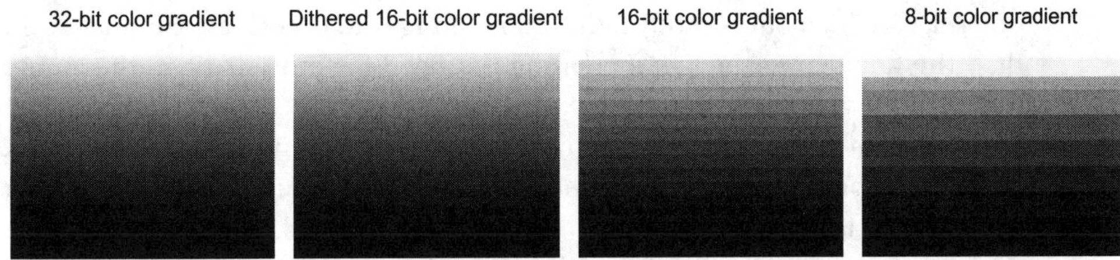

A simple gradient can appear to have lines or bands when the platform or screen is unable to show lots of color variations. Dithering (adding noise to the image) can improve the appearance without requiring more colors.

Figure 8.10 Reducing the number of colors an image includes creates the same effect as viewing the image on a device that doesn't support many colors. This is most noticeable with images having complex visuals or gradients.

Fortunately, you're unlikely to encounter a device that's only capable of displaying 8-bit graphics, or need to try to use as few colors as an 8-bit image supports, but devices with 16-bit screens are still in use. If you need to display a gradient on such a device, dithering the image (adding visual noise) hides the banding effect. The following guidelines will help you choose the best format to use for an image:

- Use WEBP files for photos if the device supports it.
- Use JPG/JPEG files for photos where WEBP isn't supported.

For images that aren't photos, use these formats (most preferred first):

- Use vector-based formats (for example, SVG) if possible.
- If you can't use a vector format, use WEBP if supported on the devices/platform the app will run on.
- If the platform your app is on doesn't support WEBP, use PNG.
- If you can't use PNG, use GIF if it's supported.
- As a final resort, and if supported, use BMP. (Note that BMP files don't support transparency, but SVG, WEBP, and GIF formats do.)

If you're not familiar with it, WEBP is a format created by Google. It's optimized to provide an image with as good a quality as an equivalent JPEG, but with a smaller file size. Regardless of the format used, optimize image files to reduce their size without affecting the quality of the image.

8.5.3 Customizing image placeholders

For images loaded from a remote source, there will often be a period when the app is displaying content without the images. It's better to show content without images than to force a person to wait for all the images to load before they see anything. Leaving a blank space or a random block of color is easy but doesn't look great. There are simple ways for you to do better.

It's tempting to try to load a smaller version of an image while waiting for the larger one to download. Displaying a blurry image that's later replaced with a clearer one is a nice idea but is rarely best. It takes longer to download the smaller image and then the final, larger image, increasing the need for more logic in the app to handle multiple downloads.

Instead of needing an extra download or using a random color as a placeholder, Pinterest popularized the technique of using the dominant colors of each image as a placeholder until it loads. This adds variety and visual interest to what's displayed onscreen before the images load (figure 8.11).

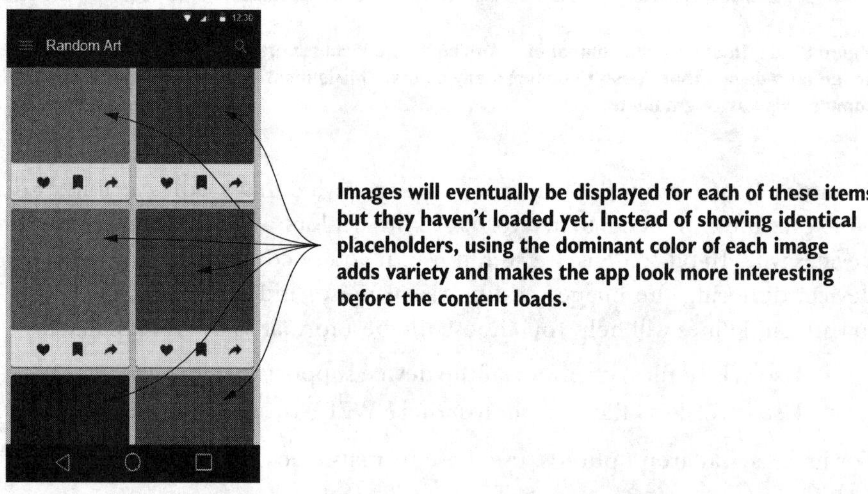

12:30
Random Art
Images will eventually be displayed for each of these items, but they haven't loaded yet. Instead of showing identical placeholders, using the dominant color of each image adds variety and makes the app look more interesting before the content loads.

Figure 8.11 Using different colors as placeholders for images that have yet to load creates visual interest.

Using unique colors as placeholders is easy to do by including the `imageColor` property in the original data payload. The following listing also includes the address of the image (`imageUrl`) to display.

Listing 8.1 Data with placeholder information to use before the image loads

```
{
"user": {
   "name": "Matt Lacey",
   "imageUrl": "http://example.com/images/3764532146873248932.jpg",
   "imageSize": "960x640",
   "imageColor": "AF927F",
   "imagePlaceholder":
    ["EAEAE3","F9F7F3","BD9586","E8E8E0","AB8255","956537","C2C4BC","F5F5F6"
    ,"8E4135","E5DAD1","AC8257","906738","B3B0A4","ABA4AA","7D4535","DDb18D"
    ,"A04D18","89633D","9D929A","B0B7C4","654033","C0977E","9D6043","583A28"
    ],
   ..... // other properties omitted
  }
}
```

The dominant color in the image is returned for use as a background until the image is loaded.

Hex values for pixels in a low-resolution version of the image are usable as a placeholder until the image loads.

The `imagePlaceholder` entry in listing 8.1 allows for creating an image like the right-most picture in figure 8.12.

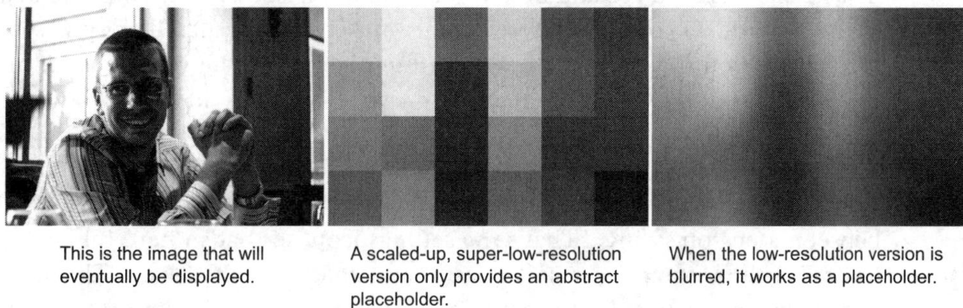

This is the image that will eventually be displayed.

A scaled-up, super-low-resolution version only provides an abstract placeholder.

When the low-resolution version is blurred, it works as a placeholder.

Figure 8.12 Using a blurred version of a low-resolution copy of an image makes an excellent placeholder until the final image can be displayed.

Blurred low-resolution placeholders are a variation of a technique first documented by Facebook. The idea is to return information for the individual pixels that make up a low-resolution version of the final image and display them with a blurred effect until the final image loads. This works well for a small number of background images, but don't use it for large numbers of images, due to the extra processing needed by the app.

When it comes to displaying images within an app, there's lots to consider, and it's best to think about each on an individual basis. For any non-trivial app, it's rare to be able to apply the same formatting, modifications, treatments, and customization to all images. You'll need to give extra consideration to a special group of images used in apps: icons. We'll look at those next.

> **Put it into practice: displaying images**
>
> - Create strategies for working with images you don't generate or whose size you don't control.
> - Optimize the physical size(s) of the images you include with the app at design time so you don't need to adjust these in the app when it's running.
> - Review the image file formats for the types and sizes of the images you're showing in the app. If possible, switch to ones that are smaller and load faster.
> - Ensure you're using image placeholders for any remotely loaded images.

8.6 Use distinct icons with specific meanings

Pictures are superior to words in many ways. Not only do they communicate more in less space (as a picture is worth a thousand words), but they're easier to recognize. You'll also avoid potential issues with inconsistent levels of literacy and the languages spoken by the people using the app. Using icons instead of (or in addition to) text makes apps easier to use and understand, but doing so needs attention to detail.

Because the OS of the device and other apps people are familiar with use icons, it's crucial that you use the same ones consistently. Even small variations can introduce the idea of the *uncanny valley* at a micro-level. This is the idea that something looks wrong, but a person can't say exactly what.

Consider the different versions of the standard icon for representing settings shown in figure 8.13. Using the standard one for the platform is the difference between a person saying, "That's the settings icon, so that's where I'll tap," or, "That looks like the settings icon, so I guess that's what I should select." This is the difference between a person having confidence in the app and how it works, instead of having doubts and uncertainty.

Any of these five icons could be used to represent settings, but only one is correct in an Android app. Can you tell which?

Figure 8.13 When an app doesn't use a distinct and specific visual style, it should use the actual versions of standard icons. Even small variations can cause uncertainty for the person using the app, as they pause to question the differences.

If your app uses a distinct, custom visual style, you'll need to create modified versions of standard icons. The icons should have the same basic image, updated to reflect the visual style and design of your app, but be sure not to change the underlying image. Continuing with the settings example, if your app used narrow lines and outlines for all icons, the settings icon should be a cog drawn in such a way. You shouldn't use a different image (for example, a series of switches) to represent a standard concept.

If creating versions of icons specific for your app, you'll need to do this for all the icons. You'll also need to create versions of each icon for all the different sizes you need for it to display clearly on all devices your app will run on. Creating icons in a vector format or as part of a custom typeface are popular ways of avoiding the need to create multiple files and still allow for different display requirements. Here are a few other guidelines for the use of icons you need to be aware of:

- Never have different versions of the same icon in different parts of the app.
- Never use the same icon to represent different things in different parts of the app.
- Never use a standard icon for a different purpose.

It's also wise to avoid using multiple icons that are conceptually similar. Consider the part of the app shown in figure 8.14. All the icons it displays for interacting with a specific piece of content are standard, but it's potentially confusing to see them all together when a lot of what they do is similar. Having fewer options makes it clearer what each is for and makes your app simpler to use.

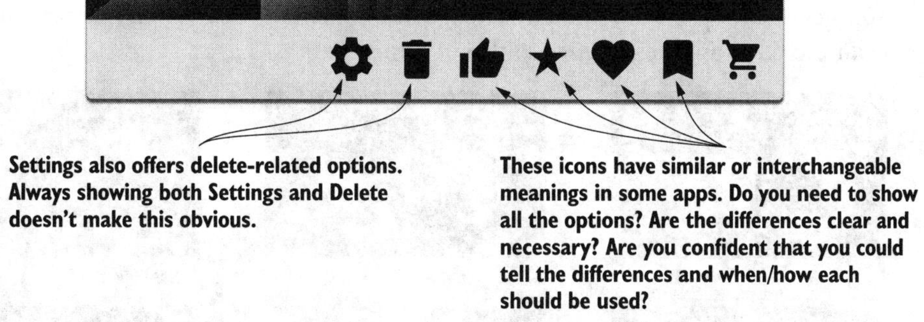

Settings also offers delete-related options. Always showing both Settings and Delete doesn't make this obvious.
These icons have similar or interchangeable meanings in some apps. Do you need to show all the options? Are the differences clear and necessary? Are you confident that you could tell the differences and when/how each should be used?

Figure 8.14 Even standard icons are confusing if given in large numbers and if it's unclear how they're different.

Icons need to be clear. Because of the size at which icons are displayed, they shouldn't include words or numbers, as the small size makes them hard to read. But, based on your testing and received feedback, you may need to add textual labels next to the icon to aid clarity. It's better to have text next to an icon to explain what it does rather than relying on a person to tap it to see what happens. When displaying many icons but where space is limited, it's common to exclude the text, having it displayed only when space allows or in response to a request from the person using the app.

> **Put it into practice: be iconic**
> If using icons like those that are native to the platform the app is running on, ensure that you're using the exact same icons, not just ones that look similar.

8.7 Allow for extremes of connectivity and content

Your app's interface will need to adapt to a variety of circumstances. If the app allows for the input of data or the retrieval of information from a remote source, you must deal with variations in that data. This includes allowing for

- Partial content that takes a long time to load
- Partial content that never loads or is otherwise unavailable
- An entire screen's worth of content that doesn't load or even exist

In this final section, I cover scenarios where you may not be able to display everything you want in the way you want. If you only design the UI for perfect content, you may miss these important scenarios.

8.7.1 Content that loads slowly or doesn't load at all

When an app has a lot of image-rich content but must load that content over a slow connection, people will end up using an app without images displayed. For the people for whom this is the case, whether regularly or occasionally, they'll benefit from and appreciate an app that's designed to work in such a scenario. Figure 8.15 shows an example of an app designed with this in mind.

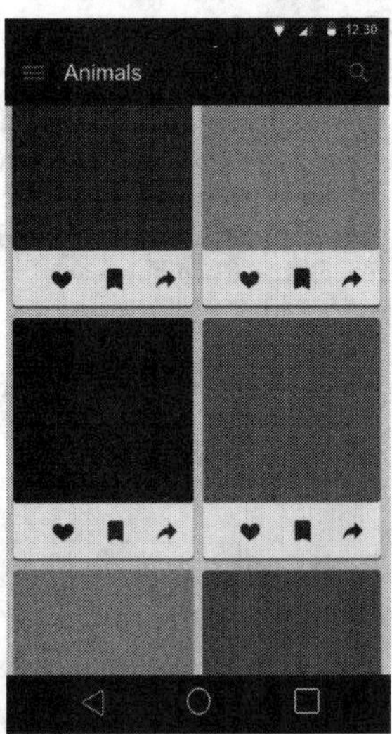

Without the images, you have to guess what each item represents.

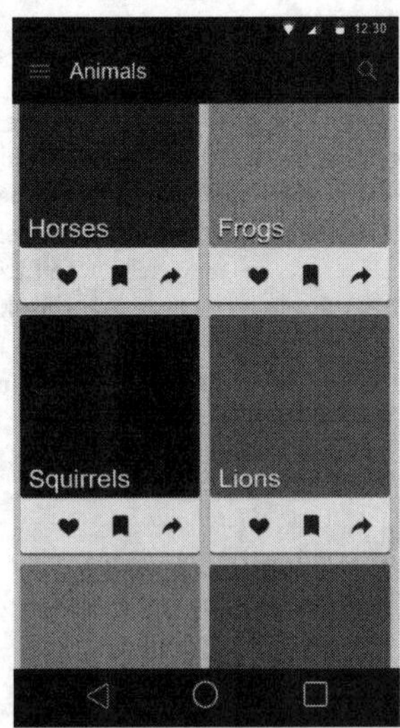

Adding text makes the options clear, even without images.

When the images are loaded, the text adds clarity.

Figure 8.15 Ensuring apps are usable even if images can't load is beneficial in many scenarios and doesn't detract when they do.

Advertisements are another form of content that may not load. For many reasons, banner ads won't display as expected (for example, if a device is offline, there are no ads to serve, or the user has an ad blocker installed). If there's no ad to display, it's a waste of screen space and can be potentially confusing when space not occupied by the ad isn't used for content instead.

8.7.2 *When content isn't available*

When there's no content to load, but space is reserved for that content, you need to preempt any questions about why that's the case. Figure 8.16 shows two versions of a list of people displaying their name and image.

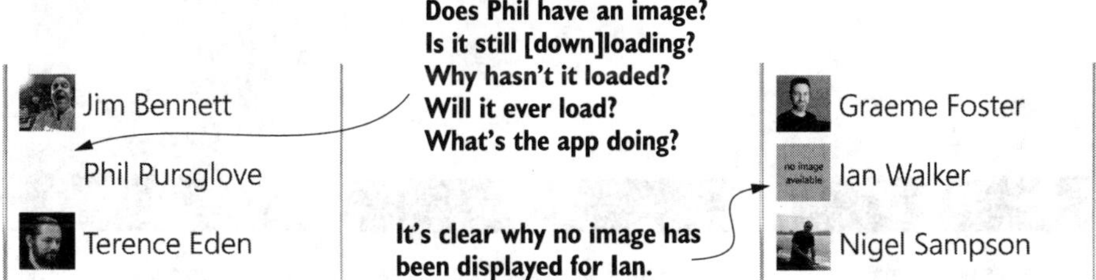

Figure 8.16 Make it clear if something is still loading or is not available.

In the leftmost version, it's not clear why there isn't an image available for each person. Should there be one? Is there a problem? Is it still loading? And if it's still loading, why is it taking so long? The image on the right avoids all those questions.

8.7.3 *Avoiding empty states*

Reasons you may not be able to show any content onscreen include these:

- The content comes from an external source and cannot load.
- The person using the app has yet to enter anything.
- There's nothing to show.

Where content is only available from an external source that can't be reached or doesn't return anything to display, and if the remote source doesn't include alternative actions to take or instructions to display, your app should show how to trigger downloading the content again. If the person using the app will enter content, you need to consider what happens in the app when there's no content to display. This can happen at various times in the use of an app, but is most common when a person uses the app for the first time. Ensure that you never display an empty screen without explaining why it's empty and what to do about it. Figure 8.17 shows some examples.

This screen gives no information and only leads to questions: Why are no messages displayed? Should some be shown? Are they still loading? Is there a problem?

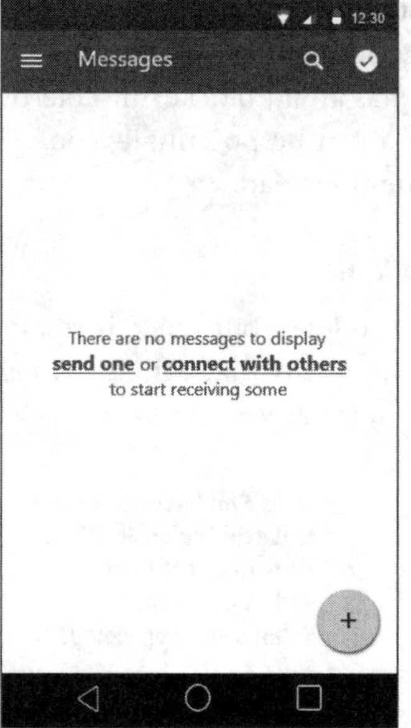

This screen acknowledges that no messages are shown but isn't clear why. By providing actions, it encourages the user to keep using the app and engage further with it and other people.

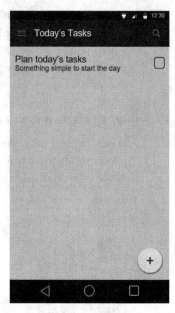

This app automatically adds a default task to each list so it's never empty. The app thus avoids any possible issues with empty lists.

Figure 8.17 Never leave the screen empty. If displaying nothing, explain why and give clear actions for adding content or attempting to reload it.

A lack of content doesn't only occur when the user hasn't entered anything. The app might not have anything to show. A common scenario where this is the case is the search results for a term that has no matches.

Empty states are another form of a dead end. As mentioned in section 8.3.2, dead ends stop the person using the app and force them to think about what to do next. As long as it's appropriate and possible, your app should keep presenting content to the person using it to prevent them from asking what to do next. A good answer to such a question might be to use someone else's app.

> **Put it into practice: empty states**
>
> If people are unable to load content, ensure that you display alternatives or instructions for accessing the missing information.

Exercise: handling extremes

Test your understanding of the last section by stating whether the following are true or false:

1. You need to design your app for when it has data or no data.
2. It's important to distinguish between content that doesn't exist and that which hasn't loaded yet.
3. Never show an empty page or list without acknowledging that it's empty.

The UI of an app is a large contributing factor to the experience of people using it. But, as you'll see in the next chapter, the output not displayed within the app plays a significant part too.

Summary

- Answering questions before they're asked is the basis of a simple, intuitive app. You can do this with what you show onscreen.
- Keep the person who'll use the app in mind when designing the UI of your app. Meeting their goals and needs is more important than what you want to show or display.
- The people who use your app come with a set of expectations about how an app should look and work. Follow the conventions of the platforms on which your app will run.
- Your app will be used on devices with different size screens. You'll need to allow for content to be sized, scaled, aligned, and laid out differently. A single, pixel-perfect layout can't be used for all devices.
- Structure the content on each screen so it follows a natural hierarchy with the most important items first.
- The alignment and proximity of elements onscreen communicates about the relationships between items.
- The consistent use of style shows the similarity between items. Break the consistency to draw attention to specific items.
- Standard navigational patterns make it easy for people to find what they want within an app. Using something different can make it hard for people to understand or find what they're looking for.
- Buttons that represent Back, Home, Cancel, Save, and Submit all have similarities, but they also represent important and separate functions. Using the wrong one can lead to confusion for the person using your app.
- Enabling people with limited or no vision, or those who speak a different language, to use your app is important for reaching as many potential users as possible.

- The images displayed in an app will need to be resized and cropped to fit the screen and available space. There's rarely a single approach you can apply to all images.
- Don't leave an empty space while waiting for images to display. Use a placeholder to show where they'll appear.
- Using standard icons for standard behaviors makes it easier for someone to understand the icon's meaning. Don't use similar icons or reuse or repurpose existing icons.
- Indicate when data or images aren't available. Don't leave a space, or you'll create uncertainty over whether something should be displayed.
- Avoid empty states. Your app should never show an empty screen or list without showing why it's empty and how or when something will be displayed there.

9 Non-visible output

This chapter covers

- Allowing for output beyond what's shown onscreen
- Creating output for other apps and hardware
- Creating effective notifications
- Using different channels to give output

If we think of the use of an app as a conversation with the person operating it, input is what the person says, and output is what the app says and does. Just as a conversation between two people involves more than words, a conversation with an app can involve more than displaying things on a screen.

Imagine you and I are talking in person. If I spoke in a monotone voice without moving or showing emotion or any facial expressions, it'd be odd and disconcerting. This is like an app that only outputs to a screen. Now consider a conversation where I'm visibly and audibly engaged and enthusiastic about what you're saying, and I later come back with further questions and information about what you've been talking about. It would be a more pleasant conversation, and you'd see I'm keen to engage with you. That's the conversational equivalent of an app that considers output beyond what's shown onscreen.

Output can also extend beyond the app and the person using it. A conversation between you and I can lead to me going and talking to someone else about the same subject, or passing on some information you've shared. A person's use of an app may also lead to the app producing output that's sent to other parties. In this chapter, I show you how to create an app that enables a rich conversation with the person using it by

- Including physical and audio output
- Sending output to other apps
- Showing appropriate output even when the app isn't running
- Communicating in other ways

Throughout this chapter, I'll also tell you about Kirstie and the lessons she learned from building apps for use within a retailer. These apps covered all aspects of the business, including distribution, warehousing, and the shop floor.

9.1 Physical and audio output support changes onscreen

We start this chapter by looking at the use of different senses to interact with an app. We interact with our environments using multiple senses; the same should be true of the way people interact with your app.

Apps can interact with three of the five senses of the people using them. Devices don't yet come with the ability to create smells or tastes, so you don't need to consider these. I'm not sure how people would feel about sniffing or licking their phones. When Steve Jobs said Apple made items onscreen "…look so good, you'll want to lick them," this isn't what he meant. Of the other senses, I discussed sight in the last chapter as it's related to what's shown onscreen. In this section, I'm going to talk about how your app can interact with the senses of hearing, by considering the sounds it makes, and touch, through physical interaction.

9.1.1 Give your app a voice

Don't leave your app silent. Audible feedback should accompany important visual information onscreen. Adding this is part of giving your app a voice. But like anyone learning to speak, you must also learn to speak at the right time and in a suitable fashion. The way your app communicates with the person using it has a lot of parallels with a conversation between two people:

- You can communicate more clearly with words and sounds, rather than by just looking.
- Certain sounds have specific meanings. Using them for something else can be confusing.

In a busy environment full of distractions, it can be easy to miss something. If you and I were both in a crowded room, you might not notice me waving to try and get your attention. But if I also shouted your name, the sound would indicate to you that there was something for you to be aware of, so you'd look around and see me waving.

A similar scenario exists with apps. If something important happens in an app, an appropriate sound can serve as an additional cue that there's something that requires your attention. Don't use sounds to alert a person to a problem, or when something has changed, but do use them to confirm an action (such as pressing a button), send a message, or change a setting.

The use of sound isn't the only way to communicate information; it serves as a complement. Just as shouting and waving worked to get your attention in a busy environment, using a combination of outputs makes it harder for the person using the app to miss. Sounds also help anyone with a limited use of a particular sense. For example, if a person has limited or temporarily restricted vision, they may miss something shown by a change in color, but would hear an associated sound. The opposite is also true. A person may be in a noisy environment and not hear an alert, but could see something onscreen.

Consider the listener and their environment

I once visited the studio of an audio engineer who specialized in making radio commercials. He had a lot of expensive and sophisticated equipment, but would listen to what he was working on with an old, cheap, low-quality set of speakers. When asked why he wasn't making use of the equipment available to him, he explained that although he had equipment capable of producing a clear sound in a room with no other noises, that wasn't the typical experience of the people who'd be listening to the ads. They would be using devices of varying quality in environments filled with other noises. He needed to be sure that what he was producing worked for them.

Ears and speakers differ from person to person and from device to device, so not everyone will hear the same thing. You need to allow for this and can't rely on testing your app in a single, controlled environment.

For the app that Kirstie was building for use in the warehouse, she was aware it was a busy environment with a lot of potential distractions. She thought it'd be necessary to have the app make noise to draw attention to important events, as they might be missed if displayed onscreen. The reality was that parts of the warehouse were so noisy that people in those areas had to wear ear defenders, so the sounds the app made wouldn't be heard. Such environments are rare, and it isn't acceptable to exclude audio output from your app purely on the basis that some people may not hear it in every situation.

As the demand for high-quality app experiences continues to grow, sound output becomes increasingly noticeable by its absence. The app Kirstie built for queue-busting in the store made a loud, clear, and reassuring beep when scanning items for sale. But it's not enough to just make any sound; sounds must be meaningful and match the context of use. You also need to consider any other sounds coming from the device. Some guidelines for this include the following:

- *Don't reuse system-level sounds for different tasks or functions.* No matter how much you like the system sound effect for receiving a message, you'll only confuse people if you use it for something else within your app.
- *Use positive sounds for positive events, and negative sounds when something fails or isn't possible.* You don't want to use an "uh-oh" sound when something is successful or a cheering sound when something fails.

  If you're creating your own sounds or are limited to using simple tones, positive sounds tend to go up in pitch, whereas negative sounds are typically deeper and of a constant pitch.
- *Avoid repeating sounds in quick succession, especially in negative scenarios.* A repeated failure sound can worsen negative emotions when a person is becoming frustrated because they can't achieve the result they want, or a task isn't possible.
- *Add sounds that are simple, impactful, and purposeful: use them intentionally and with discretion.* Too many sounds can be overwhelming and lessen their impact. If you start by adding a few, add them in ways that correspond to the most important actions and events in the app.

Sounds can also be distracting. Always have a way to control or disable them. It's more common for games to have background audio playing while the app is in use, but if your app plays background music, allow control of this separate from the use of sound effects. Additionally, if your app includes background music, don't start this automatically when launching the app, as something else may already be playing in the background. It's frustrating to be listening to music, an audiobook, or a podcast and to have it suddenly stopped when launching another app that automatically starts playing music on its own. Your app should always respect the choice of the person using it.

9.1.2 Haptic feedback starts with vibration

Haptic, or touch-based, feedback is an area where development is still taking place, so you can expect new capabilities from future devices. Even so, there are several important considerations:

- Take advantage of haptic capabilities if available on a device.
- Don't use the same vibrational pattern for all actions and events within an app.
- Avoid confusion by not reusing haptic feedback someone could mistake for something else.

Haptic feedback involves more than making the device shake. *Haptics* is the science of touch. It can allow a person to identify what they're touching or receive feedback based on shape, size, texture, and resistance. (The most advanced haptic feedback systems can give the impression of touching more than a flat piece of glass on a device, but such capabilities have yet to make it into mainstream devices.) Most devices your app will run on will be limited to using vibration, although the iPhone 7 introduced a *taptic engine* to provide more tactile sensations. You can expect more devices to include similar functionality in the future.

A small number of devices offer a high level of control over the motors that cause a device to vibrate. For these devices, you'll find libraries of predefined vibrational patterns of varying strength and duration. This allows different games to respond consistently to similar actions. But most devices are limited to allowing you to control the length of the vibration only.

If the platform your app runs on includes standard vibrational patterns, you should use these to match the behavior of your app to its context. If there's no direct equivalent, base your actions on something similar, and don't reuse a pattern that's already in use for something else. You don't, for example, want someone experiencing a vibration in your app and thinking it means they have a new email. Picking arbitrary values for the strength and duration of vibrations is unlikely to produce the best results, so you should test this with users before releasing widely.

When the app causes the device to vibrate, it's a subpar experience for this to only indicate that something has happened. Not everyone is capable of distinguishing between subtle variations in patterns, even more so when using many different patterns. At the least, you should be able to sufficiently differentiate between positive and negative events happening within the app.

Giving your app the ability to communicate to the person using it through their sense of touch means that your app can communicate an important event in three ways: visually, audibly, and through touch. By being able to communicate in multiple ways, you reduce the chance of the person missing an important event, even if they're unable to use all their senses fully. It isn't necessary to always output to all three senses, but your app should never use just one.

IMPORTANT Multiple methods of communication are essential. If one or more is disabled at a device level, you can still rely on others.

Kirstie used vibration in a novel way as part of the alert system used by senior staff within stores. When there was an important situation that required attention without alerting or causing panic among shoppers, the store would previously use coded announcements over the speaker system. For example, if Mr. Smith was asked to contact the stock room, this meant there was a potential security issue and staff should act accordingly. Once everyone had a device with them, it wasn't necessary to use a coded public announcement, as the relevant individuals could be notified directly. The challenge Kirstie had was sending notifications in such a way that they wouldn't easily be missed or ignored as "just another message." Her solution was to have such messages be accompanied by a distinctive and sustained vibration pattern. When the device in a person's pocket is vibrating vigorously, it's hard to ignore, but it isn't noticeable to others nearby.

Some people don't like their device vibrating and will disable it at an OS level. Your app must still work in this case, and you should be sure to test for this. Also allow the person using your app to control the use of vibration, and offer a setting for them to disable it.

Put it into practice: nonvisual output

- If your app/game plays background music, don't automatically start this if another audio source is already playing on the device. Allow the person using the app to listen to what they want when using your app.
- Review your app for places where adding feedback in the form of vibration would be appropriate, and make plans to add it.
- Ensure that important events and messages are communicated in more than one way.
- Ensure that you have configurable options for enabling and disabling the use of sound and vibration by the app.

Exercise: physical and audio output

Test your understanding of the last section by filling in the blanks in the following paragraph:

Apps should interact with the senses of _____, _____, and _____. By providing feedback to more than one sense, it makes it _____ that the user will miss something important if distracted by something in their environment. The feedback and output an app provides should be _____ to the scenario. Allow the person using the app to _____ the output of the app and to _____ nonessential functionality, such as sound or vibration.

9.2 Output to other apps and devices

Output to other apps and devices is becoming increasingly important. This requires you to consider

- Sharing content and data
- Integrating with and extending other apps and parts of the OS
- Testing functionality that's complicated, varied, or hidden from the user

The apps Kirstie created all integrated with the same central data source. For internal business apps, it's easy to assume that because everybody is using or has access to the same data, it removes the need for sharing. This was Kirstie's original assumption too. Even with the most advanced document-sharing systems, it's still often easier for people to share copies of what's in front of them rather than pointing to the same source.

By watching early users of the app, Kirstie noticed that people wanted to share what they saw in the app. Although they knew how to find something in the app, it wasn't always easy or possible for someone else to see the same thing. Some people even resorted to sharing screenshots to discuss data with colleagues. To address this situation, she added a way to share a link to the data on the server so it could easily be viewed by anyone within the organization.

Fewer and fewer apps exist as islands on devices. The information they show and the content they create rarely stays within the app. Regardless of whether you want it or enable it, people will try to share it. You can help influence how people do this by providing ways for them to share activities and content easily from your app. There's the potential bonus that it'll help others hear about your app too. The main reason for doing this is to make it easier for people using the app to do what they want.

When sharing from your app, there are multiple options for the type and format of sharable data. You should aim to support as many forms of data as possible by enabling more (including, but not limited to, text, HTML, images, and URIs). When you do this, you increase the ability for people to share what they want in the way they want to. Figure 9.1 shows the ability to share data with standard icons.

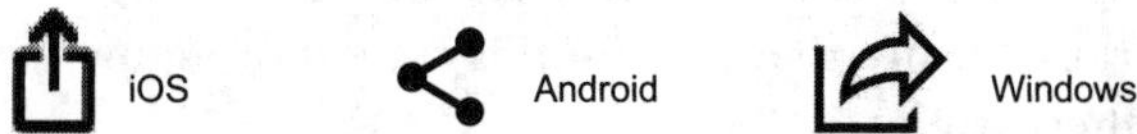

Figure 9.1 These icons represent sharing on different platforms. Because there's no universal icon and each platform uses something different, use the icon for the platform your app is running on.

Beyond general sharing, create a deeper integration with specific apps for added functionality and a smoother experience. Apps that use such functionality often make this open to any other app to integrate with, but this isn't always the case.

> **TIP** If you identify that many people using your app like to share content with another specific app, approach the producers of that app to discuss any integration options they have, but that aren't public.

Some app creators use cross-app communication to extend the functionality of individual apps by integrating them with others. One company I know has a suite of apps that are typically deployed together. These include some utility apps that exist to perform common functionality shared by other apps, such as handling account management and logging in. I've also known the developers of different games to develop a cross-promotion strategy based on sharing specific information between installed apps.

When it comes to output, the OS of the device your app's running on also provides a lot of opportunities to give extra value to the person using it. Consider integrating with other functionality or exposing information outside of the app. This includes the use of

- Widgets
- Siri/search extensions
- Map extensions
- Payment/wallet extensions
- Messaging app extensions
- Lock-screen and wallpaper provisions
- Browser extensions

The output from your app won't always go directly to the person using it. Your app may also need to send output to other services or hardware. Whether you're outputting to another organization's API or to a connected device, such as a printer or Bluetooth accessory, here are some important factors to be aware of:

- *People will interpret any problems experienced while connecting with other hardware or services as failings with your app.* Your response to this needs to allow for the correct identification of the source of any problem and appropriate messaging, and instructions for resolution.
- *With third-party services and devices, there's an increased need for your code to be incredibly robust.* Because there's a possibility for variation and change when you interact with third parties, ensure that you test this code thoroughly. It must be tolerant of faults in other systems.
- *You must protect data everywhere.* Secure anything potentially sensitive or personally identifiable during transit. Depending on what your app's communicating with, this may affect the protocol you use: encrypt it during transit, or verify the validity of the source or recipient of whatever you're sending.
- *When communication and data transfer happen in the background, there's no UI available to indicate if something goes wrong.* Be careful not to let this cause you to overlook error handling and reporting. Whether it's a case of raising notifications to the UI from a background task, automatically sending exception details to an error reporting service, or saving the details until the app is next launched, you can't ignore any problems when your app isn't viewable.

It's not just communication between your app and other apps and services that needs consideration. You also need to think about how you communicate from your own backend, as you'll see in the next section.

Put it into practice: output and other apps

- Identify content or events in your app or game that people already are sharing, or may want to share, and provide an easy way for them to do so.
- Review your testing and error handling of integration with connected hardware and third-party APIs so you're confident it's highly robust.

9.3 Communicating from your backend

This section covers what you'll need to consider when sending messages from your backend:

- Using different and multiple channels to communicate
- Sending messages that are specific, timely, actionable, and relevant (STAR)
- Not relying on the same structure and format for all notifications, but supplementing with more information where possible to communicate a lot in a simple way

For most apps, there'll be times when you want to tell the person who's using it about something, and they won't have the app open and in use. Such notifications or prompts can be sent from a background process on the same device as the app, but they're more likely to be initiated from your own server-based processes.

9.3.1 *Allowing for multichannel communication*

It used to be simple. A company or service would only have a website and an app. Now there are also chatbots, third-party app extensions, OS extensions, companion apps, and apps that change their functionality on different devices and operating systems. When communicating across multiple channels, you need to consider

- Which device(s) to send messages to
- Whether to send multiple messages
- Sending messages appropriate to the device they're received on

As figure 9.2 shows, with so many options and ways for a person and service to interact, there isn't a single way that all people interact with the service, or way the service responds to all the people who use it. You must allow for your app to be a part of this conversation.

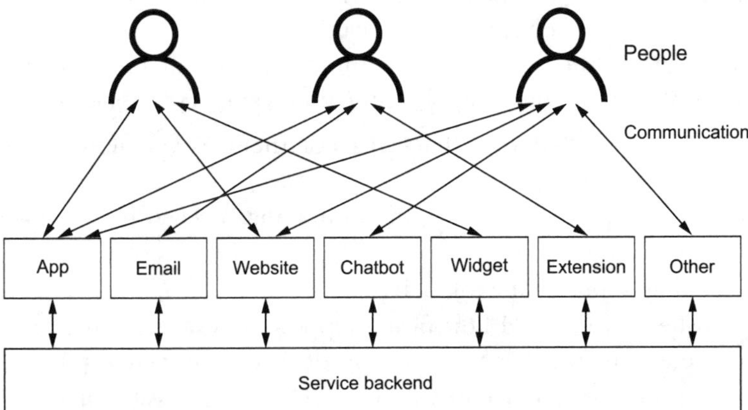

Figure 9.2 People communicate with a business or app and the services it provides in different ways.

The plethora of communication options available isn't restricted to consumer-facing apps and services. For example, the company using Kirstie's app had multiple internal systems, plus its own chatbots, browser plugins, and office add-ins. The company used email heavily, but also had an online team collaboration tool that sent messages. Even in this environment, there was still a place for in-app notifications and messaging.

Communicating across multiple channels brings complexity. If a person interacts with your service on the web and through an app, is it right to send notifications via both? One social network I use thinks it is. For every notification, I get three messages: I get a push notification on my phone, I get a browser notification on my phone, and I get a browser notification on my laptop. It all feels a bit unnecessary.

Multiple devices also bring further complexity. If a person uses your app on their phone and tablet, should you send notifications to both or just one? And, if only one, which one? It's a potentially complex problem that's affected by the number of devices involved. How do you figure out which is now in use or most likely to be used next?

If the apps on different devices have different functionality, it may not be appropriate to send the message to one or more of them. Some apps I use send messages to my smartwatch, telling me to Click To View when there's something new for me to see, but the app on my watch can't display the content. It can only tell me when there's new content to see on my phone, so the text sent by your app should reflect this. I also regularly receive notifications to the device on my wrist that don't account for the different screen size. Although there's space to display the whole message on a phone, I only see part of a message (and often this isn't enough to be useful) on my wrist.

As your apps become more sophisticated, the backend processes grow more advanced, and the number of ways a person can interact with your services increases, it's important to ensure you're delivering a great experience across all interactions and not creating confusion or extra work for the people receiving messages. Due to the variety of scenarios, there isn't a single approach that will apply to all apps, but there are specific considerations to apply to the notifications you send:

- Only send messages to devices that can act on them. Not all messages are appropriate on all devices.
- Tailor the message that's sent to the device that's receiving it. This includes length, format, and content.
- Avoid sending duplicate messages, if possible.
- Monitor where, when, and how various apps and devices are used at different times to determine which is the most appropriate channel to send to.
- Synchronize unread notifications across devices when possible, and if a notification has been read or acted upon on one device, clear it from others.
- Clear messages superseded by newer ones. That my phone continues to display notifications that app updates are available while also showing later notifications of the successful install of updates reflects badly.

Although multichannel communication is an important consideration, for now, at least, the primary method for communicating with a person outside the app is via push notifications. I discuss that next.

9.3.2 *Sending effective push notifications*

It's easy to create a bad experience with push notifications, so this section looks at how you can avoid doing so. Inappropriate content, communications sent at an inopportune time, or receiving too many messages can all cause people to disable your ability to send them anything—or, worse still, to uninstall your app.

Notifications interrupt the people who receive them. It's not only rude, it's annoying and frustrating to interrupt people too often or with irrelevant things. You don't want all these feelings and emotions associated with your app or your company. Follow these four (STAR) principles for sending notifications that people want to receive and will act on:

1 Be specific.
2 Be timely.
3 Be actionable.
4 Be relevant.

Be specific

It can be tempting to use wording that's vague or intriguing in the hope that the recipient will launch the app to find out more. Such notifications are more likely to be ignored. It's much better to send a notification about something that's nontrivial and specific to the recipient. This way, you demonstrate value and show why they should launch the app again, making them much more likely to do so.

Depending on the app, being specific can also require personalizing the content. A general message such as, "You have a new message," isn't as good as a specific one like, "Rita, you have a new message from Dave about Friday's meeting." Personalization affects more than content. It also affects what to send, what someone can do with it, and when to send it.

Be timely

Don't send messages arbitrarily. If the communication is about breaking news or something important, then it deserves to be sent immediately. For other notifications, you can achieve a greater level of response by tailoring when they are sent. I know one company that takes this to an extreme. A background process on the device receives all the notifications and controls when they are displayed. It does this based on factors including local time, network conditions, and other device information. All of this leads to notifications being acted on 15 times more often than when sent arbitrarily.

Consider the time of day for the recipient of the notification. Apps that wake me up by sending noncritical announcements in the middle of the night get deleted. Sending a message at the same time each day also isn't an effective approach, unless there's a good reason for sending at that specific time. I used to have an app that would send me the same message at 15:10 every day. There was nothing special about that time, and it was rarely a good time for me to interact with the app. For a while, it was funny, but the novelty quickly wore off and I uninstalled the app.

Also consider how long a communication is valid. Will it still be pertinent if the recipient doesn't see it for an hour? Or a day? Or a week? It can be better to show no notification than something that's out of date or otherwise no longer relevant. Sending notifications at appropriate times is not only part of being relevant, it's timely.

Depending on the version of the OS on the device you're sending the notification to, you may be able to avoid this by sending an expiry or lifetime value for the message. You'll need to send another announcement in the future to remove the original notice if not acted on.

BE ACTIONABLE

A small number of apps display notifications that can be dismissed. For most apps, the purpose of sending a message is to encourage the reopening of the app. When this is the case, it's important to connect the contents of the notice with what's first shown in the app. Consider a news app again. If you send a notification about a specific story, launching the app from that message should result in displaying that story. In this event, the app shouldn't launch the homepage, or, worse still, display a different story.

Don't send notifications that contain information that the recipient can't do anything with. Sending me a notice that tells me, "The server is currently undergoing maintenance" isn't useful. As well as not being helpful, it prompts lots of irrelevant questions like: Why are you telling me this? Can I do anything about the maintenance? Is it unavailable during this time? What's the impact of this? When will it be back? Was I supposed to be doing something this affects? None of these questions are helpful or needed.

BE RELEVANT

An unnecessary notification causes the person using the app to question the content and why it was sent. You don't need to send details of everything that's supposed to happen in your message. Doing so can result in overwhelming a person with too many notifications and ones that aren't relevant. Avoid this situation by only sending communications that the recipient needs to know and can do something about.

Notifications that are or appear to be advertising are also inappropriate. Some platforms specifically ban sending messages that are just ads. Also, some platforms allow the inclusion of images as part of a notification. Include these only if they add value to the message. Don't include them for the sake of it.

Figure 9.3 shows examples of notifications that break some of the STAR principles of good messaging practices. Breaking some principles, however, can sometimes be necessary or appropriate, and you'll need to carefully consider when to do so.

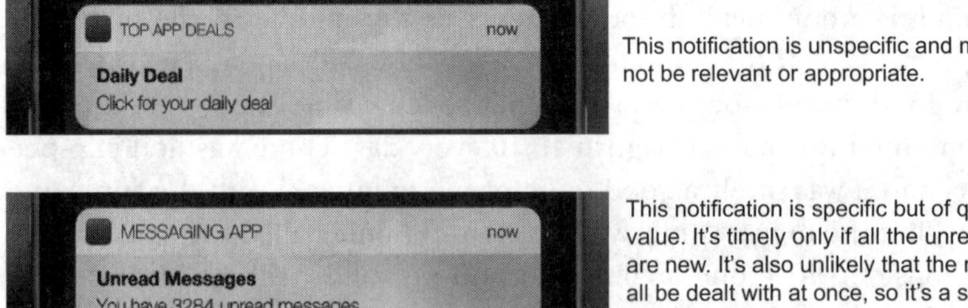

TOP APP DEALS
now
Daily Deal
Click for your daily deal
This notification is unspecific and may not be relevant or appropriate.
MESSAGING APP
now
Unread Messages
You have 3284 unread messages
This notification is specific but of questionable value. It's timely only if all the unread messages are new. It's also unlikely that the messages can all be dealt with at once, so it's a stretch to call the notification actionable.

Figure 9.3 These notifications are bad because they don't follow the STAR guidelines of being specific, timely, actionable, and relevant.

Knowing what to send and when to send it varies, based on the app and the people using it. To optimize what you send, track people acting on or opting out of your notifications.

9.3.3 *Using badges with push notifications*

Good notifications provide value quickly: a quick glance at the screen should be sufficient. Often an icon is enough to tell a person there's something new and interesting for them. A single name, number, or symbol can also provide a lot of information and indicate what a person can expect when they go to the app or even why they should. Badges also provide a great way to supplement the information in a notification.

Badges, or *notification counts*, are the little numbers added to the icons on the home screen of a device (figure 9.4). These show there's a new reason to open the app.

Badges have less value and impact when used widely.

Here, lots of apps are competing for attention by displaying badges but doing little to stand out.

Numbers can mean different things for different apps, so they aren't comparable between apps.

Numbers on their own also lack context, in terms of both app usage and the content they represent. Often, a number alone isn't enough to provide useful information. Pair numbers with other notifications.

Figure 9.4 Badges can be a simple way of indicating new content or another reason to launch an app, but their value can be questionable, as they convey little of the value that launching the app will bring.

As with push notifications, too many badges can be overwhelming, and the value of having large values becomes questionable. How useful is it to know that there are 1,284 unread messages? Is 99+ good enough, or 999+? What the specific number means will influence the answer, but using a value like 9+ can reduce the number of times the badge needs updating. This can be useful if the number value is updated by a push notification and all you want to indicate is that "lots" has changed, so there's a good reason to launch the app again.

As you can see in figure 9.5, symbols are available on some platforms as alternatives to numbers. These are better suited to indicate scenarios other than counts of new or unread items. If your app supports those platforms, use the icons when appropriate.

You can also use variations in the icons displayed to show notifications at the top of the screen in a similar way. This might include using different icons for notifications about someone liking one of your posts, compared with mentioning you in one of

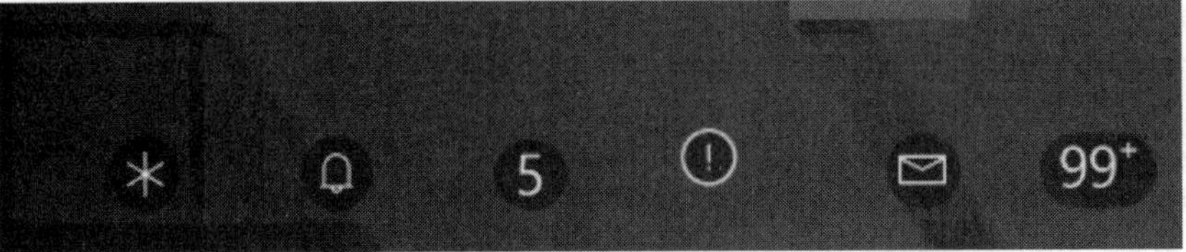

The badges on these live tiles use icons to convey more than just a number.

These notification icons are all from a single app, but the different glyphs indicate different types of messages. Providing information about the type of notification is more useful than just saying there is one.

Figure 9.5 Don't rely on numeric badges when the platform provides alternatives that can convey more information.

their own, even when they both come from the same app. Whatever the numbers or symbols on badges represent, keep them in sync with what's displayed in the app.

> **IMPORTANT** After the app is launched, you should remove notifications, clear icons, and update unread counts appropriately.

Put it into practice: output from the backend

- If you're not already sending messages via multiple channels, review how you'll need to change your apps and backends to allow this.
- Review any push notifications you send to ensure they are specific, timely, actionable, and relevant (STAR). Change them if they aren't.

Exercise: backend communication

Test your understanding of the last section by stating whether the following are true or false:

1. You don't need to consider communication with the user in ways other than directly through the app.
2. Some types of message are better suited to different communication channels.
3. The contents of push notifications should be specific, timely, actionable, and relevant.
4. Always let the user remove notifications for old messages or ones that have been read.
5. Use numeric badges and different icons as part of any notification.

9.4 Communication via channels beyond the app

You'll sometimes need to communicate with the people who use or have used the app, but you can't use the app to do this. You may want to tell people about new functionality or content to encourage them to use the app again. Or you may need to use an alternative communication method to verify identity or contact information as part of a registration process. Whatever the reason, such communication is often overlooked as contributing to the experience of using an app. The three most common channels for this, and the ones I'll cover in this section, include email, SMS, and third-party messaging services.

9.4.1 Using email to communicate with your users

Many people see email as an old and outdated form of messaging, but as a communication method, its value continues to exist due to its low cost and pervasiveness. Even other messaging and communication platforms normally require the provision of an email address as part of the sign-up process. There's only one service I use that didn't need me to give an email address during registration.

Email is also popular within many enterprises. Kirstie had this highlighted to her when the staff got devices to run the apps she was building. People asked her if the app could display email, as many they received were hard to view in the default email client. Rather than build an email client herself, it was easier to change the email templates the company used when sending mail internally.

Figures from companies specializing in sending email (including MailChimp, Litmus, Movable Ink, and Campaign Monitor) show the most popular platform for reading any kind of email is a mobile device. They claim between 34% and 86% of emails are opened on mobile devices. If sending an email as part of a process in the app, the likelihood of a person reading it on the same device goes up further still. Considering this, it behooves you to send emails that display appropriately and are easy to read on those devices, and won't appear like the ones in figure 9.6.

The following guidelines will help you create emails that work well on mobile devices:

- Keep the content short. There's no need to be verbose.
- Make them actionable, and make clear the action the recipient should take.
- Format text in a single column that's the width of the screen and is large enough to read without needing to zoom in.
- As many email clients process HTML content inconsistently, use minimal HTML in the body of the message.
- Ensure that the first few words communicate the value of the email. When displaying a list of messages, that's all that's visible.
- Allow the email to be readable and useful even if images aren't displayed, unlike the one in figure 9.7.

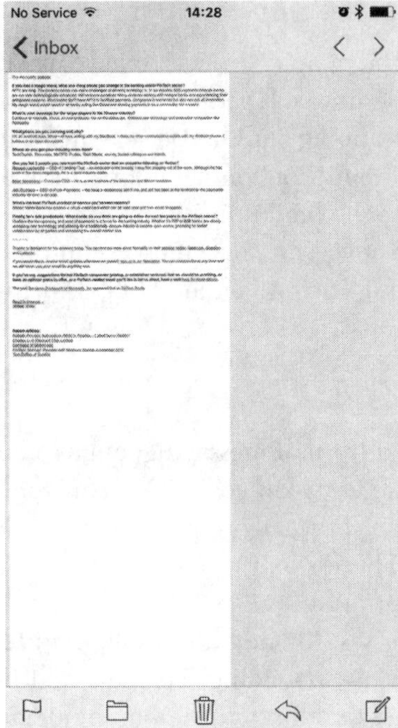

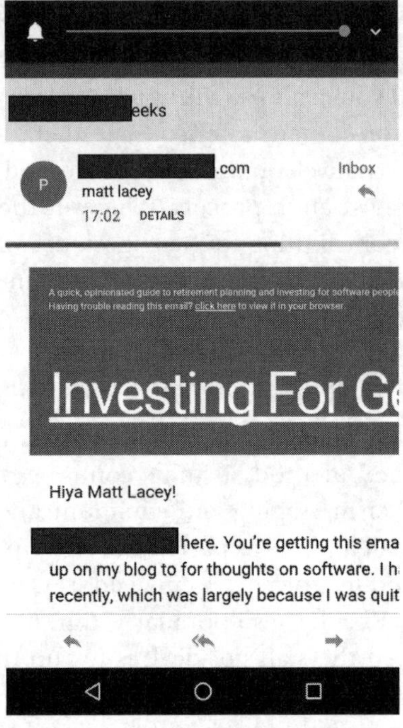

Figure 9.6 Apps that send emails should expect the recipient to read them on mobile devices, so those apps must format their emails appropriately.

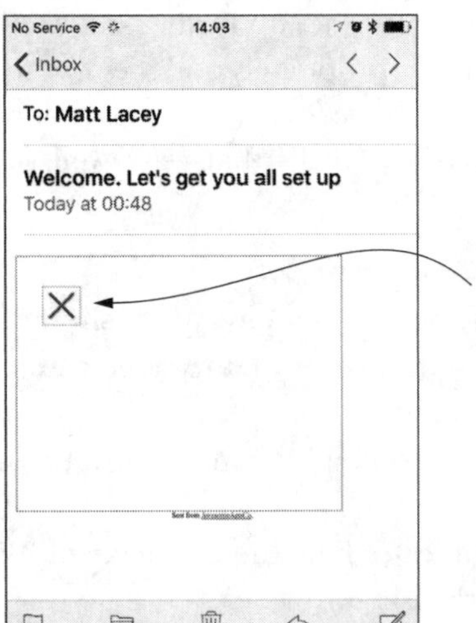

Figure 9.7 When sending emails, some recipients won't see images in the body of the message. You should design your notifications with this in mind.

Following these instructions will enable you to communicate in a medium that's likely to be read on a mobile device. We'll next look at a medium that's almost guaranteed to be viewed on such a device, SMS.

9.4.2 Using SMS to communicate with your users

Many people dismiss the use of SMS as a communication channel due to its associated costs. Although SMS messages do cost more than email or push notifications, they work on the slowest of connections. Depending on where in the world they are and the contracts they have, some people also pay to receive SMS, and this should factor into your decision to use it. Although popular as part of two-factor authentication processes, don't automatically rule out the use of SMS without fully considering the benefits:

- Like email, SMS messages work the same on all devices, so you don't need to know what device will receive the message when it's sent.
- Like push notifications, they're accessible programmatically from within an app, enabling seamless integration.

The experience of receiving an SMS is also like that of receiving a push notification for most people and creates a comparable experience. This makes it a good substitute when the sending of push notifications isn't possible. This is also a good substitute when you don't want to require a person to go into their email client to read the message, but want it accessible without having the potentially distracting action of opening another app.

9.4.3 Using third-party messaging services to communicate with your users

Unless you're creating a line-of-business app on a dedicated device, the people using your app will also use other apps. Among those other apps are likely to be one or more messaging apps. As some people dislike receiving emails or push notifications, and SMS can be expensive, integrating with the messaging service they're already using can be an appealing alternative.

It's unlikely that there'll be a single messaging service that everyone using your app also uses, but offering options that are appealing to a large proportion of the people using your app can create an improvement in the level of engagement with the messages you send.

It may be a while before options like that shown in figure 9.8 become widespread. But regardless of the mechanism you use to send notifications, ensure you're sending useful messages that give the recipient reason to come back to the app.

Everything that your app outputs and the way it does so can be affected by the app's responsiveness. I cover this in the next chapters.

Current apps provide a binary option for receiving notifications. In the future, as shown here, apps will present a variety of options for how users can receive notifications so they're more likely to engage with received messages.

Figure 9.8 Messaging services offer an appealing alternative to emails or push notifications.

Put it into practice: communicating outside the app

- Verify how the devices the app is used on display the emails you send. Do this with and without images enabled on the device.
- Explore how you could integrate with third-party messaging services as an alternative to sending emails or push notifications.

Exercise: communicating beyond the app

Test your understanding of the last section by stating which of the options in the square brackets should be used to correctly complete the sentences:

1. Test the [formatting|sending] of email on the most popular devices the app is used on.
2. SMS is [cheaper|the same price|more expensive] than sending push notifications.
3. Use third-party messaging servers because it [is the cool new thing|differentiates your app from the competition|meets the needs and desires of users].

Summary

- You need to consider direct and indirect output from your app.
- Communicate important information in (up to) three ways: visually, audibly, and physically.
- Sounds can be noticeable in their absence. At times, apps should make noise, or at least be able to do so.
- Respect any background audio that's already playing when your app is launched before you start playing something different.

- Haptics is more than simply vibration, but current screen technology doesn't yet let us take full advantage of this.
- Integrating with other apps and the OS lets you provide more ongoing value and simpler processes to the people using the app.
- Test integrations thoroughly, as they're easily affected by changes beyond your control. You'll need to deal with any negative consequences of this.
- As apps become more a part of a cross-platform experience, output needs to span those experiences.
- Notifications should be specific, timely, actionable, and relevant.
- Email is an important form of output. Optimize the emails you send to the devices you know people have and are likely to view them on.
- SMS is a valid notification channel if the economics of using it make sense.
- Third-party messaging is a growing point of interaction; consider it as a way of interacting with the people who use your app.

Part 4

Responsiveness

Responsiveness is about how the people using the app perceive the time the app takes to do something. The key word in that last sentence is *perceive*. Perception is relative to the person making the judgment. The time an action takes may always be the same, but depending on mood, time of day, or other activities, that elapsed time can feel, or be perceived to be, wildly different.

Many designers and developers will be familiar with the idea of *responsive design*, which focuses primarily on the way the UI of an app or website reacts to the space or resources available to it. In this book, I'm using a much broader definition of the term to consider all the ways people using the app can perceive its responsiveness.

It's common to link ideas about how the app responds with output, as people experience the output of an app through a "filter of responsiveness." But I draw a distinction between what's displayed (output), and how it feels while waiting for its display (responsiveness). Responsiveness has ties to more than just output. Context influences it. It can determine the appropriateness of input methods, and it'll be affected by connectivity and the use of resources.

In the next three chapters, I'll cover three important aspects that impact how the responsiveness of the app will be perceived. Chapter 10 covers the perception of time with regard to a mobile app: what influences this and how you can sway perception. Chapter 11 looks at practical things you can do during development and outside of the app to influence the perception of performance. Chapter 12 develops these ideas further and covers what you can do while the app is running to make it faster.

10 Understanding the perception of time

This chapter covers

- How perception alters time
- How quickly your app should respond
- Improving the perception of how long tasks take

In this chapter, we'll look at how people perceive time when using a mobile app and the factors that influence their perception. I'll then show you how you can positively influence perception to make your app feel quick and responsive. This allows people to believe the app is helping them achieve their goal faster and not wasting their time. In this chapter, you'll also hear about some of the ways Raymond adjusted his shopping app to allow for different perceptions of time.

As humans, we perceive time in different ways based on a variety of circumstances. You may have been on a journey and felt it took longer to get to the destination than it took to return home, when both legs of the trip took the same amount of time. You may also have experienced occasions of being engrossed in an activity or conversation without noticing how much time had passed. Or, there may have been times when a task you were undertaking or waiting for took what seemed like forever. The people who use your app will also have varying perceptions of the time it takes to perform various tasks and activities.

10.1 How people perceive mobile time

Mobile time has two common definitions. The first relates to the wider mobile industry and refers to the speed with which new features, hardware, devices, and software are released. The rate at which change happens and older systems are deprecated, or made redundant, is faster than almost any other industry. It's the implications of the second definition that are of relevance to developers. That's the idea that mobile device usage exists in a world that expects everything to be fast. If everything else operates at a normal speed, doing something on a mobile device should be even quicker. In this section, I expand on this idea and discuss

- How context influences your users' perception of responsiveness
- Additional factors that influence the perception of responsiveness
- How to be responsive with notifications
- Responses that shouldn't be too fast

People have learned from the devices and apps they've previously used that mobile software should enable them to do more, faster. And, they should be able to do that without being tied to a specific physical location.

Being responsive isn't the same as having a responsive design

Responsive design is a popular technique in web development. With that, what's displayed adjusts or responds to changes in the size (typically the width) of the screen to make the best use of the available area and screen type. In this book, I cover responsiveness from a wider perspective.

Based on device capabilities and screen size, an app shouldn't adjust only to what's displayed, but should also respond to what the people using it do and what's happening within the app. The speed with, and the way in which, it responds both impact the perception of the people using the app and reflect on the experience it provides.

10.1.1 Context influences the perception of responsiveness

We'll start by looking at the circumstances in which people using your app play a part in how they perceive its responsiveness. Specifically, there's a need to focus on

- What device is being used
- What people are using the app for

The greatest influence context plays on perception comes from the device and other apps on it. It doesn't matter if your app runs well on the latest top-of-the-range device if people are using it on older, lower-powered, or otherwise less capable devices. A low-powered device can lead to processes taking longer, and the app seeming slower.

Context isn't the only thing that influences the perception of responsiveness, but it plays a crucial part. To allow for it, you should

- Test on the lowest specified devices to ensure a good experience.
- Assume that every task must be as responsive as possible.

People won't excuse your app for being slow and unresponsive on their device even if it's fast on others. People may not see your app running on other devices, but they'll see other apps running on their device. The responsiveness of your app will be judged in comparison to the other apps used on the same device.

The task someone uses an app for impacts how its responsiveness is perceived. If I'm casually browsing an app while also watching television, the speed of the app isn't all that important. As a secondary task, its slow performance is excusable, as I'm not actively waiting for it to finish. In contrast, if I'm paying in a coffee shop with the store's dedicated app and it's slow to load and verify my balance, then the barista staring at me and the queue of people behind me make time feel like it's moving slowly, and paying is taking longer.

For most tasks, speed is important when using a mobile app. Tomi Ahonen, a famous analyst and consultant in the mobile industry, is credited with describing mobile usage as being at the "point of inspiration." Because a mobile device is always with a person, they can use it whenever they want. Want to send a message, take a picture, or look something up? You can do it right now. But that *right now* shouldn't be after a slight delay. Your app is a tool that serves the people using it. They don't need to wait for it unnecessarily.

The language people use to describe delays reflects how seriously they take them. "The app has frozen" is a common reaction by many people to even small delays. When people make this comparison with your app, they're saying that its pace is glacial when what they want is a rocket ship.

10.1.2 Perception is about feelings, opinions, and comparisons

Raymond invested a lot of effort in making the app start as quickly as possible. He took a complex startup process and was able to get it reliably down to about five seconds to complete. He was pleased with what he'd done, but the first piece of feedback he received when testing the app was that it "takes too long." Beyond context, three factors influence perception:

- It's a feeling and therefore is subjective.
- It's based on a person's opinion.
- It's based on comparison.

The amount of time it feels as though something takes is more important than how long it actually takes. How Raymond measured the five seconds, or if startup time was the same for all the people using the app, isn't as important as the feelings (perception) of the people using it. It isn't good enough until the people using it say it is.

As it's the perception of others that matters, it's important to ask people how they feel about the responsiveness of the app. Different people perceive things differently. There may be a range of opinions that will require you to adjust speeds (or the perception of speeds) to make as many people as happy as possible.

Measuring perception

Test performance and responsiveness on specific, dedicated hardware to avoid subjective opinions and varying experiences. Decide on the acceptable time for an action and then create tests to confirm that the activity is consistently within the allowed time. Run these tests throughout the development period to help identify any changes that significantly impact the time taken to complete each task. Leaving this testing to the end can make identifying and addressing the cause of any issue much harder than if caught earlier. The time taken for an app to start is a great place to begin, because start time impacts the experience of all apps and frequently increases during the development process.

Dedicated hardware is also needed, as other activity on a device can impact performance. You don't want inconsistent test results due to other apps running in the background or to be misled by performance on a simulator that isn't reflective of real devices.

A beta test period is a great time to research the opinions of the people using the software. You get feedback from the people who'll use the app, and can test on devices and environments that are reflective of app usage once launched. Be sure to capture the time taken on devices during testing and correlate this with any feedback about anything taking too long.

The importance of a task and how the app is used can also influence perception. A person casually using an app will be more tolerant of delays than a person who has an important, focused task they must complete. This information can help prioritize where to focus your efforts to improve perceived performance in an app.

Focus on those areas that people use more often, are time-sensitive, or are necessary to advance within the app. Start-up, registrations, and payment functionality are common examples of such areas, but this may differ for your app. For Raymond, it was the checkout process that required special attention, because people would fail to complete purchases if the payment process took too long.

Comparison also influences perception. People have different expectations from different devices. If you turn on your TV, it won't surprise you if it takes a few seconds before an image is shown. But if your phone behaved the same way, you'd be alarmed. Based on past experiences, you won't be surprised if you click a button to start a task in an app on your PC, and it stops reacting to further clicks or button presses until the task is completed. But the same behavior in a mobile app would be alarming, frustrating, and disconcerting.

Comparison between your app and other devices isn't as important as the comparison between other apps on the same device. It's this comparison that the people using your app will make most often and one you must prepare for. Although your belief about the perception of the app's responsiveness may differ, it doesn't make other people's opinions wrong.

10.1.3 Being responsive with notifications

Without opening the app, notifications sent to and shown on a device allow the app to be responsive. The smart use of notifications to provide information and simple interactions improves the experience.

Raymond got a lot of feedback that the notifications sent by his app weren't helpful. Originally, when the status of an order changed, a notification was sent that said, "Your order has been updated." As not all updates were as important or interesting to the people receiving them, it was frustrating that they had to open the app to see if the update was important or required any action. Once the app was revised to be more specific, Raymond received positive feedback. It was then possible to read or dismiss informational messages, but the more important ones triggered the recipient to open the app to get more details or act on a change.

When people are picking up their devices to look at them more than 100 times each day, those interactions need to be quick. Does your app provide a useful interaction to a person who's just glancing at the screen? Doing so is the ultimate in providing content in a way that responds to a person's needs and desires. At its simplest, this could be having a useful notification on the device or updating a badge to show an indicator that new content is available. Automatically updating home screen widgets also lets you display the newest content.

TIP Giving people what they need without them always explicitly asking is a great feature.

Being responsive isn't limited to what happens within the app. At times, launching the app isn't the most responsive action to take. Rich or interactive push notifications (figure 10.1) don't just show information, they also provide simple options for interacting with or responding to the message. This removes the delay between seeing something and being able to act on it. People don't need to wait for the app to load and redisplay the same content so they can respond or otherwise interact with it.

The timing of notifications also matters. It's generally preferable to send notifications as soon as possible, but there can be times when you may want to delay the sending of a message. You may want to offer this initially through your app's settings. With enough data, you may be able to find patterns in usage that allow you to perfect the experience automatically. Consider including these options:

- Group messages when sending lots in quick succession.
- Don't send or show notifications on specific subjects or from certain senders.
- Delay or suppress notifications based on knowledge about what the recipient is doing.
- Based on the type of message, adjust options for quick interaction.

It can be overwhelming to receive too many messages in quick succession or at a time when nothing can be done with them. Your app can be responsive to the needs of the people using it in the way it handles notifications.

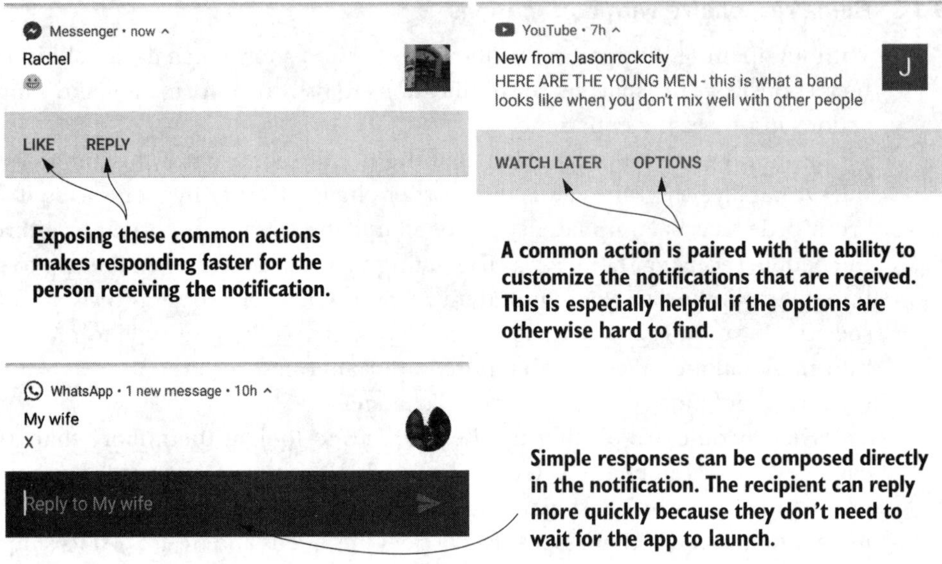
Messenger • now
Rachel
LIKE REPLY
Exposing these common actions makes responding faster for the person receiving the notification.
YouTube • 7h
New from Jasonrockcity
HERE ARE THE YOUNG MEN - this is what a band looks like when you don't mix well with other people
J
WATCH LATER OPTIONS
A common action is paired with the ability to customize the notifications that are received. This is especially helpful if the options are otherwise hard to find.
WhatsApp • 1 new message • 10h
My wife
X
Reply to My wife
Simple responses can be composed directly in the notification. The recipient can reply more quickly because they don't need to wait for the app to launch.
Each notification can be tapped to launch the app. All notifications can be dismissed with a swipe. They also all include additional options specific to the type of message sent.

Figure 10.1 Rich notifications enable a more responsive experience by allowing interaction without the delay of launching the app.

10.1.4 Meet expectations, don't just be as fast as possible

Understanding the expectations of the people who'll use the app makes it easy to create an experience that's perceived positively. The perception of responsiveness isn't always about making things faster. People don't always want or need everything to be as quick as possible. Doing that is a long, expensive, and often unnecessary task if the app is perceived as being fast enough. At times, an *illusion of labor* is necessary for tasks that people assume to be complex.

When people expect things to take time, responding too quickly will make them think something's broken or they're getting a canned reply. Identifying such areas depends on meeting the expectations of the people using the app. This must be factored into time spent understanding people's needs and verifying this during testing.

People will often attach more value to something that takes time. For example, people use search engines that search through billions of web pages to find what they need in fractions of a second, without questioning the time taken, but personalized actions are different. If someone enters specific requirements in an app that will search for the best mortgage rate, they're likely to be suspicious of an instant response. They have no way of knowing if it's the result that best meets their needs, and they have no sign of what was done to arrive at the outcome that's presented. They may, cynically, assume that the quick response was a predetermined reply or something the app is incentivized to promote.

If it isn't appropriate to educate the person using the app how it's able to return a personalized response so quickly, avoid doubts in the mind of the person by adding an artificial delay to the process, and be transparent about what the server does. Showing a series of messages (as in figure 10.2) that explain a process informs people about what's going on and gives them confidence in the process.

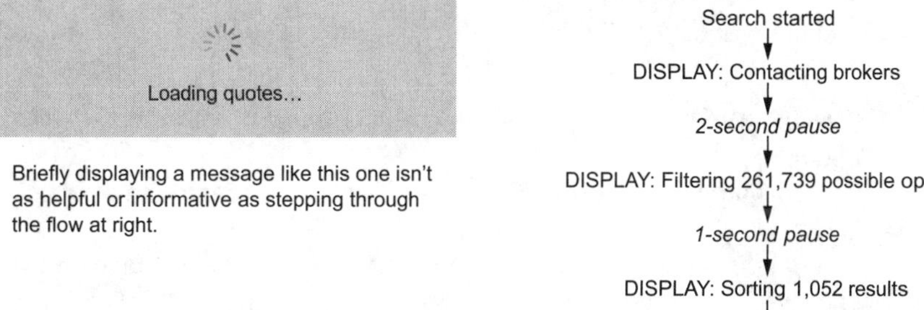

Figure 10.2 Explaining the process of producing a set of results and adding an artificial delay before displaying them gives an illusion of labor and increases confidence in their appropriateness.

Responsiveness influences people's experiences beyond the speed at which people can use an app. Consider how responsive you and the services connected to your app are in all circumstances. Are you amenable to, accepting of, and acknowledging the receipt of feedback? This could be online, in emails, via store reviews, or any other way a person using or interested in using the app can contact you. Your app may be super fast, but if someone has a reason to contact you with a question, a failure to respond quickly or at all gives the impression that you don't care or are unable to help. Causing people to feel this way will encourage them to look to alternatives and companies that are more interested in them.

Put it into practice: time perception and your app

- During testing, ask about the perception of speed.
- Understand the importance of different functions within the app so you can prioritize performance optimizations accordingly.
- Compare the performance of your app with other popular apps on the same devices.
- Test your app on the lowest-powered devices that you support, to ensure the app is responsive on them. Keep old devices you own so you can use them for testing in the future.

Put it into practice: time perception and your app *(continued)*

- Add a way to batch, group, or mute notifications sent or received by the app.
- Enable rich notifications to let people perform common interactions without having to launch the app.

Exercise: perceiving time

Test your understanding of the last section by stating whether the following are true or false:

1. Creating a *responsive* app means having a design that automatically adjusts to different screen sizes.
2. How the other apps on the device behave will impact how your app is perceived.
3. If people claim the app is slow, you should tell them how quick it actually is and how much effort you've put into making it fast.
4. Showing information or capturing a response in a notification can be preferable to launching the app.
5. Your app should do everything as fast as possible.

10.2 Influencing the perception of responsiveness

The way people perceive the responsiveness of an app can have an emotional impact on them. These emotions contribute to their experience of using the app, so it's in your best interest to create perceptions that reflect positively. In this section, we'll look at these four things you can do to alter how long people using the app perceive it to take:

- Preemptively answer questions.
- Show progress.
- Hide activity with animation.
- Make the app usable even if a task hasn't finished.

In Raymond's app, most of the items sold are nonessential. They address a want in the minds of the people using it, rather than a need. Many of the purchases are emotionally driven, so it was important that the functionality of the app contributed to the overall experience. Interviews with users during the early testing phases revealed that uncertainty over what the app was doing made it less likely for them to make a purchase, or reduced the amount of money they spent. This revelation caused Raymond to focus on ensuring the app was always clear about what it was doing and why.

10.2.1 Answer questions about what the app is doing

One major thing that intuitive and responsive apps have in common is that they don't leave the people using the app with questions. If an app is intuitive, people won't wonder how to use it, what will happen if they select certain options, or what they should do next. Similarly, a responsive app won't leave people wondering what's happening. With these things in mind, this section tells you how much information to display while the app is busy.

In order, from worst to best, here are the things an app can do when it's launched, or changed to a different view, or tries to activate a specific piece of functionality:

1. Crash.
2. Display a black screen.
3. Display an empty screen in the color scheme of the app but no content.
4. Display an empty screen in the color scheme of the app and an activity indicator.
5. Display an empty screen in the color scheme of the app with an activity indicator and details of what the app is doing in the background.

Many apps only get as far as point 4. Although this is better than options 1 through 3, it isn't as good as option 5. To demonstrate, consider the app in figure 10.3.

An animated spinner tells the user that something's (hopefully) happening.

Here, the animated spinner indicates that something's happening, the text tells the user what's happening, and the progress bar clarifies how far through the task the app is and implies how much longer it will take.

Figure 10.3 Just indicating progress isn't sufficient to explain what the app is doing.

That there's only a spinner onscreen at left in figure 10.3 suggests something's happening, but it still leaves a lot of potentially unanswered questions:

- What's happening?
- When will it finish?
- Why is it so slow?
- When can I use it?
- Could I have done something differently to avoid the delay or make it faster?
- Is it spinning because of something I've done?
- Can I stop it and try again? Or will that end up taking longer?
- Compared to my other apps, why is it taking longer to do something?

All of these questions show uncertainty in the mind of the people using the app, distract them from the task they're trying to perform, and detract from a positive experience. When the app is busy doing something, this needs to be communicated to the people using it. It provides reassurance that something's happening, and that the app's delay is related to useful and relevant activity.

The amount of information to give varies depending on what the app is doing, but it should always be specific, accurate, informative, and understandable. Displaying a message that states, "This may take a few minutes" is inadequate. It's vague, uncertain, and provides little information. It prompts further questions. What's happening? How much longer will it take? Can I leave the app and come back later to see if it's finished? Is progress being made?

Although providing inadequate information is bad, so is providing too much. Providing a lot to read or something that's hard to comprehend is not helpful. There's also no benefit in displaying lots of pieces of information in quick succession that can't be read that fast. You need to balance what's displayed based on how long it's likely to be displayed. If lots of things happen in quick succession, a progress bar in addition to text, as in figure 10.4, make it easier to see that something's happening and how close it is to finishing.

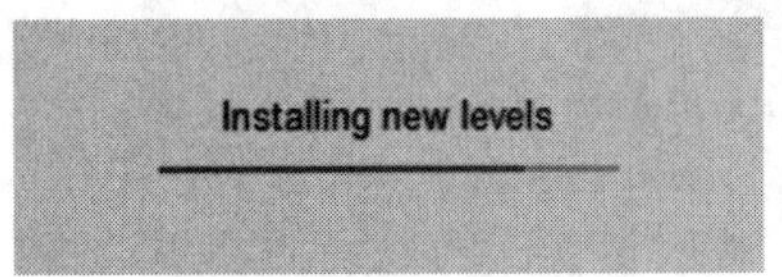

Without the accompanying text, it wouldn't be clear what the app was doing while the progress bar slowly filled.

Figure 10.4 For operations that involve many steps, a progress bar indicates that things are happening in the background and how close the task is to finishing. This is better than using only text to communicate progress.

Follow these rules when using progress bars to ensure you use them beneficially:

- Always accompany a progress bar with text to make it clear what's progressing.
- A progress bar should only ever load once. Don't reuse it as part of a larger process. For example, if downloading and then processing five items, the progress bar should have 10 steps. It shouldn't go through five steps for downloading and then restart to go through five steps for processing each item.
- Progress should never go backward. This means you can't start indicating progress until you know how many steps there will be.
- Progress bars should move in multiple, small increments rather than a few large ones. There's little value in a progress bar that only shows 50% and then 100% completion.
- Indicate 100% only when the task is complete. Don't display 100% progress while work is continuing.
- Use progress bars to indicate the number of tasks that have been completed and not an estimate of the total amount of time. When the estimated time remaining stays the same or goes up, this looks bad.

- Where possible, break tasks into equivalently sized steps. This shows a smoother advancing of progress. Only weight the size of various tasks if they're different in size and can't be made smaller.
- If using a progress bar to indicate activity while downloading a large amount of data, have it indicate how much data has been downloaded. Don't use a single step for downloading all the data.

Tasks or operations that require remote data are greatly affected by the type and availability of connectivity. I cover this in greater detail in chapter 13, but there are two important questions related to connectivity that your app must address:

- Does the device have connectivity?
- If so, what type of connection is it?

As shown in figure 10.5, you can answer both these questions by displaying the system tray or status bar at the top of the screen. If your app uses a remote connection, don't hide this important information.

The animated spinner suggests that something's happening, but there's no way to tell if a delay is due to a local connectivity issue without leaving the app.

Showing the status bar or the system tray makes it easier to tell whether any delay is due to a lack of signal. The user can see the connection strength (here, 3/5 on a 4G network) and knows there's a signal. So they'll wait a few seconds for inbox messages to load.

Figure 10.5 By displaying the system tray, any issues due to connectivity are obvious to the people using the app. That way they won't blame the app if they don't have a signal.

Even when the system status indicators are visible, it's still beneficial to make it clear when a device is offline by doing something in the app to indicate this. Don't rely on the people using the app to notice. Some potential *gotchas* to detecting if a device is online or offline follow:

- *Don't rely on connectivity indicators provided by the OS.* These may not be clear or tell the whole story.
- *Don't tell me I'm offline when the device has the flight mode setting enabled.* This can be on even when specific radios, such as Wi-Fi or cellular, are also enabled.
- *If the app is unable to connect to a specific server, it doesn't mean it's offline.*
- *If a radio is turned on or the device is connected to a specific network, it doesn't mean that your app can connect to a specific server.*

It's the nuances in the enabling of settings and the number of scenarios that could lead to data not being retrieved for a single, specific server. That means it can be tempting to try to use a single error message to indicate a failure to retrieve content. By being specific when a connection can't be made, you can help the people using the app address the problem. Similarly, you can also help them by providing relevant progress information when something is happening.

10.2.2 Show appropriate progress when something's happening

Although a general activity indicator confirms that *something* is happening, it doesn't say what or how long it's likely to take. Knowing how long something will take can be calming and reassuring to the people using the app. How to indicate something is happening depends on the length of the activity. Table 10.1 shows how to indicate activity based on the amount of time that activity takes.

Table 10.1 How to show activity based on the time it takes

#	Length of activity	How to show it
1	<200 ms	Seemingly instantaneous; no indication is needed.
2	>200ms	Display an animated activity indicator.
3	>2 sec	As with #2, plus show the potential length of wait and a progress bar.
4	>5 sec	As with #2 and #3, plus show information about what's happening and percentage complete.
5	>10 sec	As with #2, #3, and #4, plus allow people to perform other tasks while activity continues in the background; indicate when the activity completes.

TIP Don't show activity in the status bar if it's not clear what that activity is.

Many apps use the system activity indicator while network communication is in progress. It's good to indicate this, but showing activity on its own is often not enough. Make it clear to the people using the app if it will be periodically checking for updates or other new content in the background as they use the app so they don't become suspicious of what the app is doing. Providing a way of disabling or limiting such background activity is also desirable.

10.2.3 Animation can hide delays

People add animations to user interfaces for many reasons. If you do this, use functional animation techniques with clear, logical purposes. They can show an association, connect parts of a transition, or draw attention to something onscreen. Some people add them because they think it's cool or they make an app look more professional. These are good reasons, but the benefit that's relevant here is that animations take time. This can disguise the fact that work is also happening.

Consider an app that transitions from a list to a page with details of the chosen item. These four things need to happen after tapping an item on the list:

1. Load the second page.
2. Retrieve the data for the second page.
3. Indicate that something is happening while retrieving data.
4. Display the data once loaded.

If the data is retrieved in the background while the transition is taking place and the transition is animated, the time taken by the animation means less time will be spent on the second page before the data is loaded. When an activity indicator on the second page is displayed for a shorter amount of time than if no transition animation was shown, it can give the impression that the total amount of time taken is less.

10.2.4 Usable isn't the same as finished

A responsive app is usable even while it continues to perform processing or run other activity in the background. This allows people to spend more time using the app and less time waiting for it. The specific approaches I'll cover in this section are

- Loading only what's initially needed to make the app usable
- Storing data in a way that makes it quick to load
- Displaying activity indicators consistently while the app is busy
- Assuming success and updating the screen to reflect this

Some tasks take a lot of time, but sometimes it's not necessary for all parts of a task to be completed before people can use the app. Consider a messaging app. Should you have to wait for all the messages to be loaded before you can read any of them? Or, if viewing an article in a news app, should you have to wait for all the images to download before you can read the text? And should a game need to load all the levels before you can start playing it?

The way data is structured, stored, and loaded can play a big part in the impact of experiences like these. There's more on this in chapters 13 and 14, but it's important to consider how this affects the speed at which the app becomes usable. Storing all information in a single file can make loading any data slower. It can be faster to store data based on where, when, and how it's needed.

TIP Don't delay people from using the app while loading information of secondary importance.

You shouldn't update the screen and remove activity indicators before the app is usable. This is something I've seen many times: apps load the first few items in a list so the screen is now populated, but they continue to lock the app while more items load. When an app appears to have finished loading but doesn't become responsive to input, such as scrolling, it's more frustrating than when an app takes a long time to return anything.

Another way to make an app usable while activity continues in the background is to assume success. For noncritical or repeatable functionality, it isn't necessary to wait for the function to complete before allowing people to continue using the app. If you want to *like* an image someone else has posted, or add a comment to something you're reading, then it's a nicer experience if the app acts as if these actions are successful while performing them in the background.

It's frustrating to the people using the app if they must wait for every network activity to complete before they can continue using the app. Have the UI show that actions were successful and then perform the action in the background, retrying automatically if there's a problem. If the network submission never completes successfully, then you can show this to the people using the app at a later time. Hopefully, this will rarely be needed.

Assuming the success of all actions isn't always appropriate and should only be done for actions without serious consequences. Don't treat business-critical actions, financial transactions, or anything time sensitive in this way, as a failure to immediately communicate the action not being completed successfully can have serious consequences that outweigh small time savings.

Put it into practice: influencing perception

- Test the app using an artificial delay added to all network activity. Make note of any places where it's not clear what the app is doing while waiting for a response.
- Review the use of progress bars in your app. Are they in line with the rules for using them (highlighted in section 10.2.1)?
- Ensure that you're indicating activity in appropriate ways for the amount of time they take.
- Review how you store data on the device. Consider how it could be stored or loaded in different ways so you can access the parts you'll need. If loading large amounts of data, load the parts that will be visible first, and then load the rest after those are displayed.
- If using animated page/view transitions, start loading the data for the page that will be displayed while the animation is in progress.

Exercise: influencing perception

Test your understanding of the last section by using these words to fill in the blanks in the following paragraph:

doing	long	usable	connectivity
questions	specific	background	

If your app can preemptively answer the users' _____, they won't wonder what the app is doing or what they should be _____ in response. Provide access to system _____ information and be _____ in messages about connectivity problems. Adjust the way the app indicates activity based on how _____ a task is likely to take. When possible, allow the app to be _____ while it's still performing tasks in the _____.

10.3 Perceptions associated with the age of your app

It's not only the content in your app and the speed with which it loads that informs perceptions about the responsiveness of your app. Frequent updates tell people you're continuing to invest in your app by adding features and addressing issues. In this section, I'll show you

- Why updates are necessary
- How to tell people about the updates
- When is the best time to install an update
- How to inform people when to start using the new version

The frequency of updates to an app influences the way people think you respond to wider changes and your intentions around enhancing the app. People using apps not only expect evergreen content, but increasingly expect evergreen apps too.

It's rare to release an app and never update it. Whether it's fixing bugs, adding functionality, or responding to changes in a new version of the OS that the app runs on, there are lots of reasons to update an app. Whatever changes you make don't matter if the people using the app don't know about them and use them.

The most important piece of functionality you can include in your app that isn't part of its unique value proposition is a way for you to inform the people using it when a new version is available. Figure 10.6 shows one way of doing this, but how you do it isn't as important as that you do.

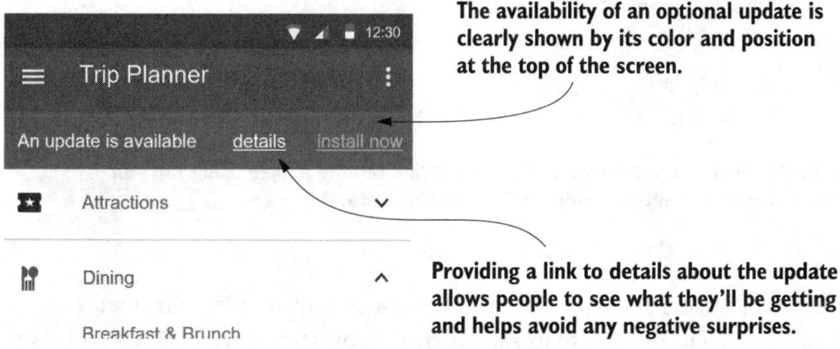
12:30
Trip Planner
An update is available
details
install now
Attractions
Dining
Breakfast & Brunch
The availability of an optional update is clearly shown by its color and position at the top of the screen.
Providing a link to details about the update allows people to see what they'll be getting and helps avoid any negative surprises.

Figure 10.6 Letting the people using your app know when a new version is available is one of the most important features of any app.

Having people update to the newest version of an app has a number of benefits:

- It reduces the bugs the people using it may encounter.
- It provides access to new or improved functionality.
- It simplifies compatibility, backend services, testing, and support by reducing the number of versions of the app that must be handled.

Because of the importance of installing updates to apps, most operating systems will now automatically attempt to install new versions of apps obtained from the app store. Even when this functionality is enabled by default, you can't rely on it taking care of the update process for you.

Back when Nokia was still making Windows phones and had this functionality enabled by default on all devices, someone who worked there told me that 50% of people disabled this capability. Three common reasons for this behavior and understanding them can help you account for these objections when updating your app:

- People fear the cost of unexpected, large data downloads.
- People are happy with how it works and don't want unexpected changes.
- People don't want to lose a feature that's removed or changed in a newer version of the app.

Even when a device has automatic installation of updates enabled, the update may not happen due to the type of connection available to the device or the level of charge in the battery. When a new update is available, tell the people using the app; have them follow a link to the store to download the update (figure 10.7). Don't automatically redirect them there without notice. People may not realize that they need to install an update and may instead think there's an error with your app.

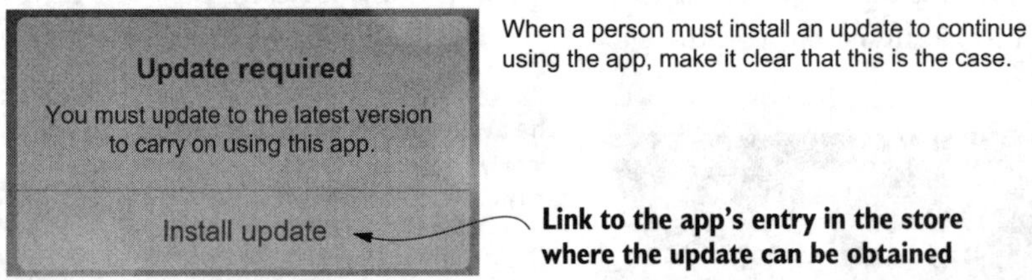

Figure 10.7 When a mandatory update is available, tell the people using the app when they launch it; don't just redirect them to the store.

To tell people using the app that a new version is available, you need to know a minimum of two pieces of information: which version they have and which version is available in the store. The simplest approach to this is to directly query the store from the app and see what version is available there. If it's different from the version of the app that's running, then prompt users to upgrade. Such a simplistic approach has two issues:

- It doesn't allow for distinguishing between mandatory and optional updates.
- It doesn't allow for a way of communicating what's new in the update or why people should install it.

These issues factor in to people disabling automatic updates. Addressing them gives people a reason and the confidence to update. When an update is made available, you need to tell the people using the app the following:

- Why they should update
- What benefit/extra value updating brings
- What happens or what alternatives they can take if they don't update now
- Any timelines or deadlines for completing the update

It's not possible to provide this information or enforce all scenarios by purely relying on information from the store. To provide appropriate information about available updates, their availability, why they should be installed, and when the update must be installed, it's necessary to create your own service to handle this. Your service will need the version number and platform the app is running on. It will then be able to determine and report whether a new version is available. If it is, you should report

- Whether the update is mandatory
- What is different between the version in use and the latest release
- Where to go to get the update (normally the store link)

A simple service will return details of the newest version, but handling this puts more logic and responsibility into the app. Making all updates mandatory is the simplest approach, but isn't ideal or even necessary in all situations. Although it's nice to have everyone using the latest version, the interruption that installing the update causes can be the reason for not launching the app in the first place. Don't force people to install an update that makes a change to an area of the app unrelated to the task they're trying to complete. The following lists different scenarios for requiring updates and considerations of when to use them:

- *Must update now*—Use this when continued use of an older version will cause issues for the people using the app or when breaking changes were made to a backend service that aren't backward compatible. It's most appropriate to employ when the app can only be used online.
- *Must update by a deadline*—If a breaking change is coming in the future, making a new version available early, but not making the update mandatory before it's necessary, allows people to use the app when they open it and then update at a time that's more convenient.
- *Minor updates optional*—If a minor update is released to fix an obscure bug or a feature that isn't widely used, it's OK to let people continue to use the version they have. It's often enough that people install the latest major version of an app, but newer, minor versions can be optional.
- *Reduced functionality if people don't update*—If an app is usable offline, this becomes available by default. That people may not have access to new functionality or fixes if offline also occurs in the other scenarios. You may choose to offer reduced functionality while online as an option to people who are particularly tied to older versions of an app and are fine with having restricted functionality and limited support as a consequence.

The final task in smoothly managing an app update is to tell the people using it when an update has been installed. If the update was installed automatically, this lets the people using the app know that things are deliberately different and aren't broken. For updates that were initiated by the person using the app, this confirms the update was successful and allows you once again to provide information about what's changed.

Don't rely on notifications from the store communicating that an update was installed. People need to know the details of the change, not just that a change has occurred. Displaying this in a prompt (as in figure 10.8) or through a feature tour when the app is next launched is recommended, but this information should also be available within the app, so people have multiple opportunities to see it.

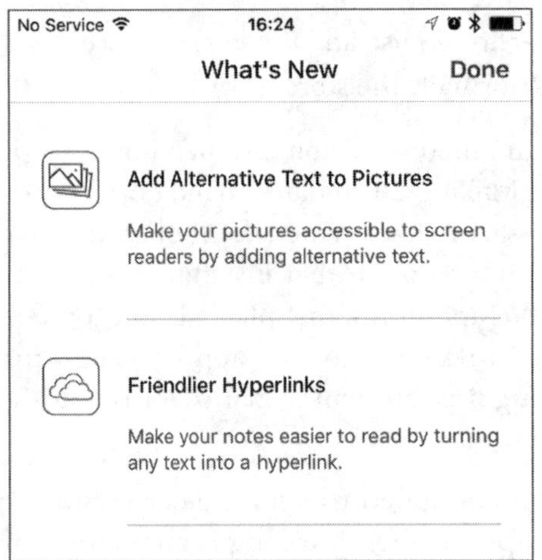

When this app is used for the first time after an update is installed, this What's New page displays a quick summary of new features. Users can tap through for more information if desired.

Figure 10.8 An example of providing information when an app is first used after being updated

Some app frameworks support the downloading of new functionality without obtaining a new version of the app from the store. In this scenario, it's still necessary to communicate that a change has taken place and what's different. This avoids confusion and any feeling of uncertainty felt by trying to use something that changes without warning.

Put it into practice: app updates

- Add an indicator when a new version of the app is available, and include details of why the update should be installed.
- Ensure that you display details of what's changed when a new version of the app is used for the first time.

How people perceive your app's responsiveness can have a big impact on the experience of using it. Now you can further improve perception by making the app faster. The next chapter looks at ways to do this before the app starts.

Summary

- People are busy and don't want to spend time waiting unnecessarily for your app to do something.
- Many factors impact the amount of time something takes, and you can influence how long something appears to take.
- Most tasks should be made to be and feel as fast as possible, but for some things, it's important to show that something's happened by taking time.
- Being responsive shouldn't be limited to just the app, but should include all interactions between the people using the app and the company behind it.
- Regarding notifications, a responsive experience may not even involve launching the app.
- The way that the app shows progress should depend on how long something takes.
- An app should preemptively answer questions about what's happening, because uncertain tasks are perceived as taking longer.
- Animation doesn't just enable a perception of a connection between states, but can also make it feel faster.
- A task doesn't always need to be finished before the app can be made usable again.
- It's important to communicate changes and updates to the app itself to ensure that these are available to the people using the app.

11 Making your app start fast

This chapter covers

- Optimizing app startup time
- Distributing content with the app
- Downloading formatted content
- Caching remote resources

The last chapter showed that having an app that's fast helps with the perception of its responsiveness. In this chapter, I'll help you think about how the startup speed of an app also helps with responsiveness. We'll look at what an app can and should do when it's started, and then move on to see how preloading and preformatting content can improve startup performance. Finally, we'll look at how to use caching to save time when launching the app and when asking for the same resource multiple times.

In this chapter, I also introduce you to Melissa, who leads a team building an app for a popular social network. I'll show you how she addressed these problems that are related to responsiveness:

- The app being slow to start
- Displaying content when used for the first time, even when the app is offline
- The time taken to download and format large amounts of content

- Removing items from the cache when they're still needed
- Not deleting cached items and taking up unnecessary disk space

People will notice the impact of what you do to improve performance when they launch the app. The speed at which an app starts is one of the first impressions it makes. Doing a little is faster than doing a lot, so let's begin by looking at what happens when an app starts.

11.1 Doing the minimum to start the app

Apps start quickly when they, the device OS, and any frameworks the app uses do little. Doing as little as possible can be hard, and it's tempting to add more things to the startup process. In this section, I'll show you how to decide what to do when starting the app, and what to show onscreen. This allows your app to be usable quickly, but without compromising functionality.

11.1.1 Deciding what to do on startup

Knowing your app should do as little as possible on startup is one thing, but that can be hard to do. This section tells how you can make things easier for yourself by

- Being deliberate about what happens when the app starts
- Considering all ways of starting the app
- Compiling and structuring the app so it can start quickly

Focusing on what happens when the app starts helps your app provide an impression that sets up expectations for people's experience with the app. If you build an app focusing on what's easiest to program, you're not likely to create the best app. Instead, you should focus on what's best for the people using the app and doing that at startup.

WHAT TO DO WHEN THE APP STARTS?

When first building an app, it doesn't have a lot of functionality, so it starts quickly. As development continues and you add more features and functionality, the startup time typically increases. Don't feel bad if this happens to you, as it's common, unless you explicitly set out to avoid this. Recognizing that everything done when the app starts has a potentially negative impact on the startup experience, you can prioritize what you do. Defer anything that isn't essential to starting the app and getting it into a usable state until later.

Although other parts of the code may have many services or resources that benefit from starting or loading before being needed, these shouldn't take precedence over allowing the app to start as fast as possible. Perform such secondary tasks only when those related to getting the app in a usable state have completed. Decide this by using events or state changes among the primary tasks.

Don't assume that because the primary tasks normally take less than *N* number of seconds, you can use a timer to wait before starting the secondary tasks. Should circumstances cause the primary tasks to take longer than the timer allows for, starting the secondary tasks could cause the primary ones to take even longer. That's because system resources become shared among more work.

Understanding and planning what should happen when starting an app is important, but it becomes more complicated when there are multiple ways of starting it. The next section looks at this.

DIFFERENT WAYS OF STARTING THE APP

It's simple, isn't it? There's an icon on the screen. A person taps it, and the app launches. That's one way an app can start, but there are many other ways to launch an app:

- Starting an app for the first time
- Starting an app when not logged in
- Starting an app with varying network conditions (good, bad, or none)
- Launching an app from a deep link on a website
- Launching an app from a push notification
- Launching an app via a custom protocol
- Launching an app to open a document (based on file type or extension)
- Launching an app to use something shared from another app

Each of these scenarios uses different parts of the app's codebase and takes different actions, which can impact startup times. Not considering all of the ways to launch an app can mean that sometimes your app doesn't start quickly.

ARCHITECTURE AND COMPILATION IMPACT STARTUP PERFORMANCE

Because Melissa's app is so large, the OS takes a lot of time to load it into memory before it starts. This is an issue she wants to improve. For Melissa, removing functionality to reduce the size isn't an option, nor is splitting areas of functionality into separate apps (as Facebook did with Messenger). Rather than remove items from the app entirely, she chose to rearchitect the app to limit what needed to be loaded into memory when starting. Instead of a single package containing all the functionality of the app, she broke it into multiple smaller modules.

As in figure 11.1, starting the app only needs to load the *app boot loader* part of the code. This holds only the core parts of the app needed for communication with the server and a placeholder UI. When the server responds, the app loads modules based on the person's account status and how they launched the app. The parts of the app that aren't needed never get loaded into memory. Any that are needed are small and load quickly.

Having functionality separated into different modules in this way also helps enforce logical separation of code and prevents dependencies from growing wildly. Another positive side effect of this is that it makes testing easier.

I worked on the app for a social network that struggled with a complex and large set of dependencies. The level of connectivity between different parts of the app was so complicated that the dependencies made it difficult to track the creation of all the objects and processes, or the starting of services when launching the app. The many

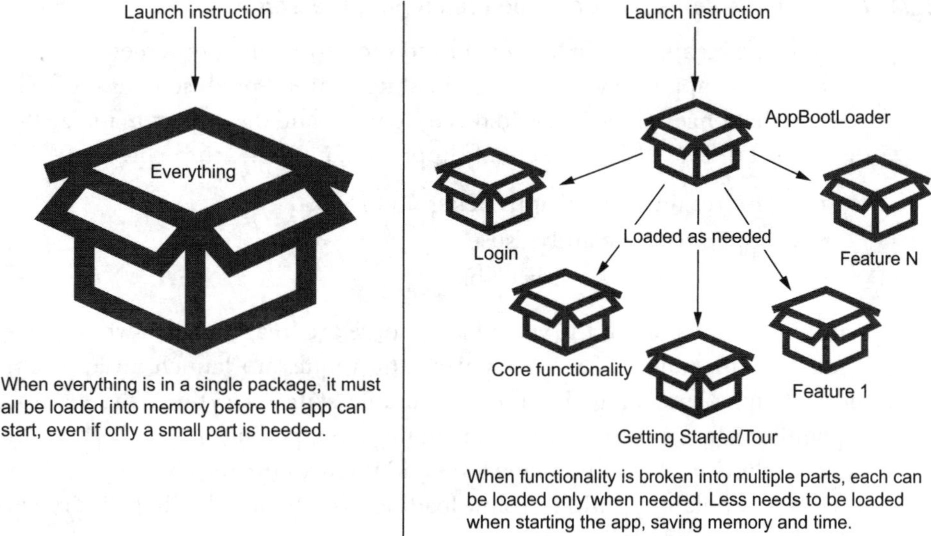

Launch instruction
Everything
When everything is in a single package, it must all be loaded into memory before the app can start, even if only a small part is needed.
Launch instruction
AppBootLoader
Login
Loaded as needed
Feature N
Core functionality
Feature 1
Getting Started/Tour
When functionality is broken into multiple parts, each can be loaded only when needed. Less needs to be loaded when starting the app, saving memory and time.

Figure 11.1 Breaking an app into multiple, smaller modules reduces the amount the OS or any framework must load when the app starts.

internal processes could take up to five seconds to all start, but they weren't all necessary to begin using the app. To prevent the startup time from becoming a problem, we added automated monitoring to ensure it didn't increase as a side effect of other changes.

Even if dependencies between created items aren't an issue in your app, it's still good to monitor app startup time. And it's best to do this from early in the development process, because it tends to creep up as an app gains functionality. It's easier to fix delays when you introduce them rather than to wait until development is almost complete, as changes can have significant consequences due to more added dependencies. Early monitoring lets you know when delays are added to your app. I've yet to hear of an app that reached the end of development, found that startup times were too slow, and quickly achieved an easy way to improve them.

It's also possible to improve startup times based on the use of different compilers and settings. Different platforms have various options available that control the compilation and packaging of your apps. This, in turn, can affect startup performance. These options regularly change with the release of new versions of development tools. Different versions of some tools restrict more advanced options, so they're only available with more expensive versions. Understand the available options for the platforms you're building for and the tools you have so you're getting the best performance available.

Remember to test versions of the app built for submission to the store. Including debug information and functionality in your app makes them slower and isn't representative of what the people using the final version of your app will experience.

11.1.2 Displaying a splash screen when launching the app

If launching an app takes a few seconds to show something onscreen, the people wanting to use the app may wonder if it's loading or not. Splash screens are an attempt to prevent that uncertainty. They do this by loading and displaying an image before starting to load the app. It's a reasonable approach, but it has three problems:

- It ignores the issue of apps being slow to load.
- It's open to abuse and misuse.
- Better alternatives are available.

Static splash screens are the worst kind. These are images shown while the app loads. They show that the OS has recognized the request to launch an app, but nothing more. If fully launching the app to a usable state takes time, there's no feedback explaining why and no sign that anything is happening. It can be tempting to use them, as they're simple and many tools add them automatically. But avoid static splash screens as a default solution to slow loading; use them only when you're certain they won't be displayed for long.

The only scenario where it's OK to have a splash screen is when it shows progress information when loading an app or game that must be online to be usable. In this situation, you need something to show that the app is trying to connect and that progress is being made. For such cases, show loading progress in small increments and have explanatory text in a progress bar to explain what's happening.

I've known management to raise issues with apps because the splash screen wasn't displayed long enough. The team asked for the addition of a delay to ensure the splash screen displayed for a longer period. This misses the point. A splash screen isn't an ad and shouldn't be a way of forcefully exposing the people using the app to logos or brand messages. Never add artificial delays to the time it takes to start the app. And don't put lots of text on a splash screen that's not shown for long.

A popular trend is to include a piece of information or a tip on the splash screen. This is a way of sharing useful information with the people using the app and gives them something to look at while waiting for the app to load. If you do this,

- *Use different messages.* When people see the same messages repeatedly, they quickly lose value.
- *Ensure that the information is also available elsewhere in the app.* Don't rely on people to read a particular splash screen message and know how to perform a task or know that a piece of functionality exists.

The best splash screen is no splash screen. Rather than show something while the app loads, it's better to have the app load quickly and use placeholders while retrieving content. Apps like the ones shown in figure 11.2 are better than ones that don't allow people past a splash screen if offline. These apps use existing functionality to display error messages or retry notices if there's a connectivity problem. They also allow access to any other parts of the app that aren't dependent on connectivity.

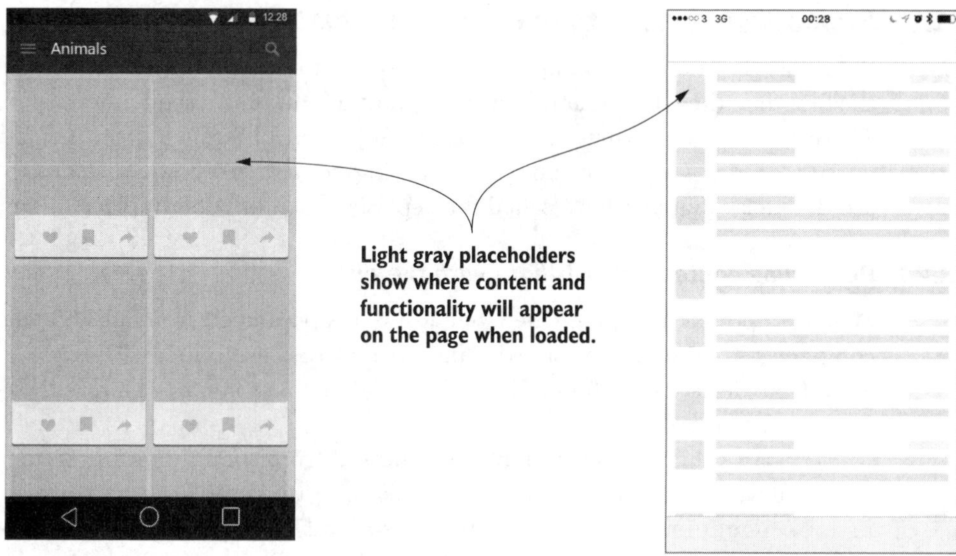

Figure 11.2 Apps showing placeholders while retrieving content are preferable to those using splash screens.

Given everything I've said in this section, you still might need to have a splash screen. If your app runs on devices that have older, slower processors or relatively small amounts of memory, it might not be possible to have your app start without a delay. If this is the case, you should have a splash screen. But only include one when you can't make the app start instantly. Including one isn't an excuse for having an app that takes a long time to get to a usable state.

Put it into practice: making your app do the minimum on startup

- Measure how long it takes between launching the app and being able to use it. How does it compare with popular and similar apps? Get feedback on this from the people who use the app.
- Periodically track the *time until usable* so you become aware of and can react to any changes in the app that increase this interval.
- Track the *time until usable* for all the different ways of launching the app.
- If you have a large app that's slow to start, consider how you could divide it into separate modules, components, or assemblies that don't all need to load on launch.
- Review the startup of the app and the information given to the user in relation to table 10.1 in the last chapter. Add more information or placeholders as necessary.

11.2 Preloading content to make the app faster

When people launch your app, they want to use it right away. They don't want to wait the first time they start it, and they don't want to wait on subsequent occasions either. These two scenarios (first use and later use) need different effort. And if the app doesn't need a *live* server connection, having content ready when opening the app avoids a delay that may have called for a splash screen or content placeholders.

11.2.1 Preloading content to distribute with the app

Melissa's app has a company news section that's populated from an RSS feed on the company's website. The business required that this section should never be empty, even if the device was offline. There should always be some news about the company for people to read.

Melissa's solution, as you may have guessed from the title of this section, was to distribute some content with the app. This wasn't just the latest information at the time of submitting to the store, but was specially chosen to provide important or general information about the company. With content available, there's also no need to handle a scenario where nothing can be retrieved and lists would otherwise be empty.

As a concept, distributing content is straightforward. But many people are quick to find objections or reasons why they think it won't work for them. The following are solutions and alternatives to the most common objections:

- *Content is often updated, so anything distributed with the app quickly becomes out of date*—Include examples of the most popular content or content that shows the capabilities and features of the app. Revise this periodically and when updating the app for any other reason.
- *The app only works with online data*—Include sample and training content with the app. Not only will this mean the app is never empty, but it can also be a helpful reference in the future.
- *The app needs online configuration before first use*—Include defined configurations for common scenarios for use offline. Or include a demo mode that allows people to try out the app with specific configurations.
- *Content files are too large to distribute through the store*—Include smaller, sample pieces of content with the app. This way a person can instantly see the app in use, and they can view something more exciting than a progress bar while downloading the remaining content.

Always include some content with your app when you distribute it. Use this initial content to populate a cache (discussed in section 11.4) or instead of it. This way your app will never be empty, even if launched while offline or if there are server or connectivity issues.

11.2.2 Preloading content for the app's next use

When starting an app, it can be frustrating to have to wait for it to launch and then for it to retrieve the latest data to display. If you've already loaded the latest data, you enable the app to be usable faster, and you create the impression that the app has anticipated the needs of the people using it.

At one level, giving the impression that the app is running in the background while the person isn't using it is beneficial because it allows the app to be usable more quickly. At another level, such effort is also potentially wasteful as it means the app did lots of work that may not be needed or seen. Such wasted effort can also be costly, as it unnecessarily runs down the battery or may use an expensive data connection. Having the app continually run while not used is neither practical or possible in all situations. Instead, consider these two options for your app:

- Have the app periodically check for new content and download it.
- Send the app a notification when new content is available.

These two options are known respectively as *pulling* and *pushing* the content, and we'll look at those next.

PULLING NEW CONTENT INTO THE APP

When new content becomes available on a predictable schedule or for an app used at regular times, it's practical and realistic to retrieve the content in advance. That way you'll have it ready when a person opens the app. By using background tasks, jobs, or services, it's possible to retrieve the content before it's needed.

Consider an app that publishes a news summary at 7 A.M. and 7 P.M. each day. These would be great times to automatically retrieve data that will be ready for the next use of the app. Or consider a business app for a system that updates prices or stock levels each night. Rather than have the person using it wait for this information to download when they first start or open the app each morning, have the app download this data before the person starts work.

The following can help you avoid unnecessarily downloading content that's not wanted or needed. These actions can also help decrease unnecessary resource usage:

- *Only preload the minimal usable content*—For example, only download the text associated with an item, and save the loading of any associated images or videos until after the app loads.
- *Stop preloading content if people don't use the app*—For an app previously used daily and then not used for a week, stop preloading content until the app is next used.
- *Use patterns to preload content*—If you can identify patterns of usage for the app, either for individuals or for all people using the app, use those to indicate when to preload content.

The use of some apps and the content they show mean it isn't practical to use a form of periodic polling for new content. Instead, it's better for the server to tell the app when there's new content to display.

PUSHING NEW CONTENT TO THE APP

Push notifications offer a simple, well-understood way to tell the people with the device there's something for them to look at in your app. Many developers are unaware that it's possible to send push notifications that can be processed by the app on the device that receives them before they are displayed, or to suppress their display entirely.

By intercepting the received message and doing additional work before the notification is displayed, you can avoid situations like the one in figure 11.3. A notification is received by a device, but the app can't handle the action associated with the notification. Often this happens if connectivity is lost between the time that the notification is received and the attempt to open the app.

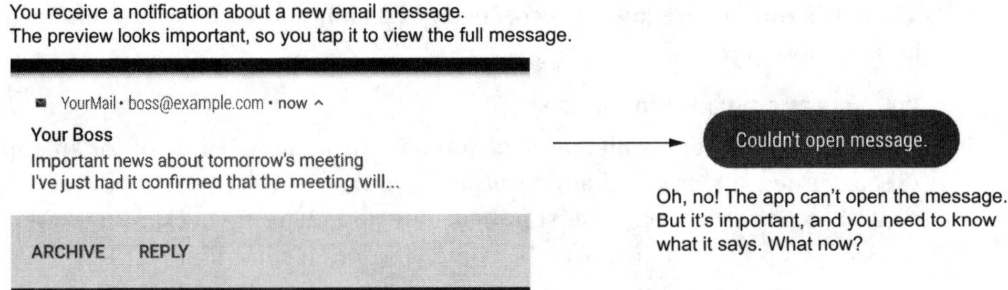

Figure 11.3 Notifications about new content are more helpful if displayed when the content they show is available in the app.

To avoid this scenario, you can send a notification to an app that isn't shown, but only to tell the app there's new content. If the content is small, include it in the notification payload. For larger content, receipt of the notification can trigger the app to download the new content. After downloading the new content in the background, it can wait there until the app is launched or the background process that downloaded the content displays a message to let the person know there's new content when they launch the app.

You can't always preload everything. You must also allow for loading content when the app starts, so the people using the app always have access to the latest content. When you don't preload content, you can still make the app fast by preformatting the content the app retrieves. We'll look at that next.

> **Put it into practice: preload content in your app**
>
> - Identify where preloaded content could be beneficial. Using the app without a network connection is one way to do this. Make plans to create and include appropriate content with the app when distributed.
> - If content takes time to download when the app starts, add a background process to periodically check for and download new content while the app isn't in use. That way, new content is available when the app is started.
> - Intercept remotely sent push notifications so you can download any related content before displaying a message that it's available.

11.3 Preformatting content retrieved by the app

Melissa's app retrieves the content for the news section from an RSS feed and then converts it for display using the UI controls native to the platform that the device is running on. This causes two issues. First, the RSS feed includes a lot more than it shows in the app, so it's downloading unnecessary data. Second, the content is HTML-based and isn't always correctly formatted.

Web browsers are tolerant of poorly or strangely formatted HTML, but custom code written to convert it to native controls is notoriously hard to make as resilient. The consequence of this is a regular need to update the reformatting code to cope with new scenarios.

Melissa's team created a new endpoint on their server that acted as a proxy between the app and the feed to avoid needing to download the entire contents of the RSS feed. The app connected to the new endpoint that returned a version of the RSS feed with the unneeded content removed. This smaller payload had a smaller network cost and was quicker to download and process.

To address the second issue of converting the content for display, Melissa built on the first step by having their server code be responsible for reformatting the content for device-specific controls. She then provided this to the app. Moving the responsibility for formatting the content to the server meant her app had to do less, and changes could be made on the server rather than updating the app. Consequently, a fix for the formatting was rolled out to all users in under an hour without any of them ever knowing there was a problem. This was a big positive for Melissa. It's also infinitely preferable to the consequences of a week with all users experiencing a bug that causes the app to crash while the app store certifies an update with the bug fix.

As Melissa saw, it's not only content distributed with an app that benefits from formatting, transforming, or manipulating before an app uses or displays it. Preformatting content that an app downloads provides the following benefits:

- It makes the app faster.
- It can reduce the amount of content downloaded.
- It makes it easier and quicker to detect and fix any issues with content formatting.

By moving the task of formatting content onto the server, your app doesn't need to do that work. It can take what the server gives it and show it. The alternative is to take the raw content, transform it for display, and then show it. As table 11.1 shows, this is the difference between a two-step process and one taking five steps.

Table 11.1 The steps involved in displaying unformatted and preformatted content

Displaying unformatted content	Displaying preformatted content
1 Download content. 2 Parse downloaded content. 3 Transform content to a device-specific format. 4 Handle any errors in the parsing and transforming steps. 5 Load content for display (and handle any errors).	1 Download content. 2 Load content for display.

For anything other than trivial transformations of content, do the work centrally on a server. Not only is this faster for the people using the app, but it means expending the effort once on the server, rather than on every single device running the app.

> **Preformatting is like precompiling**
>
> Preformatting downloaded content is comparable with apps built with interpreted versus natively compiled code. With interpreted code, each machine it runs on must compile it. This makes it easier to run that code on different devices, but means each device must take the time to do this when it starts. Natively compiled code, like preformatted content, is created once and runs faster on the machines that use it.

It's not just complex reformatting tasks that experience a benefit. Advantages exist for simpler formatting tasks too. Consider a piece of text interspersed with images of varying sizes. If the server can provide the dimensions of each image, the app can allocate enough space for a suitable placeholder until the image is retrieved. This is preferable to updating the layout after downloading the image, which causes the content onscreen to move or flicker. The first scenario may also save space and memory by decoding the image at the correct size for the space allotted.

Downloading content for the app to transform can mean downloading data that's unnecessary or not needed. Removing this can result in an overall reduction of size, even if the natively formatted content is larger. Content formatted for display with native controls will be larger than plain text, but is usually comparable in size with HTML-formatted content. Any size saving will vary based on the content, but this isn't the biggest benefit of this approach.

The final benefit to moving the formatting of content out of the app is potentially the most valuable, and relates to handling changes to the formatting logic. If the original content changes in previously unidentified ways that the logic is unable to handle, distributing a fix would mean changing the app code and distributing the update to all via the store. If content from a third party is causing your app to crash or fail in other ways that make it unusable, you don't want to be waiting for the app store to approve and distribute the fix. If the formatting logic is on a server you control, you can distribute the fix within seconds of creating it.

If you don't have control of the data your app consumes, adding the ability to preformat what it downloads means you may need to provide your own server infrastructure to act as a proxy for the app. The cost and amount of extra effort involved in doing this may be prohibitive, but providing what's best for the people using the app doesn't always mean doing what's cheapest or easiest to develop. In addition to what was previously mentioned, it also has potential other benefits, such as the ability to improve caching and compression of data.

Put it into practice: preformat content used by your app

If you download content that you transform before displaying it in the app, consider the costs and benefits of moving the transformation work to a server.

Exercise: preloading and preformatting content

Fill in the blanks in the following paragraph to confirm your understanding of the last two sections:

Preloading content helps the app start ______, ensures content is available when ______, and ______ the need to handle having nothing to show. Preformatting content moves ______ and ______ from every device to a single server. It allows the app to be ______, downloads to be ______, and bug fixes to be deployed more ______.

11.4 Caching content to save time and money

Caching is another way of using the idea that doing nothing is faster, cheaper, and easier for an app. This applies to the starting of the app and also extends to its ongoing use. You can display content faster by using what you've already retrieved. You need less network traffic and can support offline scenarios by removing the need for a network connection.

When retrieving something repeatedly from somewhere with a cost (time, money, or data), you can realize savings by only making the request once, keeping a copy of what's returned the first time, and using that for later identical requests. This is the fundamental principle of caching, which is simple and useful, at least in part, in any app. To make the best use of caching in your app, consider the following:

- Where and how to store the cached items
- How to check for new versions of items you've cached
- When to get rid of cached items

While the principle is simple, there are some potentially challenging scenarios to consider. What is right for one piece of data may not be right for another. Even within the same app, you need to carefully examine the different ways you cache content.

11.4.1 Using in-memory and disk-based caches

If you only retrieve something once, you don't need to consider caching it. Nor should you cache something guaranteed to be different when you want it again; you don't want to show old data even if clearly indicating it as old. For everything else, it's worth considering caching. You can store cached items in memory or on disk, and each approach has its pros and cons, as shown in table 11.2.

Table 11.2 Pros and cons of keeping cached data in different locations

Location	Pros	Cons
In memory	■ Fast to access and update ■ Available when using the app offline	■ Limited by how much can be stored ■ Not preserved between app restarts
On disk	■ Available even if you start the app offline ■ Preserved between app restarts ■ Size is only limited by available disk space	■ Slower to access than memory ■ Can result in lots of disk I/O ■ Need to manage amount of disk usage

Whether you store cached data in memory or on disk isn't an exclusive decision. It's possible to use both, but this makes the logic around retrieving data and keeping caches up to date more sophisticated.

Figure 11.4 shows the decisions for both returning cached items and checking the server for new content. If the server does return new content, this means that a single request for data can result in more than one response. Writing code that can handle one or more responses is more complicated than code that will only ever return one, but is an approach worth taking. Not only does it make it easier to create a responsive app that starts quickly and updates with the latest data, but it also makes it simpler to handle the manual or periodic refreshing of data too.

Having at least some content in a disk-based cache can mean that your app will always have content to display when combining this approach with the preloading of content discussed earlier. It also enables an app to start while offline, but this doesn't mean that all functionality in the app will be possible or available. Chapter 13 explores this scenario in more depth. The use of a flow that displays locally cached content and then checks the server is a good start, but it skips over the question of whether to also query the server. I'll answer that question next.

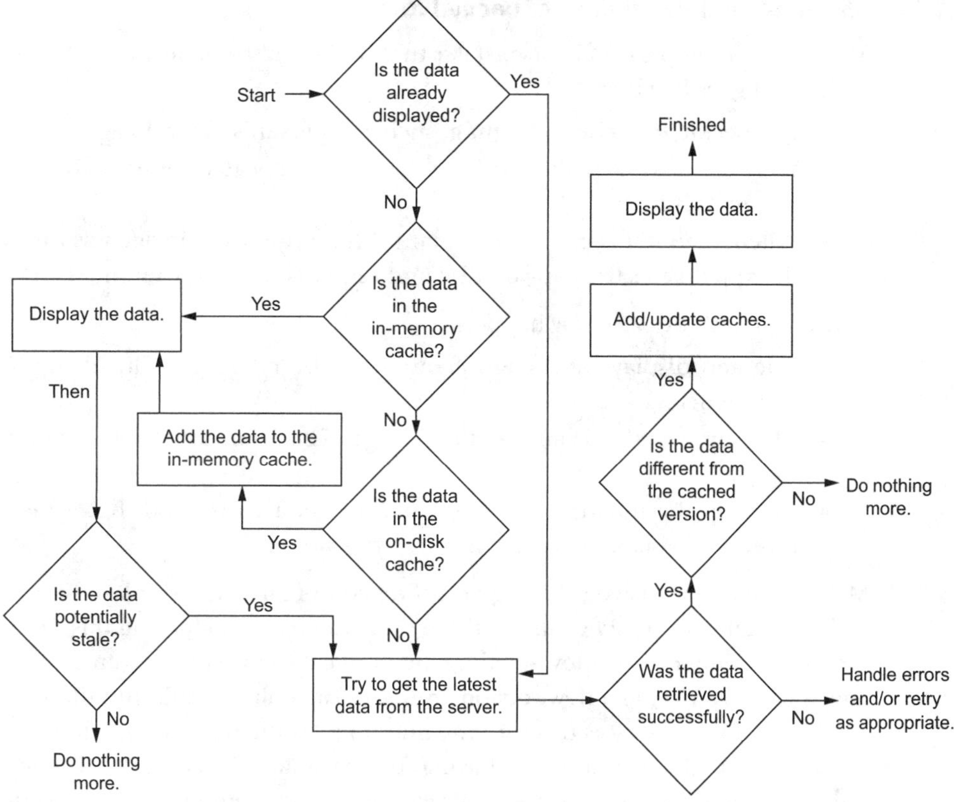

Figure 11.4 A workflow for deciding when and how to retrieve from the cache, server, or both

> **Exercise: where to cache**
>
> We've looked at the ways you can store items in a cache and how to retrieve them. Verify that you know which approach to use when by deciding if you should cache each of the following in memory, on disk, or not at all:
>
> 1. A large image relating to an item displayed in the app
> 2. A list of the latest messages received within the app
> 3. Items shown on the first page of the app when it's launched
> 4. Details of the logged-in user
> 5. The high score record of the current user
> 6. A global online scoreboard
> 7. A list of content subcategories retrieved in the app

11.4.2 Checking for new versions of cached items

Many app developers make a mistake that Melissa also made when they start using caching. It goes like this:

- You decide to cache something, such as a person's avatar image.
- You keep a copy on disk and use that for all repeated requests for the image in the next 24 hours.
- When a request is made more than 24 hours after the image was first asked for, the app deletes the copy on disk and requests it again from the server.

One of three things will now happen:

- The app displays no image if one can't be retrieved. This degrades the UI experience.
- The app downloads an identical image. This is an unnecessary duplication of effort.
- The app downloads a new, updated image. This is good, but a new image is rarely available more often than every 24 hours.

Melissa's goal was to avoid having an *old* version of an avatar displayed for more than 24 hours. This is a noble goal, but there's a better way of achieving this. It's a way that avoids the unnecessary downloading of duplicate content, prevents displaying no image while retrieving a new version, and uses capabilities built into the HTTP protocol. Figure 11.4 addresses this with the question, "Is the data potentially stale?"

Consider an HTTP request as having four parts: a verb (GET, POST, and so forth), the URL, some headers, and sometimes some body content. The response has two parts: some headers and sometimes some body content. Many developers overlook the headers, but they enable many powerful options and pieces of functionality. With regards to caching, it's necessary to understand the following headers that may be part of the response from the server:

- `Cache-Control`—Indicates whether and how long (in seconds) before the content should be considered stale
- `ETag`—An identifier (often a hash) of the content
- `Expires`—The date/time after which to consider the content stale
- `Last-Modified`—The date/time that the requested object was last changed

First, these headers tell you if the server can support caching. Second, they tell you how to avoid having the server return the same content even if it hasn't changed. A second request for the same URI and passing the `ETag` from the first response in the `If-None-Match` header returns the `304 Not Modified` status code and no content if it hasn't changed, or a `200 Ok` status and the new content if it's different. Alternatively, you can ask the server if the content has changed since a specific date/time using the `If-Modified-Since` header. This returns the 304 or 200 status previously described, depending on if the content has changed. Figure 11.5 shows examples of multiple requests and the differing responses returned.

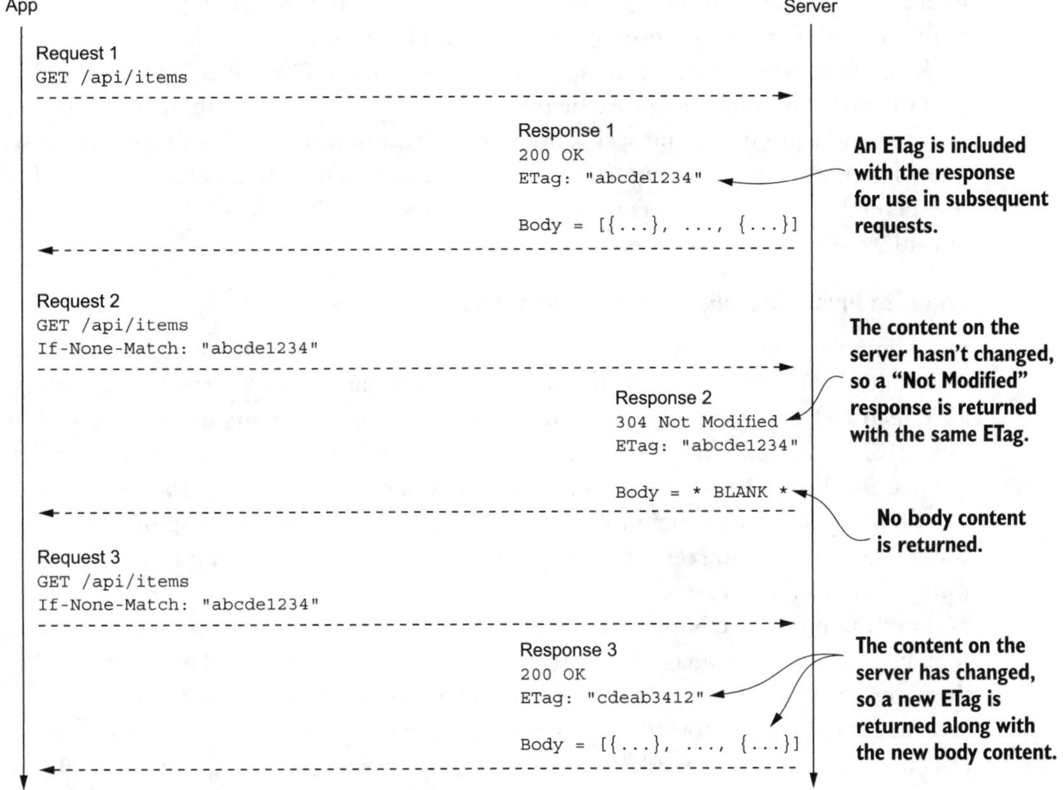

Figure 11.5 How using `ETag`s avoids downloading duplicate content that hasn't changed

Returning to the story about caching avatar images at the start of this section, here's how Melissa improved the app:

- Request the image and store the response on disk along with the information used to identify its age or changes (`ETag`, modified date, expiry date, expiry time, or a combination of these).
- When the image is needed again, show the version from disk.
- After loading the cached version and if it's stale, make a call to the server to check for a new version.
- If a new version isn't available, there's nothing to do, as the app already shows the current version.
- If a new version is available, update/overwrite the file on disk and update what's displayed. This way you can always display something, even if offline.

Be aware of many other HTTP headers and status codes, some of which also relate to caching. The ones mentioned previously will cover most cases and are enough for you to enable the caching of HTTP responses in your app. It's also important to be aware of the preceding solutions, even if you chose not to use them yourself.

Some frameworks, networks, and operating systems automatically act as a caching proxy if you don't include any cache-related headers in your requests. They do this to reduce bandwidth usage and save battery life. If you find that you're making requests but not getting the latest data from the server, this could be what's happening. That the server can tell you when content hasn't changed or when to check again is useful, but still leaves the issue of when to get rid of items you've cached.

11.4.3 When to invalidate and delete cached items

As Melissa learned of the benefits of caching, she added it throughout her app. Although this brought benefits to the app's performance, she started receiving negative feedback about the amount of disk space the app was taking up. It was creating lots of files on disk, and Melissa hadn't considered the potential negative consequences of this. Because of the benefits of disk-based caching, Melissa wasn't about to stop using it. Instead she implemented a step in her team's development process: she added a new feature to the app that reviewed if the team should cache something, and, if so, for how long.

Early attempts at creating a caching policy led to lots of different requirements and soon became hard to manage. Because of this, Melissa's team switched to a simple policy that considered anything cached as either high or low priority. The addition to the app of a background task enforced the policy by daily deleting any cached items with low priority if the amount of free disk space fell beneath a certain percentage, or the total disk space used by the cache grew above a certain percentage. These simple rules proved effective for Melissa, but she reviews their approach to caching on a periodic basis to ensure that they're doing what's best for their app as it grows and evolves.

I've heard it said that the biggest challenges in software development are these:

- Naming
- Cache invalidation
- Off-by-one errors

Naming and off-by-one errors are beyond the scope of this book, but cache invalidation is relevant, important, and worth your consideration. Because it's hard doesn't mean you should avoid it. It's hard because there are few scenarios where you can guarantee that you know someone will need the same resource, data, or image again, and it won't have changed in the meantime. The challenges are

- Identifying what can be removed from the cache
- Knowing whether to take something from the cache or check for a new version from the remote source

Even though there aren't absolutes, there are approaches you can take to provide a *good enough* solution. No rules will apply to every app and every situation, but here are some guidelines to help you figure out what's best for your app:

- *Don't depend on cached data.* By remembering that anything from a cache is a bonus and not a necessity to the functioning of the app, it's not the end of the world if you remove something from the cache but later need it again.
- *You don't need to cache everything.* The best type of data to keep on the device is data that doesn't change often or is hard or time-consuming to obtain or format.

If the app is usable without images, only cache the text content. If data changes often or is only valid for a short time, there's little benefit to caching it. Similarly, there's lots to gain from caching things that you need with every use of the app. You can avoid purging these from the cache if you regularly check for updates after using them.

Not all cached data is the same. Just as you shouldn't cache everything, not everything you cache will expire at the same time. If the server providing the content offers a lifetime for the content, use that. If the provider of the content doesn't tell you when to consider it stale, you'll need to make this decision based on the expected lifetime of the data, the expected frequency of change, and the amount of data to cache. If in doubt, as shown in figure 11.6, cache things that change regularly or you have a large number of for one day, and those that you have a few of and infrequently change for one week.

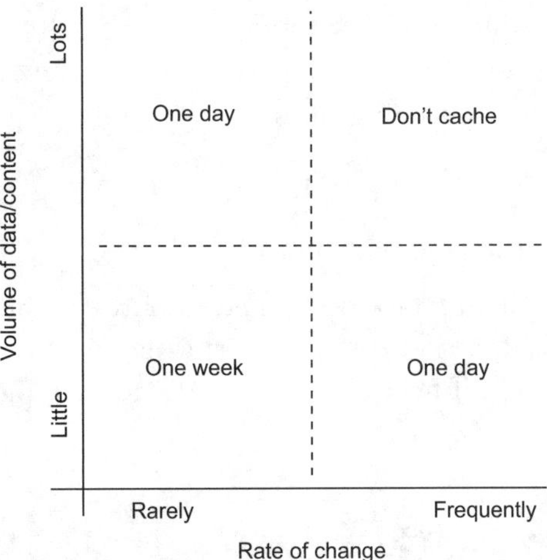

Figure 11.6 Default caching periods to use if no other information is known about the content and its use

The values in figure 11.6 are guidelines if you don't have information about when to consider items stale. If you don't have sufficient knowledge of the content used by the app, you should monitor this as the app is used and revise the values as necessary.

The type of data also affects where to store it. Store anything that isn't critical to offline use, such as cached information about the logged-in user, in temporary folders on the device so the OS can automatically delete the files if disk space starts to run low. If you store all data in locations exclusive to the app, its removal becomes *all or nothing* when it comes to management of the app by the OS or the settings app. You should also allow people to control the files created by the app from within the app. Although the OS may provide a way to delete files created by the app, you should also provide this within the app.

There may not be space to always save everything. If free space on a device is limited, you benefit by not using all of it. A full disk can cause apps to run slowly and make devices behave in unexpected ways while the OS tries to free up some space. Avoid contributing to the problem by only saving essential items when space is low and by deleting anything you don't need. Not using lots of disk space will also help your app when the OS prompts the person to free up space. If your app isn't using lots of space, it's less likely to be uninstalled to free up space and allow the device to continue being usable.

Allow people to bypass and control cached data. You may have displayed data from a cache that isn't stale, but if a person using the app specifically asks for a refresh or reloading of data, you should go to the original source to check for updates. Also provide a way to clear temporary and cached data created by the app. This is useful if a person experiences unexpected behavior within the app, as well as if disk space on the device becomes limited. The managing of cached items is a balancing act between

- The lifetime of the content
- The likelihood of needing something multiple times
- The disk space used for storing content
- The overhead of managing complex caching rules
- Offline support
- The speed of loading content
- The avoidance of duplicate requests and data transfer

If you're in doubt about the value of caching or have limited resources to dedicate to it, start simple and track how effective it is. It's better to start with a few simple rules applied everywhere and later revise them if necessary than to do no caching because you may need a complicated solution.

Put it into practice: cache content used by your app

- Identify content that the app retrieves multiple times, and evaluate the benefit of caching it on disk or in memory.
- If you already cache something, don't automatically delete it if it's stale. Ensure that you check for a new version first.
- Check the HTTP response headers from all the sources of your remote data to see which already support caching. Make use of those that do.
- Test your app's ability to cope with caching when the device it's on is low on free disk space.
- Test how your app handles cached files being deleted when the device removes temporary files.

Exercise: caching, true or false?

Check that you understand caching by stating whether the following are true or false:

1. Cache everything from a remote source.
2. Delete anything from the cache that's more than one week old.
3. If an app only works when online, there may still be benefits to caching.
4. Delete stale content when it's no longer current.
5. Content in an app can always be treated with the same caching rules.

After improving the performance of your app before people start using it, the next step is to make it faster while it's running. I'll show you how to do that in the next chapter.

Summary

- People don't use your app because they want to watch animations or look at your logo. They launch the app to get some value. You should make it as quick and easy as possible for them to get that value.
- Don't use splash screens to show ads or make them the only place you display helpful information.
- The best splash screen is no splash screen.
- An app that displays content should always have something to show. Even if it's offline when first used, include content with the app.
- Monitor startup times throughout the development process so you can identify when adding any delays.
- Formatting content once on a powerful machine takes a lot less effort than relying on every slow device that uses the content to format it.
- Formatting content on the server rather than in the app makes it much quicker to fix any formatting or processing issues for everyone using the app.
- Creating your own proxy server for content from third-party sources lets you improve the app experience.
- Cache any content from remote sources to avoid retrieving duplicate content and wasting resources.
- Use the existing capabilities of HTTP to handle request caching. Don't invent your own.
- Cache invalidation is a complex subject. You must balance the length of time something will be valid for, the likelihood it'll be needed again, and the amount of space used to keep a copy.

12 Making your app run fast

This chapter covers

- Preloading data
- Treating multiple operations as one
- Performing multiple operations simultaneously

In the last chapter, I showed you actions you can take before and during app startup to improve its responsiveness. In this chapter, I'll continue this theme and look at ways to improve the speed and responsiveness of an app while in use. Specifically, I'll cover three techniques:

- *Eager loading*—Lets people avoid having to wait for data to be retrieved.
- *Combining requests and responses*—Fewer requests take less time.
- *Making asynchronous requests*—Reduces the time spent waiting.

In this chapter, I'll also introduce you to Elliott. He has a shopping app where the primary use case involves finding items through a search function. I'll show you how he used each of the three techniques to address the following challenges:

- Search results that can't be preloaded
- Returning results slowly, leading to less use and fewer sales

- A chatty functionality with lots of requests and responses
- The need to retrieve data from multiple sources

12.1 Using eager loading so people don't have to wait

Avoid forcing people to wait while the app does something, as this negatively affects the experience of using the app. Eager loading is one way to do this. As a concept, eager loading is simple: you load something before it's needed so that it's available when required. The opposite of eager loading is lazy loading, which is when you wait until you need something before retrieving it. Both are useful, but in different ways and for different reasons. Chapter 14 includes more details on where and how lazy loading can be beneficial.

Eager loading is most appropriate when loading an item that may take some time. It's often used when loading large files from disk or when retrieving external resources, but you can use it anywhere. As with most simple ideas, there are places where eager loading is more appropriate than others, and so it shouldn't be applied to everything. I'll show you where, when, and how to use it shortly, but first, let me tell you how Elliott used eager loading to make his app and business more profitable.

Elliott's shopping app makes his company money when people make purchases through the app. The most popular way for people using the app to find what they want is through the search feature. The problem for Elliott was that the search was slow, and his company's analytics supported the belief that the longer it takes to complete a transaction, the higher the number of people who don't complete a purchase. His search process involved the following steps:

1. A search term was entered.
2. A list of result items was returned and displayed.
3. A result item was selected.
4. The full details of the selected item were retrieved and displayed.

It wasn't possible to predict and eagerly load search results before the user entered a search term in Elliott's app, but it was reasonable to load the data eagerly for the second request. Through the analytics already in the app, Elliott could see that in over 80% of the searches, people tapped one of the top three search results. With this insight, he changed the app to automatically retrieve the full details of the top three search results in the list. Although this was a small change, the company was able to attribute a measurable increase in sales. Figure 12.1 shows the difference in app logic and the potential time saved when eagerly loading the result details.

It's worth remembering that the performance of an app isn't always due to the app itself. All systems involved in providing content or value to a person through an app can impact the experience. If you're using third-party systems, there may be little you can do to change them. But if you or your company are also responsible for the server, you should consider the possibility of making improvements there too.

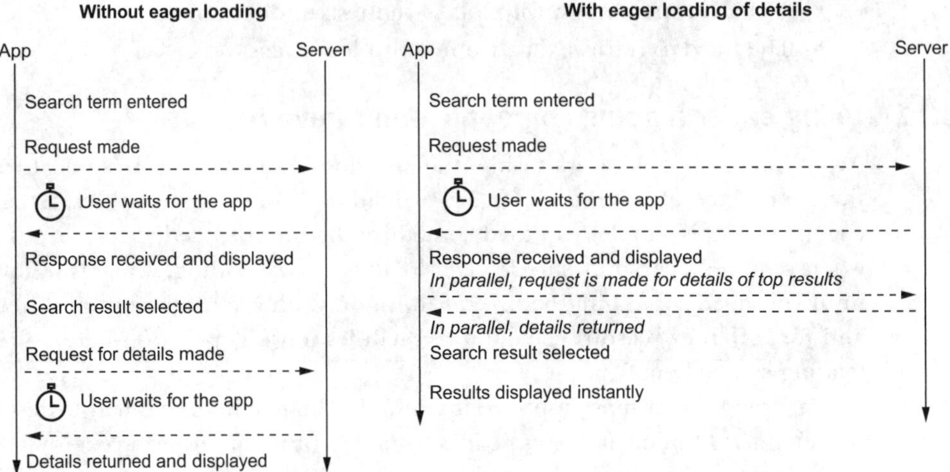

Figure 12.1 Comparing the activity flow for viewing search result details with and without eager loading

NOTE The performance of an app that retrieves data from a server is impacted by the effectiveness of the server too. Although performance optimization of websites is beyond the scope of this book, many other resources focus on that.

Some examples of improvements that could be made to a search functionality include the caching of common responses so that a database lookup isn't needed for each request, accounting for misspellings and typos, and searching for autocompleted terms rather than a provided value. For example, imagine the search function in a clothing app returning the results for "jumper" when a person has only entered "jum."

12.1.1 Eager loading complements preloading content

Eager loading for an app's next use is comparable with preloading content (as covered in chapter 11). Both are ways of reducing the time a person spends waiting before the app can show them what they want. With remote content, the difference between the two approaches is that preloading better suits more general content. Conversely, it's possible to eagerly load data specific to the current task when an app is running.

Whereas both eager loading and preloading are good ways to work with content from a remote source, only eager loading is appropriate for large amounts of data that will be loaded into memory. To go back to Elliott's app, it may make sense to preload remote items for display when opening the app, while eagerly loading the top search results in an active way.

As you saw in chapter 11, caching can happen in memory or on disk. When the app isn't running, however, only disk-based caching is possible. Figure 12.2 is a variation of figure 11.4. It shows eagerly loading (or *priming*) the in-memory cache before it's needed. Doing this is useful when something takes too long to load otherwise.

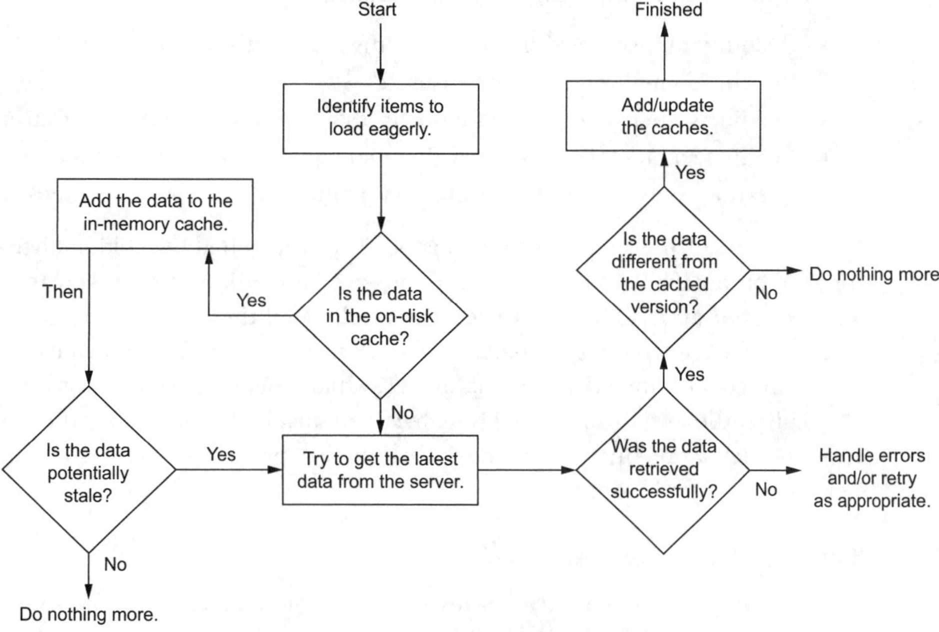

Figure 12.2 A workflow for priming the cache with eagerly loaded data

Priming the in-memory cache is often useful when working with large files. If your app needs the contents of a large file, then it's wise to start accessing it before it's needed. Splitting large files into multiple smaller ones can also help, but that isn't always possible. Many games take the time when they're launched to load all images into memory to avoid having the game stutter or pause when loading more graphics while playing.

It's not just in accessing files where you can apply the principles of eager loading. Some processes have time-consuming initialization steps that take longer when first used. If it takes longer to return a result the first time you query a database or use a specific API, do these things when starting the app and ignore or discard the results. Then, when the app needs to use them, they'll load quickly.

You can also consider automatically refreshing content as a form of eager loading. Doing this can have negative consequences, though. Frequently replacing content that's never shown to anyone can be unnecessarily wasteful. Also, changing displayed content without making it clear that, and why, it's changed can cause confusion. These are potential issues with being too eager, which we'll look at next.

12.1.2 Beware of being too eager

Being too eager can lead to the wasting of limited resources (possibly at the user's expense) and affects the performance of your app, as well as other apps that run on the same device. If you find your app doing any of the following, you may be too eager and should consider adjusting the app appropriately:

- Loading multiple versions of something before it's needed
- Loading something that's never used
- Loading something every time the app starts, but that's only used rarely
- Loading so much into memory that managing memory becomes an issue
- Creating so many temporary files that managing disk space becomes an issue

As with many of the suggestions in this book, you may need to add analytics to your app to monitor if any of the previous points are happening. It's unlikely that the people using your app will be able to accurately tell you if these things occur.

A lot of eager loading scenarios mean doing more work when starting the app. This conflicts with the advice in chapter 11, which encouraged doing as little as possible to allow the app to start quickly. A balance must be found to give the best experience in each app. But, in the next section, I'll point out some guidelines when considering eager loading.

12.1.3 Knowing what to load eagerly

Knowing what to load eagerly can involve a delicate balance of doing too much versus not doing enough. You want the app to be fast, but not cause the device to get hot from doing too much processing or waste money by transferring unnecessary data. As a general guide, start by eagerly loading for the three following scenarios. Then adjust to add more based on the priorities and the performance impact in your app:

- *Essential functionality*—Eagerly load anything you can that wouldn't cause the person using the app to wait unnecessarily before using the primary functionality of the app.
- *Bottlenecks highlighted by analytics*—Use analytics to track the time the person spends waiting for the app before they can continue with their task. Delays in the most commonly used features and those that are time-consuming are good candidates for eager loading.
- *When continuing offline*—If the app has functionality or use cases that involve starting a task while online but continuing without access to a network or the internet, eagerly load what's needed offline. Such scenarios are more common in enterprise apps or those related to travel, but can happen elsewhere too.

Eagerly loading content can take time and impact device resources. For this reason, it's important to load content eagerly in the background and not block the UI thread or impede a person's ability to interact with the app. You should make these requests in parallel with other activity; that's what I'll cover next.

Put it into practice: eagerly load content used by your app

- Identify anything that would benefit from eager loading on startup, and enable it.
- Where a workflow in the app involves a sequence of operations, and where possible, automatically start the next step so it's ready when needed.
- Identify places where a person has to wait for some content to download or load, and, if possible, start the retrieval process early.
- For anything that's slow on first use, do it once in advance and discard the results so that it'll be fast when needed.
- Add analytics that track how long a person must wait for the app, and then act to remove any bottlenecks that are highlighted.

Exercise: when to load data eagerly

Test your understanding of eager loading by looking at the following scenarios and stating if they should load eagerly:

1. The top story in a news app that has preloaded the list of stories
2. The purchase history in a shopping app
3. The details of customers with upcoming appointments in an app for salespeople
4. Level information for all levels in a game
5. Recently captured photos for an image-sharing app

12.2 Parallel operations take less time

Imagine you have two tasks to perform, and each takes five seconds to complete. Doing one after the other will take a total of 10 seconds. When the aim is to make things as fast as possible, it's better to do them at the same time and avoid making someone wait five unnecessary seconds.

To perform something *in parallel* means doing it at the same time as something else. It could be making a request or performing a task at the same time as making another request, or it could be while doing something completely different. The search feature of Elliott's shopping app has some functionality that would benefit from running in parallel.

In the last section, I said that over 80% of the people using the search feature in Elliott's app would select one of the top three entries in the results, but the actions performed before selecting a result weren't always the same. Approximately half of the people who used the app would tap one of the immediately viewable results. The other half would always scroll down, tap Load More, and look at those results before selecting an option to view in more detail, even if the option they chose was one of the first few originally displayed. That they had to wait while more results loaded was a potential bottleneck.

The app also loaded results from different sources for different categories of products within the app. It loaded each category in turn, with the order based on past preferences. Elliott improved the speed of the app in both these areas by performing operations in parallel. On receiving the first set of results, the app would begin downloading the second page of results in the background, while displaying the first page. This meant that anyone scrolling down and pressing Load More didn't have to wait as long, or at all, before seeing more results. Because user behavior was so consistent (people would either scroll down and load more or never scroll), after using the search feature a couple of times, a hidden settings flag indicated if people were a scroller or not. If they weren't, the app did not automatically retrieve the next page of results, and so avoided requesting data they'd never see.

Although the Load More scenario was parallelized by making a request when the user was doing something else, improving the speed of retrieving multiple search results involved parallelizing multiple concurrent requests. Rather than make the requests one after the other, they were all made at the same time and displayed when returned. Figure 12.3 shows the changes in Elliott's app.

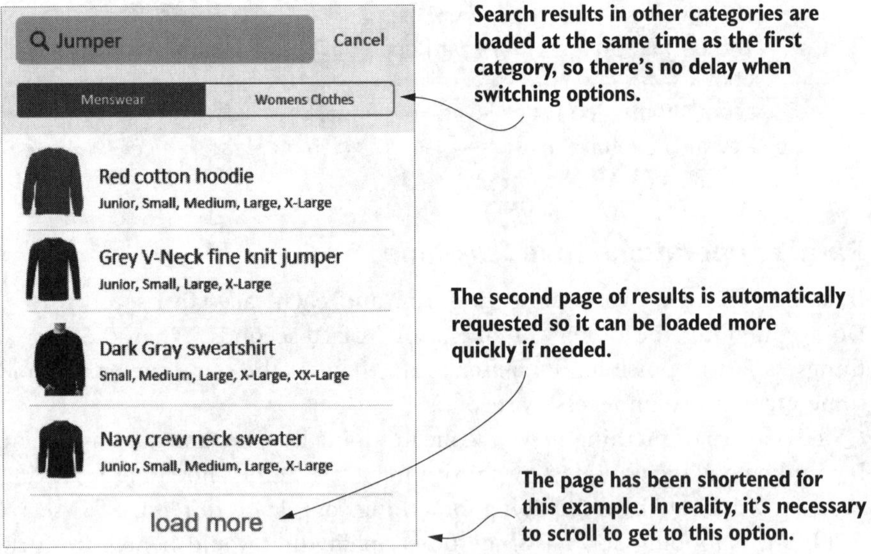

Figure 12.3 The search page in Elliott's app and how it was enhanced

> **Parallelism and concurrency**
>
> Throughout this chapter, I talk about doing things *at the same time* as a catchall phrase for operations that happen either concurrently or in parallel. The difference between the two is that parallel activities happen literally at the same time, and concurrent operations appear to happen at the same time. As device specifications improve to include more CPU cores, a device's ability to perform truly parallel operations also gets better.
>
> My experience has been that there's rarely a need to distinguish between parallel and concurrent operations in an app. If you run into issues with simultaneous activity, it's likely to be due to the number of I/O operations or network connections that can be made at the same time. These are easily addressed by queueing requests.

12.2.1 Synchronous and asynchronous operations

It isn't always possible or necessary to do everything in parallel. There can be reasons for and benefits to not doing multiple things at the same time. It's important that you understand the advantage of each approach and when to use them. Performing operations in parallel means doing them all at the same time. The opposite of this is doing them sequentially, or one after the other.

Sequential and parallel operations are roughly equivalent to synchronous and asynchronous coding patterns. With a *synchronous* request, the caller waits for a response before continuing. With an *asynchronous* request, the caller isn't blocked while waiting for a response and can continue to perform other tasks. The way different platforms and programming languages implement asynchronous capabilities varies, but the principles are the same.

> **The async keyword**
>
> Both JavaScript and C# languages use the keyword `async` that allows them to create asynchronous requests using promises and tasks. These aren't the only types of asynchronous requests possible with these or other programming languages. They're syntactic sugar that enables writing asynchronous methods that look like synchronous ones. Some programming languages don't use this keyword, which avoids confusion in this area.

After learning the benefits of doing things asynchronously, it can be tempting to use it for everything. But like any tool, there are advantages and disadvantages to doing something in parallel or sequentially. Table 12.1 lists the pros and cons of such operations.

Table 12.1 Comparing parallel and sequential operations

	Pros	Cons
Sequential/Synchronous	Necessary when dependencies exist between actions. Easier to write and debug code in this format.	Total time to complete all actions is longer, which makes the app slower.
Parallel/Asynchronous	Time needed to complete all tasks is shorter. Can avoid blocking the UI or preventing the person from continuing to use the app for another task.	Can be harder to code and debug, although some languages and tooling make this easier. Harder to follow flow through code when multiple things happen at once. The possibility of race conditions, as there's no guarantee of the order of execution. Higher likelihood of thread safety issues and deadlocks. Harder to manage things finishing at different times.

12.2.2 Advice when working in parallel

You'll find many quirks and gotchas when you move to doing things in parallel. In this section, I'll point out areas to pay special attention to, so you can ensure a great experience with your app.

The number one rule of asynchronous operations is to never block the UI thread. If for no other reason, you should use asynchronous operations to ensure that the person using the app can continue to interact with it, and the app doesn't appear to have frozen. If that's the case, this might frustrate the person using the app, or it could lead to the termination of your app by the OS. Seeing dialogs like the one in figure 12.4 doesn't inspire confidence.

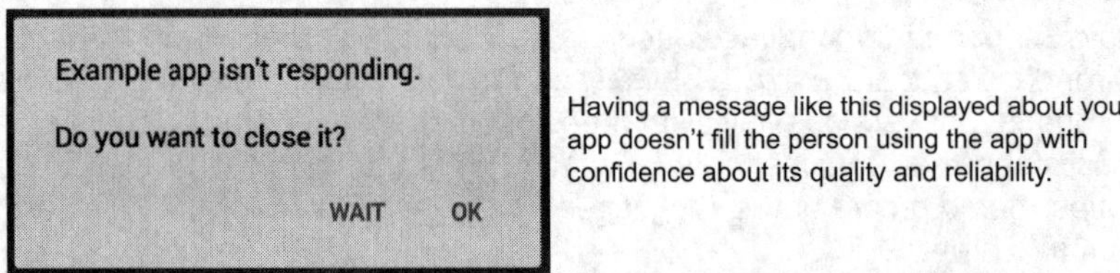
Example app isn't responding.
Do you want to close it?
WAIT
OK
Having a message like this displayed about your app doesn't fill the person using the app with confidence about its quality and reliability.

Figure 12.4 Android dialog showing that an app appears to have frozen

Keep the people using the app informed of what's happening. This is true of single operations, but even more so with multiple parallel operations. Passive indicators of activity, like a busy indicator in the task bar, are useful as subtle signs of activity when doing something in the background.

The level of information you give when making multiple parallel requests should be as specific as is necessary to be useful. It's more helpful to provide general rather than specific information. A simple Loading Data message is better than long descriptions of all the data the app is retrieving. This applies to exception messages too. Displaying a prompt that the loading of a specific piece of data failed when making multiple requests in parallel can raise more questions than it answers, especially if it isn't possible to retry only the failed request.

NOTE It's better to fail silently when trying to eagerly load something in the background than to display a message unrelated to what a person is doing.

Loading data from multiple sources at one time also isn't an excuse for not having an app that loads data quickly. Don't let the loading of any initial data suffer at the expense of reducing the time to load all data. It's rare that a person needs all the data before they can get any value from an app. Get to content quickly. If loading a long list or multiple pages of data, load enough to fill the screen first and then load the rest in the background.

The best number of items to initially load and display in a list depends on the number that fit onscreen at one time, the time it takes to load more, and the number retrievable at the same time. As a general guide, get twice the number that fit onscreen at once, but adjust this if necessary to your circumstances.

When working with data requests that may first return cached data and then an updated version of that data from the server, the calling code has to deal with either one or two responses. Handling two responses is more complicated, but things can get even more difficult when needing to handle multiple pages of results and retrieve multiple results at the same time. Reactive programming (Rx) and the use of the observer pattern offer a solution to this.

At a simplified level, Rx allows you to say, "On receiving data, handle it this way." A single function can then handle any number of responses. It requires thinking about the received data as more of a stream than a response to a single request, but can be powerful. To learn more about Rx, see the following titles:

- Timo Tuominen, *Grokking FRP* (Manning, 2016)
- Paul P. Daniels and Luis Atencio, *RxJS in Action* (Manning, 2017)
- Tamir Dresher, *Rx.Net in Action* (Manning, 2017)

In addition to asking for data before the person using the app requests it, you can also improve the perceived speed of uploading files or data before the person presses Send. Consider this workflow:

1. Capture a video or image.
2. Enter information, such as a title, description, tags, and so forth.
3. Upload all the information.

In this workflow, there's no reason to wait for all the information to be entered before starting the uploading of media, thereby doing points 2 and 3 in parallel. Uploading a large image or video can be time-consuming. Doing some or all of that work while the other information is entered reduces the time spent waiting for the app to finish the entire upload. Working like this requires a backend that supports sending data this way and one that can handle data never being sent. Sending the image first is a bit more work, but that can improve the overall experience.

Instagram adopted this pattern of sending the image before the associated data. It set a new standard among its competitors for how fast image uploading should take. In some cases, the apparent speed of the upload was so fast that some users thought it couldn't possibly have successfully completed in that time. Instagram had to adapt the UI to make it clear that it was that quick.

NOTE You should consider any data privacy or security issues about uploading content before it's explicitly requested.

Don't restrict your thinking about parallel operations to network-based activities. They apply to disk-based ones too. As with remote data, this applies to both the retrieval and persistence of data. Don't load data while doing something else. Consider also saving, possibly automatically, data or settings while the person using the app is concerned with other tasks.

Making asynchronous requests can reduce the total time multiple requests take, but making fewer requests can be faster still. One way of reducing the number of requests made is by combining them. The next section covers this.

Put it into practice: making asynchronous requests

- Look for sequential operations that can be performed in parallel, and change them to work this way.
- Ensure that you give a visual indicator of background network activity.
- Ensure appropriate communication when one or more parallel requests fail.
- Ensure that you never block the UI. Test with an artificially long delay added to any activity that could potentially be time-consuming. The OS should never stop the app while performing any lengthy activity.
- Research a reactive approach to data retrieval, and explore how it can work for you.
- Review places where you upload or save data, and, if appropriate, make plans to do this in parallel with other user activity.

Exercise: acting asynchronously

Fill in the blanks in the following paragraph to confirm your understanding of what you've read about asynchronous operations:

Performing activities in ______ can be faster than doing them sequentially. This allows the person using the app to spend ______ time waiting while it's busy. Parallel operations can apply to the ______ and persistence of both local and ______ data. Doing everything sequentially can be simpler for the person ______ the app but can ______ affect the overall experience.

12.3 Combining requests for improved speed and control

Making fewer requests in your code can lead to faster data retrieval and an app that has simpler code. These are factors that make the app faster for the people using it. It also helps you increase the reliability of the code, which reduces support and maintenance costs. To do that, in this section I cover the following:

- How controlling the server the app connects to leads to a better app
- How combined requests are faster than multiple requests
- How combined requests simplify the code in the app
- How requests for data on the device can be combined

Making fewer requests can be faster and simpler than making many requests, even when making those requests in parallel. If the requirements of the app mean that you must retrieve multiple pieces of information, then it's better to get them all with a single request.

In Elliott's app, even after he enhanced the search feature to be faster by using eager loading and parallel requests, the app was still making more requests than necessary. The app

- Retrieved the summary search response and individual item details separately
- Made at least two requests when a person scrolled through the search results
- Made separate requests to each of the search providers

To address the first issue, Elliott changed the search results so that the full details of the top three items were included. This meant that for 80% of cases, the app could allow someone to perform a search and show the complete details of the desired item while needing to only make a single request to the server.

Addressing the second issue required increasing the number of items returned in each page of results, so the need to load more was removed for most people who scrolled down the list. The internal setting to identify a person as a scroller was used to only return the larger page size if it was likely to be relevant. In either case, the ability to load more was still available when more results were requested.

Returning results from all search providers at once was more complicated. It involved a trade-off between the simplicity of functionality and the time to get content into the app. Rather than make multiple calls, it's much easier for the app to make one call and have the server aggregate the different provider results. But this requires getting responses from all the providers before they can be combined and the results returned.

12.3.1 Controlling the server your app connects to

Having full control of the external requests your app makes can lead to simpler code on the client and to faster communication with the server, leading to a more responsive app. In chapter 11, I recommended creating your own server endpoint for your app to talk to and act as a proxy between the ultimate source of the data the app requests. In addition to the benefits listed previously, having your own proxy server offers the ability for you to combine requests. The need to combine requests and the way of combining them is often app-specific and not something offered widely. The ability to combine communication with different servers is also only something you can do yourself.

> **NOTE** The API that a server provides isn't an excuse for your app having to work in a way that isn't how you'd like it to. Create the API you want for your app, not just what the server returns. This also protects you from unexpected changes in what the server returns.

Because not all the combined requests may be successful, you'll have to deal with a response that may be partially successful. This might seem daunting at first, but should be no more complex to handle than making multiple parallel requests that may not all complete successfully. In addition to combining requests by having your own server return data to your app, you can also introduce further benefits and optimizations such as caching, compression, or even changing the protocol used for communication. Your communication doesn't have to be JSON over HTTP. Data in a binary format over a socket connection can be preferable in some circumstances.

12.3.2 Getting faster responses by combining requests

When making multiple requests to a server, even the same server, there are steps in establishing the connection that must be repeated for every request. Steps such as enabling the radio may be unsurprisingly slow, but even multiple DNS resolutions and protocol handshaking can add up. Removing this unnecessary duplication makes the app faster.

To show how much time you can save by combining requests, I created a simple app that would retrieve content from four different URLs and then display the size of the body in each response. I implemented the functionality in four different ways to show the difference in results:

- *Sequential*—Made a request for first URL, got a response, requested the next, and so on.
- *Parallel*—Made all requests at the same time.
- *Proxied*—Made one request to the server including the list of URLs. The server then made individual requests (in parallel) and returned all the results at once.
- *Optimized*—Taking everything from this chapter and chapter 11, the server not only cached responses from the other servers but also cached responses to requests. It also did some processing, so it only returned the size of each response, not the whole body.

All requests were made from a single device over a 3G network connection, and timing was done with the clock timer on the device. I made all attempts to avoid any third-party proxies and caches that could have impacted the results. All testing was done over a period of a few minutes. Strict lab conditions weren't available, but everything was as consistent as I could get in my house. Figure 12.5 shows the times taken by each of the different approaches when making the requests 10 times.

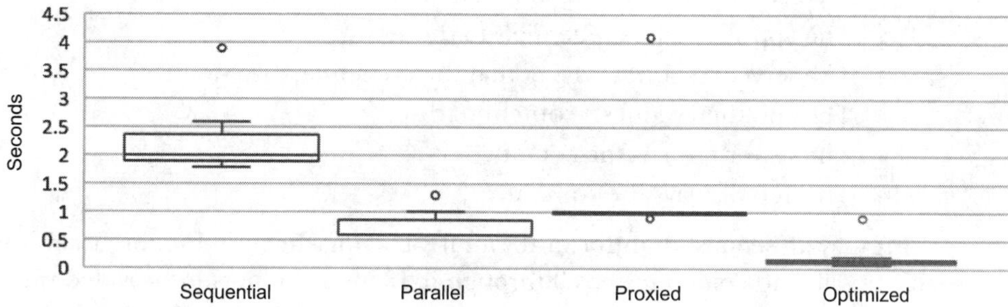

Figure 12.5 The response times of different approaches to making multiple requests. The parallel and proxied approaches are twice as fast as the sequential approach, but the fully optimized requests are more than 10 times as fast.

By making requests in parallel, the total time taken was more than halved. But when combining the requests and adjusting the response to be only what the app needs, the total time taken was cut by 90%. When the speed of response matters, it's clear that you can make potentially significant savings by optimizing what's sent and received and how it's packaged. Table 12.2 summarizes the key values.

Table 12.2 Average times for retrieving data using different techniques

	Sequential	Parallel	Proxied	Optimized
Mean time (secs)	2.24	0.73	1.29	0.212
Median time (secs)	2.0	0.6	1.0	0.14

As an alternative to rolling your own solution for combining responses from the same server, HTTP/2 also offers some capability for this. An explanation of the full features of HTTP/2 is beyond what I can offer in this book, but there's a good introduction in *Web Performance in Action* by Jeremy L. Wagner (Manning, 2016).

12.3.3 Simplifying the client by combining requests

In the tests in the last section, the optimized version moved the logic to the server. It was simple logic for measuring the length of some text, but it meant that logic didn't need to be in the app. That logic was trivial, but the code for manipulating server responses can be complex, and moving it to the server reduces client app complexity. Reduced complexity in the client reduces the risk of bugs, which saves on maintenance and support costs.

The other way that combining requests can simplify client code is by combining sequential requests. There's a benefit for designing apps based on how the data the app uses is available. Consider this common scenario:

1. A person enters their sign-in credentials.
2. The app sends the credentials to the server.
3. The server responds, saying that the credentials are valid.
4. The app then requests content to display.
5. The server returns the content.
6. The app displays the content.

This may all seem straightforward, but it's making the app do more than it needs to. It's possible to combine steps 3 through 5. If, after the person provided valid credentials, the server responds by saying, "Those credentials are valid AND here's the content you'll need next," it removes the need for the client to ask separately. Yes, the client still needs to handle failures and exceptions, but there's a reduction in the work it needs to do, combined with a speed improvement from making fewer requests.

In addition to sign-in processes, you can use this approach anywhere the client would wait for the response from one request before making another. A common scenario where I've seen apps that could benefit from this is when the app displays more content from a collection than the server returns in a single page of results. Rather than have the client request the first page, wait for the results, and then get the next, the app could get them all at once. If you can control the server the app talks to, you can avoid such constraints.

Beware of premature optimization

Optimizing your code and the communication it makes with a server can bring lots of benefits, but it can also be more work. Optimizations for the sake of it are normally a bad idea. Test and measure what you're considering optimizing before doing so. By prioritizing areas with known issues and quantifying the improvements, you avoid wasting effort.

Optimized code is also normally longer or more complicated, increasing the effort needed to support and maintain it. This extra effort should be factored into decisions about what to optimize.

12.3.4 Combining requests and local files

As with all data access, don't ignore local file access and think exclusively of remote communications. The opportunity of improving performance also exists for combining, or not, local file access.

If you need only a small amount of data, you don't want to have to open and load a large file to get it. Similarly, if you need a large amount of data, you shouldn't have to access lots of small files. As you consider the format you use to store data, also think about how you'll access it if you decide to store it in separate files. As with all things, you should test to find the appropriate sizes for your app, but, as a general guideline, consider dividing files once they reach 300 KB in size.

A compromise is also possible with large amounts of data stored in a single file: keep a copy of the most recent or important data in a separate, smaller file. Load and display the content of the smaller file first so that useful, actionable content can be displayed in the app while loading the rest of the data in the background.

Put it into practice: combine requests

- Weigh the costs, benefits, and risks of creating your own proxy server to marshal communication between the app and any other remote endpoints. If cost effective and possible, make plans to do this.
- Find any sequential requests that can be done in parallel, and change them to run in parallel.
- Look for parallel or sequential requests that you can combine, and do so.
- Evaluate the size of files created on disk. Combine small ones, and split up any large ones as appropriate.

Exercise: combining requests, true or false?

Test your understanding of combining requests by stating whether the following are true or false:

1. Your app must communicate with your own server to be able to combine requests.
2. When using combined requests, your app still has to deal with all the requests not returning successfully.
3. The combining of requests requires support from the server you're connecting to.
4. You can only combine requests made in parallel.
5. All apps should combine all requests.

Much of the detail in this chapter has related to data retrieved from a remote source. Access to a remote source depends on connectivity, and that's what the next chapter is about.

Summary

- Eager loading is based on the same idea as the preloading of data. Get the data before it's needed so a person isn't left waiting for the app to retrieve it.
- Load anything that enables the use of the app as quickly as possible.
- For actions that take a long time when first performed, do them once before they're needed so that they respond.

- Not everything can or should be eagerly loaded. The most important data to eagerly load includes that which slows down essential functionality in the app, is widely used but slow to retrieve, or is necessary for working offline.
- Prefer parallel operations over sequential ones. Code that performs many actions in parallel can be harder to write and debug, but the benefits of an app that works this way outweigh the negatives.
- Give a visual indication when doing something in the background, especially if connecting remotely.
- Never block the UI thread while executing a task.
- The API that a server provides isn't an excuse for your app having to work in a way that isn't how you'd like it. Creating your own proxy server allows you to optimize the API your app communicates with.
- Parallel and sequential operations can be combined to make them both faster and simpler.
- You can improve the loading of both local and remote data by accessing it eagerly, doing it in parallel, and combining multiple small operations into one operation.

Part 5

Connectivity

More than 90% of all mobile apps connect to the internet in some way. Based on what I've covered so far in this book, you should be aware that having an app communicate with you over the internet must be the default, with very few exceptions. That way you can receive analytics information even if the app doesn't need to connect to a remote service or data source.

For many of us, ready access to high-speed Wi-Fi and 4G LTE connectivity is a given, but there's no guarantee of this for all people, in all places, and at all times. For this reason, it's important that you consider how changes and variations in connectivity will impact the experience of using your app.

As with everything else, connectivity doesn't exist in isolation. Context has a big impact, and the consequences of connectivity affect the perception of responsiveness. In the next chapter, I'll teach you how to think about and handle the variety of connectivity situations that your app will inevitably meet.

13 Coping with varying network conditions

This chapter covers

- How network conditions vary
- Network connections and what to expect
- Working with different periods or conditions
- Providing great experiences with limiting conditions

Users of modern mobile devices expect to access content at any time and in any location. They expect your app to work and don't want to think about connectivity. Many factors influence the ability to connect to and use a network to access content and services; these factors can make people's expectations unreasonable. Rather than trying to justify why some things are hard, you'll create the best experience for the people using your app if you focus on improving the experience for all scenarios.

Throughout this chapter, you'll learn how to cope with the connectivity variations that your app will encounter, and how to ensure the best experience you can even with a limited connection. You'll then learn how to balance the quality of the experience with the currently available connection, keeping the people using the app informed and in control, so they remain positive about their experience with your app.

In this chapter, I'll also introduce you to Rosa. She developed an app for capturing and sharing images and videos. These were specifically aimed at local events and activities for people around the world, who normally wouldn't be aware of such happenings. You'll see how she overcame connectivity issues affecting both the download and upload of large files, and how she made sure the app was always able to provide value, even when offline or experiencing poor network conditions.

13.1 Not all connections are the same

Connections vary with regard to security, speed, and cost. Each of these variations can influence the experience of using your app, and not allowing for them can lead to a poor experience for some of the people using it. In this section, I look at how the three ways a connection may vary can impact your app. You'll learn what you can do to ensure the best experience for your users.

13.1.1 Securing your connection

The security of your connection is important for the privacy of the people whose data you're transmitting. Always use secure forms of communication, if available. For most situations, this means using HTTPS rather than HTTP. For some platforms, this is a requirement, but even if it isn't, its use can avoid other side effects.

Rosa had an issue that was the result of not using HTTPS for the images displayed in her app. Some people complained about the poor quality of the images when viewed in the app. The issue was the result of transmitting the images over the mobile network of an operator that automatically re-encoded the images to a smaller size. The operator did this to save on the amount of data sent over its network. The downside for Rosa's app was a reduction in image quality. Switching to sending the images over HTTPS meant that the network couldn't change them.

The use of HTTPS can be a little expensive and requires more work to set up, but it's worth the time and effort to ensure that you always use a secure connection for all communication, even during development and testing. If you have circumstances or scenarios where you deem it OK to use insecure connections, it's too easy for one of those to end up in the live app. If you never allow the use of unsecured connections, then you remove the possibility of an accidental security breach.

The privacy of data for the people using your app is important when storing data on the device and when sending it over a network, but data in transmission has other potential considerations. As Rosa discovered, the servers, networks, and devices data can pass through on its way to the app can affect the data if not secured. Re-encoded and downgraded images are one issue, but the consequences can be more serious. Not securing the content in transit can lead to its modification in other ways. There have been cases, maliciously or otherwise, of the following content changes:

- Removal of ads from the content
- Adding extra ads to the content

- Changing URIs so that embedded links point to different sites or add extra tracking details
- Changes to caching headers with the potential to change application behavior

Always using HTTPS for your communications not only protects the security of the data, it safeguards the integrity of the content of your app. The use of HTTPS on its own isn't enough, however. You must also check that the data you receive has the proper signature, and it must be from the correct certificate.

13.1.2 Connection speed can vary

The speed of the available data connection can vary dramatically. Also, assumptions about always having a high-speed connection can lead to a poor usability experience when the assumption is wrong, as Rosa soon discovered.

Rosa's app downloads a lot of images. When she was developing and testing the app, this wasn't a problem. But after the release of the app, she received lots of reports about the app being slow to get into a usable state. Whereas Rosa was using a high-speed, broadband data connection, many of her users were on much slower mobile networks that took longer to download the images. Rosa solved this issue by adding custom placeholders for the images based on the main color of the graphic, as mentioned in section 8.5.3. More importantly, she became aware that she needed to consider and test for the ways a variation in connection can impact an app. In the following sections, we'll look at the ways variations in connection speed can affect your app and how to test for these.

HOW CONNECTION SPEED VARIATIONS CAN AFFECT YOUR APP

If your app only transfers small amounts of text-based data over a network, the speed of the connection can have little impact. The inclusion of images and other media in apps, however, makes it increasingly rare that apps only transfer a small amount of data.

The speed of data transfer can be as low as 40 KB/sec on 2G mobile networks and up to 100 MB/sec, or even more, on broadband or Wi-Fi connections. But more factors can affect the bandwidth available:

- *Network throttling*—Some networks, especially mobile, limit the available bandwidth to a specific device so it can't get data as fast as it's capable of.
- *Total network traffic*—When lots of people use a network at the same time, it requires dividing the total available bandwidth into smaller amounts for each person and device. Dividing bandwidth can have an impact on local as well as wider networks.
- *Network architecture and hardware capabilities*—This can mean a reduction of the speed of a local network to that of the slowest router in the network. I've known companies to get better performance in their apps by upgrading their routers than they did by rewriting the apps.
- *Geographic distance to the server*—This can be a factor for apps with a global user base. The use of a content delivery network (CDN) or multiple servers in different

countries can mean that the app isn't waiting for electrons to travel halfway around the world for each request.

- *Server speed*—The speed of the server hosting the content can often have the biggest influence on the overall time taken to obtain data. If possible, consider optimizations that can be made on the server, as well as what it sends over the network.

Before transferring a large amount of data (either upload or download), check the available speed. Don't rely on the type of connection. A tethered device might report as connected over Wi-Fi while still using a mobile network for internet access. If you can choose the type of connection to use, and with no other information available, favor Wi-Fi over a mobile network. But check the speed presently available before starting a large transfer, and warn the user if it's likely to take a long time, or longer than usual.

TESTING FOR CONNECTION SPEED VARIATIONS

The ability to reliably test over different connection speeds requires structuring the code of the app. Although many emulators and simulators offer the ability to mimic different connection speeds, there are times when you need to test on a device.

If the app's code has a single place where all network requests are made, it's easy to use this part of the codebase to add artificial delays for each request to simulate slow connections. As a start, it's a simple way to test different connection speeds. Extending this with the ability to inject random delays can be useful, but it's also necessary to record and to replay such delays if you find any errors when doing this.

In addition to specifically testing for speed issues, you can benefit by regularly using your app at slower speeds to become familiar with what the people using your app experience. Although there are benefits to developing and testing with the fastest machines and environments available, it's important to understand the realities of the people who use your app. An example of this is Facebook's 2G Tuesdays. Once a week, staff are encouraged to use a simulated 2G connection to better understand the experience of users in emerging markets, where high-speed connections aren't available.

13.1.3 Connection cost can vary

As data charges for different networks can vary dramatically, it's important to consider this to make sure the costs for the people using the app aren't large, and that the app will still work if someone has disabled mobile data usage to save money. In this section, I'll cover the key areas to consider and what you can do about each. First, let's look at Rosa's app.

Rosa encountered a problem with her app in this area when a background process used by the app to upload video got stuck and repeatedly tried to upload the same large file. The consequences were a large data bill for the user and an unhappy customer. Having the same file uploaded repeatedly was a bug that needed fixing. But it also highlighted the cost of mobile data for some of her users. In response to this,

Rosa added a capability for users to opt into having files automatically uploaded over a metered connection.

Many people pay for mobile data, and the amount can vary around the world. Relative to income, this can be so expensive that some people will disable mobile data usage on their device and rely only on Wi-Fi when available. The cost of data when roaming between networks can also be much higher and can be a reason for people to disable data use. This is another reason to ensure that, as far as is possible, your app can work without a data connection, but it doesn't have to be all or nothing when it comes to data use:

- Consider getting user confirmation before using a metered connection.
- Allow the user to control data within the app when using roaming connections.
- Where possible, use the connection method that's most likely to be the cheapest.
- Warn the user before transferring (uploading or downloading) large amounts of data.
- Allow the deferring of the downloading of data until on a cheaper, or faster, connection when such a connection isn't presently available.

The amount of data your app uses isn't a secret. As shown in figure 13.1, the OS can show the amount of data each app uses. Using more than the user expects can cause suspicion and concern from the owner of the device and the person who's paying for all the data.

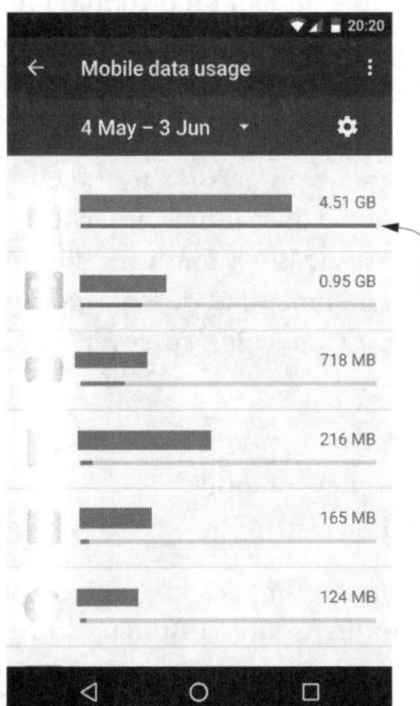

This app has been using a considerable amount of data. If this isn't appropriate to the function of the app, it could lead to an unhappy person. (The apps here have been anonymized to protect the innocent and the guilty.)

Figure 13.1 A device can show how much data has been used by each app, making it hard to hide wasteful usage of someone's potentially expensive data.

Put it into practice: allowing for connection variations

- Switch to using HTTPS if you can. Make plans for how you'll do this if you can't change right away.
- If you have a widely distributed user base, move static content to a CDN.
- Include the ability to add artificial delays on each network request as a way of simulating slower connections when testing on physical devices.
- Make testing on slower devices and connections a regular part of your development and testing practices.
- Add settings to avoid sending large amounts of data over a metered connection without the user's approval.

13.2 Occasionally connected is the norm

In this section, I'll show you how to approach connections that

- Can't be made
- Are lost while the app is in use
- Vary over a session with the app

It's easy and can be convenient to think about connections as consistent and always available, but that isn't reality. A common response to the potential variations in connectivity is to try to allow for the loss of connections. But it's normally simpler to approach it from the position of not having a connection and then adding functionality when a connection is possible.

13.2.1 Connections may not be possible

Many factors influence connectivity, from the available networks to the current state of the server you're connecting to. For apps that need an online connection, the value they provide may depend on the ability to connect. But value isn't absolute. Even though you may not be able to provide value all the time, that doesn't mean that your app can't be useful, even when a connection isn't possible. To cover this scenario, these three approaches can provide value:

- Save things to send later.
- Have default content available so the app is never empty.
- Save content displayed when the app was last used.

Lots of people who used Rosa's app would capture images and videos in remote areas where they had no signal. Without the ability to upload them at the point of capture, they could lose the content. The solution was to save the captured content and then automatically upload it later when a suitable connection was available. I cover that next.

SAVE THINGS TO SEND LATER

I previously claimed that thinking about being offline first was preferable for making a better experience, and these are great examples. Consider these two scenarios for when the app captures an image:

- *The device is offline, so it's not possible to upload the image.* The app stays on the upload screen, waiting for the user to press the Retry button when a connection is available. The user can't continue using the app until the upload is complete or risks losing the image they've captured.
- *The app places the image in a queue, ready to upload when a suitable connection is available.* The main UI and app logic can continue once the image is in the queue. A background process manages uploading items from the queue and reports progress.

In the second scenario, a lack of connectivity doesn't stop the ability to navigate around the app or progress through a task. This approach works well whenever this connectivity scenario exists. If the app works while offline, it can cope with any variation in connectivity, and, for whatever reason, when a connection isn't available.

HAVE DEFAULT CONTENT AVAILABLE, SO THE APP IS NEVER EMPTY

In chapter 11, I suggested including default content with the app when shipping so that there's always cached data to show when first starting the app. This content can also be useful if using the app while offline.

SAVE CONTENT DISPLAYED WHEN THE APP WAS LAST USED

People switch between apps and tasks regularly. Someone may leave your app partway through a task or when consuming a piece of content and expect to return and resume where they left off. Except for streaming media, a change in connectivity shouldn't prevent someone continuing where they were when they last used the app. By following these simple guidelines, you avoid unnecessarily taking away content from a person while they're consuming it:

- Keep a disk-based cache of displayed content when someone leaves the app.
- Don't discard what was previously shown.
- Avoid automatically loading new content when a session is resumed.

Two other points to consider when thinking about the use of an app when no network connection is available are monetization and web-based content. If you're monetizing your app with remotely served advertising like pictures or videos, be aware that the app is essentially being used for free when offline. It's also not uncommon for people to engage flight mode while using some apps and games to avoid being distracted and delayed by having to see ads. If this is an issue, you may need to consider alternative or supplementary monetization strategies. The ability to work offline doesn't limit apps built purely with native UI technologies. Even embedded web apps or apps that use web technologies for some or all of their functionality should be able to work when offline through HTTP caching, the use of service workers to preload content and manage caches, and local storage for storing content.

13.2.2 Connections may be lost

If a connection is available when the app starts, it might not be there later in the session. I once worked with a piece of desktop software where the company that developed it took the approach that if something went wrong because of a dropped connection between the PC running the software and the server holding the database, it wasn't the software's problem. The company assumed that a connection between the app and the server should always be there. If there were any side effects from a dropped connection, it was "tough luck" for the people using the software. I'd argue that such an approach to connection reliability is not acceptable in any environment. It's certainly not acceptable with mobile apps.

Murphy's Law says, "Anything that can go wrong, will go wrong." You should take this approach to connections when it comes to mobile apps. What can go wrong?

- You'll lose the connection partway through downloading important data.
- You'll lose the connection partway through requesting multiple items.
- You'll lose the connection as someone presses a button to complete a process or to make a purchase.
- You'll lose the connection after the server receives a request but before the app receives the response.
- The app will be closed after sending a request and before receiving a successful response.

Your app needs to handle all these scenarios. To do this requires that every time you write code that connects to a server, you need to make sure the app (and the code, in particular) can manage these scenarios:

- What if a connection isn't possible right now?
- What if the device loses connection while this request is in progress?
- What if the request fails?

You don't just need to plan for these situations, you also need to test for them. Third-party tools and frameworks can help with much of this, but you can expect to write some code to re-create and test some situations.

13.2.3 Connections may change

A connection may not be possible when starting the app, or it may be lost while the app is in use. You're not limited to these two scenarios. Connections may change in other ways while the app is in use, and your app must allow for this. Let's see how Rosa handled this. Rosa tried to account for the app having to work with and without a connection by checking for connectivity when the app was started. She then set a flag to indicate if the app was in online or offline mode. On the surface, this seems like a reasonable strategy and makes things easy for the developer, but it doesn't allow for reality.

The reality of mobile connections is that they change while the app is in use, so Rosa ran into issues where the app was acting like it was online but it didn't have a connection. People using the app also complained that if the app started in offline mode and then gained a connection, there was no way to take advantage of this. In the end, Rosa had to change her app to allow for changes in connectivity.

That the device will switch between cell towers, Wi-Fi access points, or between cell and Wi-Fi networks without manual intervention is great for general usability, but can hide issues with changes in the speed and the cost of the connection. If this matters to the people using your app, then you'll need to adjust your app accordingly. Use the following techniques to account for connection changes:

- Indicate within the app when a connection isn't available.
- Consider adjusting the image or video quality to account for changes in connection speed.
- Detect changes in the type of connection so you can change behavior or ask for user confirmation if switching to a more expensive connection.
- Handle connection changes reported by the device, and automatically send queued messages when a connection becomes available.

The next section focuses on different things you can do to improve an app in subprime conditions. The ability to automatically retry failed requests (section 13.3.5) is particularly important when allowing for connections changing, dropping, and coming back.

Put it into practice: allowing for occasional connections

- Ensure that your app can launch when offline or unable to connect to any necessary servers.
- Allow captured content to be queued and sent later.
- Cache displayed data to be shown again when the app is next used.
- Test the app to be sure it copes with losing connections while in use.
- Test changes in connectivity while using the app, and ensure it adapts appropriately.

Exercise: occasional and varied connections

Test your understanding of the last two sections by stating whether the following are true or false:

1. Secure connections are only important if an app sends or requests personal or financial data.
2. Connection speed can be affected by local and network-wide conditions.
3. Everyone has a fast, cheap, reliable internet connection, so you don't need to think about connectivity.
4. Connections can come and go at any point while using the app.
5. Your app should handle connection changes without needing the user to do anything.

13.3 Optimizing for subprime conditions

The last section made it clear that the only thing we can say about a mobile connection is that it won't always be fast, cheap, and available. For any combination of factors that means the device doesn't have perfect connectivity, I call the situation *subprime.* This section shows you how to allow for the variations of subprime conditions by building for the worst scenarios. Doing so provides a great experience in good scenarios. But building an app assuming the best scenario and then adding code to handle all the exceptions takes more work.

Rosa, like many developers, initially tested her app while in her office with a fast, reliable broadband connection. Everything seemed fine with the app until it was given to some early beta testers. Testing in real-world environments highlighted many issues with the app when connections changed, were unavailable, or weren't as fast as in Rosa's office. Addressing these issues took lots of work and some major changes to the app's code. Had she considered these scenarios initially, it would have meant less work overall and taken less time.

> **TIP** Don't wait until development is thought to be nearly complete, such as when reaching a beta testing phase, before adding code to handle subprime conditions.

Techniques discussed in earlier chapters, such as transcoding requested content, also apply here, but now we'll look at some other techniques that can help. To reduce the effort required by the people using the app, you'll learn about the use of caching and compression to reduce the amount of data transferred, batching and deferring operations for times when a good request is available, and automatically retrying failed requests.

13.3.1 Caching improves the experience in subprime conditions

Caching content reduces the amount of network traffic an app uses. Having to transfer a smaller amount of data is beneficial in all network conditions. When Rosa began caching the large, high-quality images displayed in the app, it not only saved on bandwidth, but also meant they were available when offline.

As mentioned in chapter 11, HTTP contains built-in functionality for handling caching that you can and should take advantage of. Additionally, you can remove the need for caching by minimizing eternal default resources and including them in the app bundle.

13.3.2 Compression improves the experience in subprime conditions

Smaller amounts of data are faster and cheaper to transfer. This is beneficial regardless of the network conditions. Rosa, in addition to gzipping the content downloaded by the app, added a server process to re-encode and resize the images uploaded to the backend. This reduced the size of the downloaded images.

> **NOTE** Compressing content sent over HTTP is commonplace and simple to implement. Always request compressed content if the server supports it.

Not all image formats will benefit from additional compression, because they're already compressed internally. You may be able to reduce their size further by reducing their displayed dimensions. It's unnecessary to download something larger than is necessary, only to make it smaller when displayed. So if you can create versions of images appropriate to the size of the screen that will display them, this can be beneficial in reducing the amount of data transferred.

13.3.3 Deferring actions increases what's possible in subprime conditions

Saving operations until conditions are good can help you avoid losing information or preventing the ability to use some functionality when conditions are poor. Users of the first version of Rosa's app would capture images and videos when offline. Because there was no way to save them, the app would lose these if they weren't immediately uploaded. Rosa's solution was to save the content captured on the device and upload it when a suitable connection was available. She also added a configurable option to the app to control whether large amounts of data could be uploaded over a mobile network, as this expense was a concern for some users.

Separate the processes of preparing content to send and sending it. Not only is the separation of different pieces of programming logic good practice, but it also makes it easier to change and compose the way pieces of functionality work together. Consider the code needed to capture a photo and then upload it. If these are tightly integrated, then it later becomes more work to add other functionality, such as alternatively loading an image from disk, adding extra optional information, or uploading multiple images together.

Whether uploading images, placing orders, posting an update for your followers, or doing anything that isn't time critical, your app should be able to save the content and send it later if it's unable to send it when requested. When implementing this functionality, also make it possible to see a list of queued items, as well as to cancel them or retry on demand.

13.3.4 Batch operations in subprime conditions

Performing multiple actions in batches can improve their chances of successful completion and simplify retry logic. After Rosa implemented the ability to defer the uploading of content captured in subprime conditions, that process became quite slow and involved uploading each item in turn. She improved the speed of uploading multiple files by zipping them all together and sending them as a single request.

Although sending one large file reduces the number of requests, it potentially introduces another issue: if it fails part way through, it's necessary to send the whole file again. This approach is good if you have lots of small items to send, but not so good if you have many large files to upload. With large files there's also an opportunity to break them into smaller pieces to be reassembled on the server. This leads to more requests, but means you can avoid sending the whole file again if the upload fails or connection is lost partway through.

13.3.5 Automatic retries improve the experience in subprime conditions

It's better to have the app do things it can do by itself and not make the people using the app be responsible for those things. People are forgetful and have better things to do than manually or repeatedly trying to upload content.

For Rosa, automatically retrying a failed upload was important. She wanted the people using the app to be able to just press Send and then know the app would take care of uploading and sharing their content. The approach Rosa took is applicable in most situations where content is uploaded. It follows these steps:

1. The app stores content in a queue on disk and not in memory, as the content might be unsent when the app is closed.
2. A background process is then told to try to send any queued items.
3. The background process attempts to upload the content and uses an automatic retry approach should the transfer fail (figure 13.2).
4. The background process is also told to try to send any queued items when a person returns to the app or when a system-level event is received indicating that a network connection has become available.

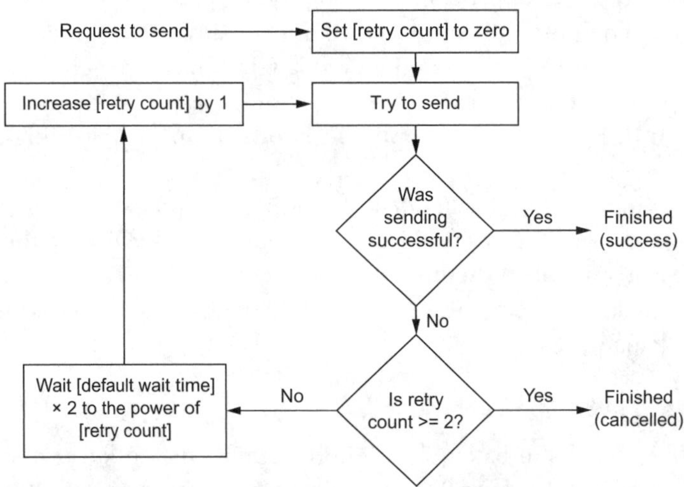

Figure 13.2 A simple logic flow for attempting to resend content to a remote server when the task can't be completed. The logic flow tries a total of three times, waiting an increasing amount of time between each attempt.

Although using a retry approach like the one in figure 13.2 is a good start, it can also be extended to account for being, or going, offline at any point, or to allow for different server responses and manually requesting the sending of the data. Having an automatic retry policy is useful even when network connections are normally good, as it can handle transient network or server errors. This makes it worth considering for all apps that send content. An automatic retry without a long wait can also be useful for trying to retrieve content. As a person using an app, would you rather be told, "Unable to retrieve the content. Try again later," or, "I was unable to retrieve the content but will retry for you"?

Put it into practice: allowing for subprime network conditions

- Use HTTP caching as supported by the server.
- Request compressed versions of HTTP content if available.
- Consider batching multiple small requests together or splitting up large file uploads if a connection isn't reliable.
- Enable automatic retrying of failed requests.

Exercise: coping with subprime network conditions

Test your understanding of this section by matching the strategy with the scenario:

Strategies

- Cache past responses.
- Request compressed data.
- Defer requests until later.
- Batch content together.
- Automatically retry failed requests.

Scenarios

1. Inability to complete a request now due to connection issues
2. Avoiding downloading the same thing multiple times
3. Wanting to make the app seem reliable to avoid having the people using the app do things the app can do itself
4. Wanting to minimize the amount downloaded
5. Wanting to minimize the number of requests made to upload multiple items

13.4 Balancing usability and a poor connection

In this section, we'll look at two principles that can help you create better experiences when the connection is poor. Using these principles as a guideline, you'll be able to make smart, informed decisions about how to ensure your app provides the best experience it can, regardless of connectivity:

- Prioritize important activities when conditions are poor.
- Adjust network usage based on current conditions.

You can't always have everything you want all the time. This is true with app experiences that rely in whole or part on having an available network connection. This means providing the best experience you can, based on the circumstances.

13.4.1 Prioritizing important activities in poor conditions

Not all functionality within an app is equally important, and your app shouldn't be all or nothing. Only apps that must constantly be connected to a server to provide any value at all can attempt to justify not allowing the app to start without a connection.

It would be easy to claim that Rosa's app should only work with a connection. Its two main functions are viewing content that others have shared and sharing content with other people. Both core functions require connecting to a backend server. But there are lots of ways that the app can provide value when a connection isn't possible.

To prioritize the important activities in an app first requires deciding what's important. Two clear indicators of that are

- It's part of the core functionality of the app.
- It's a part of the app the person is actively using. This means that foreground tasks take priority over background tasks, and anything relating to the displayed page takes priority over all.

Together, these approaches should cover every part of an app; there shouldn't be things in your app that no one uses. This isn't a trick. You need to think about all parts of your app and how to optimize them for poor connectivity. Depending on the context of use, even the most underused parts of an app can be the most important to some people.

Once the important areas have been identified, you need an approach for handling poor conditions. Consider these three questions:

- Is something better than nothing?
- Are there any alternatives?
- Can you start it now and finish it later?

Answering these questions will help you to find appropriate approaches to addressing the different connectivity scenarios that your app will encounter. Let's look at how the answers can be applied.

DOING SOMETHING IS BETTER THAN DOING NOTHING

Consider these common approaches to offering some functionality under poor conditions. First, showing some content means that the app is still usable. Second, loading low-resolution, thumbnail versions of images not only saves on bandwidth, but can still indicate the full image. And, finally, allowing the sending of only simple text-based content, rather than uploading images or videos, is better than nothing.

OFFERING ALTERNATIVES IS BETTER THAN DOING NOTHING

As an alternative to doing nothing, having a Browse Only mode allows viewing of content even when the connectivity needed to interact with items isn't available. Another approach is showing cached historical data (if indicated as such), which can provide value even when the app can't show current data. And, when it's not possible to view new items, a person may still get value from being able to view saved copies of items they've previously bookmarked or favorited.

STARTING NOW AND FINISHING LATER IS BETTER THAN PUTTING IT ALL OFF UNTIL LATER

Start uploads as early as possible, so there's a chance for them to complete before a connection is lost. Consider also composing content and saving it for sending later, or queue requests until a connection becomes available (like the example in figure 13.3). These are all popular approaches to starting now and finishing later.

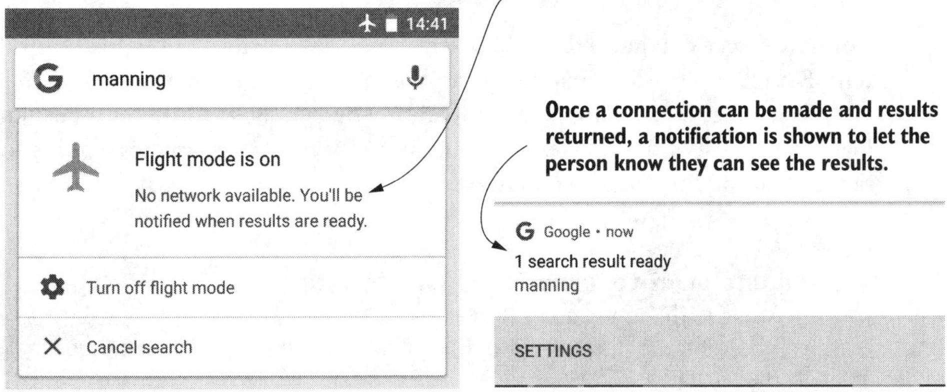
When the person using the app attempts a Google search but no network is available, the request is automatically saved and retried when a connection is possible.
14:41
manning
Flight mode is on
No network available. You'll be notified when results are ready.
Turn off flight mode
Cancel search
Once a connection can be made and results returned, a notification is shown to let the person know they can see the results.
Google • now
1 search result ready
manning
SETTINGS

This image shows what happens in flight mode, but the experience is the same if the person using the app is unable to search for any reason.

Figure 13.3 When attempting to search for something when offline, the app remembers the request and automatically retries once a connection becomes available.

Combining the techniques for handling poor conditions will allow your app to always work as well and quickly as circumstances permit. What we'll look at in the next section is how it's also necessary to adapt as circumstances change.

13.4.2 Adjusting network usage based on network conditions

Subprime conditions can impact the app in different ways, and it's not a binary state of having good or bad conditions. You can have your app adapt to changing conditions in various ways. These ways all help deliver the best experience to the user.

When Rosa was first demoing her app internally, she set the frequency at which it would poll for new content to every five seconds. She did this to highlight the availability of new content within the app, because the company felt it was more important to highlight the ability of the app to let the user know when new content was available. The reality was quite different.

Rosa also found out that polling at that frequency was inefficient, as most of the requests didn't return anything new. This meant making lots of requests for no benefit. By increasing the polling interval, fewer wasted requests were made, and by reducing the polling frequency on potentially expensive mobile data connections, the financial impact on the person using the app was also lessened. The following are several other popular ways to adjust the way your app uses the network based on the state of the connection:

- Make automatic polling for new or updated content configurable.
- Make automatic polling configurable based on the type of connection (for example, only refresh over Wi-Fi).
- Reduce the number of parallel connections in slower conditions.
- Prioritize requests when queued.

Content directly requested by the user should take priority over loading other content. For example, while loading a list of items and related images, one item is tapped to view its details. The app should load anything related to the chosen item before loading the rest of the images. It should not wait until it completes loading all images before loading the requested content.

Put it into practice: usability in poor conditions

- Assess the functionality in the app that's dependent on a network connection to identify if it could be done partially, differently, or completed later when used offline.
- Adjust the automatic polling frequency to account for network conditions.
- Enable the prioritization of important requests when queuing many.

13.5 Keeping the user in control when conditions are poor

Keep the people using the app informed and in control when conditions aren't perfect. It gives them confidence that nothing has gone wrong and all is going as well as possible. Originally, Rosa's app displayed a spinning activity indicator when it was loading. Some people complained that the startup time was too slow. Rather than change the time it took to start the app, she changed the loading process to indicate what was happening during startup: "Connecting to server," "Checking for updates," "Getting the latest shares," and so forth. The result of this was enough to stop people complaining about the time the app took to load.

A key aspect of creating a positive experience with an app is to set expectations, remove doubts, and preempt any questions the people using it might have. These guidelines apply to all aspects of an app, but they're important when the app is suffering the consequences of poor network conditions. If the people using the app ask any of these questions, it's an opportunity for you to improve the experience:

- What's happening?
- Why is it slow?
- When will it be finished?

- What can I do to make it faster?
- What should I do with the information you're giving me?

That last one is especially important. It's not enough to present some information to the person using the app; the app must explain the problem and be actionable. The transient error message displayed in figure 13.4 is a great example of what not to do. When displayed in an app I was using, it didn't seem to have any negative effect on the app's ability to function correctly and so probably wasn't worth showing.

The word "Error" and the exclamation point make it seem important. Shouldn't it also be important to explain the consequences of the error and any action that can or must be taken to rectify it? Or will the app somehow try to address the error itself?

What does "net::ERR_SPDY_PROTOCOL_ERROR" mean? Should the user know? Or do they need to know? Should they go find out?

There's an error, but what does it mean? This message disappears after a short time. Does that mean the error has gone away, too? Has it been fixed? Has the error been reported to the makers of the app? Should it be? And if so, how should that be done? What if this error happens again, or every time?

Figure 13.4 A message indicates that there was an error, but the meaning and consequences of the error are unclear. How, if at all, should the person respond to seeing this?

As a rule, you should hide problems from the user. This isn't to pretend they don't exist, but to avoid concerning users with things that are irrelevant or they can't do anything about. Your app should look to do the following:

- *Indicate if a connection can't be made and the app is in an offline scenario.* Allowing the OS to display the default connectivity indicators at the top of the screen is a simple way of doing this.
- *Indicate when network activity is taking place.*
- *Control periodic polling.* Allow polling to be turned off, made infrequent, or limited to certain connection types.
- *Add an option for handling queued events.* If queuing items for sending later, allow the user to attempt to send them immediately.
- *Make messages about failed connections specific to the reason for the failure.* It's not enough to only ever say, "Check your connection and try again later."

Following these guidelines will help you make the best of bad situations and avoid the people using the app becoming frustrated that they don't know what's happening or how to do anything about it.

Put it into practice: keep the user in control

Review all displayed error messages to ensure that they're clear, necessary, and actionable.

Exercise: communicating app activity

Which of the statements shown beneath the figure are true or likely to be true about this app?

- The app is doing something.
- The task is nearly finished.
- The task will only take a short time to complete.
- The user needs to wait for this task to complete.
- The task is taking the expected length of time.
- The user can do nothing to speed up this task.
- The app is connecting to a remote source to retrieve data.
- The device is online and able to connect to the remote server.
- Whether the task is successful or not, the app will be able to continue.

Summary

- Secure all HTTP connections, even during testing and development.
- Allow for variations in connection speed, and ensure your app works on slow connections.
- Allow for variations in network costs and for people who'll want to use minimal data sets or only use data in some conditions.
- Allow for the use of the app when offline, as some people may not have control over their ability to connect.
- Being offline may be more complicated than being unable to reach a single URL. Error messages and the automatic retrying of requests may need to consider if any connection is possible or any specific error conditions are present before being deemed offline.
- Connections can change or be lost at the most inconvenient times. Test your app to allow for this.
- Use caching and compression of HTTP(S) requests to reduce the size and frequency of requests and to improve the offline and subprime connection experiences.
- Rather than send data when there's a poor or no connection, save the data and send it when you have a good/fast/cheap connection.
- Batch or group requests together, and send when there's a good connection.
- Automatically retry when a request fails so the user doesn't have to.
- Prioritize what you request and send based on the available connection.
- Match the frequency of automatic requests to the type of connection available.
- Keep the user informed when using the network and when connections are slow or unavailable.
- Allow the user to control what happens in subprime network conditions.

Part 6

Resources

The capabilities and functionality of mobile devices continue to grow, but there will always be limits on what can fit inside a device and what people are willing to pay for. The resources available on a device are dependent upon the hardware and connected services. Both can vary between devices, operating systems, and carriers. Allowing your app to support variations in available resources enables it to work and provide good experiences on more devices.

In addition to whether the app uses resources, how it uses them can also have a big impact on a person's experience with your app and their device in general. Resources on a mobile device are finite. If you allow your app to consume them all, it can affect other apps, as well as your own.

The final chapter looks at how to approach the use of resources in your app in a way that will not only give you the greatest benefit from their use, but at a minimal cost to the person using the app, and with the least impact on the other apps on the device.

14 Managing power and resources

This chapter covers

- Power management and resource usage
- When and if to load data and resources
- Responsible resource usage and disposal

Despite advances in technology that mean batteries last longer, disks are bigger, processors are more powerful, and devices have additional sensors, mobile devices are constrained. Resources are finite and often less than what's available on a laptop, PC, or server. In this chapter, I cover the specifics of what you'll need to consider for responsible power and resource usage, and how to ensure that you don't negatively impact the experience of using your app or the device it's running on. To do that, I'll address four types of resources: power, disk space, processors, and sensors.

Power is limited by the capacity of the battery. When every action an app performs uses energy, there's a trade-off between the value of the action and the device's ability to use that power for something else. Because of this, it's the most valuable resource to manage. Until new, longer-lasting battery technology is widespread, or all devices can be charged passively, it's necessary for all apps to ensure they're not wasting power.

The capacity of the disk in a device is often a big factor in influencing its price. This causes many people to purchase devices with smaller disks. The fact that many devices don't support removable or extended storage also increases the number of devices with limited space. A lack of space can prevent apps from working correctly or preclude the installation of other apps. It can also increase costs to the user when they can't download more content and so may have to stream it repeatedly.

The capabilities and availability of processors and sensors vary between devices. It might be simple to ask the processor on one device to perform a task; but while on another, it may take a lot of effort, which takes time, uses a lot of power, and produces more heat. Similarly, sensors work differently on different devices and impact app responsiveness and power consumption in different ways. The use of various sensors can also affect other apps and their ability to use the sensor. For example, an app or game that depends on location and movement detection may behave another way on devices with location sensors that support different movement thresholds, or on those that can only provide a latitude and longitude, but not altitude and velocity.

Everything an app does affects the use of resources. In this way, this chapter has a lot of overlap with earlier chapters. Think of this chapter and the consideration of resource use as a reality check and potential counterpoint to the ideal plans you have for your app. For example, you may want to have lots of animation in the UI (as discussed in chapter 10), cache everything to disk (as discussed in chapter 11), and maintain a constant connection to a server (as discussed in chapter 13). The impact these things have on resources, however, may mean they're inappropriate.

Throughout this chapter, I also share Frank's experiences to illustrate these concepts. Frank developed an app for the drivers of a delivery firm. Because the app is essential for people to do their jobs, it was important that Frank didn't waste resources, which might result in a dead battery. That would mean fewer deliveries, with expensive consequences for the business.

The importance of resource usage is often amplified in business apps, but also applies when people are using devices with lower specifications, as is common in locations where many users have old or secondhand devices. Applications that are used for extended periods of time or do a lot of work in the background need to be careful about their resource usage too. And, apps that track location or potentially transfer large amounts of data also need to plan their resource usage carefully. Let's begin our look at the use of resources with a lesson from my childhood.

14.1 When it's gone, it's gone

When I was young, I had a lot less self-control than I do now. If there was some candy, I'd constantly be asking for more. If I had money, it would burn a hole in my pocket, and I'd ask for permission to spend it. Often this would be on something I didn't want or need; I just wanted to use it because I could. In these situations, the response from my father was often the same: "Okay, but when it's gone, it's gone!"

The lesson my father was trying to teach me was to accept responsibility for the consequences of the use of available resources. If I quickly ate all the candy, there wouldn't be any left when I wanted some later. If I spent all my money on something I didn't need, I wouldn't have any left for when there was something I really wanted. It was an important lesson and one that I still remember and apply to the use of resources in mobile apps. If all the power in the battery goes to nonessential tasks, then there's no power left for anything important. If the disk is full of things that don't matter, there's no space left to store the important items.

Frank had to take power consumption seriously in his app. The delivery drivers needed to use the app often through a 14-hour shift. They'd sometimes forget or be unable to charge their devices during that time. If the power ran out, they'd have to use a manual backup processes, which was slow, frustrating, and meant less work was possible while in the field. The effect of this was a drop in morale. Because drivers were unable to make as many collections and deliveries, the company lost money. The challenge for Frank was to extend the battery life of the devices so they would last for a full shift. As he couldn't change the capabilities of the battery, this meant minimizing battery consumption while still providing the functionality for drivers to do their jobs effectively.

Although Frank's challenge of battery optimization was an extreme necessity, he still managed to achieve it by analyzing every aspect of the app and use of the device. He not only controlled when to make network requests, but also turned the individual antenna on and off to prevent power consumption when not needed. By controlling brightness, the output to the screen made minimal use of battery power. To aid visibility in poor light, a driver could change the screen's brightness for easy reading before it automatically dimmed again. Frank even optimized the way data was structured on disk to minimize disk I/O.

While Frank had to take full responsibility for maintaining battery life, in most scenarios, some responsibility exists with the people using the app. If they use their device actively for several hours, then it won't come as a surprise if the battery is low. This, however, doesn't mean you can ignore the power usage of your app. Even if someone is using their device a lot, they'll still want the battery to last as long as possible.

A person's desire for the battery to last increases as the amount of power gets lower. For this reason, operating systems have many built-in ways to avoid wasting power. The most important one for you to consider is the battery saver or low power mode. The OS enables this mode when the battery charge falls below a certain percentage. Reducing functionality has a big impact on battery life. Your app also needs to react to the device in battery saver mode to avoid unnecessarily using limited power. You can do this by

- Reducing the frequency of network activity
- Disabling UI animations
- Using cached data longer

Taking note of being in battery saver mode can be more widely defined as the need to reduce functionality when resources become limited. Beyond power usage, this can mean you cache less (or nothing) on disk, or invalidate data faster. Or it may mean asking less of a low-power processor.

> **Improving battery life with more or less caching**
>
> It may seem contradictory, but in some situations, more caching can make the battery last longer; in others, less caching can reduce power consumption. Caching attempts to save time and resources by keeping a copy of something rather than having to load it again. It's a balancing act where you weigh the cost of the extra work in creating and maintaining the cache against the potential savings.
>
> Consider caching the response from a web request. If you don't cache a copy of the response on disk, you avoid using the power needed to create the file. If you do cache the response, you avoid needing to repeat the web request. If reading from disk uses less power than requesting from the web, then caching saves power.
>
> What's best for your app depends on more than just power consumption, but it should be a factor in your decision making. If power is low, it can be better to have the app work for a little bit longer and make no web requests than to have it run for a short time with all the online capabilities.

Frank's final solution was dependent on the ability to control almost every aspect of the device the app was on. For most consumer-facing apps, it's not possible or appropriate to restrict the use and functionality of the device in such an extreme way. People will know what their device is capable of and will want to use the available features and functionality. You can't and shouldn't try to stop people from using the functionality that exists on the device, but you should make use of all that's available to you:

- If the device can give you an accurate location, then use it; don't estimate.
- If the device has two cameras, don't limit people to only using one.
- If the device has fingerprint or other biometric identification capabilities, don't force people to use a short numeric PIN.
- If the device has a high-powered CPU and GPU, use them.

Provide a rich, engaging app that makes use of the capabilities available, unless it contributes to an overall negative experience with the device. Just as a simple process that does the minimum necessary to give value can be extended to provide a fuller and more engaging experience, you can reverse that same process to be less resource intensive. A static map image may be enough to show a location. But an interactive map that shows the person's current location and traffic conditions may be more helpful and provide a richer experience when the device can get the current location, connect to a network to get the traffic information, and has the available power to show this without compromising the wider device experience by draining the battery.

To help you understand which functionality to prioritize and how to consider the associated resource usage, the rest of this chapter considers three questions:

- Do you really need it?
- How often are you going to use it?
- Do you still need it?

Your app doesn't need to do everything. It can do less and still give value, even if it's only doing the least amount necessary; that may be enough. With all that's possible, it's easy to forget the most important aspect of your app is the value it provides to the people using it.

Put it into practice: managing battery life

- Ensure that your testing process includes monitoring power consumption.
- Ensure that you're using all the functionality, features, and sensors on a device, rather than forcing the manual entry of data or creating alternative methods of gathering information.
- Provide ways of giving value to the people using the app even when device capabilities are limited.
- Ensure that your app responds to the device in battery saver mode in a way that avoids using limited power unnecessarily.
- Allow the user to disable background polling or any other periodic activity to save power and reduce network activity.

14.2 Do you really need it?

Frank's delivery company had a lot of historical information about the places delivered to. This included special instructions about how to get to a location, and, in some cases, how to access a property. When the same driver delivered to the same area repeatedly, they knew such details and wouldn't need the information displayed onscreen. In that case, the device didn't have to transfer and store all the data. When drivers changed routes or someone was filling in due to illness or a holiday, this information proved to be invaluable. Drivers unfamiliar with the location didn't have to spend time looking for specific properties. It saved valuable minutes to know that to get to 37 Harper Drive, they needed to access it via Beechnut Avenue. But this was only valuable in a small number of cases. Not including this information for every delivery saved disk space and reduced the time needed to transfer and process the data.

Just as having unnecessary data stored on disk can cause problems, having extra data held in memory can also slow down a device—or, even worse, cause the OS to terminate the app. A mobile OS cannot afford for a single app to take control of all the available memory without losing the ability to function correctly. The enforcement of strict limits prevents an app from causing the whole device to stop functioning.

One way to reduce memory usage is not to load something until it's needed. This is known as *lazy loading*.

14.2.1 Lazy loading reduces wasted effort

To load something lazily is to wait until you need it before accessing it. This approach can be applied to almost anything and includes data, images, and screen elements. Additionally, lazily loading into memory reduces wasting that resource. By assuming you won't need something, you can simplify the loading process, thereby lowering resource usage.

The next question to answer is, how long do you keep things? The general rule for keeping what's loaded is the reverse of how to choose what and when to load something. Unload it when you're finished with it and won't need it again, or if it's large but quick and easy to reload. Keep things loaded that you'll need to repeatedly access, or those that will be slow to reload. Figure 14.1 summarizes this logic.

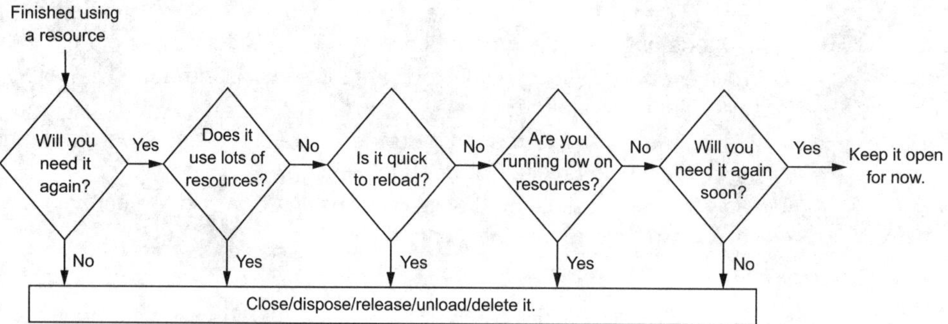

Figure 14.1 Decision tree showing the questions to ask of a resource

You can apply lazy loading to the use of sensors and system resources by not accessing them until needed. Accessing sensors or other resources will need more processing power and, therefore, battery use. It can also cause the device to prompt the user to permit resource use. It's not a good experience to be asked for permission to access a resource that isn't related to what a person is currently doing with the app.

Screen real estate is also a resource of finite supply. You can't always display everything, so you should only display what you must and what's presently relevant. Don't try to load or display everything that's newest. Getting this wrong can have serious consequences.

The first automated dispatch system for an ambulance service in the UK worked by displaying addresses that the crew needed to go to. The next address to visit was at the top of the list, and new entries were added at the bottom of the screen. The screen could show up to five entries at a time. All worked well until a crew had six addresses they needed to visit. The one they were expected to attend to next, and the earliest received, was pushed off the top of the screen when all six addresses loaded. At this point, it was up to them to remember the details and trust that the entry hadn't been assigned to another crew. Once this issue was identified, and due to the potential risk to life, it was quickly addressed. Although you may not be creating apps with potential life-and-death consequences, this example shows the importance of not loading information before it's needed, and the consequences of misusing limited space onscreen.

Eager and lazy loading: opposite, yet complementary

Section 12.1 covered the idea of *eager loading*. That's loading something before it's required, so it's ready when it's needed. Eager loading is the opposite of lazy loading. Both approaches to loading items are useful for different things, at different times, and in different ways. Most apps benefit from using a combination of the two approaches. The following table shows the pros and cons of each approach.

Pros and cons of loading data at different times

Loading approach	Pros	Cons
Eager loading	Allows the app to be faster when used Hides the time necessary to load large or complex items	Can make startup time slower Uses more resources and can be wasteful
Lazy loading	Saves resources Can make the app start faster Good for things that may never need to load	Can make the app slower when used Not good for things that are slow to load

14.2.2 *Using alternatives to save resources*

There's rarely only one way of doing something, and different methods and techniques use different resources. If the result is the same, then you should use the approach that requires fewest system resources. To classify alternative approaches to using an expensive resource, consider the following:

- Use a simpler approach.
- Defer an action until later.
- Offload computation to reduce effort.
- Use an approximation.

Frank used several approaches to reduce the resources used by his app when sending data between the server and the devices while in use on the road. He had the server provide data preformatted to reduce the amount of processing in the app. The server also reformatted the output from the app at the end of a shift. Data was sent to and from the app when the device was in the depot at the beginning and the end of the shift, because this was fast and cheap. It sent only minimal data over the mobile network during the day.

A SIMPLER APPROACH THAT USES FEWER RESOURCES IS PREFERABLE

Section 11.4 covered caching as an approach to simplifying resource usage by keeping a copy of something, rather than asking for it every time it's needed. This also has the benefit of reducing the resource usage when getting values from sensors. Compared with the effort of keeping the value in memory, this is a simple approach to saving resources.

Another simple approach is to ask for the manual entry of data, rather than reading it from sensors. With this approach, you can support devices without those sensors. It also allows the capturing of data in different or potentially more appropriate formats. For example, a location sensor may provide a latitude and longitude, but it doesn't help with getting the current street address. It may be simpler to ask for it directly rather than approximate or look it up based on latitude and longitude.

Combining activities can also reduce resource use. Rather than make multiple requests for each item in a collection, it's quicker and simpler to ask for the items all at once, thus avoiding a huge amount of waste.

DEFER THINGS THAT YOU CAN DO LATER

Doing less is faster, cheaper, and consumes fewer resources. It's neither appropriate nor helpful to do nothing. If you don't have to do a process when resources are low or limited, it can be beneficial to wait for better circumstances. For example:

- Wait until the battery is sufficiently charged or plugged in before performing power-intensive tasks, to avoid negatively impacting the app experience.
- Don't send large amounts of data over slow or costly networks if speed or cost of connectivity is important. Wait until a suitable network is available.

The impact on battery and network consumption is why it's common for apps that download large amounts of data, such as podcast apps, to update overnight, when a device is likely to be plugged in and charging, and when access to a home's Wi-Fi network is available. Although it can be good to have things done and out of the way, it's better to avoid the risk of wasting limited resources if using them later would prevent any potential issues. A final approach to performing work when the impact on resources is minimal is to pass the work on to other apps or devices with specialized capabilities, targeted optimizations, or different constraints.

OFF-LOAD COMPUTATION TO REDUCE EFFORT AND RESOURCE USAGE

Your app can only do some things while on a device, but this doesn't have to be everything. The lower specifications of older devices meant that it was unrealistic to try to perform advanced computations or image manipulation on the device. Newer devices are capable of more advanced processing, but just because they can perform these actions doesn't mean they should.

Suppose your app is capturing data that can be manipulated and processed by a backend. Having the app upload the raw data not only saves the app from doing the processing, but also makes it easier to handle situations where the backend wants to do something different when it has the original, raw data. Having the server manipulate the content that's sent to the device also allows a more powerful machine with fewer constraints to do the heavy lifting of reformatting the data. For data sent to multiple devices, it also means that data transformation is only done once, rather than on each device that receives it.

You can also make your app simpler by off-loading work to other apps on the device; for example, suppose you want to gather feedback from the people using it. Rather than handle the entry and sending of the message, it may be simpler to launch the email app with some fields already populated. A dedicated email app should already have the capability to send the message at an appropriate time and handle retries and offline scenarios without you needing to do anything.

BALANCE APPROXIMATIONS, ACCURACY, AND EFFORT

Doing work in the app or on a backend server needn't be an all-or-nothing scenario. It may be appropriate to only do some of the work, or a simplified version of it, on the device, as in Frank's case.

In addition to delivering parcels, drivers at Frank's company also took legal paperwork to people to be signed. In some cases, waiting until the next day for the original signed paperwork was too slow, so it would be scanned or photographed and sent that way. To get the signature confirmed as quickly as possible, the driver used the app to take a picture of the signature before sending it. On the driver's return to the depot, they scanned and sent all the documents to the office. This compromise was enough for the company's needs and matched business requirements with workforce and device resources.

When lower-power devices were more common, image-manipulation apps would often fake effects and filters by overlaying a semitransparent image on top of a photo, rather than manipulate it directly. Then they would upload the original image and the effect to apply. A process on the server would alter the image that was posted and shared online. Modern devices are now more than capable of manipulating images directly, but they don't have to. A server process can do the work.

Just because you can use sensors to get specific data doesn't mean you must. An approximation is often good enough, rather than doing all the work or having the most exact data. Again, using cached data is an example of not always needing the most detailed and current data. If it's not essential that data is 100% accurate and up to date, then it's not worth the cost and effort of trying to provide such data.

Put it into practice: resource alternatives

- Look at the way you retrieve data. Obtain resources in your app, and confirm you're using lazy or eager loading appropriately for each instance.
- Verify that you're using sensors to supplement or replace data capture when possible.
- Defer any actions that don't need to be done immediately, and perform them in batches or in response to other events in the use of the app.
- Move the preparation and formatting of data to the server that provides it.
- Move the processing of data captured by the app to the server it's sent to.

Exercise: doing what's needed

Test your understanding of the last two sections by stating whether the following are true or false:

1 An app should only use eager or lazy loading, but never both.
2 If you load something lazily, you don't need to think about when to unload it.
3 Your app doesn't have to always do everything at once.
4 Your app doesn't have to do everything itself.
5 People using apps always need the most accurate and up-to-date information.

14.3 How often are you going to use it?

How many times you plan to use something should affect how you interact with it. Don't default to assuming you can treat all similar resources in the same way. It's likely to be inappropriate to treat the things you only use once in the same way as those you'll use many times.

14.3.1 Managing resources that are only used once

A resource may be used once per session or once in the lifetime of the app. Each scenario has different considerations. This section describes those differences.

Resources used once per session

Tasks only performed once in a session are normally done at the start. Combining these actions makes them faster and simpler to manage. If you need to load some information from disk at the start of the session, putting all of it in one file can make it faster to access than loading lots of separate files. Or, if you need to make multiple network requests, combining them makes them faster and reduces resource usage.

Frank's app, for example, got most of the information about the deliveries a driver needed to make at the start of a shift. It loaded the relevant data into memory. Under normal circumstances, there would be no need to reload the data, but a copy was kept on disk in case it was needed again.

For data stored on disk but only used once, it may be more appropriate to save space by compressing the data. It makes the data slightly slower to read or write, but because it's only accessed once, that makes little difference compared with files that are accessed or updated frequently.

RESOURCES ONLY EVER USED ONCE

It's important to carefully manage resources that will only be used once by an app, because they consume power needlessly. The most common reason to only use a resource once is if it's used as part of the registration or sign-up process. It can be helpful if the app accesses the device's sensor to detect a location to simplify a registration process, but it shouldn't retrieve the location every time the app starts.

Similarly, an app may try to query information about the device it's installed on for analytics or to detect if an unofficial, hacked, or pirated version has been installed. Such information only needs to be retrieved once and then can be cached for future use, if necessary. The make and model of the device on which the app is installed won't change. If you've verified it's an official version, the app won't have been uninstalled and a hacked or bootlegged copy installed in its place the next time it's run.

14.3.2 Managing resources that are used repeatedly

When you use resources repeatedly in a session, treat them differently from those used once. If you're making frequent requests, it can lead to increased battery drainage. By combining or batching network activity, it's possible for the OS to manage the power to the antennae more efficiently. Similarly, don't hold a network connection open on the chance of a response when one isn't likely.

Frank's app sent a lot of messages about the deliveries made or attempted by the drivers. Rather than keeping a single file or database updated with the status of all the data, it was stored in memory, and individual messages about each delivery attempt were written to disk before sending. After sending, individual message files were moved to a separate directory. If necessary, the state of all deliveries could be recreated based on the original data and all subsequent messages, but this wasn't a regular need. This way of working with multiple files was less resource intensive than repeatedly loading a large file to change a single value.

Storing all data in a single file on disk can make it slow to access a small piece of that data. In general, it's slower to access a single large file than many smaller files, but there's no absolute rule about where to draw the line. As a starting point, I recommend using multiple files and keeping data that's used together in the same file, and then adjusting if you encounter any performance issues.

When working with files on disk, it's also important to ensure that any corruption in them doesn't break the app. It's easy to forget that files aren't perfect; they may become corrupt when read or written. Or, they may have been changed or deleted by a third party while the app wasn't running. Always validate the structure and contents of the file if possible. It can also be useful to help when debugging any issues to store files with descriptive file extensions. If it's an image, save it to disk with an extension that shows the format. It's easy to think this is unnecessary, but it can save a lot of time when debugging any issues with the contents of a file if it's clear what it's meant to contain.

Put it into practice: how often you use resources

- Treat resources used once separately from those used repeatedly.
- Cache data if you know it won't change and you only need to retrieve it once.
- Store data on disk in a way that corresponds to how frequently you'll need to read, update, and write it.

Exercise: frequency of use

Test your understanding of the last section by stating which of the options in the square brackets should be used to complete the sentence correctly:

1 It's [appropriate|inappropriate] to treat resources you only use once in the same way as those you'll use many times.
2 Combining network requests can [increase|reduce] overall network traffic.
3 It's more appropriate to put data used [once|frequently] in a single, compressed file.
4 [Keep|Don't keep] connections open indefinitely to make future use faster.
5 Files on disk [may|won't] change after you write to them.

14.4 Do you still need it?

When you've established that the use of a resource is necessary to the value your app will provide, and the cost is justified, ensure that you're not then wasting that resource by doing more with it than is necessary. At the start of this chapter, I shared a lesson from my childhood. Two more lessons from the same time in my life are to put things away when I'm finished with them and not to use more than I need. I'll know where the things I put away are when I want them again. Plus, if I don't use all of something if I don't need to, I'll have some for later if I need it then.

As mentioned at the start of this chapter, Frank had to take the management of resources into account in everything the app did, to preserve the battery life for as long as possible. Although your app may not be used in as tightly constrained situations, this isn't an excuse to avoid thinking about how it manages resource use. Here are some simple things you can do avoid waste:

- Turn off sensors when you're finished with them.
- Respond to changing circumstances.

It's good to not be wasteful. Just as you'd turn off the lights in a room if no one is in it, your app should disconnect from or turn off sensors when it's finished with them. If you turn off or disconnect from a sensor when it's no longer needed, other apps will be able to connect to it instead, and you'll still be able to connect to it later. Also, if you've been doing something that consumes a lot of power but don't need to anymore, stop so that there will still be some power available when it's needed later.

14.4.1 *Turning off resources when finished*

When your app no longer needs a resource, the app should disconnect from it, turn it off, or otherwise disassociate from it. After retrieving the data, close the file handle or the network connection. If your code creates separate tasks, threads, or processes to perform different pieces of functionality, release or stop them once they've completed. Also, be sure only to start them if they're needed.

Polling creates unnecessary requests and can prevent the OS from managing power and resources efficiently, so avoid using it for new information. Rather than repeatedly looking to see if some new data is available or a sensor has new information, have external services push new information when it becomes available, or subscribe to events indicating new or updated information.

> **Third-party libraries and resource management**
> Check that any third-party utilities and libraries you use in your app also handle resources as carefully as you do. It's not unusual for these to be optimized for whatever benefits them the most. This may not correspond with your desire to provide the best experience for the people using your app.

The importance of transparency in resource usage impacts not only battery life and network costs, but also data privacy. Device manufacturers are starting to take this issue more seriously, and, as figure 14.2 shows, are exposing information about background activity more clearly.

The message indicates that an app named Animals is accessing the device's location in the background.

Figure 14.2 Showing which apps are accessing location information is important for data privacy concerns. It also shows the app may be wasting resources by performing background activity and using resources when it shouldn't.

Hardware and sensors can use lots of power. Bluetooth is notorious for its high level of power consumption, so you should disable it when it's not needed and where possible. Powering the screen also uses a lot of resources. Apps that can work without the need to look at the screen should be able to be used in this way. For example, if an app is tracking location or providing audio output, working with the screen off provides value without wasting power.

Other common culprits that use resources when no longer needed are animations that continue to run once they're no longer visible. It may be that they have scrolled out of the visible part of the screen or another UI element is covering them. Continuing the animation wastes resources, and it isn't always obvious that this is happening. Monitor and test for this to prevent it from becoming an issue.

14.4.2 Responding to changing circumstances

To avoid the need to poll for information constantly, most sensors provide an event-based mechanism your code can use to retrieve the information needed. If you need to know where the device is located, how the person is holding it, or which way it's facing, then subscribing to events from the location sensor, gyroscope, and compass will allow you to update the UI appropriately without continually asking the sensors for data.

Your app may benefit from responding to other available sensor and system events. The full list of options available will vary by platform and device, but the most common ones include the following:

- *Battery events*—These tell you when the device is entering or exiting battery saver mode so you can respond in ways appropriate to your app. Events relating to battery charge levels or if on external power can also be relevant.
- *Connectivity events*—Rather than checking for the type of connectivity available every time a connection needs to be made, you can make your app more efficient by having it respond to events that indicate a change in the available network connections, or when it enters or leaves flight mode.
- *File system events*—If your app uses data that the OS may automatically synchronize between devices, it's important to know when a synchronized file or setting changes so your app can respond accordingly.

Some sensors periodically need recalibration. If appropriate, your app should handle this, rather than reporting an error with the sensor.

Put it into practice: do you still need it?

- Ensure that you don't load things you don't need.
- Confirm that any third-party libraries used in your app don't waste resources or perform actions more often than needed.
- Use system and sensor events to obtain information and find out when the data changes. Don't poll to see if data has changed.

Exercise: changes and turn offs

Test your understanding of the last section by using the words below to fill in the blanks in the following paragraph:

usage finished pushed maintain

responsibly subscribe inefficient

Close connections or handles to resources as soon as you're _____ with them. Every app must use resources _____ to ensure the best experience with a device. It's important to be transparent with your resource ______ for privacy reasons as well as to _____ battery life. Polling for changes is _____. If possible, respond to changes in remote data by having new details sent or _____ to the device. For changes on the device, _____ to appropriate events to be told of changes.

Summary

- Mobile devices are constrained in terms of power and resources. Treating power and resources as infinite can lead to bad app experiences and unusable devices.
- Reducing your use of system resources doesn't mean creating a lower-quality app.
- You can use lazy loading of data and resources to reduce waste and make your app faster.
- It's often necessary to use a combination of eager and lazy loading within a single app to create the best experience.
- Performing operations on other devices or only under certain conditions is often the best use of resources.
- An app shouldn't use resources longer than necessary.
- Apps must respond to changing circumstances and adjust resource usage accordingly.

appendix A Exercise answers

Chapter 2 Who's using the app?

2.1.3 Know that you're different

1. True. You should always plan and research the people who will use an app and what they'll want before you start building it.
2. False. People do care about bugs in your app and won't excuse them easily.
3. True. You don't need to know about a subject to make an app for it, but, if that's the case, you should get help from people who do.
4. False. As the developer of an app, you're far from being a typical user of that app.
5. False. Just because you've built an app doesn't mean you'll automatically have a good understanding of who uses the app and how they do so. Any guesses you make about this are likely to be wrong.

2.3.3 Being aware of people's differences

Differences in abilities that affect how people interact with your app can be *temporary* or permanent and can potentially affect *anybody*. Make your apps inclusive and accessible to avoid *discrimination* and to meet moral and *legal* responsibilities. The expectations people have for your app will be based on other *devices* they've used and other *apps* on the same device. By defining and communicating the goals the app will help with, you make it easier to ensure you help people *achieve* what they want and make them *happier*.

2.4.2 Learn about and from the people using the app

1 Add *analytics* to your app to see which features or parts of the app are used.
2 Use *automatic exception reporting* so you can be proactive about addressing any errors or crashes.
3 Monitor *support requests* and *store reviews* to learn what changes to the app people want.
4 Look at *details from the store* to learn about user demographics.

Chapter 3 When and where is the app used?

3.2.2 Regional and location impact

The location where an app is used affects all the options listed except *formatting dates, times, and numbers for storage and transmission.* Always use the same standard formats for storage and transmission of data to avoid issues during conversion.

3.3.4 When the app is used

People may use an app differently or for different purposes and at different times of the *day*. Some apps are more relevant or will be used more at specific times of the *year.* Adjusting the app based on the time of year or in relation to special *events* can be a simple way to create interest and show personality. Anything relating to specific times or dates should be *tested* carefully before release. How *often* and for how long an app is used can impact many factors of its *design* and commercial viability.

3.4.4 Activities influencing the app

1 True. What a person is doing while using the app affects how they hold it, and this influences whether you should support the use of the app in landscape and portrait orientations.
2 False. It isn't OK to capture location and connectivity status when the app is launched and use that information for the whole session. If the person is likely to move to a new location, the new location can affect the content or behavior of the app.
3 False. Adding integration between your app and another shouldn't be avoided. If integration encourages a person to spend more time in the other app, rather than yours, it doesn't matter if your app provides unique value.
4 True. If an app is used on different types of devices, it may be used in different ways or for different tasks.
5 True. The needs of someone using an app while sitting at a desk might be different from someone walking in a field.

Chapter 4 What device is the app running on?

4.2.4 Understanding different operating systems

It's important to know about the OS your app will run on so can take *advantage* of unique capabilities it may offer to your app. The OS can also impose *restrictions* on what's possible. The different stores you use to distribute your app can also *prevent* your app from doing some things. Your app will *benefit* if it looks like it was designed for the version of the OS it's running on. Matching the conventions of the OS the app is running on is *important* in making an app easy to use. It's *less* important to match OS conventions for internal business apps.

4.3.3 Brand identity and differentiation

1. False. Internal business apps don't always need to look the same even if running on different operating systems, but creating them this way is more likely to be acceptable than in consumer-facing apps.
2. True. A brand is about more than colors, fonts, and logos.
3. True. Feelings and emotions toward a company or app are a valuable part of its brand.
4. True. The quality of a company's app reflects on the company's brand.
5. False. You don't need to sacrifice brand identity to make your app look like it belongs to a specific OS.

4.4.3 Varying hardware and software capabilities

1. It's important to know about the *hardware and software* that your app runs on.
2. The *hardware* can influence who uses a device and how it's held.
3. When displaying content onscreen, you need to think about *hardware and software.*
4. Test for the presence of specific *hardware and software* before trying to interact with it in your app.
5. The *software* of a device can change over time, and you must allow for this.

Chapter 5 How people interact with the app

5.2.2 Appropriate gestures

1. Use a *long press* as a shortcut to actions on an item in a list, without having to open a separate view of that item.
2. Use a combination of *single and double taps* to handle large and small changes to a value with a single button.
3. Use a *swipe* gesture to access a single common operation that isn't the primary (tap) action on an item in a list.

4 Use a sustained *long press* to repeat an action multiple times without needing multiple taps.
5 Use a *long press* to select an item without adding any specific selection UI.

5.3.2 The truth about challenging touch input

1 False. Even if you only use standard control events, you do need to think about touch-related input.
2 True. There is a semantic difference between touching something onscreen to trigger navigating to another part of the app and displaying more information on the same screen, and this can impact how the app should be coded.
3 True. You should always consider what happens if someone taps something twice in quick succession, as this may have unintended or unexpected consequences, such as immediately canceling or confirming an action.
4 True. You should always consider what happens if someone taps on something to make it disappear and then taps the same point on the screen, so it doesn't have unintended negative consequences.
5 False. As soon as someone makes contact with something onscreen, it shouldn't be treated as an action on that item. They may want to start a gesture or move their finger off that item before removing it from the screen as a way of canceling.

Chapter 6 User-entered data

6.1.3 Minimizing input

1 True. Prefer shorter forms to improve the likelihood they'll be completed, and completed correctly.
2 False. Asking for important information to be entered twice doesn't avoid accidental typos if the entry is pasted. Don't rely on this as the only way to prevent mistakes.
3 True. Only include default selections from a list if there's a strong likelihood that they'll be correct.
4 True. You should avoid asking for information you can easily obtain from other sources.
5 False. Text entry is not the most appropriate method for gathering all information.

6.2.5 Evaluate this login form

1 The username may be an email address or it may not. Let's hope the people using the app know if they can use their email address.
2 A username is probably mandatory. It's reasonable to assume that's what the asterisk means, but it's not explicitly stated. If that's not what the asterisk represents, it's very unclear what it does mean.

3. The password is probably not optional. The app (and related service) wouldn't be very secure if not providing a password was allowed. This question only seems relevant because the Username field has an asterisk with no explanation.
4. It's not possible to tell if there are any special restrictions on the contents of the password. If there are, and they're entered, then hopefully they'll be indicated before submitting the form.
5. It's not clear what to do if someone has forgotten their username or password. It may be that instructions are provided after a failed login attempt, but this wouldn't help someone who knows they've forgotten their credentials.

Chapter 7 Data not from a user

7.1.2 Data from the web

It's important to consider both how you *request* data and what the app should do when it can't be *retrieved.* It's normally better to show *old* data rather than no data, as long as this is clearly indicated. Include data with the app when it *ships* so that it'll always have something to show. Show *activity* while the app is doing something. Provide clear *explanations* when something fails and what, if anything, can be done to address the problem. Test how your app copes with *corrupt* data or data in an *unexpected* format. Ensure that you *format* content so it displays appropriately for the space available.

7.2.3 Data from the device

1. True. PIM data can be an appropriate source of data for apps that involve contacting other people or appointments.
2. False. Files your app writes aren't guaranteed to still be there or unchanged the next time your app needs them. Even files inside a sandboxed area of the file system can become corrupt or deleted to free up space.
3. True. You should treat the contents of a file in the same way as you would data typed into the app. You can't be sure there's nothing in the file that might cause a problem or otherwise be invalid.
4. True. Your app should make it easy to share data.
5. False. It's necessary to allow your app to support the copying and pasting of data. There's no benefit to the user if you do this, only the opportunity for frustration if you don't.

7.3.2 Data from sensors

1. It's *better* to get user consent before using a sensor.
2. A prompt to ask to use a sensor should be *clear.*
3. The format of the response from sensors on different devices *won't* always be the same.
4. Different makes of a sensor *aren't* guaranteed to provide the same level of accuracy.
5. Access to a sensor *can* change between sessions.

Chapter 8 Displaying items in the app

8.1.4 Visual fundamentals

1. Good visual output comes from focusing on *the person using the app.*
2. The people using your app expect it to behave *like other apps they use.*
3. Handle different screen sizes by *considering the impact on each view in the app and adjusting accordingly.*
4. It's better for an app to look *like it matches the conventions of the device it's running on.*
5. It's better to *follow common design patterns.*

8.3.2 Navigation

Good navigation aids *discoverability* and provides *signposting* to help the user know what's possible and where they are. By following common navigational *patterns*, you'll help people find and access the information and functionality they want. Give special consideration to handling the *Back* and *Home* buttons, and when someone *returns* to the app.

8.7.3 Handling extremes

1. False. It's not enough to only design your app for when it has or doesn't have data. You should also consider loading and error states.
2. True. It's important to distinguish between content that doesn't exist and that which hasn't loaded yet.
3. True. Never show an empty page or list without acknowledging that it's empty.

Chapter 9 Non-visible output

9.1.2 Physical and audio output

Apps should interact with the senses of *sight*, *sound*, and *touch*. By providing feedback to more than one sense, it makes it unlikely that the user will miss something important if distracted by something in their environment. The feedback and output an app provides should be *appropriate* to the scenario. Allow the person using the app to *control* the output of the app and to *disable* nonessential functionality, such as sound or vibration.

9.3.2 Backend communication

1. False. You do need to consider communication with the user in ways other than directly through the app.
2. True. Some types of message are better suited to different communication channels.
3. True. The contents of push notifications should be specific, timely, actionable, and relevant.

4. False. Your app should automatically remove notifications for old messages or ones that have been read.
5. True. Use numeric badges and different icons as part of any notification.

9.4.3 Communicating beyond the app

1. Test the *formatting* of email on the most popular devices the app is used on.
2. SMS is *more expensive* than sending push notifications.
3. Use third-party messaging servers because it *meets the needs and desires of users.*

Chapter 10 Understanding the perception of time

10.1.4 Perceiving time

1. False. Creating a responsive app is different from having a design that automatically adjusts to different screen sizes.
2. True. How the other apps on the device behave will have an impact on how your app is perceived.
3. False. If people claim the app is slow, it doesn't matter how quick it actually is and how much effort you've put into making it fast.
4. True. Showing information or capturing a response in a notification can be preferable to launching the app.
5. False. Your app doesn't need to do everything as fast as possible. Some things are better perceived if they take time.

10.2.4 Influencing perception

If your app can preemptively answer the users' *questions*, they won't wonder what the app is doing or what they should be *doing* in response. Provide access to system *connectivity* information and be *specific* in messages about connectivity problems. Adjust the way the app indicates activity based on how *long* a task is likely to take. When possible, allow the app to be *usable* while it's still performing tasks in the *background.*

Chapter 11 Making the app start fast

11.3 Preloading and preformatting content

Preloading content helps the app start *quickly*, ensures content is available when *offline*, and *removes* the need to handle having nothing to show. Preformatting content moves *complexity* and *processing* from every device to a single server. It allows the app to be *faster*, downloads to be *smaller*, and bug fixes to be deployed more *quickly.*

11.4.1 Where to cache

1. A large image relating to an item displayed in the app should *not be cached* if it's unlikely to be displayed in multiple uses of the app. Large images can also take up a lot of disk space, so it should be possible to use the app without them.

2 A list of the latest messages received within the app should be *cached on disk* so that those don't all need to be loaded for each use of the app.
3 Items shown on the first page of the app when it's launched should be *cached on disk* so the app can start quickly and be usable offline.
4 Details of the logged in user should be *cached on disk,* as these will be needed each time the app is used. Details should also be *cached in memory* if frequently used within the app.
5 The high score record of the current user should be *stored on disk,* as that will be needed with each use of the app.
6 A global online scoreboard should only be *stored in memory,* as it can't be used offline and is highly likely to change between uses.
7 A list of content sub-categories retrieved in the app should be *stored on disk,* as it will be needed every time the app is used and is unlikely to change frequently.

11.4.3 Caching, true or false?

1 False. Only consider caching something if you're likely to need it again.
2 False. Only delete something from the cache once it's invalid or unlikely to be needed again.
3 True. Apps that must be online to work can still benefit by caching content that doesn't change to avoid downloading it multiple times.
4 True. If something is stale, that means it might not be valid. Check if it's been superseded before deleting it.
5 False. Different content will change at different frequencies and be useful for different lengths of time. You can't always treat everything in the cache with the same rules.

Chapter 12 Make the app run fast

12.1.3 When to load data eagerly

1 *Do eagerly load* the top story in a news app, as this is highly likely to be viewed by all people using the app.
2 *Don't eagerly load* the purchase history in a shopping app, as this isn't functionality that's regularly accessed.
3 *Do eagerly load* customer details for upcoming appointments for sales people, as they'll need this and will require it even if offline.
4 *Don't eagerly load* the details of every level in a game, as they're unlikely to all be needed at once. Having the next level loaded and ready for use, however, could be very useful.
5 *Do eagerly load* recently taken photographs in an image-sharing app, as their use within the app is highly likely.

12.2.2 Acting asynchronously

Performing activities in *parallel* can be faster than doing them sequentially. This allows the person using the app to spend *less* time waiting while it's busy. Parallel operations can apply to the *retrieval* and persistence of both local and *remote* data. Doing everything sequentially can be simpler for the person *developing* the app, but can *negatively* affect the overall experience.

12.3.4 Combining requests, true or false?

1. False. Your app doesn't need to communicate with your own server to be able to combine requests, but it does require support from the server you're connecting to.
2. True. When using combined requests, your app still has to deal with all the requests not returning successfully. As with multiple requests made in parallel, don't throw away the results of any successful requests just because one or more has failed.
3. True. The combining of requests requires support from the server to which you are connecting, whether it's your own or someone else's.
4. False. You can combine sequential and parallel requests, but in different ways.
5. False. Not all apps should combine all requests because it may not be possible or cost-effective to combine them.

Chapter 13 Coping with varying network conditions

13.2.3 Occasional and varied connections

1. False. Secure connections are important for all apps, not just those that send or request personal or financial data.
2. True. Connection speed can be affected by local and network-wide conditions.
3. False. Not everyone has access to a fast, cheap, reliable internet connection, so you do need to think about connectivity.
4. True. Connections can come and go at any point while using the app.
5. True. Your app should handle connection changes without needing the user to do anything.

13.3.5 Coping with subprime network conditions

1. Can't complete a request now due to connection issues—*defer requests until later*
2. Avoid downloading the same thing multiple times—*cache past responses*
3. Wanting to make the app seem reliable to avoid having the person using the app doing things the app can do itself—*automatically retry failed requests*
4. Wanting to minimize the amount downloaded—*request compressed data*
5. Wanting to minimize the number of requests made to upload multiple items—*batch content together*

13.5 Communicating app activity

- The app is doing something—hopefully true.
- The task is nearly finished—false. There's no indication of this.
- The task will only take a short time to complete—false. There's no indication of this.
- Waiting for this task to complete is necessary—hopefully true.
- The task is taking the expected length of time—hopefully true, but not indicated.
- The user can do nothing to speed up this task—hopefully true, but there's no indication of this.
- The app is connecting to a remote source to retrieve data—false. There's no indication of this.
- The device is online and able to connect to the remote server—false. We can't see this for sure. While an icon in the system tray indicates a network connection, we don't know about a remote server.
- Whether the task is successful or not, the app will be able to continue—false. That there's nothing shown while this task is in progress suggests otherwise.

Chapter 14 Managing power and resources

14.2.2 Doing what's needed

1. False. An app can benefit from using a combination of eager and lazy loading.
2. False. You need to consider the loading and unloading of items and resources separately.
3. True. Your app doesn't have to always do everything at once. It may not be able to, or it may be more efficient to wait or batch multiple operations.
4. True. Your app doesn't have to do everything itself. It may be easier and preferable to offload tasks to other apps or do work on the backend.
5. False. For many scenarios, people don't always need the most accurate and up-to-date information. Approximations, cached, or old values can be good enough or better than nothing if clearly indicated as such.

14.3.2 Frequency of use

1. It's *inappropriate* to treat resources you only use once in the same way as those you'll use many times.
2. Combining network requests can *reduce* overall network traffic.
3. It's more appropriate to put data used *once* in a single, compressed file.
4. *Don't keep* connections open indefinitely to make future use faster. Doing so can waste power.
5. Files on disk *may* change after you write to them. Don't assume they won't have been changed or become corrupt.

14.4.2 Changes and turn offs

Close connections or handles to resources as soon as you're *finished* with them. Every app must use resources *responsibly* to ensure the best experience with a device. It's important to be transparent with your resource *usage* for privacy reasons as well as to *maintain* battery life. Polling for changes is *inefficient*. If possible, respond to changes in remote data by having new details sent or *pushed* to the device. For changes on the device, *subscribe* to appropriate events to be told of changes.

appendix B *Put it into practice*

Throughout this book there are many sections entitled "Put it into practice." Here they're all gathered for your reference.

Chapter 2 Who's using the app?

2.2.6 Know your users

- Answer these questions (there may be multiple answers, but be specific):
  - Why are you making this app?
  - Who's it for?
  - What are these people trying to do that the app will enable? (What's the value they'll get from the app?)
- Create personas to represent the different people who'll use the app. Where the people who may use the app are different from you, pay attention to any particular abilities, expectations, or goals they may have.
- Identify the targeted audience. If the eventual number of people who'll use the app matters, estimate how many people could potentially use the app. This is important if there are prerequisites or other requirements for using the app, or it may have a niche appeal.
- Understand your possible finances relating to the app. If the app is expected to make money, do some calculations to see how many people you'll need using it for it to be profitable. Then see how changes in lifetime value and user-acquisition costs cause these figures to vary.

2.4.2 Analyze app usage

- Add analytics to the app.

  Capture exceptions and page views. You can start by looking at the information you get from the store(s) where the app is available or look to a third-party service. You can always build your own system if you have special requirements or want to easily relate the analytics to other information you're capturing as part of the app. Spending time building your own tools for this at the start, however, risks becoming a distraction from building and improving the app.

Avoid trying to capture analytics about everything, as you risk becoming overwhelmed by the volume of data. Instead, identify the things you're most interested in and add analytics to allow you to understand those first. Add more over time as the need arises.

Update or add a privacy policy about the data collection and retention of analytics information.

- Monitor feedback.
  Have everyone involved in the app regularly read reviews and support requests relating to the app so they can see what the people who're using it think and gain insight into their perspectives. Ways you do this could be a weekly appointment in everyone's diary to look at reviews, regular time spent answering support requests, or having reviews automatically added to your internal group chat system (if you have one).
- Conduct a simple guerrilla user research study.
  Find someone who uses the app and ask them to show you how to (they) use it. Receive extra credit for any other (stealth) user observations or interviews you can do.

Chapter 3 Where and when is the app used?

3.1.2 Location of app usage

Answer these questions:

1. Where in the world will people use your app? Be careful about saying "everywhere" if you mean that nothing in the app would prevent it from being used by a particular group of people based on their location. Even if you do make your app available in all countries, it's often more helpful to first think about people in a few parts of the world. Keep this in mind as you answer the next question, too.
2. What are the differences and similarities between people and their circumstances in different countries?
3. What types of buildings or locations are people likely to be in when using the app?
4. Are there any special considerations you must make for these locations?

3.2.2 Regional impact on your app

- Make plans to support multiple languages in your app if you don't already do so.
- Identify the places in the app where numbers, dates, and times are used:
  - Where they're stored or manipulated, ensure that these aren't dependent upon a specific regional format.
  - Where they're displayed in the app, ensure to format them appropriately based on the device's settings.

3.3.4 When the app is used

- Consider how time affects the use of the app, and identify how to adapt the app to those differences.
- Identify the common activities or scenarios a person may be involved with while simultaneously using the device. Identify the ones that make using the app harder. Consider alternative ways the app could behave or interact with the person using it in those situations.
- Add or update analytics for your app to track the following:
  - What country the people who use your app are in
  - Time of day or night (local to the person using the app)
  - How long the app is in use
  - Language and regional settings configured on the device
- Update or add a privacy policy about the data collection and retention of analytics information.

Chapter 4 What device is the app running on?

4.2.4 Knowing the OS your app runs on

Complete the following tasks to solidify your understanding of the devices people are or will be using to run your app, and to help you make plans for applying it to the apps you work on.

- Answer these two questions as precisely as possible:
  - On which devices do, or will, people use your app?
  - Which versions of which operating systems are on those devices?

  If you don't already have it in place, add analytics to monitor this in the future.
- Review all the features of the operating systems (and related development SDKs) that your app runs on. Identify any features or functionality that could add extra value to the users of your app or improve the experience of using it. Then make plans to add them.
- Add details of planned announcements and events by all major OS and device manufacturers to your calendar. You may have to make plans for changes to your apps in response to anything that's announced. The announcement can also provide information about new opportunities or ways to enhance your

app. Even if your app doesn't currently run on that device or OS, what you can learn could help you in the future or provide ideas for your app anyway. Not being prepared for a potentially major change or opportunity can have a big impact on your plans. It's therefore wise to at least prepare for the need to do something.

4.4.3 Device differences

- Review the capabilities of the devices that your app is used on. Identify anything that could improve or extend the usefulness of your app, and make plans to add it.
- Ensure that your designs and test plans correspond with the devices that people are using to run your app. If they don't, change them so they do.
- Ensure that your app is at least usable with the different scaling and text size settings that are available on the devices that people use with your app. Any improvements beyond just being usable will likely be appreciated by the people using such settings.

Chapter 5 How people interact with the app

5.1.3 Different input devices

- Find a small device and someone with large fingers and watch them use your app. Are there any parts they find hard to use or places where items are too close for them to tap correctly with confidence? Adjust any layouts to increase sizes and spacing as appropriate.
- Verify that all parts of your app can be fully used with different input devices. Make plans to address any issues you discover.
- Add analytics to detect if people are using different input devices with your app, assuming your app runs on an OS that lets you detect this. Ensure you update your test plans to include the devices people are using with your app. Consider any enhancements you could make for specific devices, and implement them as appropriate.
- Ensure that any important information displayed in the app isn't obscured by normal use, such as a thumb hovering over the lower part of the screen.

5.2.2 Gestures and multi-touch input

- Ensure that any gestures in the app that involve more than a single tap or swipe are discoverable.
- Identify functionality that requires using more than a single finger. Monitor usage of this functionality (with analytics, support requests, and feedback), and provide an alternative way of using or accessing it if needed.
- Consider adding gestures for functionality that's often used (based on your analytics) but not easily accessible.

Chapter 6 User-entered data

6.1.3 Align your form with user goals

Do the following to ensure you make your forms as intuitive and easy to use as possible:

- Identify everywhere data is entered or changed in your app.
- Understand the business implications of removing any optional or unneeded fields. Remove all that the business doesn't need, and then remove anything that's duplicated or can be combined.
- Don't ask for what you can get automatically or from the device.
- Auto-advance the focus on any fields that have a fixed length and that length is reached.
- Support use of the Enter key to advance focus through a multi-text-field form.
- For any pages, screens, or views in which the only task is to enter text, set the focus appropriately on accessing the page.

6.2.5 Optimize your forms

Do the following to ensure you make your forms as intuitive and easy to use as possible:

- Ensure that lists of options are ordered appropriately for the information you're asking for. For large lists, if a few options are selected significantly more than others, include a copy of those options at the top of the list.
- Allow a person to type to filter the list or jump to the options starting with the typed character(s).
- Position labels above the fields they relate to.
- Ensure that any hints about the required formatting of data are visible when the text box has the focus or is partially complete.
- Set all keyboards appropriate to the data being asked for.
- Add masking to input where appropriate.
- Ensure that default values are used appropriately. Add any you can; adjust any you must.
- Add smart validation to email addresses. But beware of using simple regular expressions, due to the large number of edge cases and international/Unicode domains to consider.
- Add tracking to analyze what's selected from large lists to keep common summaries up to date.
- Analyze validation failures to see what issues are being encountered, and address them.
- Indicate errors inline and not in a summary at the top or the bottom of the form, where they may be scrolled out of view.

Chapter 7 Data not from a user

7.1.2 Data from the web

- If your app relies on remote content, identify and add placeholder content to ensure that there's data that can be displayed on the first use of the app, even if the remote content source cannot be accessed.
- Ensure that the app handles cases where no content, unexpected content, or corrupt content is received.
- Ensure that the messages displayed when there are problems provide advice specific to the issue. Include actionable instructions on how, if possible, they can be addressed.
- If old or cached data is displayed in the app when new content can't be obtained, confirm that this is indicated as such.
- Look to identify options for moving functionality into any notifications sent, to minimize the need for people to open the app to access functionality.
- If sending notifications about specific items or contents, ensure that the app will open on these if accessed from the notification.
- If notifications you send have a natural lifetime, remove them from a person's device if they aren't acted on in that time frame.

7.2.3 Data from the device

- If the app requires the entry of PIM data, consider adding the ability to obtain this directly from the device, in addition to allowing it to be manually entered.
- Review the extensions and advanced integration options available from the operating systems that your app runs on.
- If you're using the filesystem for data storage and retrieval, ensure that you're adequately testing for and handling changes, corruption, and missing files.
- Confirm that files are stored in appropriate locations on disk so that a person using the app won't lose anything important if temporary files are deleted, and that non-essential files aren't kept longer than they need to be.
- Enable the sharing of data with and the receipt of data from other apps as appropriate.

7.3.2 Using sensors for input

- Explain why and how any data or device resource will be used before asking for permission to access it.
- Ensure that the use of all data from the device and sensors is covered by the app's privacy policy.
- If you can, make it possible to use the app without the use of any sensors or data that require additional permissions from the person using it.

7.4.2 Giving people what they want without asking

Identify analytics that could help you understand how the app is used and improve the experience of using it for the people who do this. Then start recording the data.

Chapter 8 Displaying items in the app

8.1.4 Visual fundamentals

- Understand and document the goals of the people using your app. These should be high-level goals of things they want to get from using the app and not how to use it. Evaluate your app against these goals, and address any inconsistencies.
- Verify consistency as part of your testing process. There should be no unexpected or unintended changes in the UI within the app or between releases.
- Familiarize yourself with the design guidelines and store submission rules for the platforms your app will run on.
- Regularly use devices like the ones your app will run on. Become familiar with the conventions and standards of the popular apps and platforms of those devices. You won't know if you're breaking expectations if you don't know what is "normal."

8.2.3 Be consistent with layout

- Review anything that you display in a list or grid. Remove any whitespace that implies groupings that don't exist or any falsely implied association due to proximity.
- Where variations between items onscreen are shown with visual differences, ensure that the difference is enough so it's identifiable with a quick glance.
- Use less whitespace within sub-elements of an item than between items. Ensure consistent spacing between groups to avoid the impression of subgroups that don't exist.

8.3.2 In-app navigation

- Pay special attention to devices that have a Back button provided by the platform and how that works in combination with a Back (or equivalent) button presented in the UI.
- Remove any unnecessary Home buttons from your apps.
- If you treat a person returning to the app in the same way as when launching it, review the analytics on what they do in each situation and gather feedback on which behavior they prefer.

8.4.2 Avoid discrimination

- Support system settings relating to DPI or color schemes (including high contrast).
- Try using the app with a screen reader. Ensure that all functionality is usable.

- Ensure that nothing in the app is only indicated by a change in color.
- When using color, check the meaning of that color in the countries where you'll distribute your app.

8.5.3 Displaying images

- Create strategies for working with images you don't generate or whose size you don't control.
- Optimize the physical size(s) of the images you include with the app at design time so you don't need to adjust these in the app when it's running.
- Review the image file formats for the types and sizes of the images you're showing in the app. If possible, switch to ones that are smaller and load faster.
- Ensure you're using image placeholders for any remotely loaded images.

8.6 Be iconic

If using icons like those that are native to the platform the app is running on, ensure that you're using the exact same icons, not just ones that look similar.

8.7.3 Empty states

If people are unable to load content, ensure that you display alternatives or instructions for accessing the missing information.

Chapter 9 Non-visible output

9.1.2 Nonvisual output

- If your app/game plays background music, don't automatically start this if another audio source is already playing on the device. Allow the person using the app to listen to what they want when using your app.
- Review your app for places where adding feedback in the form of vibration would be appropriate, and make plans to add it.
- Ensure that important events and message are communicated in more than one way.
- Ensure that you have configurable options for enabling and disabling the use of sound and vibration by the app.

9.2 Output and other apps

- Identify content or events in your app or game that people already are sharing, or may want to share, and provide an easy way for them to do so.
- Review your testing and error handling of integration with connected hardware and third-party APIs so you're confident it's highly robust.

9.3.2 Output from the backend

- If you're not already sending messages via multiple channels, review how you'll need to change your apps and backends to allow this.
- Review any push notifications you send to ensure they're specific, timely, actionable, and relevant (STAR). Change them if they aren't.

9.4.3 Communicating outside the app

- Verify how the devices the app is used on display the emails you send. Do this with and without images enabled on the device.
- Explore how you could integrate with third-party messaging services as an alternative to sending emails or push notifications.

Chapter 10 Understanding the perception of time

10.1.4 Time perception and your app

- During testing, ask about the perception of speed.
- Understand the importance of different functions within the app so you can prioritize performance optimizations accordingly.
- Compare the performance of your app with other popular apps on the same devices.
- Test your app on the lowest-powered devices that you support, to ensure the app is responsive on them. Keep old devices you own so you can use them for testing in the future.
- Add a way to batch, group, or mute notifications sent or received by the app.
- Enable rich notifications to let people perform common interactions without having to launch the app.

10.2.4 Influencing perception

- Test the app using an artificial delay added to all network activity. Make note of any places where it's not clear what the app is doing while waiting for a response.
- Review the use of progress bars in your app. Are they in line with the rules for using them (highlighted in section 10.2.1)?
- Ensure that you're indicating activity in appropriate ways for the amount of time they take.
- Review how you store data on the device. Consider how it could be stored or loaded in different ways so you can access the parts you'll need. If loading large amounts of data, load the parts that will be visible first, and then load the rest after those are displayed.
- If using animated page/view transitions, start loading the data for the page that will be displayed while the animation is in progress.

10.3 App updates

- Add an indicator when a new version of the app is available, and include details of why the update should be installed.
- Ensure that you display details of what's changed when a new version of the app is used for the first time.

Chapter 11 Making your app start fast

11.1.2 Making your app do the minimum on startup

- Measure how long it takes between launching the app and being able to use it. How does it compare with popular and similar apps? Get feedback on this from the people who use the app.
- Periodically track the *time until usable* so you become aware of and can react to any changes in the app that increase this interval.
- Track the *time until usable* for all the different ways of launching the app.
- If you have a large app that's slow to start, consider how you could divide it into separate modules, components, or assemblies that don't all need to load on launch.
- Review the startup of the app and the information given to the user in relation to table 10.1. Add more information or placeholders as necessary.

11.2.2 Preload content in your app

- Identify where preloaded content could be beneficial. Using the app without a network connection is one way to do this. Make plans to create and include appropriate content with the app when distributed.
- If content takes time to download when the app starts, add a background process to periodically check for and download new content while the app isn't in use. That way, new content is available when the app is started.
- Intercept remotely sent push notifications so you can download any related content before displaying a message that it's available.

11.3 Preformat content used by your app

If you download content that you transform before displaying it in the app, consider the costs and benefits of moving the transformation work to a server.

11.4.3 Cache content used by your app

- Identify content that the app retrieves multiple times, and evaluate the benefit of caching it on disk or in memory.
- If you've already cached something, don't automatically delete it if it's stale. Ensure that you check for a new version first.
- Check the HTTP response headers from all the sources of your remote data to see which already support caching. Make use of those that do.

- Test your app's ability to cope with caching when the device it's on is low on free disk space.
- Test how your app handles cached files being deleted when the device removes temporary files.

Chapter 12 Making your app run fast

12.1.3 Eagerly load content used by your app

- Identify anything that would benefit from eager loading on startup, and enable it.
- Where a workflow in the app involves a sequence of operations, and where possible, automatically start the next step so it's ready when needed.
- Identify places where a person has to wait for some content to download or load, and, if possible, start the retrieval process early.
- For anything that's slow on first use, do this once in advance and discard the results so that it'll be fast when needed.
- Add analytics that track how long a person must wait for the app, and then act to remove any bottlenecks that are highlighted.

12.2.2 Making asynchronous requests

- Look for sequential operations that can be performed in parallel, and change them to work this way.
- Ensure that you give a visual indicator of background network activity.
- Ensure appropriate communication when one or more parallel requests fail.
- Ensure that you never block the UI. Test with an artificially long delay added to any activity that could potentially be time-consuming. The OS should never stop the app while performing any lengthy activity.
- Research a reactive approach to data retrieval, and explore how it can work for you.
- Review places where you upload or save data, and, if appropriate, make plans to do this in parallel with other user activity.

12.3.4 Combine requests

- Weigh the costs, benefits, and risks of creating your own proxy server to marshal communication between the app and any other remote endpoints. If cost effective and possible, make plans to do this.
- Find any sequential requests that can be done in parallel, and change them to run in parallel.
- Look for parallel or sequential requests that you can combine, and do so.
- Evaluate the size of files created on disk. Combine small ones, and split up any large ones as appropriate.

Chapter 13 Coping with varying network conditions

13.1.3 Allowing for connection variations

- Switch to using HTTPS if you can. Make plans for how you will do this if you can't change right away.
- If you have a widely distributed user base, move static content to a CDN.
- Include the ability to add artificial delays on each network request as a way of simulating slower connections when testing on physical devices.
- Make testing on slower devices and connections a regular part of your development and testing practices.
- Add settings to avoid sending large amounts of data over a metered connection without the user's approval.

13.2.3 Allowing for occasional connections

- Ensure that your app can launch when offline or unable to connect to any necessary servers.
- Allow captured content to be queued and sent later.
- Cache displayed data for showing again when the app is next used.
- Test the app to be sure it copes with losing connections while in use.
- Test changes in connectivity while using the app and ensure it adapts appropriately.

13.3.5 Allowing for subprime network conditions

- Use HTTP caching as supported by the server.
- Request compressed versions of HTTP content if available.
- Consider batching multiple small requests together or splitting up large file uploads if a connection isn't reliable.
- Enable automatic retrying of failed requests.

13.4.2 Usability in poor conditions

- Assess the functionality in the app that's dependent upon a network connection to identify if it could be done partially, differently, or completed later when used offline.
- Adjust the automatic polling frequency to account for network conditions.
- Enable the prioritization of important requests when queuing many.

13.5 Keep the user in control

Review all displayed error messages to ensure that they're clear, necessary, and actionable.

Chapter 14 Managing power and resources

14.1 Managing battery life

- Ensure that your testing process includes monitoring of power consumption.
- Ensure that you're using all the functionality, features, and sensors on a device, rather than forcing the manual entry of data or creating alternative methods of gathering information.
- Provide ways of giving value to the people using the app even when device capabilities are limited.
- Ensure that your app responds to the device in battery saver mode in a way that avoids using limited power unnecessarily.
- Allow the user to disable background polling or any other periodic activity to save power and reduce network activity.

14.2.2 Resource alternatives

- Look at the way you retrieve data. Obtain resources in your app, and confirm you're using lazy or eager loading appropriately for each instance.
- Verify that you're using sensors to supplement or replace data capture when possible.
- Defer any actions that don't need to be done immediately, and perform them in batches or in response to other events in the use of the app.
- Move the preparation and formatting of data to the server that provides it.
- Move the processing of data captured by the app to the server it's sent to.

14.3.2 How often you use resources

- Treat resources used once separately from those used repeatedly.
- Cache data if you know it won't change and you only need to retrieve it once.
- Store data on disk in a way that corresponds to how frequently you'll need to read, update, and write it.

14.4.2 Do you still need it?

- Ensure that you don't load things you don't need.
- Confirm that any third-party libraries used in your app don't waste resources or perform actions more often than needed.
- Use system and sensor events to obtain information and find out when the data changes. Don't poll to see if data has changed.

appendix C
Recommended reading

By the nature of the fact that you're reading this book, I'm going to assume you'll be interested in reading other, related books too. These are my recommendations for the ones that can have the biggest impact and are most widely applicable.

Badass: Making Users Awesome – Kathy Sierra (O'Reilly, 2015)

This is a great book about how to focus on what will make your product (app) invaluable to the people who use it. The focus isn't on apps, but you can easily apply the lessons of this book to apps and games to help make them better. Read this book if you want to create something people will love.

Design for Hackers: Reverse Engineering Beauty – David Kadavy (John Wiley & Sons, 2011)

This is a great book full of useful, practical instructions for creating beautiful, well-designed interfaces. The focus of the book is primarily for web design and development, but it highlights fundamental principles that developers can easily apply to the UI of apps. Read this book if you're not a designer, but would like to improve your design skills.

Elements of User Experience: User-Centered Design for the Web – Jesse James Garrett (New Riders, 2002)

This book provides an accessible introduction to the world of user experience (UX). Like many of the other books listed here, it focuses on web development, but also shows how to apply what it teaches to other areas too. The book provides an overview to UX and has a structure for explaining its key components (elements). Read it if you want to learn more about the formal discipline of UX.

Mobile Design and Development: Practical Concepts and Techniques for Creating Mobile Sites and Web Apps – Brian Fling (O'Reilly, 2009)

This is probably the best book about mobile development I've ever read, and my copy has more pages with notes, highlights, and folded corners than any other book I own. It's a little dated now, as it was written at a time when there were more feature phones than smart phones, and the idea of building apps for iPhone or Android was still new. Don't let its age fool you. While the practical parts of this book focus on web development at a time when mobile browsers were way behind what we have now, the fundamental principles and concepts it teaches are just as valid today. Read this if you're doing any mobile development.

Rocket Surgery Made Easy: The Do-It-Yourself Guide to Finding and Fixing Usability Problems – Steve Krug (New Riders, 2009)

This is the follow-up to Steve's earlier book, *Don't Make Me Think!* The earlier book was an introduction to the importance of usability in websites; this book explains how you can run usability tests yourself. This is another book written for people developing for the web, but it's also widely applicable to mobile app development. Read this book to learn how to begin performing your own usability testing.

The Design of Everyday Things – Donald A. Norman (MIT Press, 1988)

This book is a classic introduction to design. It's about more than just how things look and work, as it also considers the importance of understanding how they affect the people who use them and the businesses that create them. Read this to learn more about the principles of design and how they affect everything you use and create.

appendix D *Bibliography*

The contents of this book have been informed by personal experiences, conversations with other app creators, using many apps, watching videos and tutorials, listening to talks and podcasts, and lots of reading. The reading has come from many sources, including blogs, websites, magazines, and books. Of all these, the easiest for me to reference and for you to seek out if you so desire are books. Here is a list of the books (physical or in an electronic format) that have in some way helped me to write this book:

Agar, John. *Constant Touch: A Global History of the Mobile Phone.* Icon Books, 2003.

Ahonen, Tomi T. *The Insider's Guide to Mobile.* TomiAhonen Consulting, 2010.

———. *Mobile as 7th of the Mass Media: Cellphone, Cameraphone, Iphone, Smartphone.* Futuretext, 2008.

Ajit, Jokar, and Tony Fish. *Mobile Web 2.0: The Innovator's Guide to Developing and Marketing Next Generation Wireless/Mobile Applications.* Futuretext, 2006.

Allen, Christopher, and Shannon Appelcline. *iPhone in Action.* Manning, 2008.

Allen, Sarah, et al. *Pro Smartphone Cross-Platform Development: iPhone, Blackberry, Windows Mobile and Android Development and Distribution.* Apress, 2010.

Allums, Skip. *Designing Mobile Payment Experiences.* O'Reilly, 2014.

Alvarez, Cindy. *Lean Customer Development: Building Products Your Customers Will Buy.* O'Reilly, 2014.

Anderson, Jonathan, et al. *Effective UI: The Art of Building Great User Experience in Software.* O'Reilly, 2010.

Baines, Jeremy, and Clive Howard. *UX Lifecycle: The Business Guide to Implementing Great Software User Experiences.* CreateSpace, 2016.

Ballard, Barbara. *Designing the Mobile User Experience.* John Wiley & Sons, 2007.

Banga, Cameron, and Josh Weinhold. *Essential Mobile Interaction Design: Perfecting Interface Design in Mobile Apps.* Addison Wesley, 2014.

Bank, Chris. *Mobile UI Design Patterns.* UX Pin, 2014.

Baxter-Reynolds, Matt. *Death of the PC: The Authoritative Guide to the Decline of the PC and the Rise of Post-PC Devices.* The Platform, 2013.

Baxter-Reynolds, Matthew. *Cracking Windows Phone and BlackBerry Native Development: Cross-Platform Mobile Apps Without the Kludge.* Apress, 2011.

Beer, Paula, and Carl Simmons. *Hello App Inventor!* Manning, 2014.

Bennett, Jim. *Xamarin in Action.* Manning, 2017.

Berkowski, George. *How to Build a Billion Dollar App: Discover the Secrets of the Most Successful Entrepreneurs of Our Time.* Piatkus, 2014.

Binkley-Jones, Timothy, et al. *Windows Phone 7 in Action.* Manning, 2012.

———. *Windows Phone 8 in Action.* Manning, 2013.

BlackBerry. *BlackBerry Browser: Content Developer Guide.* Research In Motion Limited, 2007.

Blake, Joshua. *Natural User Interfaces in .NET.* Manning, 2012.

Boling, Douglas. *Programming Microsoft Windows CE .NET.* Microsoft Press, 2003.

Borowska, Paula, and Thomas Laurinavicius. *Mobile Design Book: The Extended Version.* 2014.

Bratton, Alex. *Billion Dollar Apps: How To Find & Implement a Winning Mobile Strategy.* Innovation Networks, 2014.

Brooks, Frederick. *The Design of Design: Essays from a Computer Scientist.* Addison-Wesley Professional, 2010.

Brown, Dave. *The iPhone App Design Manual: Create Perfect Designs for Effortless Coding and App Store Success.* Ilex Press, 2014.

Buley, Leah. *The User Experience Team of One: A Research and Design Survival Guide.* Rosenfeld Media, 2013.

Buxton, Bill. *Sketching User Experiences.* Morgan Kaufmann, 2007.

Cameron, Rob. *Pro Windows Phone 7 Development.* Apress, 2011.

Cartman, Joseph, and Richard Ting. *Strategic Mobile Design: Creating Engaging Experiences (Voices That Matter).* New Riders, 2008.

Carver, Matthew. *The Responsive Web.* Manning, 2014.

Castledine, Earle, et al. *Build Mobile Websites and Apps for Smart Devices.* SitePoint, 2011.

Chimero, Frank. *The Shape of Design.* Frank Chimero, 2012.

Chisholm, Wendy, and May, Matt. *Universal Design for Web Applications.* O'Reilly, 2008.

Clark, Josh. *Tapworthy: Designing Great iPhone Apps.* O'Reilly, 2010.

Colborne, Giles. S*imple and Usable Web, Mobile, and Interaction Design (Voices That Matter).* New Riders, 2010.

Cooper, Alan. *The Inmates Are Running the Asylum: Why High Tech Products Drive Us Crazy and How to Restore the Sanity.* Sams, 2004.

Danger Gardner, Lyza, and Jason Grigsby. *Head First Mobile Web.* O'Reilly Media, 2011.

Davidson, Neil. *Don't Just Roll the Dice.* Simple Talk Publishing, 2009.

Dawes, Adam. *Windows Phone 7 Game Development.* Apress, 2010.

Dutson, Phil. *Responsive Mobile Design: Designing for Every Device.* Addison Wesley, 2014.

Esgar, Justin. *Appitalize On Your Idea: Bringing Any Idea to Fruition.* Justin T. Esgar, 2013.

Ferraro, Richard, and Murat Aktihanoglu. *Location-Aware Applications.* Manning, 2011.

Fling, Brian. *Mobile Design and Development: Practical Concepts and Techniques for Creating Mobile Sites and Web Apps.* O'Reilly, 2009.

Frederick, Gail Rahn, and Rajesh Lal. *Beginning Smartphone Web Development: Building Javascript, CSS, HTML and Ajax-Based Applications for iPhone, Android, Palm Pre, Blackberry, Windows Mobile and Nokia S60.* Apress, 2010.

Gajda, Karol. *What I Learned Losing $7,211 in the iPhone Apps Business: 13 Lessons to Stop from Becoming a Mobile App Store Failure.* Karol Gajda, 2014.

Garrett, Jesse James. *The Elements of User Experience: User-Centered Design for the Web and Beyond (Voices That Matter).* New Riders, 2010.

Goodman, Elizabeth, et al. *Observing the User Experience: A Practitioner's Guide to User Research.* Morgan Kaufmann, 2012.

Gothelf, Jeff. *Lean UX: Applying Lean Principles to Improve User Experience.* O'Reilly, 2013.

Greenfield, Adam. *Everyware: The Dawning Age of Ubiquitous Computing.* New Riders, 2006.

Greever, Tom. *Articulating Design Decisions: Communicate with Stakeholders, Keep Your Sanity, and Deliver the Best User Experience.* O'Reilly, 2015.

Griffiths, Dawn, and David Griffiths. *Head First Android Development.* O'Reilly, 2015.

Gustafson, Aaron. *Adaptive Web Design: Crafting Rich Experiences with Progressive Enhancement (Voices That Matter).* New Riders, 2015.

Hanington, Bruce, and Bella Martin. *Universal Methods of Design: 100 Ways to Research Complex Problems, Develop Innovative Ideas, and Design Effective Solutions.* Rockport, 2012.

Hinman, Rachel. *The Mobile Frontier: A Guide for Designing Mobile Experiences.* Rosenfeld, 2012.

Hoober, Steven, and Eric Berkman. *Designing Mobile Interfaces: Patterns for Interaction Design.* O'Reilly, 2011.

Hughes, Jeffrey. *iPhone and iPad Apps Marketing: Secrets to Selling Your iPhone and iPad Apps (Que Biz-Tech).* Que Publishing, 2011.

Jackson, Wallace. *Pro Android UI.* Apress, 2014.

Jaokar, Ajit, and Anna Gatti. *Understanding the Impact of Open Mobile: Implications for Telecoms/ Devices, Web, Social Networks, Media and Personal Privacy.* Futuretext, 2009.

Jensen, Derek. *Xamarin Forms Succinctly.* SyncFusion, 2015.

Johnson, Jeff. *GUI Bloopers: Don'ts and Do's for Software Developers and Web Designers (Interactive Technologies).* Morgan Kaufmann, 2000.

Jones, Matt, and Gary Marsden. *Mobile Interaction Design.* John Wiley & Sons, 2005.

Kadavy, David. *Design for Hackers: Reverse Engineering Beauty.* Wiley, 2011.

Klein, Laura. *UX for Lean Startups: Faster, Smarter User Experience Research and Design.* O'Reilly, 2013.

Kosmaczewski, Adrian. *Mobile Javascript Application Development.* O'Reilly, 2012.

Krause, Jim. *Color for Designers: Ninety-five Things You Need to Know When Choosing and Using Colors for Layouts and Illustrations (Creative Core).* New Riders, 2014.

Krug, Steve. *Don't Make Me Think, Revisited: A Common Sense Approach to Web Usability.* New Riders, 2014.

———. *Rocket Surgery Made Easy: The Do-It-Yourself Guide to Finding and Fixing Usability Problems (Voices That Matter).* New Riders, 2009.

Kuniavsky, Mike. *Smart Things: Ubiquitous Computing User Experience Design.* Morgan Kaufmann, 2010.

La, Rajesh. *Digital Design Essentials: 100 Ways to Design Better Desktop, Web, and Mobile Interfaces.* Rockport, 2013.

Lee, Henry. *Beginning Windows Phone 7 Development.* Apress, 2011.

Lidwell, William, et al. *Universal Principles of Design: 100 Ways to Enhance Usability, Influence Perception, Increase Appeal, Make Better Design Decisions, and Teach Through Design.* Rockport Publishers Inc., 2007.

Little Springs Design. *Mobile Operators: Application Store Ecosystem.* Little Springs Design, 2009.

Lockton, Dan, et al. *Design with Intent: 101 Patterns for Influencing Behaviour Through Design.* Equifine, 2010.

Lovell, Nicholas, and Rob Fahey. *Design Rules for Free-to-Play Games.* GAMESbrief, 2012.

Lowdermilk, Travis. *User-Centered Design.* O'Reilly, 2013.

Luton, Will. *Free-to-Play: Making Money From Games You Give Away.* New Riders, 2013.

McKay, Everett N. *UI Is Communication: How to Design Intuitive, User Centered Interfaces by Focusing on Effective Communication.* Morgan Kaufmann, 2013.

McNeil, Patrick. *The Mobile Web Designer's Idea Book: The Ultimate Guide to Trends, Themes and Styles in Mobile Web Design.* How Design Books, 2013.

McWherter, Jeff, and Scott Gowell. *Professional Mobile Application Development.* Wrox, 2012.

MediaCT, and Google. *The Mobile Movement: Understanding Smartphone Users.* Google Think Mobile, 2011.

Mehta, Nirav. *Mobile Web Development.* Packt Publishing, 2008.

Mendoza, Adrian. *Mobile User Experience: Patterns to Make Sense of It All.* Morgan Kaufmann, 2013.

Metzger, Monty C M, et al. *Mobile Future @mocom2020.* Books On Demand, 2009.

Microsoft Corporation. *Designing Web Sites for Mobile Browsers.* Microsoft Corporation, 2010.

———. *Inclusive: A Human-Led Design Practice.* Microsoft Corporation, 2015.

Miller, Tom. *XNA Game Studio 4.0 Programming: Developing for Windows Phone 7 and Xbox 360 (Developer's Library).* Addison-Wesley Professional, 2010.

Mobile Marketing Association. *Consumer Best Practice Guidelines for Cross-Carrier Mobile Content Programs.* Mobile Marketing Association, 2008.

MobiThinking. *Designing Usable Pocket Rockets: A Three Step Guide to Usability on the Mobile Web.* MobiThinking, 2009.

Moll, Cameron. *Mobile Web Design.* Cameron Moll, 2008.

Moore, Todd. *Tap, Move, Shake: Turning Your Game Ideas into iPhone & iPad Apps.* O'Reilly, 2012.

Moule, Jodie. *Killer UX Design.* SitePoint, 2012.

Mureta, Chad. *App Empire: Make Money, Have a Life, and Let Technology Work for You.* Wiley, 2012.

Nathan, Adam. *101 Windows Phone 7 Apps, Volume I: Developing Apps 1-50.* Sams, 2011.

Neil, Theresa. *Mobile Design Pattern Gallery.* O'Reilly, 2012.

Norman, Donald A. *The Design of Everyday Things.* 2d ed. MIT Press, 2013.

Nudelman, Greg. *Android Design Patterns: Interaction Design Solutions for Developers.* Wiley, 2013.

O'Farrell, Michael, et al. *Mobile Internet for Dummies.* John Wiley & Sons, 2008.

Petroski, Henry. *To Engineer Is Human: The Role of Failure in Successful Design.* Vintage Books, 1992.

Petzold, Charles. *Creating Mobile Apps with Xamarin.Forms.* Microsoft Press, 2014.

———. *Programming Windows Phone 7.* Microsoft Press, 2010.

Pickering, Heydon. *Inclusive Design Patterns: Coding Accessibility into Web Design.* Smashing Magazine, 2016.

Pierce, Taylor A. *Appreneur: Secrets to Success in the App Store.* Apress, 2012.

Raskin, Jef. *The Humane Interface: New Directions for Designing Interactive Systems.* Addison Wesley, 2000.

Reid, Jon. *jQuery Mobile.* O'Reilly, 2011.

Reis, Eric. *The Lean Startup.* Portfolio Penguin, 2001.

Rogers, Scott. *Swipe This!: The Guide to Great Touchscreen Game Design.* Wiley, 2012.

Saffer, Dan. *Designing for Interaction: Creating Smart Applications and Clever Devices (Voices That Matter).* New Riders, 2006.

———. *Designing Gestural Interfaces: Touchscreens and Interactive Devices.* O'Reilly Media, 2008.

Salz, Peggy Anne. *The Everything Guide to Mobile Apps: A Practical Guide to Affordable Mobile App Development for Your Business.* Everything, 2013.

Schlatter, Tania, and Deborah Levinson. *Visual Usability: Principles and Practices for Designing Digital Applications.* Morgan Kaufmann, 2013.

Shackles, Greg. *Mobile Development with C#.* O'Reilly, 2012.

Sierra, Kathy. *Badass: Making Users Awesome.* O'Reilly, 2105.

Spolsky, Joel, and Dave Winer. *User Interface Design for Programmers.* Apress, 2001.

Stanley, Morgan. *The Mobile Internet Report: Key Themes.* Morgan Stanley, 2009.

Stevens, Chris. *Appillionaires: Secrets from Developers Who Struck It Rich on the App Store.* Wiley, 2011.

Tenner, Edward. *Why Things Bite Back: Technology and the Revenge of Unintended Consequences.* Vintage Books, 1997.

Tidwell, Jenifer. *Designing Interfaces: Patterns for Effective Interaction Design.* O'Reilly, 2005.

Tiffany, Rob. *Mobile Strategies for Business: 50 Actionable Insights to Digitally Transform Your Business.* Blackcomb Press, 2016.

———. *Windows Mobile Data Synchronization with SQL Server 2005 and SQL Server Compact 3.1.* Hood Canal Press, 2007.

Tondreau, Beth. *Layout Essentials: 100 Design Principles for Using Grids.* Rockport, 2011.

Various. *Designing for Android.* Smashing Magazine, 2012.

———. *Designing for iPhone.* Smashing Magazine, 2012.

———. *Essentials of Mobile Design.* Smashing Magazine, 2012.

———. *Mobile Design Patterns.* Smashing Magazine, 2012.

———. *Real-Life Responsive Web Design.* Smashing Magazine, 2015.

———. *The Mobile Book.* Smashing Magazine, 2012.

Vaughan, Daniel. *Windows Phone 8 Unleashed.* Sams Publishing, 2013.

Walter, Aaron. *Designing for Emotion.* A Book Apart, 2011.

Weinschenk, Susan. *100 Things Every Designer Needs to Know About People (Voices That Matter).* New Riders, 2011.

Weiss, Scott. *Handheld Usability.* John Wiley & Sons, 2002.

Welinske, Joe. *Developing User Assistance for Mobile Apps.* lulu.com, 2014.

Wigley, Andy, et al. *Microsoft .NET Compact Framework (Core Reference) (Developer Reference).* Microsoft Press, 2003.

———. *Microsoft Mobile Development Handbook.* Microsoft Press, 2007.

Wildermuth, Shawn. *Essential Windows Phone 8 (Microsoft Windows Development Series).* Addison-Wesley Professional, 2013.

Williams, Chris, and George Clingerman. *Professional Windows Phone 7 Game Development: Creating Games Using XNA Game Studio 4.* Wrox, 2011.

Williams, Robin. *The Non-Designer's Design Book.* Peachpit Press, 1993.

———. *The Non-Designer's Design and Type Book (Deluxe Edition): Design and Typographic Principles for the Visual Novice.* Peachpit Press, 2007.

———. *The PC Is Not a Typewriter: A Style Manual for Creating Professional Level Type on Your PC.* 1st ed. Peachpit Press, 1995.

Wise, Wendy L. *Anyone Can Create an App.* Manning, 2017.

Wooldridge, Dave. *The Business of iPhone and iPad App Development: Making and Marketing Apps that Succeed.* Apress, 2011.

Wroblewski, Luke. *Mobile First.* A Book Apart, 2011.

———. *Web Form Design.* Rosenfeld Media, 2008.

Yarmosh, Ken. *App Savvy: Turning Ideas into iPad and iPhone Apps Customers Really Want.* O'Reilly Media, 2010.

Yocco, Victor S. *Design for the Mind.* Manning, 2016.

Zhou, Z, et al. *Windows Phone 7 Programming for Android and iOS Developers.* Wrox, 2011.

Zwick, Carola, Burkhard Schmitz, and Kerstin Kühl. *Designing for Small Screens.* AVA Publishing, 2005.

index

Symbols

@ symbol 133
% (percentage sign) 67
. (period) character 69

Numerics

304 Not Modified status code 262

A

actions, deferring
  for saving resources 316
  poor network conditions 297
  saving content displayed when app was last used 293–294
  saving things to send later 293
  starting now and finishing later vs. putting it all off 301
activities, influencing apps 81
address entry field 146
advance until submit 130
advertising 39
all-or-nothing removal 265
analytics data 50, 97, 325
animation, to hide delays 240–241
API (application programming interface) 156
app boot loader 250
app experience components 6–17
  connectivity
    email client example 12
    news app example 14
    overview 9
    tower defense game example 16
  context
    email client example 11
    news app example 13
    overview 6–7
    tower defense game example 15–16
  importance of
    differentiation 17–20
    meeting user expectations 20–21
    planning for success 21–23
  input
    email client example 11–12
    news app example 13
    overview 7–8
    tower defense game example 16
  output
    email client example 12
    news app example 14
    overview 8
    tower defense game example 16
  resources
    email client example 13
    news app example 14–15
    overview 10
    tower defense game example 17
  responsiveness
    email client example 12
    news app example 14
    overview 8–9
    tower defense game example 16
application programming interface (API) 156
applications
  activities influencing 81
  considering cost of 37, 39
  EULA, including with 50
  evaluating 29
  regional impact on 70

applications *(continued)*
  session length in 76
  sharing content between 54
  situations affecting usage 45
appointments, finding 163
artificial delays 290
aspect ratios 194
async keyword 275
asynchronous operations 275
Atencio, Luis 277
audio output 208–210, 212, 329, 342
auto advance 130
auto-complete 129
auto-focus 130
automatic exception reporting 325
automatic polling 302
automatic retries, poor network conditions 298–299
auto-suggest 129

B

Back button 188–189
backend APIs 156
backend communication 220
Badass (Sierra) 348
badges 219–220
batch operations, poor network conditions 297
battery events 322
battery life
  managing 313
  overview of 347
boredom 18
bottlenecks 272
brand identity 90–93
  branding vs. visual identity 91
  maintaining OS conventions while still reflecting brand 93
  separating brand from OS 91–92
branding 84

C

caching
  content 259–267
    checking for new versions 262–264
    in-memory and disk-based caches 260
    invalidating and deleting cached items 264–267
    overview of 330–331, 344–345
  poor network conditions 296
cameras 100
Campaign Monitor 221
capitalization, adjusting 144
capturing non-user data 155–173
  devices 161–166
    filesystem 163–164
    OS 162–163
    other apps 164–166
    overview of 328, 340
  heuristics and inference 171–173
    based on an individual's usage 171–172
    based on usage of all people 172
  overview of 341
  sensors 166–170
    overview of 328, 340
    transparency and permission when using sensor data 166–168
    variations in input 168–170
  web-based resources 156–161
    directly requested 156–158
    overview of 328, 340
    pushed to app 158–161
capturing user data 126–154
  alternative inputs 136–138
  defaults and suggestions 134–135
  forms 138–153
    arrangement of 138–143
    fixed set of options 149–150
    overview of 327–328, 339
    password entry 146–149
    text entry 143–146
    validation and required fields 151
  goals of users 127–128, 339
  minimizing input 128–134
    avoiding duplication 132–134
    effort involved in providing input 129–130
    overview of 327
    reducing required input 130–132
CDN (content delivery network) 289
character recognition 136
chat interface 146
code, errors in 47
color schemes 93, 197
combining input 129
combining requests and responses 279–284
  combining requests and local files 282–284
  controlling server 279–280
  faster responses 280–281
  overview of 332, 345–346
  simplifying client 281–282
common data 165
common icons 46
communication 211, 213, 220
compression, poor network conditions 296–297
concurrency 275
configurations 168
connection variations 292

connectivity 202–205, 287–305
availability 203
balancing usability and network conditions 299–302
adjusting network usage 301–302
overview of 333, 346
prioritizing important activities 300–301
email client example 12
empty states 203, 342
keeping user in control 302–305, 346
loading speed 202–203
movement and 78
news app example 14
optimizing for network conditions 296–299
automatic retries 298–299
batch operations 297
caching 296
compression 296–297
deferring actions 297
overview of 332, 346
overview of 9, 329
tower defense game example 16
variations in network conditions 288–295
connection cost 290–291
connection speed 289–290
connections may be lost 294
connections may change 294–295
connections may not be possible 292–294
overview of 332, 346
securing connections 288–289
contacts, finding 162
content
compressing 296
sharing between apps 54
unexpected 158
content delivery network (CDN) 289
context
email client example 11
news app example 13
overview of 6–7
tower defense game example 15–16
control layout 181–185
alignment and hierarchy 182–183
consistency 183
overview of 341
proximity 184–185
corruption 158
costs, considering 37, 39
crash reports 50
cross-app communication 213
cross-platform tooling 85
cultural associations 193
custom fonts 93
cutting data 165

D

Daniels, Paul P. 277
deep linking 165
default content, for display when network conditions are poor 293
deferring actions
for saving resources 316
poor network conditions 297
saving content displayed when app was last used 293–294
saving things to send later 293
starting now and finishing later vs. putting it all off 301
DemoApp 168
demographic information 40
demographic targeting 39
Design for Hackers (Kadavy) 348
The Design of Everyday Things (Norman) 349
detecting inactivity 80
developers, users vs. 28–33
average user 31–32
effects on thinking 32–33
knowing what other people want 28–29
overview of 324
tolerating rough edges 29–31
development costs, considering 37, 39
devices 83–102
brand identity and differentiation 90–93
branding vs. visual identity 91
maintaining OS conventions while still reflecting brand 93
overview of 326
separating brand from OS 91–92
cameras on 100
capturing data from 161–166
filesystem 163–164
OS 162–163
other apps 164–166
overview of 328, 340
CPU and GPU on 100
fingerprint scanners on 100
internal hardware capability 97–100
available sensors 99
inclusion or absence of physical buttons 97–99
overview of 326, 338
multi-handed operation of 119
one-handed operation of 119
operating systems 86–90
enterprise usage 89–90
looking like app belongs on OS 87–88
OS-imposed restrictions 86–87
OS versions 89
overview of 326, 337–338

devices *(continued)*
output to other devices 212–214, 342
physical sizes 94–97
how device is held 95–96
overview of 326, 338
what can be displayed 96–97
who uses device 94–95
pointing 106
software variations 100, 326, 338
testing on 98
touch-screen 105
tracking details 97
user interface 179
write once, run everywhere (WORE) solutions 84–86
dictation 136
differentiation 17–20, 90–93
alternative apps 18–19
branding vs. visual identity 91
maintaining OS conventions while still reflecting brand 93
no competition 19–20
non-app alternatives 19
separating brand from OS 91–92
direct input 8
discoverability 186, 329
discrimination 191–193
communication 192–193
overview of 341–342
physical abilities 191–192
disk space 13
disk-based caches 260
displaying images 200
double tapping 112, 116, 326
DPI settings 192
drag gesture 116
drawer pattern 187
Dresher, Tamir 277

E

eager loading 269–273
determining what to load eagerly 272–273
downside of 272
overview of 315, 331, 345
preloading content and 270–271
Elements of User Experience (Garrett) 348
email client example 11–13
connectivity 12
context 11
input 11–12
output 12
resources 13
responsiveness 12
email, communication with users via 221–223
empty states 204
End User License Agreement (EULA) 50
enterprise app usage 42–43
environments, influencing apps 81
errors 47, 162
ETag 262–263
EULA (End User License Agreement) 50
evaluating apps 29
expectations, meeting 45

F

false consensus effects 31
feature usage, tracking 50
file extensions 165
filesystem events 322
fingerprint scanners 100
Fitts's law 95
flick gesture 116
float label pattern 141
fonts, custom 93
formatting, unexpected 158
forms 138–153
arrangement of 138–143
fixed set of options 149–150
default values 149–150
making likely options easy to find 150
reducing options 150
overview of 327–328, 339
password entry 146–149
text entry 143–146
easy to enter correct data 143–144
hard to enter incorrect data 144
simple to provide multiple pieces of data 145–146
validation and required fields 151

H

haptic feedback 210–211, 329, 342
hardware capabilities 101
heuristics and inference 171–173
based on an individual's usage 171–172
based on usage of all people 172
Hick's law 150
high-level navigation 95
hint text 140
Home button 189–190
hub and spoke pattern 187
Humanizer 67

I

icons 46, 89, 200–201, 342
If-Modified-Since header 262

If-None-Match header 262
illusion of labor 234
image spacing 185
imageColor property 198
imagePlaceholder entry 199
images 193–199
  displaying 200
  formats and formatting 196–198
  overview of 342
  placeholders 198–199
  sizing 193–196
in-memory caches 260
inactivity, detecting 80
in-app navigation 191
informed consent 50
input 126–154
  alternative inputs 136–138
  combining 129
  defaults and suggestions 134–135
  difficulties with, raw input events 123
  email client example 11–12
  forms 138–153
    arrangement of 138–143
    fixed set of options 149–150
    password entry 146–149
    text entry 143–146
    validation and required fields 151
  goals of users 127–128
  minimizing 128–134
    avoiding duplication 132–134
    effort involved in providing input 129–130
    overview of 327
    reducing required input 130–132
  multi-touch 120
  news app example 13
  overview of 7–8
  tower defense game example 16
  user interaction 116–120
    gesture-based input 116–119
    multi-touch input 119–120
    overview of 326–327, 338
Instagram, image uploading by 278
interaction 105–125
  difficulties with 121–124
    overview of 327
    raw input events 123
    unintended touch events 121–122
  input 116–120
    gesture-based input 116–119
    multi-touch input 119–120
    overview of 326–327, 338
  pointing devices 106–116
    mice and keyboards 114–116
    overview of 338
    styluses 112–114
    touch 107–112
internal enterprise apps 19, 42
International Organization of Standardization (ISO) 69
intuitiveness 5
invalid data 152
iris scanning 148
ISO (International Organization of Standardization) 69

K

Krug, Steve 52

L

labels 140
landscape orientation 139
languages
  formatting dates 68–70
  formatting numbers 67–68
  formatting words 65–67
  multiple language support 61–65
lazy loading 314–315
libraries, third-party 321
line-of-business apps 19, 42
Litmus 221
local data 165
location 57–61
  macro-geographic level 58–60
  micro-geographic level 60–61
  overview of 325, 336–337
  regionalization 61–70
    culture and locale 65–70
    multiple language support 61–65
long press gesture 116, 326
lowest common denominator approach 85

M

MailChimp 221
master/detail pattern 187
media playback, manipulating 98
MIME types 165
minimizing input 138
Mobile Design and Development (Fling) 349
mobile devices, resource constraints of 10
mobile time 230–236
  context and 230–231
  feelings, opinions, and comparisons 231–232
  notifications 233
  overview of 330, 343
  user expectations 234–236
monetization techniques 76

Movable Ink 221
multichannel communication 215–216
multi-finger gestures 117
multi-handed operation 119
multi-touch input 120

N

native sharing 165
native UI 84
navigation 186–190
  Back button 188–189
  common patterns 186–188
  high-level 95
  Home button 189–190
  overview of 329, 341
  returning to app 190
negative experience, creating 4
negative numbers 68
negative sounds 210
network conditions 287–305
  balancing usability and 299–302
    adjusting network usage 301–302
    overview of 333, 346
    prioritizing important activities 300–301
  keeping user in control 302–305, 346
  optimizing for 296–299
    automatic retries 298–299
    batch operations 297
    caching 296
    compression 296–297
    deferring actions 297
    overview of 332, 346
  variations in 288–295
    connection cost 290–291
    connection speed 289–290
    connections may be lost 294
    connections may change 294–295
    connections may not be possible 292–294
    overview of 332, 346
    securing connections 288–289
network throttling 289
network traffic 289
news app example 13–15
  connectivity 14
  context 13
  input 13
  output 14
  resources 14–15
  responsiveness 14
news bubble 14
no splash screen 252
non-visible output 207–225
  audio 208–210, 329, 342
  communicating from backend 214–220
    multichannel communication 215–216
    overview of 329–330, 343
    push notifications 216–220
  communication via channels beyond app 221–223
    email 221–223
    overview of 330, 343
    SMS 223
    third-party messaging services 223
  haptic feedback 210–211, 329, 342
  to other apps and devices 212–214, 342
notification counts 219
notifications, responsiveness 233

O

occasional connections 295
off-loading computation 316–317
one-handed operation 119
optional information 152
optional updates 245
OS (operating system) 86–90
  capturing data from 162–163
    OS integration 163
    PIM data 162–163
  enterprise usage 89–90
  looking like app belongs on OS 87–88
  OS-imposed restrictions 86–87
  OS versions 89
  overview of 20, 36, 65, 83, 326, 337–338
output 207–225
  audio 208–210, 329, 342
  communicating from backend 214–220
    multichannel communication 215–216
    overview of 329–330, 343
    push notifications 216–220
  communication via channels beyond app 221–223
    email 221–223
    overview of 330, 343
    SMS 223
    third-party messaging services 223
  email client example 12
  haptic feedback 210–211, 329, 342
  news app example 14
  non-visual 212
  overview of 8
  to other apps and devices 212–214, 342
  tower defense game example 16
  user interface (UI) 177–206
    avoiding discrimination 191–193, 341–342
    control layout 181–185, 341
    extremes of connectivity and content 202–205, 329, 342
    fundamentals of 178–181, 329, 341

output *(continued)*
icons 200–201, 342
images 193–199, 342
navigation 186–190, 329, 341
overconfidence 31

P

parallel operations 273–278
advice regarding 276–278
overview of 332, 345
synchronous and asynchronous operations 275
parallelism 275
passwords
entering 146–149
overview of 134
protecting 148
recovering 148
pasting data 165
pattern libraries 180
percentage sign (%) 67
perception 232
period (.) character 69
permissions, sensor data 166–168
personality information 40
personas 40–42
phone number entry field 145
PhoneGap/Cordova 84
physical output 212
PIM data 162–163
pinch/stretch gesture 117
pixel density 109
placeholders 140, 198, 253
plain text files 64
pluralization 66
pointing devices 106–116
fingers 107–112
mice and keyboards 114–116
overview of 338
styluses 112–114
portrait orientation 139
positive sounds 210
Postel's law 151
power and resource management 309–323
battery life 347
consequences of usage 310–313
lazy loading 314–315
resources only ever used once 319, 333, 347
resources only used once per session 318–319, 333, 347
resources used repeatedly 319–320, 333, 347
responding to sensor and system events 322–323, 334
saving resources 315–317
balancing approximations, accuracy, and effort 317
deferring actions 316
off-loading computation 316–317
overview of 333, 347
simpler approaches 316
turning off when finished 321–322, 334
power source 10
precompiling content 258
preformatting content 257–259, 330, 344
preloading content 254–256
eager loading and 270–271
for app's next use 255–256
pulling new content 255–256
pushing new content 256
overview of 330, 344
to distribute with app 254
premature optimization 282
pressure sensitivity 113
primary goals, vs. secondary goals 127
priming 271
privacy 50, 97
progress indicators 240
proxied requests 281
proxy APIs 156
pseudo-loc translation 62
push notifications 216–219
actionable content 218
badges 219–220
overview of 159
relevance 218–219
specificity 217
timeliness 217–218

R

Raskin, Jef 128
React Native 84
reactive programming (Rx) 277
regionalization 61–70
culture and locale 65–70
formatting dates 68–70
formatting numbers 67–68
formatting words 65–67
multiple language support 61–65
requests, combining 283
required information 152
required sensor 168
resetting passwords 148
resources 309–323
battery life 347
consequences of usage 310–313
email client example 13
lazy loading 314–315
news app example 14–15

resources *(continued)*
only ever used once 319, 333, 347
only used once per session 318–319, 333, 347
overview of 10
responding to sensor and system events 322–323, 334
saving 315–317
balancing approximations, accuracy, and effort 317
deferring actions 316
off-loading computation 316–317
overview of 333, 347
simpler approaches 316
tower defense game example 17
turning off when finished 321–322, 334
used repeatedly 319–320, 333, 347
responsiveness 229–247
app updates 243–247, 344
email client example 12
influencing perception of 236–242
animation to hide delays 240–241
indicating what app is doing 236–240
overview of 330, 343
progress indicators 240
usable vs. finished 241–242
mobile time 230–236
context and 230–231
feelings, opinions, and comparisons 231–232
notifications 233
overview of 330, 343
user expectations 234–236
news app example 14
overview of 8–9
run speed 268–284
combining requests and responses 279–284
eager loading 269–273
parallel operations 273–278
tower defense game example 16
rich notifications 234
Rocket Surgery Made Easy (Krug) 349
rotate gesture 117
rubber finger tips 108
run speed 268–284
combining requests and responses 279–284
combining requests and local files 282–284
controlling server 279–280
faster responses 280–281
overview of 332, 345–346
simplifying client 281–282
eager loading 269–273
determining what to load eagerly 272–273
downside of 272
overview of 331, 345
preloading content and 270–271
parallel operations 273–278
advice regarding 276–278
overview of 332, 345
synchronous and asynchronous operations 275
Rx (reactive programming) 277

S

scaling fallacy 96
screen elements, scaling 96
screen orientations 139
screen scaling 109
SDK (software development kit) 50, 68, 337
secondary goals, vs. primary goals 127
security 148
sensors
capturing data from 166–170
overview of 328, 340
transparency and permission 166–168
variations in input 168–170
responding to sensor events 322–323, 334
server speed 290
settings 168
sharing content, between apps 54
short session lengths 76
shortcuts 129
signposting 186, 329
simultaneous activities 325
distraction 79–80
movement 78–79
connectivity 78
interaction 79
location 78
posture 81
single finger gestures 117, 326
single tapping 112
slide gesture 116
SMS, communication with users via 223
software capabilities 101
software development kit (SDK) 50, 68, 337
sounds
negative 210
positive 210
system-level 210
spacing images 185
specific, timely, actionable, and relevant (STAR) 214, 220, 343
speech bubbles 109
speech-to-text interface 145
splash screen 252–253
stack pattern 187
STAR (specific, timely, actionable, and relevant) 214, 220, 343

startup time 248–267
  caching content 259–267
    checking for new versions 262–264
    in-memory and disk-based caches 260
    invalidating and deleting cached items 264–267
    overview of 330–331, 344–345
  optimizing 249–253
    architecture and compilation 250–251
    deciding what to do on startup 249–250
    different ways of starting app 250
    overview of 344
    splash screen 252–253
  preformatting content retrieved by app 257–259, 330, 344
  preloading content 254–256
    for app's next use 255–256
    overview of 330, 344
    to distribute with app 254
stealth user 336
store reviews 325
stylus 113
support requests 325
swipe gesture 116, 326
synchronous operations 275
system-level sounds 210

T

tab pattern 187
tap and hold gesture 116
tap events, canceling 123
tapping gesture 112, 116
taptic engine 210
targeted advertising 39
test performance 232
testing on devices 98
text entry 136
text, pseudo-localizing 63
third-party apps 19
third-party libraries 321
third-party messaging services, communication with users via 223
time 70–77
  day of week 72–73
  length of session 75–77
  number of times used 74–75
  overview of 325, 337
  responsiveness 229–247
    app updates 243–247, 344
    influencing perception of 236–242, 330, 343
    mobile time 230–236, 330, 343
  run speed 268–284
    combining requests and responses 279–284, 332, 345–346
    eager loading 269–273, 331, 345
    parallel operations 273–278, 332, 345
  startup 248–267
    caching content 259–267, 330–331, 344–345
    optimizing 249–253, 344
    preformatting content retrieved by app 257–259, 330, 344
    preloading content 254–256, 330, 344
  time of day 70–72
  time of year 73–74
    impact on all apps 73–74
    impact on specialized apps 73
time until usable 253, 344
touch input
  fingers 107–112
  gesture-based input 116–119
  multi-touch input 119–120
  overview of 326–327, 338
  unintended touch events 121–122
touch-screen devices 105
tower defense game example 15–17
  connectivity 16
  context 15–16
  input 16
  output 16
  resources 17
  responsiveness 16
tracking, device details 97
traditional icons 46
transit test 143
translation
  avoiding 64
  pluralization of words 66
transparency, sensor data 166–168
Tuominen, Timo 277

U

UI (user interface) 177–206
  avoiding discrimination 191–193
    communication 192–193
    overview of 341–342
    physical abilities 191–192
  control layout 181–185
    alignment and hierarchy 182–183
    consistency 183
    overview of 341
    proximity 184–185
  extremes of connectivity and content 202–205
    availability 203
    empty states 203, 342

UI (user interface) *(continued)*
loading speed 202–203
overview of 329
fundamentals of 178–181
devices 179
focus on user and user goals 178
overview of 329, 341
standards and conventions 180–181
user expectations 178–179
icons 200–201, 342
images 193–199
formats and formatting 196–198
overview of 342
placeholders 198–199
sizing 193–196
navigation 186–190
Back button 188–189
common patterns 186–188
Home button 189–190
overview of 329, 341
returning to app 190
uncanny valley 200
updates 243–247
usability 1–5
app success factors 3–5
defined 2–3
importance of 2
intuitiveness 5
usage 57–82
determining 49–54
automated monitoring 49–51
manual observation 51–52
monitoring support and reviews 53
multiple apps for wider tasks 53
soliciting feedback 52–53
devices 83–102
brand identity and differentiation 90–93, 326
internal hardware capability 97–100, 326, 338
operating systems 86–90, 326, 337–338
physical sizes 94–97, 326, 338
software variations 100, 326, 338
write once, run everywhere (WORE) solutions 84–86
interaction 105–125
difficulties with 121–124
input 116–120, 326–327, 338
overview of 327
pointing devices 106–116, 338
location 57–61
macro-geographic level 58–60
micro-geographic level 60–61
overview of 325, 336–337
regionalization 61–70
simultaneous activities 78–82
distraction 79–80
movement 78–79
overview of 325
posture 81
sharing of data or functionality 80–81
time 70–77
day of week 72–73
length of session 75–77
number of times used 74–75
overview of 325, 337
time of day 70–72
time of year 73–74
user experience (UX) 2–3
user interface. *See* UI (user interface)
user needs, meeting 4
users 27–54
capturing data from 126–154
alternative inputs 136–138
defaults and suggestions 134–135
forms 138–153, 327–328, 339
goals of users 127–128, 339
minimizing input 128–134, 327
determining how app is used 49–54
automated monitoring 49–51
manual observation 51–52
monitoring support and reviews 53
multiple apps for wider tasks 53
overview of 335–336
soliciting feedback 52–53
developers vs. 28–33
average user 31–32
effects on thinking 32–33
knowing what other people want 28–29
overview of 324
tolerating rough edges 29–31
differences between 43–48
abilities 44–45
expectations 45–47
goals 47–48
overview of 324
expectations, meeting 45
identifying 33–43
enterprise app usage 42–43
overview of 325, 335
personas 40–42
potential user base 35–36
quantity of users 36–39
targeting groups 39–40
value 34–35

utilities, third-party 321
UX (user experience) 2–3

V

validation 151
varied connections 295
vertical stacking 140
vibration 210–211
visual identity 84
voice input 136

W

Wagner, Jeremy L. 281
web-based resources 156–161
  directly requested 156–158
    input not being received 157
    malformed or unexpected input 157–158
  overview of 328, 340
  pushed to app 158–161
whitespace 341
wizard pattern 187
WORE (write once, run everywhere) solutions 84–86

X

Xamarin 84

RELATED MANNING TITLES

Design for the Mind
Seven Psychological Principles of Persuasive Design
by Victor S. Yocco

ISBN: 9781617292958
240 pages, $39.99
June 2016

Progressive Web Apps
by Dean Alan Hume

ISBN: 9781617294587
200 pages, $39.99
December 2017

Irresistible APIs
Designing web APIs that developers will love
by Kirsten L. Hunter

ISBN: 9781617292552
232 pages, $44.99
September 2016

Cross-Platform Desktop Applications
Using Node, Electron, and NW.js
by Paul B. Jensen

ISBN: 9781617292842
312 pages, $49.99
May 2017

For ordering information go to www.manning.com